# INFORMATION TECHNOLOGY FOR COMMON MAN

## Books by the same Author

* *Dynamics of Formulating Policy in the Government of India* (co-author)
* *Operational Analysis and Indian Defence*
* *Information Management in Government*
* *Management Perspectives*
* *Computer Applications for Techno-Economic Development* (Ed.)
* *Computer Management and Planning*
* *Computer, compiler*!
* *Computer Applications for Rural Development* (Ed.)
* *Management Information System: A Framework* (co-author)
* *Common Man's Guide to Computers*

# INFORMATION TECHNOLOGY FOR COMMON MAN

*Edited by*

UTPAL K. BANERJEE

COMPUTER SOCIETY OF INDIA
and
CONCEPT PUBLISHING COMPANY, NEW DELHI-110059

First Published 1992
Reprinted 2002



*Published and Printed by*
Ashok Kumar Mittal
**Concept Publishing Company**
A/15-16, Commercial Block, Mohan Garden
New Delhi-110059 (India)
*Phones:* 5648039, 5649024
*Fax:* 091–(11)–5648053
*E-mail:* publishing@conceptpub.com

*To*
*All Those*
*Professionals,*
*Researchers,*
*Voluntary Agencies*
*and*
*Corporate Sector Organisations*
*Striving to Make*
*Information Technology*
*Relevant*
*to*
*Every-Day Life*
*of*
*the Common Man*

# FOREWORD

The discovery of Computers and the subsequent development of Information Technology is one of the most significant achievements of the present century. The role of this new technology as an instrument of progress and development is also now widely recognised all over the world. There is no doubt that usage of Information Technology will lead to major social and economic benefits for mankind and will have an important bearing on the life styles of the society at large.

There is a lot of scope for the application of Information Technology in India also for the overall national development. There is a growing all-round awareness in the country in this regard and it is generally agreed that Information Technology can play a useful role in accelerating the process of development. Several applications have been evolved in the last few years to open up new areas for the usage of computers. The employment of computers is thus becoming common place and is being extended rapidly to encompass several facets of our daily lives.

Computers can be employed gainfully in several important fields such as education, agriculture and weather-forecasting. Computers are also being used already for railway and air-reservation, banking and insurance as well as for the billing of the electricity and telephone charges. The existing applications in areas such as health services, conduct of examinations and crime-detection can be augmented further and there is considerable scope for the enlarged usage of computers in several segments of public administration.

The concept of computer networking has also added a new dimension for harnessing the full potential of computers. The growth of computer networking has given rise to Local Area Networks for the improved functioning of the offices. The introduction of Wide Area Networks has similarly led to the design of systems which cater for instantaneous flow of information over long distances. The equipping of offices with facilities such as PC-telex and PC-FAX has resulted in further modernisation of the office environment. The evolution of Information Technology has thus been a great boon and has become a major factor for enhancing the efficiency and productivity of the working places and offices.

It is, however, generally believed that the usage of Information Technology in India is confined to the metropolitan cities and the urban sector only. In this context, it must be remembered that nearly 80 per cent of our population lives in the villages. It is, therefore, necessary that the benefits of modern technology should be extended to the rural sector as well.

It is also often argued, albeit incorrectly, that people in the rural sector are not interested in any computer-based activity. To dispel this myth, it must be emphasised that computers are not meant for the elite only. Today the knowledge of the English language is also not necessary for handling computers and computer displays and printouts are available in all regional languages. People in the villages would welcome any programme of computerisation which would cater for information of special interest to them such as information pertaining to land records. Such information to be fully useful should be made available in the prevalent regional language. Perhaps in not too distance future, computer-based Information Centres would be set-up for groups of villages to provide information of vital interest to the village community in the local language. Such a step would go a long way for spreading the message of computerisation throughout the country.

Information Technology can be specially useful in imparting literacy in the rural sector. Demonstrations have shown that the process of teaching and learning can be substantially speeded up by using computer-aided techniques for this purpose. These techniques can be used with great advantage for the removal of adult illiteracy, in particular, in the rural sector.

The role of Information Technology in the service ot the handicapped sections of our society is another important area which needs greater attention. The Computer Society of India has been one of the pioneers in this context. A project has been initiated by the CSI at Bombay in collaboration with the Indian Guild for the Handicapped, with support from the Department of Electronics of the Government of India, for the training of the blind in the use of computers. Projects are being planned on similar lines for other handicapped persons also, such as the paraplegic and the spastic persons.

There is, however, a mistaken impression that computers deprive people of job opportunities. This common misconception has retarded the growth of computer culture and has been partly responsible for the slow progress of the plans for the introduction of computerisation in the country. It is, therefore, necessary that this misconception should be removed effectively by highlighting the role of computers in the creation of new job opportunities.

Many ancillary industries have come up throughout the country due to the introduction of computers. It must also be emphasised that any large-scale programme of computerisation would further encourage the production, marketing and maintenance of ancillary items and equipment needed by the Information Technology industry.

Ancillary industries connected with items such as standby generators, voltage stablisers and UPS, air-conditioning and fire alarm systems and printing and supply of special stationery and other consumables such as floppy diskettes and printer ribbons have received considerable impetus due to the growth of computer related activity. If we consider the job openings which have arisen due to these ancillary industries, then it would be obvious that, on the whole, instead of depriving people of job opportunities, computers have played a positive role in the creation of new jobs. Introduction of computerisation should therefore be welcomed from every angle and it is in our interest that we should exploit this new technology for the common good of all sections of our population.

The book *Information Technology for Common Man*, has covered a wide spectrum of computer applications which are of relevance to us in our day to day lives. This book is based on the proceedings of a pre-Convention Working Conference which was organised by the Computer Society of India for a detailed discussion of the theme of the Annual Convention (CSI-91) which was held at New Delhi from 29 September to 02 October 1991. A large number of status papers were presented in this Working Conference by various experts to cover a wide range of applications for a variety of socio-economic benefits for our society.

As the Convenor of the Working Conference, Dr. Utpal K. Banerjee was responsible for organising a very comprehensive discussion of the theme of CSI-91. I would like to commend the painstaking efforts of Dr. Banerjee in editing this book. The publication of this book was feasible entirely due to the sustained hardwork and untiring efforts of Dr. Banerjee. I am sure that readers interested in studying the role of Information Technology, both in the overall development of the country as well as in improving the quality of life of our people at large will find this publication immensely useful.

BRIG. SVS CHOWDHRY (RETD)*
*Chairman,*
Conference Committee
Computer Society of India

New Delhi
April 1992

---

* Since taken over as President of Computer Society of India.

# ACKNOWLEDGEMENTS

On behalf of Computer Society of India, its President, Dr. Rattan K. Dutta and Vice President, Brig. S.V.S. Chowdhry suggested the holding of the Working Conference and requested the undersigned to be its Convenor. Shri S.K. Sharma, Chairman of Organising Committee, CSI-91, provided organisational guidance, approved financial support and rendered great help in copy-editing. Department of Science and Technology, Government of India provided free use of its auditorium and infrastructure facilities. Col. Vinay K. Khanna coordinated the administrative arrangements from beginning to end, and helped in measurably to make the Conference a success.

Brig. V.M. Sundaram, Col. B.K. Rai, Prof. R.K. Arora and Mr. Subash Pani chaired the various morning and afternoon Panel Sessions and User Review Sessions. Dr. Vinay K. Dharmadhikari and Dr. B.C. Kailay acted as Rapporteurs for the entire Conference and summarised the findings during the User Review Sessions.

To all of them and to the very large number of user departments, organisations and institutions, who participated and shared their views, grateful thanks are due.

New Delhi
April 1992

UTPAL K. BANERJEE
*Editor*

# CONTENTS

# LIST OF TABLES

# LIST OF FIGURES

# LIST OF CONTRIBUTORS

*Dr. Utpal K. Banerjee,*
Director Incharge,
Forum for Information
Technology of India,
C-563, Sarita Vihar,
New Delhi - 110044

*Shri N. Vittal*
Secretary,
Department of Electronics,
Electronic Niketan,
CGO Complex, Lodi Road,
New Delhi - 110003

*Dr. N. Sheshagiri,*
Director General,
National Informatics Centre,
'A' Block
CGO Complex, Lodi Road,
New Delhi - 110003

*Dr. Rattan K. Datta,**
President,
C.S.I.,
C/o Deptt. of Science &
Technology,
Technology Bhawan,
New Mehrauli Road
New Delhi - 110016

*Dr. M. Rai* (& Colleague)
Asstt. Dir. General,
Indian Council of Agricultural
Research
Krishi Bhavan,
New Delhi - 110011

*Dr. Vinay Dharmadhikari*
Director
Department of Electronics,
Lok Nayak Bhavan,
Khan Market,
New Delhi - 110003

*Shri A.D. Mohile*
Chief Engineer,
Central Water Commission,
SEWA Bhavan,
R.K. Puram, Sector I,
New Delhi - 110066

*Shri A. Ramakrishnan,*
Director,
Land Reforms,
Ministry of Agriculture,
Krishi Bhavan,
New Delhi-110001

---

* Since handed over Presidentship to Brig. S.V.S. Chowdhry.

*Shri D.C. Mishra*
(& Colleagues)
CRISP Project,
National Informatics Centre,
7th Floor, 'A' Block,
CGO Complex,
Lodi Road,
New Delhi - 110003

*Shri M. Moni* (& Colleagues)
Addl. Director (DISNIC),
National Informatics Centre,
7th Floor, 'A' Block,
CGO Complex,
Lodi Road,
New Delhi - 110003

*Shri B.M. Chhabra,*
Deputy Director General,
Indian Meteorological Department,
Mausam Bhavan,
Lodi Road,
New Delhi - 110003

*Mr. Harjit Singh*
Advisor,
Ministry of Environment and Forestry,
Parivahan Bhawan,
CGO Complex,
Lodi Road,
New Delhi - 110003

*Prof. J.G. Krishnayya,*
Executive Director,
Systems Research Institute,
Gultekdi,
Near Golibari Maidan,
Pune

*Shri M. Srinivasan*
Knowledge Engineering and Consultancy Pvt. Ltd.,
2, Ragavan Road,
Tata Nagar
Madras - 600017

*Dr. A.K. Jain,*
Jt. Director (Corporate Building),
Steel Authority of India Limited,
Ispat Bhavan,
Lodi Road,
New Delhi - 110003

*Shri B.N. Talukdar*
Advisor,
(Production & Geo Sciences),
Oil India Corpn. Ltd.,
17, Sansad Marg,
New Delhi - 110001

*Shri P.K. Mittal,*
Director,
Geo Data Processing &
Interpretation Centre,
Oil & Natural Gas Commission,
Tel Bhavan
Dehradun - 284195

*Shri S.K. Chand,*
Deputy Chief Mining Engineer,
Coal India Limited,
407, Surya Kiran Building,
Kasturba Gandhi Marg,
New Delhi - 110001

*Shri M.I. Beg,*
Member (Planning),
Central Electricity Authority,
SEWA Bhavan,
R.K. Puram,
Sector-I
New Delhi - 110066

*Shri B.B. Saxena,*
G.M. (SNT),
State Bank of India,
New Administrative Building,
Madam Cama Road,
Bombay - 400021

*Shri V.S. Dhruv,*
GM,
General Insurance Corporation,
Industrial Assurance Building,
Church Gate,
Bombay - 400020

*Dr. Sujoy K. Guha,*
Head, Centre for Bio-Medical Engineering,
IIT, Hauz Khas,
New Delhi - 110016

*Dr. R.P. Gupta,*
Coordinator,
National Council of Educational Research &
Training (NCERT),
Sri Aurobindo Marg,
New Delhi - 1100016

*Shri Gopal Dass,*
GM (C&T),
Mahanagar Telephone Nigam Ltd.,
Chandralok Building,
10th Floor, Janpath,
New Delhi - 110001

*Ms. Deepika Saxena,*
CMC Ltd.,
A-5, Ring Road,
South Extension Part-I,
New Delhi - 110049

*Shri R.K. Jain,*
Traffic Superintendent,
Delhi Transport Corporation,
Indra Prastha Estate,
New Delhi - 110002

*Shri R.D. Saklani*
Executive Director,
Centre of Railway Information System,
Chanakya Puri
New Delhi - 110021

*Shri S.K. Bose,*
Manager, EDP,
Indian Airlines Corporation,
Indira Gandhi National Airport,
New Delhi - 110010

*Shri S.K. Sharma**
Director General,
National Crime Records Bureau
West Block,
R.K. Puram, Sector-1,
New Delhi - 110066

* Since Retired

*Col. P.P. Varma,*
Deputy Director,
National Crime Records Bureau
West Block,
R.K. Puram, Sector-I,
New Delhi - 110066

*Shri S.R. Majumdar* (& Colleague)
Directorate General of Employment & Training,
Ministry of Labour,
Rafi Marg,
New Delhi - 110001

*Shri Pradeep Gupta,*
MD
CYBRE Media,
810, Meghdoot,
94, Nehru Place
New Delhi - 110019

*Shri Y. Venkateswarlu*,
Director (Engineering),
Doordarshan,
Mandi House,
New Delhi - 110001

*Shri Sugata Mitra,*
Computer Application Research Division
NIIT Ltd.
8, Balaji Estate
Guru Ravi Das Marg,
Kalkaji Extension,
New Delhi - 110019

*Shri Subash Pani,*
Chairman,
Orissa Computer Application Centre
TDCC Building, 2nd Floor,
Janpath,
Bhubaneshwar - 751007

*Shri B.C. Kailay*,
Head, Cultural Information Unit,
NIC, Room No. 246,
Vigyan Bhavan Annexe,
New Delhi - 110011

*Dr. V.V.S. Murthy*
Principal Systems Analyst,
NIC, Sports Authority of India,
Jawaharlal Nehru Stadium,
New Delhi - 110003

# PART I

# INTRODUCTION

# 1

# AN OVERVIEW

UTPAL K. BANERJEE

## Introduction

Over the last two millennia of human history, the society has evolved continuously from its pre-industrial to industrial and finally to post-industrial manifestation. Another way of looking at the evolving society is to divide it among the following sectors:

(i) Primary Sector – with a focus on nature;
(ii) Secondary Sector – with a focus on material;
(iii) Service Sector – with a focus on community;
(iv) Leisure Sector – with a focus on individual.

While different strata of human society have lived overlappingly through the various sectors, there has been a perceptable shift of labour as well as capital from the primary society to the service society, and now to leisure society. This trend has been as much evident in the developed world as in the newly industrialising world of India.

It is interesting to note that technology has provided continually the underpinning in this social evolution. Alongside the technology, the role of information has been an increasingly predominant one from the primary society to the leisure society, so much so that many call it a gradual evolution towards information society. Computers have also been increasingly involved in this evolutionary process, thus almost metamorphosing even the primary, secondary, service and leisure societies.

Agriculture, for instance, is an indispensable part in the primary sector. In the USA today, it is the largest industry which makes heavy use of computers and even involves genetic manipulation and biotechnology. It relies there an up-to-the-minute planning in management and sales. It also demands the best in high-technology communication and the most sophisticated marketing strategies.

**Working Conference**

It was decided by the Computer Society of India to hold the Working Conference in September 1991 in Delhi as a precursor to the main convention of CSI-91, on the broad theme of "Information Technology (IT) in Everyday Life". The purpose of the Working Conference was to cover the following:

(a) Comprehensive presentation by subject-area specialists from related organisations over all the four sectors as above;
(b) Consolidation of findings for action by, and recommendations to, Department of Electronics (DOE), CSI and other related public and private agencies.

In order to serve the above purpose, more than fifty organisations from the Government departments, public and private sectors, organisations and institutions were formally invited to share their ideas and activities in IT–related areas. The unique point about the Working Conference was that the heads of the organisations were invited to send their organisational representatives for an authoritative coverage of their role in IT, instead of asking anyone for general contribution of papers or invited talks.

**Participation Profile**

The tone was set by the principal participants from the triumvirate: Department of Electronics, National Informatics Centre and Computer Society of India. While the DOE – Secretary inaugurated the Working Conference, the NIC – Director General provided the key-note on its theme and the CSI – President gave the call to professionals for their contribution.

The participation profile was as follows:

(i) *Primary Sector (Focus on Nature)*

Crops and Seeds : Indian Council of Agricultural Research (ICAR)

| | | |
|---|---|---|
| . Agriculture | : | Department of Electronics |
| . Water Resources | : | Central Water Commission |
| . Rural Development (General) | : | Ministry of Agriculture |
| . Rural Development (CRISP) | : | National Informatics Centre (NIC) |
| . Decentralised Planning (DISNIC) | : | National Informatics Centre (NIC) |
| . Weather & Environment | : | India Meteorological Department |
| . Environment | : | Ministry of Environment & Forestry |
| . Desk-top Mapping | : | Systems Research Institute |

(ii) *Secondary Sector (Focus on Material)*

| | | |
|---|---|---|
| . Manufacturing | : | Knowledge Engineering & Consultancy Services |
| . Steel | : | Steel Authority of India (SAIL) |
| . Oil | : | Oil India Limited (OIL) |
| . Oil & Natural Gas | : | Oil & Natural Gas Commission (ONGC) |
| . Coal | : | Coal India Limited |
| . Power | : | Central Electricity Authority (CEA) |

(iii) *Service Sector (Focus on Community)*

| | | |
|---|---|---|
| . Banking | : | State Bank of India (SBI) |
| . General Insurance | : | General Insurance Corporation of India (GIC) |
| . Health | : | Centre for Bio-Medical Engineering, IIT, Delhi & All India Institute of Medical Sciences (AIIMS) |
| . Education (CLASS Project) | : | National Council of Educational Research & Training (NCERT) |
| . Telecommunications | : | Mahanagar Telephone Nigam Limited (MTNL) |

| | | |
|---|---|---|
| . Intelligent Building | : | CMC Limited |
| . Road | : | Delhi Transport Corporation (DTC) |
| . Railways | : | Ministry of Railways |
| . Airlines | : | Indian Airlines |
| . Police (General) | : | National Crime Records Bureau |
| . Police (Finger-print Identification) | : | National Crime Records Bureau |
| . Employment | : | Directorate General of Employment & Training (DGE & T) |

(iv) *Leisure Sector (Focus on Individual)*

| | | |
|---|---|---|
| . Newspapers & Magazine | : | Cyber Media Limited |
| . Television | : | Directorate General of Door-darshan |
| . Books | : | NIIT Limited |
| . Indian Languages | : | Orissa Computer Application Centre (OCAC) |
| . Art & Culture | : | National Informatics Centre and Indira Gandhi National Centre for the Arts (IGNCA) |
| . Games & Sports | : | National Informatics Centre and Sports Authority of India (SAI) |

In all, 35 organisations participated with the hospitality of the Department Science and Technology and deliberated over the two days on the profound implications of IT in everyday life in all the four sectors. The structured panel discussions were followed on each day by a strong user review session, where many senior users of IT came specially to participate and offer their valuable views.

**Recommendations**

The 35 participant Organisations (out of 51 invitees) interacted closely with each other through structured panel discussions and strong user review sessions over two days. A number of success stories came out from such organisations as SAIL and the Railways, while there were a few stories of not achieving the goals, namely, Delhi Transport Corporation (DTC) and Computer-aided Literacy and Studies in Schools (CLASS) project. Many clear recommendations emerged suggesting action by DOE and CSI, apart from the user community. It was also perceived that there was much scope of concerted studies by government and non-government agencies.

The recommendations could be classified under five sections as follows:

A. *Achievements and Experience*

(i) Achievements in key economic sectors for use of IT should be focused upon;
(ii) Documentation and publication were needed to highlight tangible benefits from utilisation of IT;
(iii) Loss saved and service improved by Food Corporation of India (which moved annually grains for Rs. 12,000 crores), by using NIC services, should be computed for public information.
(iv) SAIL experience should be recorded regarding efficient resource utilisation and productivity improvement with minor investment in IT;
(v) SAIL experience to make IT vendor equipment work through standardisation, vendor qualification and rate contracts also needed highlighting.

B. *IT Use Strategy*

(i) A national time-table was needed for police network (POLICENET) across the States;
(ii) There was scope of adopting pre-planning in the employee-orientation models in the banking and transaction intensive sectors based on the Railway experience;
(iii) Ministry of Surface Transport should develop a comprehensive IT plan after examining the efforts made by BEST, APSRTC and other city transport corporations;
(iv) NIC'S experience on Electricity Construction Projects should bear upon the operations of Central Electricity Authority (CEA);

(v) The grand plan for IT usage worth Rs. 4,000 crores, which did not come off in a public sector undertaking, needed a "Trojan Horse" approach;

(vi) Accountability was needed for political and for bureaucratic commitments made for CLASS programme of DOI and NCERT (Ministry of HRD);

(vii) IT user forum was needed urgently for all technical, managerial and vendor-related IT uses.

C. *Integration of IT Material*

(i) Comprehensive village-level data-base was needed instead of each department or agency doing its separate survey;

(ii) Twenty-nine state level departments, which at present collected information at village and district level, should be integrated into the DISNIC scheme of the NIC;

(iii) CSI should present tariff-reduction suggestions to Raja Chelliaya Committee;

(iv) Ministry of Water Resources and various State Departments should integrate the action plan of Central Water Commission (CWC) into a national schedule;

(v) IT use plan was needed to be involved and publicised by all ministries as part of a national-level IT Action Plan;

(vi) CSI should help in formulating the above plan for wealth generation and improvement in quality of life.

D. *Training and Standardisation*

(i) CSI should provide a check list of all preparations needed before purchase of computers and publicise the same;

(ii) DOE should intervene in laying down good documentation standards for implementation of all hardware and software vendors;

(iii) CSI should determine a *Code of Ethics* for all IT vendors;

(iv) Special incentives should be considered for computer workers, along with a certification of training;

(v) A training institute for banking information was urgently needed to be established;

(vi) Computer-Aided Instruction Centres, being created by the NIC by using multi-media technology and capable of 32,000 trainees per year, needed 'prioritisation' segment by segment to have the maximum visible impact on training.

E. *Action Plan*

(i) A time bound action plan was needed to facilitate full utilisation of all *Public domain* software developed by using Government of India and State government support and grants;
(ii) A single "Clearing House" was needed to avoid unconscious overlap of similar development projects;
(iii) The NIC resources should be made available for all non-profit organisations, NGO sector and research agencies;
(iv) Major software projects (like "CAM" and "CAD" carried out under UNDP support) should make their documentation available for others to use.

**Conclusion**

To summarise, IT's all-pervading impact in all sectors is being felt today from the pre-industrial society to the post-industrial society across the entire sub-continent of India. This fact came out clearly in the working conference in its authoritative deliberation covering as many as 35 premier organisations of the country. Alongside, a clear mandate was also given to both DOE and CSI to orchestrate as well as catalyse a lot of disjointed IT efforts in the country, even including those in the government sectors. One only hopes that this mandate will be heeded by the various authorities and agencies concern with IT in India.

# PART II

# GENERAL

# 2

# INAUGURAL NOTE

N. VITTAL*

## Introduction

We live in an age dominated by technology. Information Technology (IT) is perhaps one of the most influential of the present technologies because it is a *meta* resource. There is no aspect of life or no sector of industry or services which cannot benefit by the application of IT. By IT, we mean that sector of electronics where we operate mainly on the systems based on computers (hardware and software) linked with communications. This powerful combination of computers and communications has emerged as an instrument for improving the performance of any sector of activity, be it manufacturing, education, rural development entertainment, process control, etc.

## IT : Strategy and Applications

We can approach the theme of IT in everyday life from two angles. One is just listing out and identifying the areas where information technology can be applied. The second is to go into the question of evolving a strategy by which such application of IT could be achieved. We shall focus more on the second angle. This is because we find that we Indians are very good in theory but when it comes to action, we are nowhere near being champions. Of course, while tackling a natural disaster or other emergency we are perhaps able to come up with solutions. At such times, we have no time for argumentation or for vested interests to play their role. But for this exception, by and large, we are, as Dr. Paul Appleby said in his review of Indian

* Secretary, Department of Electronics, Government of India.

Administration during the early years of our independence: "action-shy".

We already have IT being used in some departments of the Government of India as well as industry. We have already in position the NICNET. We had a glimpse of what NICNET can do during the recent elections, in getting information from all parts of the country. The National Informatics Centre (NIC) is based on the concept of developing data-bases at the district level which can be used for development of district level planning. The Department of Revenue is going in for a major application of computer systems in administration of customs and excise.

When it comes to applications affecting large sections of the public, we have the successful example of application of computers in railway reservation systems. Of course, airlines also have computerised systems. In banking also, there could be substantial progress but thanks to the fears entertained by the unions, the progress is not as much as it could be. What is happening in banking is also an example of how, even though a developing country like Indian can have access to IT, even though we may have the technology, its actual application may be delayed by other factors.

An attempt was made to inject an element of computer literacy in general education by the CLASS Programme (Compute Literacy in Schools), but by an large, the performance of this programme has been sub-optimal.

We have application of instrumentation and computerised systems in the manufacturing sector. The recently built fertiliser, cement and textile plants have gone in for the application of electronic control systems in a significant way. Numerically controlled machines (CNC's) also became familiar from the 60s, so far as the machine tool industry is concerned. These are large areas in the manufacturing sector where we can apply electronic control and instrumentation systems. However, till recently, we had not made any systematic industrywide, nationwide effort to achieve this. A case in point is the 20-year old appropriate automation programme of the Department of Electronics (DOE). The DOE has been funding research in different sectors for development of control and instrumentation systems. Most of them have remained at the laboratory level or, at best, confined to some selected plants. No effort to bring this knowledge to the notice of the industry across the board and also tackle the problem of transferring the research findings to industry was launched. In the last six months, this lacuna is being removed. The DOE has launched at vigorous drive to send technical reports directly to the chief executives of power generation, tea, textiles, sugar paper and pulp and cement industries.

Consumer electronics is another area where again IT has played a part. In fact may people identify electronics with television and VCR. Unfortunately, this in turn had led to a perception that the TV and VCR are items of conspicuous consumption, they are luxury items, they are for the elite etc. As a result, we find that the TV industry has been facing a negative growth in the past three years. The black and white TV production has gone down from 4.4 million to 4 million and 3.6 million in the years 1988-89, 1989-90 and 1990-91 respectively.

**New Approach to IT**

What are the new areas where we can apply electronics and IT? In fact, practically there is no activity where we cannot apply electronics and IT. Pilzer makes the point that modern business is not longer a case of "find a need and fill it" but it is a game of "imagine a need and create it". (*Unlimited Wealth — The Theory and Practice of Economic Alchemy* by Paul Zane Pilzer). This is totally applicable to IT. If we are asked what the role of IT is in everyday life, we would say that the application is limited only by our imagination. We live in the age of technology or what Pilzer would call the age of economic alchemy and it is only our imagination that limits the application of this bounty. We would, therefore, round up this part of talk regarding IT for everyday life by saying that we have made very little use of IT in our country so far. We have barely scratched the surface. A part of the reason for our poor show is that there are vested interest who see a threat to their interests and thereby impede the growth of IT. We also have the perennial problem of resources, in making good use of IT.

That last observation can be challenged. Are we really short of resources when it comes to applying IT? The thought on resources brings us to the next aspects of IT in everyday life. Normally we adopted only an economist's approach to the issue of development of an industry or application of technology and so on. In the recent months especially, economic issues have grabbed the headlines. For a change they have replaced the political issues as the number one item in the nation's agenda and debates in the media. It is, therefore.

worthwhile to recall at this stage what a perceptive observer like Pilzer says in his book. The rest of my talk, therefore, is an attempt at giving a glimpse of what Pilzer has said about the alchemical role of technology. We shall then go on to see to what extent we can apply these principles of Pilzer in achieving our basic objective of a better life for the people of this country, by applying IT in everyday life.

Pilzer says: "Underlying the Theory of Alchemy is the notion that technology has liberated us from the zero-sum game of traditional economics. Instead of finding better ways to slice up the same old pie, in the alchemic world, you concentrate on baking a new pie big enough for all to share. In short, an Alchemist creates wealth; an economist merely moves it around." He then goes on to comment on some of the new realities of today, these are:

(a) The only enduring business is the business of change;
(b) The market has no corners;
(c) No business is an island;
(d) The first law of modern business is no longer "find a need and fill it", but "imagine a need and create it"; and
(e) Labour is capital.

Each one of the above observations calls for deep thinking in our country, we tend to think of issues like population and resources from traditional, generally negative, and important points of view. We would suggest that we should change this approach and look at these problems as opportunities. For instance we are likely to consider labour, especially organised labour, as a problem. In fact, we can look at labour as capital and see how best we can motivate people to give their best. Let us not forget that IT ultimately is the supreme example of intellectual capitalism. It is the culmination of what Alwyn Toffler would call the *power shift* from violence to wealth to knowledge.

**IT as an Alchemist and its Laws**

Our basic point is that IT can play the role of an alchemist in helping us to overcome our economic problems. In order to appreciate how this can be achieved, a look at the six laws of economic alchemy as enunciated by Pilzer will not be out of place. Here are these laws:

The *first* law of alchemy is that "technology determines the nature of physical resources". The *second* law is "technology determines the supply of physical resources". The *third* law explains what controls the advance of technology and hence contains the key to wealth. Mathematically it can be expressed as $W = PT^n$, where $W$ stands for wealth, $P$ for physical resources, $T$ for technology and $n$ is exponential.

By enabling us to make productive use of a particular raw material, technology determines what constitutes a physical resource. Technology determines our supply or existing physical resources by determining both the efficiency with which we use the resources and our ability to find, obtain, distribute and store them. The rate at which the society's technology advances is determined by the relative level of the ability to process information.

The *fourth* law of alchemy is "by providing us with raw materials and service, and changing the way in which we live, technology determines what constitutes a need and hence the nature of consumer demand." The *fifth* law is "technology determines the level of consumer demand by determining the price at which the goods can be sold". The *sixth* and final law is "the immediate economic potential for an individual an industry or a society can be explained by examining the technology gap, the best practices possible and the current knowledge and the practices in actual use."

**Technology and Physical Resources**

We would, therefore, suggest that if we want to see that the IT is made applicable in every day life, we should make full use of these six laws of economic alchemy as enunciated by Pilzer. Let us begin with the *first* one. Technology determines the nature of physical resources. IT can help in making the best use of the resources we have. Especially in the area of manufacturing, for instance, the application of process control systems can save substantially in energy and raw materials. We have done this exercise so far as instrumentation and control is concerned and our estimate shows that by applying process control systems and appropriate automation that has been developed as a result of DOE funded research in the past 20 years, substantial savings are possible as shown in Table 2.1.

What is coming in the way of applying this technology is lack of awareness and lack of resources. In order to overcome the problems

TABLE 2.1: Projected Potential: Costs and Benefits of Increased Electronics Usage in Selected Industries

| | Steel | Cement | Ferti-lizer | Paper | Elect-ricity | Total |
|---|---|---|---|---|---|---|
| Production (1988-89) | 8.3 M.t. | 42 M.t. | 11 M.t. | 1.8 M.t. | 221 B. kWh | |
| Capital cost of electronification (Rs. crores) | 565 | 140 | 330 | 35 | 100 | 1170 |
| Additional Production | 0.68 M.t. | 1.05 M.t. | 0.9 M.t. | 0.084 M.t. | 22 B. kWh | |
| Capital cost of additional production (Rs. crores) | 1700 | 126 | 2800 | 125 | 750 | 5501 |
| Annual energy savings (Rs. crores.) | 125 | 92.5 | | 8.7 | | |
| Present value of energy savings @ 12% (Rs. crores) | 790 | 585 | | 55 | | 1430 |
| Total cost savings from electronification (Rs. crores) | 2490 | 711 | 2800 | 180 | 750 | 6931 |
| Net Savings from Electronification (Rs. crores) | 1925 | 571 | 2470 | 145 | 650 | 5761 |

of awareness, we in the DOE have started a massive programme of writing from the Secretary, DOE, to the individual chief executives of units in different sectors like power generation, tea, steel, textile, sugar, paper and pulp, cement, etc. There has been an enthusiastic response to our letters which were sent with the appropriate technical reports on the industry concerned. This will be obvious from the figures given in Table 2.2.

This is just the beginning. We will have to tie up the resources. The Risk Capital Finance Corporation has come forward to fund, in selected industries, the application of these systems so that this can become a model for others. Other financial institutions like IDBI, ICICI, etc., also have shown a positive interest.

The *second* law of alchemy is that technology determines the supply of physical resources. The Prime Minister while giving away the DOE's "Excellence in electronics" Awards on 24th August, 1991 made the telling point that we must apply computers and IT in government. He started with reference to the recent UPSC examination scandal where the question papers leaked out. He indicated that the government was thinking in terms of applying IT and computer network so that instead of printing the papers in advance and running the risk of leakage, information could be released all over the country simultaneously using the national network. Here, we find that IT can completely replace the vast physical resources involved by way of paper, printing and distribution etc. by cheaper alternative and more importantly a more secure system. Another example the Prime Minister pointed out was the processing of pension papers in the defence services. At present, a lot of man-hours are used and even then the documents are not completed in time. It is learnt that already so far as the civilian side is concerned, processing of pension papers in the Government of India is being done through through application of computer technology. Out of nearly a lakh of cases processed, there are hardly 300 complaints about calculation of pensions, etc. The same thing has been extended now to the army pension papers. There could be substantial savings in paper. This in turn would mean indirectly some marginal beneficial impact on the environment because paper is one of the industries which places a severe strain on environment because of the need to cut trees to get the raw material.

TABLE 2.2: Electronic: Retrofit Report (Period 1-4-1991 to 31-7-1991)

| Sl. No. | Description | Sectors | | | | | | |
|---|---|---|---|---|---|---|---|---|
| | | Tea | Cement | Paper & Pulp | Textiles | Power | Sugar | Total |
| 1 | 2 | 3 | 4 | 5 | 6 | 7 | 8 | 9 |
| 1. | Total No. of letters sent | 60 | 65 | 117 | 116 | 29 | 79 | 466 |
| 2. | Responses received | 19 | 14 | 11 | 7 | 3 | 4 | 58 |
| 3. | Responses attended to/replied | 13 | 10 | 5 | 5 | 2 | 4 | 39 |

## Key to Economic Wealth

The *third* law of alchemy explains that the wealth of a nation is equal to the product of the physical resources and technology raised to the power of *'n'* ($W=PXT^n$). It is here that we should look upon IT has a saviour for the country. We are today without much of rupee resources, and in foreign exchange situation, we have a crisis. This means that we should think in terms of making the best use of the physical assets we already have. Take, for instance, an area like information in libraries. Many educational institutions are short of resources and especially foreign exchange to subscribe to costly foreign magazines. If we can have a national network connecting all the libraries, there will be a significant contribution through the educational infrastructure. The educational and research network (ER Network) of the DOE is trying to do this. As of now we have got around 55 institutions registered in the ER Network, catering to about 3000 institutions. Our objective must be to cover practically every educational institution in the country. This, in turn, would contribute to greater intellectual stimulation, saving in terms for subscriptions to costly foreign magazines and technical journals and above all, savings substantially in time because, with access to the databases all over the world, it will be possible for our people to be as up to date as anywhere else. We have today the technology and we have the constraint today because of the lack of resources. IT can help us to not only overcome this problem but also to build the basis for a wealthier India.

The same can be said about the application of IT in improving the production performance, cutting down rejection rates, improving quality in the manufacturing sector of industry. We have already mentioned about the DOE-funded appropriate automation programme. If in every sector of industry there is a systematic attempt in terms of applications of IT-based central systems there will be substantial improvement. We will save on costs and energy and improve the productivity and competitiveness of the Indian industry.

**Need and Nature of Consumer Demand**

This brings us to the *fourth* law of economic alchemy, i.e., by providing us with new products and services and changing the way in which we live, technology decides what constitutes a need and hence the nature of the consumer demand. It is here that we would like to appeal to all those who are concerned with IT in particular and electronics in general about the need to change the perceptions of the public. In a democracy, perceptions are very important. Public opinion is based on perceptions. Public opinion ultimately decides what political stances are going to be. Political stances decide policies about where the resources would be spent. They also decide the shape of regulations and laws. The perception today for instance is that a TV or a VCR is a luxury item. On the other hand, the TV and VCR as an audio-visual infrastructure has a tremendous potential for education. Imagine a TV and a VCR in every school in this country and a system of telecasting, which experts like Shri P.S. Deodhar have been talking about. Shri Deodhar in his recent book, *The Third Parent* brings out a blue-print about how we can use the existing Doordarshan network for distance learning process and projecting educational TV in a much more effective manner. At the same time, because of the perception of TVs being luxury items, the tariff is such that they are going beyond the reach of even the middle class people.

It is here that there is a challenge to the technocrats and professional bodies like the Computer Society of India. For instance, is it not possible to combine the TV as a monitor with the computer, or convert the TV itself into a more value-added instrument so that the perception that it is an elitist luxury item to be shunned, is first removed?

The *fifth* law of technology appropriately is that, the level of consumer demand is determined by technology because it is technology which determines the price at which the goods can be sold. It is here that we should concentrate our efforts. Secondly, the higher cost of the equipment limits the market. We have come across instances in the West where the cost problem was tackled by a creative approach for deciding the level at which the product should be marketed. In his book, *Father, Son & Co.*, Tom Watson Jr. points out how, when IBM shifted to transistors from thermionic valves, they found that the cost of the transistor was about $2.16. Unless this was brought down to $1.5, they could not mass produce the computers built on transistors. Accordingly, an arrangement was made with Motorola to put up a transistor factory. IBM gave an assurance that 90 per cent of the production would be lifted by IBM, provided, the cost was $1.5. Ultimately, the factory was built and transistorised computers were built. The rest is history.

Why is it then that our Indian electronic industry and those concerned with IT cannot sit together and evolve a similar strategy? Let us do an element of reverse engineering in a marketing sense. If the market for both the PC or the PC linked with a TV can be brought down to say Rs. 3000-4000, the demand will sky-rocket. Why not work out a manufacturing arrangement in such a way that the full potential of this country and the full growth potential of the electronics and IT technology country is utilised?

Otherwise, we are caught in an eternal *Catch 22* situation. May be, because of the protective atmosphere we have had and the plethora of licensing we had adopted in the past, the industry is generally united only to plead for concessions from the government. Probably, more innovation was shown in getting best benefits out of the loopholes in the law rather than technological innovations! Now that the government have liberalised the trade and industrial policies, why not apply the strategies like the learning curve, which is so well-described by Pilzer in his book, and come out with a programme for cost reduction? Unless such innovations are made, we will be only scratching the surface. The Prime Minister, while addressing the Award winners for excellence in electronics, particularly mentioned that so far, we have only scratched the surface. Unless IT and electronics become wide-spread and practically a part of every-day life, it will continue to be perceived as an elitist item.

**Resistance to Technology**

A problem which was mentioned in passing while reviewing the growth of IT in the country is the resistance from the groups who feel threatened by the onward march of technology. In the area of transportation, the horse-drawn carriages were replaced by cycle-rickshaws and then auto-rickshaws. This was relatively smooth because the horse-drawn carriage was not in the organised sector. On the other hand, when IT is sought to be applied in the banking sector, we find that the progress is not so smooth. This is because the labour is organised and there is a perception that jobs will be threatened.

How do we meet this situation? Technology about which we have mentioned above can be one solution. Another solution can be adopting strategies which have worked successfully in other areas. For instance, communism succeeded in China, when Mao Tse Tung adopted the strategy of encircling the cities from the villages. If there is resistance in certain organised sectors, the logical choice for those concerned with information technology would be to take those areas where there is no resistance and apply IT. In the process, it may also be possible to prove the value of IT. When Swami Vivekananda was asked how he could prove that a particular line was crooked, he said that he would draw a straight line and people could immediately appreciate the difference. Because of history, it may happen that under the labour laws, efficiency is debarred or even made illegal. Why not be think of those areas where there are no such laws against efficiency? A case in point is the growth of courier system in the United States. As the postal systems could not deliver the services faster, the courier system developed. If we want to be successful in spreading IT in every walk of life, we should target markets and sectors, where we will not be confronted with vested interests or legal restrictions. This, apart from the application of the fifth law of Pilzer, should help us.

**Our Economic Potential**

Finally, we come to the *sixth* law, i.e., the economic potential of an individual or an industry or a society is explained by examining the technology gap, the best practices possible, the current knowledge and the practices in actual use. It is here that a seminar like this can explore sector by sector, and then identify what are the technologies that can be immediately implemented, and the areas where it can be done. The DOE's initiative in the area of appropriate automation is just an example of how technologies are available locally and could be applied to the local industry. There may be other similar applications. For instance, in many areas of government itself, it should be possible to introduce IT. Postal service is one such area. It is said that nearly 80 per cent of the postal budget is on manpower. Suppose we take advantage of concepts like electronic mail and funds transfer and electronification of postal services, we will not only be giving a better service to the public, but, there will also be substantial savings. A transmission of money order by the satellite network will be cheaper than the manual system of money orders by 22p per money order. The same thing can also be done in the area of police administration also. We have already mentioned the application of IT in UPSC examination or in Army Pensions. Land records is another area where we can apply IT in a big way. Who knows this can also help partly to check corruption because, at the village level, getting land records is a perennial source for corruption.

If we take a look at national planning, we find that for the past 40 years, we have adopted an energy and resource intensive paradigm. IT can help us to break out of this and have an information intensive paradigm. A plea for such a switch has been made by Shri Krishanlal Sondhi (who was connected with the Planning Commission) in his recent book *Beyond Mass Communication*.

We have so far highlighted the resistance to technology that may come from vested interests and the bottlenecks of law on the one hand, and the economic aspects like price on the other. Ultimately you need financial resources. How to generate financial resources? One method would be, so far as government is concerned, to look at every sector and department, and earmark certain percentage of the budget for systematic application of IT. Of course, in a department like electronics, we are already undertaking an exercise for zero-based budgeting so that our limited resources can be deployed in areas where they are needed. For instance, we found a potential for export in software and one of the bottlenecks was lack of availability of telematic infrastructure. Therefore, we have done an internal exercise to provide Rs. 5 crores from our limited budget for buying of the earth stations and the TDMA systems and so on. A similar exercise can be done right through the government both at the centre and in the states. This can be done in every educational institution and university so far as education is concerned. As regards the manufacturing sector of the industry, a similar exercise can be undertaken. If this is done we will find that inspite of the generally perceived shortage of financial resources, we will come up with enough resources.

**Conclusion**

The above analysis attempts to share some ideas about how IT can be used substantially in every walk of life. We have particularly focussed on the *six laws of economic alchemy* which Pilzer has advocated. If we can apply those laws, we will have a more pragmatic solution to the daunting problems which our nation faces, and ensure that IT becomes an effective instrument for the people of this country to face those problems successfully.

# 3

# KEYNOTE

DR. N. SESHAGIRI*

**Introduction**

Information Technology (IT) has now become a scientific discipline emerged out of the research and development activities in the field of computer technology, database technology, software technology, television technology and communication technology. For IT professionals and end-users, it holds promises as a "productivity tool". "The real challenge comes in delivering quality information – the information that people really need, and often need quickly, in order to do their jobs — and facilitating information sharing".

**Information Technology in India**

Information concepts and technologies are changing very rapidly and the economic importance of "information" has grown steadily. The growing "informatisation" of economy is facilitating the global integration of national and regional economics. National and international computer-communication networks are emerging with remote access to host computers; and distance and geographical barriers are becoming virtually irrelevant either in the cost or operational sense.

Computer Policy-1984, Electronic Policy-1985 and Software Policy-1986 laid the foundations for the liberalised growth of IT industry in the country. IT industry, user groups and professionals who require organised information flow for multi-disciplinary R&D, await the declaration of a comprehensive National Informatics Policy by the government, and also setting up of national policy level committees.

Use of IT has brought in confidence as well as sincerity in the

---

* Director General, National Informatics Centre, Planning Commission, Government of India.

"Public Administration" to provide quality service. This is evident from the development of Computer-Communication Networks (NICNET, INDONET, ERNET, I-NET, etc), banking computerisation, computerised railways reservation system, Airlines reservation system, and database development for decision-making in the government and in the country. Impact of live coverage of the Parliament Election-91 results analysis using NICNET facilities and Doordarshan was tremendous among the people in India.

Better policy decision needs better information and formulation of policy requires increasing knowledge of ground reality. In fact, IT is an important tool of cooperation within the government and the public; and exceedingly relevant for the "common public" in everyday life. It is essential to create a national focal point to coordinate the development and assimilation of IT in government operations. Existing frameworks within the government may have to be restructured to take the opportunities offered by IT.

**IT for Social Transformation and Development**

Our country has different types of terrain, resources, climate, socio-economic levels, distinct problems, etc. Socio-economic conditions in more than 50 per cent of the villages are far from satisfactory. The Seventh National Development Plan has laid emphasis on the importance of "decentralised planning" and "effective planning" at district level, for working out schemes based on the actual requirement of people in rural areas.

Major component of the decentralised planning is rural development. Actual implementation of all development projects and administrative tasks "starts from and is monitored by" district authorities. IT is thus essential for planning and implementation of rural development programme. Fusion of IT, biotechnology and space technology will bring in the necessary S&T inputs for required regional rural development in the country.

**Development of Informatics for Decision Support in Government**

National Informatics Centre (NIC) is the nodal S&T organisation of the central government for informatics development for decision support in government, using the NICNET facilities available at district, state and the central government departments. There are about 2000 informatics professionals of NIC involved in this national effort. NICNET is a satellite (INSAT-1D) based computer-communication network.

Effective institutional arrangements such as (i) NIC-Ministry Coordination Committee (NMCC) in the central government ministries, (ii) NIC-State Coordination Committee (NSCC) at the state level, and (iii) NIC-District Coordination Committee (NDCC) at the district level, are already established to assist in working out short-term and long-term IT plan for the development of computer-based information systems and data-bases in various sectors of importance and also to give possible guidance for implementation.

*A. Land Records Computerisation Programme*

In accordance with the importance given by the central government for "land records and land reforms and streamline systems and procedures for effecient land management', NIC has undertaken the land records computerisation programme at 15 pilot districts (Burdwan, Rewari, Ropar, Bishanpur, Sanitpur, Tirvananthapuram, Gulbarga, Salem, Wardha, Dungarpur, Kangra, Deoria, Tripura (North), Imphal and Thoubal) selected by the Central Rural Development department.

*B. Informatics Development Programme at District Level (DISNIC)*

DISNIC programme provides a framework for the development of district information system in about 27 sectors for each district and the programme is operational in about 450 districts across the country.

GIS software tools (GISNIC) using state-of-art GIS concepts were developed to facilitate the development of geographic information system for enabling spatial planning for rural development in the country. NIC would like to have collaboration with ISRO in the area of GIS activities for the development of natural resource management system using remote sensing data at the district level.

*C. Treasury Level Computerisation*

Treasury computerisation programme using NICNET facilities are undertaken in the states of Maharashtra, Himachal Pradesh, Kerala, Karnataka, Tamil Nadu, Haryana, Bihar, Rajasthan, Uttar Pradesh, Orissa and Tripura, to facilitate the development of integrated financial management information system for state governments. This programme is operational in all the districts in the states of Himachal Pradesh and Maharashtra. NIC acknowledges the cooperation and participation of the State governments extended to

NIC in implementing the programme.

*D. Common Power Database*

Development of common power database on NICNET for the benefit of the Central Electricity Authority (CEA), Regional/State electricity boards, power corporations, the Central Energy Department, and the Planning Commission is under implementation. The Department of Power, Government of India has issued instructions to all the State power departments to utilise NICNET for this purpose.

*E. METLINK on NICNET*

Development of NICNET-based water resources management information system (surface water, ground water, etc.) and METLINK on NICNET for 400 meteorological stations to facilitate the meteorological information flow to the India Meteorological Department (IMD) would be given necessary support.

*F. Design Informatics*

Computer-aided design group, one of the R&D groups of NIC, supports various government organisations and public sector undertakings in design informatics area including specialised HRD and expert support to improve design productivity. Development of utility mapping (Urban GIS) has been undertaken in Delhi under NORAD technical cooperation programme between Norway and India.

*G. NICNET-Based Project Monitoring (NICPROM) Programme*

The main objective of this programme is to provide project monitoring facility to the project monitoring committees to enable them to monitor the progress of various projects covering different sectors of the economy which are in progress in different parts of the country. NICPROM Programme facilitates (i) establishment of NICNET close user groups (CUGs), (ii) macro-level plan monitoring, (iii) microlevel project monitoring and (iv) World Bank project monitoring.

NICPROM enables the Government of India to effectively monitor large projects (Costing Rs. 100 crores and above), with respect to reducing the delay and optimum use of available resources. Under NICNET CUGs Programme, Organisations like SAIL, NTPC, FCI and IFFCO use NICNET for their projects monitoring.

*H. Enhancement of NICNET Facilities*

NICNET is expected to be enhanced with the latest state-of-art techology during the Eighth Five-Year Plan period (1992-97) to cover about 5300 blocks/tehsils (sub-district level administrative unit) throughout the country to facilitate grass-root level development planning and administration. Negotiations with the World Bank for financial assistance to the tune of about US$ 150 million for the expansion of NICNET programme to the block level are at an advanced stage.

**IT Training and Human Resources Development**

IT is a human resource intensive activity. Any national strategy should address (i) education and training of managers and users, (ii) training and retraining of IT specialists, (iii) instituition of training facilities for IT personnel, and (iv) improvement of training cost-effectiveness [APO90*].

NIC has scheduled about 160 IT courses under its "Government Informatics Training Programme" during 1990-91 for government employees and more than 10,000 participants have attended. It has been planned to set-up computer-aided instruction (CAI) facilities using multi-media technology to train the government staff at NIC regional centres to enable the government staff to use the IT facilities set-up in various government departments effectively.

National planning for "training and re-training" of IT users is to be given thrust in the country and the organisation like CMC Ltd should provide catalytic support for banking computerisation and IT training and education; and also undertake coordinated efforts to associate private and public organisations for collosal amount of training on IT in banking industry with the agreement of bank employees unions. The Department of Electronics is expected to give matching grant to the IT training institutes to undertake this national effort.

**Establishment of POLICENET**

Establishment of POLICENET is long overdue in the country. Both central and state police organistations and various investigation

---

* APO Symposium on IT in Government, held at Seoul, Republic of Korea on 5-8 November 1990.

agencies could promote the POLICENET and derive benefit by information sharing among themselves. NIC would certainly give its technical expertise in this regard, if asked for, and also extend software support to the police departments in the area of "law and order".

But NIC has constraints in allowing police and defence to use NICNET. This is due to the fact that defence, police and intelligence organisations have been made to keep outside the purview of NICNET and NIC Programmes, as NIC receives financial assistance from various international and multinational organisations for the promotion of informatics development programme for development planning and administration.

**Conclusion**

NIC institutional facilities and infrastructural facilities (NICNET) could act as a "launching pad" for private and public sector database industry in the country. Informatics development programme for decision support in government at the national level, State level and district level is already getting implemented by NIC. This coordinated national effort has the promise of facilitating development planning and responsive administration to improve the socio-economic conditions of the "common public" at the grass-root level in the country.

Integrated development of informatics for the government is required. Development of computerised information systems and databases and the utilisation of IT resources is a matter of strategic importance for the effective growth of government services today. Coordinated development and assimilation of IT in government operations through the national focal point is essential.

# 4

# PRESIDENT'S NOTE

DR. RATTAN K. DATTA

## Introduction

A Famous Painter, found sitting under the shade of the Eiffel Tower in Paris, when queried, said "this is the only place where I cannot see the Damn thing".

I quoted the Eiffel Tower, because I wanted to see the day Byte Singh and Bias Lal complain they have had too much of IT! That will make my life worth it. At the risk of being a cliche-monger, passing through the stone age, other ages, the wheel and industrial revolution, society has now entered an information revolution "Third Wave" and so on. Before we discuss the impact of IT it is necessary to answer a question: what kind of a beast is IT?

First, one can describe information and then technology related to information. To describe information one starts with the low level data (events, occurrences, etc., which by themselves carry no meaning) linking with the environment, the circumstance, etc. and analysis of which leads to information (on which we can act); then esoterically one talks about all that linkage from information to knowledge and then on to wisdom (God help us!)

Information has now a "place in the Sun"; the new *paradigm* of management puts it as the prime resource (displacing cash) from which one can derive every other necessity; coming thus, to my pet slogan, "Information is as important as *Roti, Kapra* aur *Makan* (bread, clothing and housing)," because, from information we can derive all the necessities of life.

The next logical question that arises is how do we juggle with information and to the rescue came technology of two Cs —

------------------

* President, Computer Society of India

Computers and Communication. These two Cs from two distinct streams have become highly interdependent, so that progress on either is mutually beneficial. A merger of the two is a happy marriage leading to IT, a great impetus being provided by integrated circuitary (the now Ubiquitous "Chip"). The pace of progress in this area is so fast that what was achievable in the pre-chip era in a matter of years is now possible to accomplish in a matter of days if not hours, minutes and so on. "Science update", a few months ago, while listing the ten most spectacular inventions of the century, came up with three top items the microprocessor, fibre optics and the satellite.

All the above are fundamental components of modern "IT". *Fantasies* of "Mahabharat" became real through the CNN channel during the Gulf War. "Trojan Horsing" on Microprocessors. IT has so pervaded every human activity that one should be most concerned if a typical human endeavour does not use "IT"! Some protagonists of IT, like me, would even go to the extent to say unequivocally that the present political world order, whose many myths are tumbling like the proverbial house of cards, has also been influenced by the "IT". We may keep on debating that issue, but the facts are there for everyone to see!

**IT Scenario in India**

IT revolution, though tangible in India, has been a rather late starter and the progress slow; there is a high degree of inertia and many dyed-in-the-wool feitishes overcome. In the sixties, there were all types of — perhaps legitimate — apprehensions from the trade unions and the workers on one side and the management on the other. Central to the whole trouble was ignorance and half knowledge. Whatever applications were started were, in most cases "vendor driven" or for the "prestige" for management, because they had seen it (rather superficially) happening in some other parts of the World; the well know "Jonese-S Syndrome"!

The CSI started with a degree of vendor incentive (user group) but it soon picked up true professionalism and was able to present to the government, industry and the public, objective perspectives. Doubts and taboos started falling on the way, and consolidation of IT started picking up by the eighties. Initially, computers were meant for only scientific usage, but by the eighties they have come into use not only for routine and other mundane activity, but also for enhanced operations efficiency.

Mr. Rajeev Gandhi came to the helm of affairs in 1984 and the country saw a phenomenal growth, nay, an explosion. He had the unflinching faith in a gospel that IT is the primary tool for increasing national productivity and creating a better quality of life for its citizens. Efforts of CSI in propagating IT as an indispensable tool for the common man got a fillip. A great ally was the increase in the speed of computing and transaction power that increased ten-fold every five years, with an astonishing comparable price fall. One could buy, in 1985, a computer more powerful than the most powerful computers of the sixties and seventies at a price of almost one hundredth of that price. PCs, which were designed and launched for personal use, picked up power, so that these became significant application tools in the office. Today these have even penetrated into the environs of progressive farmers in villages, no more as a prestigious gadget or a status symbol, but as an indispensable tool for growth and productivity.

Intellectuals in the country, who were looking for a niche in the national and world market, found IT and in particular software as a significant vehicle. CSI again played a pivotal role in convincing the government that it would be desirable to declare this as an industry and provide all the incentives. Can we not be global players in the trillion dollar software market? Professionals from India, when abroad, are able to perform miracles within a short time, but at home the same work takes ages. Titillatingly a "food for thought" – what is the secret portion? – touchstone? a magic word or a catalyst, that is lacking? Is it the climate? Is it the environment? Probably a lack of synergy? CSI is convinced on the last score. To stimulate that symbiosis, CSI is propagating the creation of a consortium: one of industries, professionals and CSI. There is bound to be resistance but we have to keep pushing and I am sure, one day, not too far distant, we will succeed in an edifice of efficiency that will tower over the global software market. My hunch is that the future lies with software – be it on PC, the workstation, distributed databases, network and massive parallel computing.

## IT is Paras

*Paras* is a Sanskrit/Hindi word which refers to a stone that can convert any base metal into gold, under the science of alchemy unlike the proverbial Midas who got the gift. This is a slogan, again started by the CSI to focus attention of the public, government and industry on the use of IT. To illustrate that it is just not a slogan but "doable", I often quote a few examples. Take the case of railway reservation system. Before the computerised reservation, it used to take an average person anything from two to four hours to buy a ticket, to meet which need, he shuffled from one window to another; today he just gets a ticket and reservation from one window and that, at most, in half an hour. Issue of each ticket thus saves time of anything from one to three hours. For Delhi station alone, there are 80,000 tickets issued daily, a saving of the nation's time of the order of 200,000 hours a day and in terms of money it could be Rs. 20 lakhs per day or over Rs. 60 crores every year! Considering all the big cities in the country, one can say that the nation is saving a few hundred thousand crores of rupees through the introduction of railway reservation system whereas money spent for computerisation will be a mere fraction of that.

Another example one could take when we add one more C with two Cs — process control. When Hindustan Zinc Ltd. started process control the quality improved, as also the production, by 1.8 to 2 per cent. In Thermal Power it is said that by spending 1000 crores on process control, we save 10,000 crores on the many facets. One can keep on giving such examples to prove that IT could be self-generating and truly *paras*.

We should not forget the other societal applications like IT in disaster management during tropical cyclones when, besides the saving of wealth, one is able to minimise agony and human lives — a priceless commodity. One can talk of increase of agricultural production in the IT way; but it is an entirely different view of IT when it helps designing artificial limbs very close to natural one, or when IT provides aid for the handicapped, like the visually handicapped and spastics, in supporting their independence and self-respect. IT is thus not only for us but also God's gift to the needy and handicapped.

**Each One, Teach a Chunk — IT Way**

Soon after Independence, the Government of India launched a campaign "each one teach one" but the performance did not come up to expectation. Prof. Yash Pal, as Chairman of University Grants Commission, even proposed a one-year moratorium to classes and suggested that all students and teachers take up a campaign for adult education to bring our nation to a level of 100 per cent literacy; people laughed and jeered ! Kerala has shown the way to do it. CSI, however, believes that through IT we can convert the slogan "each one, teach one" into "each one teach a whole chunk like a village".

Whenever I am at any student function, I extract a vow from the students of computer science to donate one month of their life to literacy campaign; the response has been very encouraging. I have been requesting new and old chapters of CSI to pledge a few days, if not a year, for this campaign. Miracles, I am told, happen when a slogan is put into practice. A few professionals like Dr. Thrimurthy, have already developed programmes for teaching Gujarati. Our aim is not as exhaustive as the "CLASS" programme, but limited in scope to start with, teaching local language alphabets, numerals and own signatures. We have faith that once this is accomplished, it will be contagious or act like an addiction and a large per cent of self-learnt personnel will multiply and will learn more. This is our hope; volunteers please come forth to take this challenge.

While on one side we, in CSI, are launching a campaign for literacy in a limited sense, on the other side, we are also building up facilities for all who want an open university environment for learning of professional courses up to the level of M. Tech. This scheme, now known as DOE accreditation scheme, was launched by DOE with the active support of CSI and in close collaboration with IETE. They say, well begun is half done, the first of the tasks was very successfully completed by the holding of "O" level examination in a mere eight months from the launch in Nov. '90 to an examination in July '91 with all the hurdles thrown in. Any such certification is a hard task, but more so in IT, where obsolescence and new inventions are very rapid. We have, therefore, to keep the whole system under dynamic review.

## Conclusion

In conclusion, we are today in an era of IT. It is not the capital or the managerial or entrepreneurial skill which can bring a revolution to the quality of life, but it is the information power. Information power is all technology on intellectual power and uses very little raw material. "The goddess Lakshmi will come only after the goddess Saraswati" is an old saying. Forget the old myth that Saraswati and Lakshmi do not co-exist. It is not that money begets money, but it is the information power which will bring in that lot of gold at the end of rainbow.

# PART III

## PRIMARY SECTOR

(Focus on Nature)

# 5

# CROPS AND SEEDS

DR. M. RAI and S. MAURIA*

## Introduction

The Indian Council of Agricultural Research (ICAR) is the apex body to undertake aid, promote and coordinate agricultural, horticultural, animal husbandry and fisheries education, research and its frontline application in the country. It has to act as a clearing house for research and general information relating to diverse associated matters. The organisation is functioning through 42 Central Institutes, 4 Bureaux, 20 National Research Centres, 9 Project Directorates, 69 All India Co-ordinated Research Projects and 26 State Agricultural Universities. It is also endeavouring to strengthen the regional research capabilities in different states to tackle the location-specific research problems by establishment of Zonal Research Stations in each of the 120 agro-climatic zones under its National Agricultural Research Project. The size and multi-disciplinary nature of the organisation, as depicted in Fig. 5.1, thus, could itself give an idea of the quantum of information that is needed to be handled in this giant set-up. The related complexities in management of the information are also obvious and pin-points the need for greater efforts and strengthening, including that of the Indian Agricultural Statistics Research Institute (Fig. 5.2).

The quantity and complexity of information is a major factor to be given due consideration while deciding for any information management system to streamline the working. Since a major share of the work in the Council revolves around crop sciences and related aspects, the volume of information is maximum here. For this forum,

---

* Indian Council of Agricultural Research, Government of India.

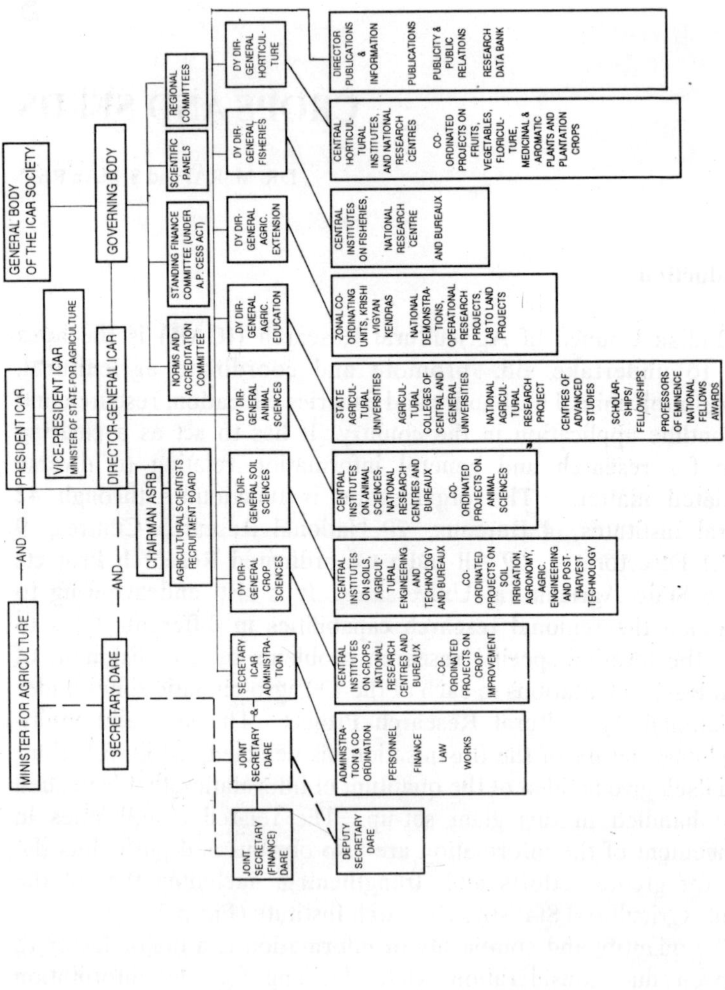


FIG. 5.1: Organisation of Department of Agricultural Research and Education (DARE) and Indian Council of Agricultural Research (ICAR)

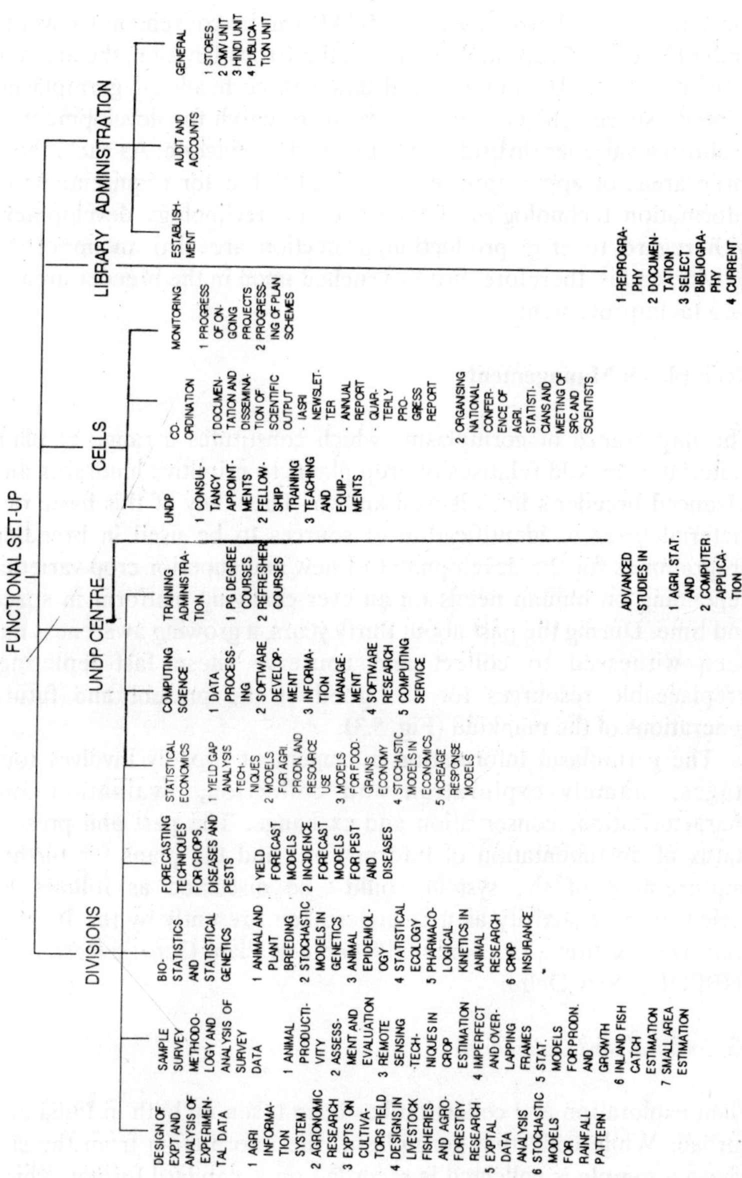


FIG. 5.2: Indian Agricultural Statistics Research Institute Functional Set-up

the activities of Crops Division in ICAR can be conveniently covered under the title, "Crops and Seeds". In the Crops Division, the areas of activities can be broadly covered under three heads (i) germplasm-related aspects, (ii) crop improvement research for development of promising varieties/hybrids, and (iii) seed production. As such, these three areas of application are discussed below for requirements of information technologies. Researches on technology development with regard to crop production/protection are also an important activity, and is, therefore, briefly touched upon in the breeder area of varietal improvement.

## Germplasm Management

The importance of germplasm, which constitutes a range of plant material from wild relatives of crop plants to primitive landraces and advanced breeder's lines is well-known. The study of this basic raw material leads to identification of sources to be used in breeding programmes for the development of new and superior crop varieties depending on human needs on an ever-changing platform in space and time. During the past about thirty years, a growing awareness has been witnessed to collect and conserve these fast-depleting, irreplaceable resources for the good of the present and future generations of the mankind (Fig. 5.3).

The germplasm information management broadly involves four stages, namely exploration and collection, evaluation and characterisation, conservation and exchange. The past and present status of documentation of information, and the plans for further improvement of the system could be discussed as follows by reviewing each activity as it is undertaken presently by the ICAR's concerned institute, i.e., National Bureau of Plant Genetic Resources (NBPGR), New Delhi:

### *Exploration and Collection*

Plant exploration and collection has been taken up both in India and abroad. While collecting germplasm, the information from the site where a sample is collected is recorded on a standard format, which is called the 'passport data sheet'. The information about the location of the site, environmental and ecological variables and population structure etc. is collected. Such data are available for explorations

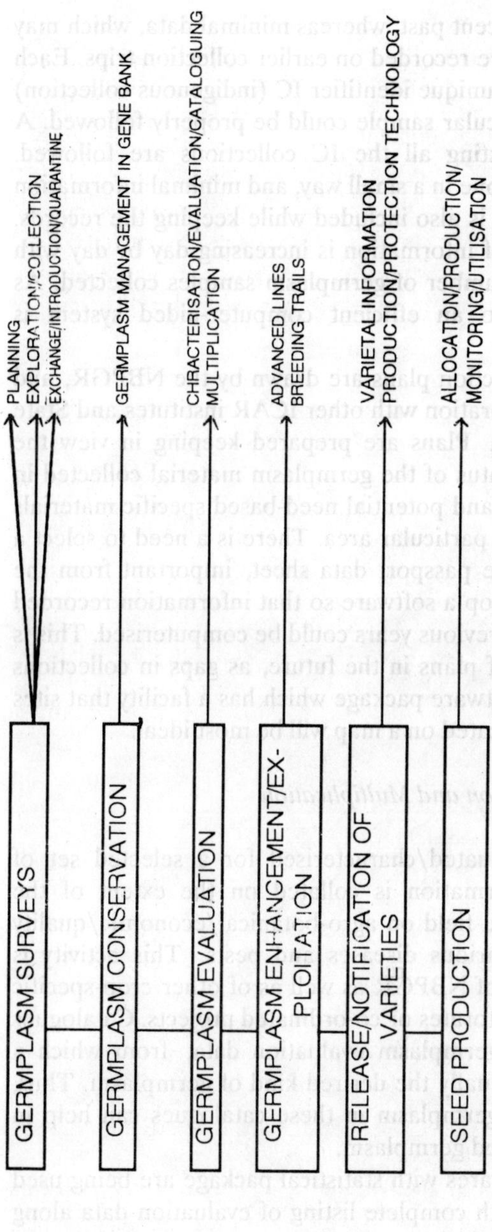


FIG. 5.3: Subsequence for Information Management in Crops and Seeds

undertaken during the recent past, whereas minimal data, which may not be available now, were recorded on earlier collection trips. Each collection is later given a unique identifier IC (indigenous collection) number so that the particular sample could be properly followed. A centralised system of listing all the IC collections are followed. Presently it is manually done in a small way, and minimal information from passport data sheet is also included while keeping the records. However, the quantum of information is increasing day by day with regular increase in the number of germplasm samples collected. As such, a change over to an efficient computer-aided system is essential.

Exploration and collection plans are drawn by the NBPGR, and are undertaken in collaboration with other ICAR institutes and State Agricultural Universities. Plans are prepared keeping in view the areas covered and the status of the germplasm material collected in the previous years/trips, and potential need-based specific materials likely to be available in a particular area. There is a need to select a few descriptors, from the passport data sheet, important from the point of utility, and develop a software so that information recorded in all the data books of previous years could be computerised. This is crucial for formulation of plans in the future, as gaps in collections could be identified. A software package which has a facility that sites of collections could be located on a map will be most ideal.

*Evaluation, Characterisation and Multiplication*

Crop germplasm is evaluated/characterised for a selected set of descriptors so that information is collated on the extent of the variability observed in the field on agro-botanical/economic/quality traits and reaction to various diseases and pests. This activity is undertaken by scientists of NBPGR as well as of other crop-specific institutes or project directorates or co-ordinated projects. Catalogues are prepared from the germplasm evaluation data, from which a breeder can pick up manually the desired kind of germplasm. Thus, the classification of the germplasm in these catalogues can help in identification of the needed germplasm.

In recent times, softwares with statistical package are being used to prepare catalogues with complete listing of evaluation data along with the estimates of variability and correlation and regression parameters, frequency distribution in respect of quantitative as well as qualitative traits, and answers to certain simple and complex queries regarding the database on useful traits or combination of traits. These programmes developed in dBase III plus, leads to selection of the needed kind of germplasm.

However, due to certain limitations in this software, some of the information requirements are not fulfilled. If advanced statistical packages are an inbuilt feature of the programme information could be retrieved to have more meaningful derivations. For example, a package with cluster analysis facility can help in appropriate grouping of the germplasm in separate sub-groups to understand the affinity of relationship indifferent accessions or group of accessions. Similarly, an additional facility of principal component analysis can give still better analysis of the germplasm. Networking of this information system among different concerned centres/institutes can greatly help in making available all the information at the doorsteps of all concerned scientists. This can reduce the workload of one centre doing the job of screening germplasm information every time the request is received.

*Conservation*

The total number of germplasm accessions all over the country at different institutions, including the materials with individual breeders, may number around three lakhs. There is a national repository for long-term conservation at NBPGR, holding over 1,35,000 accessions. In addition, medium-term conservation facilities are built or proposed for about 30 research stations. These germplasm data are to be maintained on some important descripts namely crop name, genus and species, identification number, germination percentage, moisture content, month and year of storage etc. At NBPGR, a database is being developed on these aspects to ensure monitoring of information, periodically.

*Exchange and Quarantine*

Information needs to be maintained on import and export of germplasm, and quarantine aspects. Some of the requirements for imports are:

(i) an upto-date record of contact addresses of possible donors, from different countries along with the names of the crops (varieties, breeding lines) offered for supply;

(ii) information on the kinds of plant material and the appropriate time when the materials should be sent to India; and

(iii) records on incidence of diseases, pests and nematodes occurring in the exporting countries on the crop plants under reference.

All plant introductions when received, pass through plant quarantine and on their release are entered in National Register of Exotic Collections. Each introduction is given a serial EC (Exotic Collection) number, by which it is always referred in future citations. This EC number is the unique identifier and is not given to any other introduction. Other information on botanical/varietal name, donor's accession number/varietal name, its special traits, conditions of the material, remarks of quarantine unit, name/address of the donor and of the Indian Scientist/institute to whom supplied are also recorded. Collection of data on introduced materials needs to be done so that the information could be arranged/retrieved in any manner required.

An import quarantine register dealing with the import number, country, material, case number, consignee, quarantine history, etc., is another requirement to the documented. A set of records is kept on the materials, number of samples in a consignment, EC numbers, presence or absence of phytosanitary certificate and additional declaration thereof, source of supply, pre-treatment, fumigation history, urgency of clearing, method of maintenance/storage conditions under quarantine clearance, nature of packing on receipt and general health of the material, comments of different quarantine disciplines, number and kind of samples rejected and the reasons thereof, interceptions, post-quarantine treatment and follow-up instructions, post-entry precautions, etc. Similar records, as stated for imports, are also to be maintained for the material under export. Incoming requests are registered serially. The outgoing supplies are entered in the export quarantine register. Export quarantine forms are prepared and details on various descriptors similar to the import quarantine are recorded. The dates of despatch, packing used and other information is recorded.

Since the information on the introduction of germplasm from exotic sources for use by the breeders in India is one of the regular activities of NBPGR, the entire information is compiled and a Plant Introduction Reporter (PIR) is published on a quarterly basis. Germplasm of different crops introduced into India is compiled from time to time and published as Crop Inventories. Similarly, the quarantine records, as discussed above, are required to be systematically documented.

Overall, there is a need to develop a Germplasm National Information System in the country. The national system has to cater to the needs of crop-based institutes, co-ordinated projects, agricultural universities, and other user agencies in India as well as abroad. As such, a thorough system analysis is needed in terms of identification of inputs and outputs of information and then generation and standardisation, information flow, security/protection against misuse, hardware and software, communication facilities, etc.

**Varietal Development**

The selected germplasm is exploited through conventional and non-conventional breeding techniques for varietal development. The finished products are systematically evaluated at different stages of testing through Co-ordinated Research Networks to assess their potentialities for enhancing the productivity of the existing and potential cropping systems in the changing agricultural scenario in different parts of the country. After a thorough evaluation of the material in terms of yield, quality attributes, resistance/tolerance to various biotic and abiotic stresses, varieties are identified at the Annual Workshops of research scientists and agricultural development officers, which subsequently are considered for release by the State Variety Release Committees and/or Central Variety Release Committee, depending on the suitability of the variety for a state, region or the country as a whole. Finally, released varieties are notified by the Central Government after the recommendation of the Central Sub-committee on Crops Standards, Release and Notification of Varieties.

For varietal development, the information systems are required mainly on two aspects. Once the technical programmes on research is finalised at the workshops, there follows an automatic and for management of its conductance at different centres of the co-ordinated programme. Later, at the end of completion of any particular research programmes, appropriate database systems are needed to systematically project the recommended research technologies.

*Technical Programme Management*

There are broadly two kinds of experimental trials : (a) for varietal identification, and (b) for matching technology development. For identification of varieties in the coordinated system, improved and stable advanced materials pass through stages of initial and advanced varietal evaluation trials. Thus any material is identified for recommendation as a variety only after a thorough evaluation at many research centres. In this endeavour initial traits are conducted cutting across zones with common test entries while zonal trials involve only those entries which have initially proved their worth in a specified zone.

On the other hand, experiments involving associated disciplines viz. agronomy, pathology, entomology, etc., are designed with the aim of arriving at suitable crop production and protection technologies to exploit the genetic potential of newly evolved varieties. These experiments are also conducted at a number of locations of the co-ordinated system, before any recommendation is finalised for extension to the farmers. Obviously then, there is a requirement of information systems which can handle the management of co-ordinated research. A networking of the centres associated in any co-ordinated programme can greatly help in information management, and considerably reduce the time lag by avoiding information transmission by post as also manual compilation and analysis of data. The system would obviously help to a great extent in drawing reliable conclusions over years and locations.

In this area, proformae have been standardised for uniform recording of observations in various co-ordinated trials of different crop improvement programmes. In addition, there are proformae on assessment of co-ordinated trials at various locations and recording the observations of assessment. Thus computerisation of data and standardisation of data retrieval system would be of paramount significance to provide much needed impetus to crop improvement programmes.

*Management of Recommended Research Technologies*

One area is management of information on different crop varieties.

Since inception of the research efforts for organised varietal development, release and notification, over 1800 varieties/hybrids of different crops have been released and notified for commercial cultivation in the country. A publication 'Handbook of Cultivars' providing salient features of each of the varieties was published in 1986. This publication needs to be regularly updated to add new varieties and describe the status of old, obsolete and denotified varieties. While it is a useful compilation, there are deficiencies in the included information. This is obvious owing to the fact that the whole exercise is done manually.

There is a need of a database wherein detailed information on the status of the varieties, the general information with regard to genesis and suitability of each variety, and special features associated with the varieties including standard attributes for identifying various varieties/parental lines/hybrids are properly documented. This documentation can particularly save a lot of time of research managers who are to routinely provide information on urgent basis. Further descriptors and precise identifying features would be of great help to the seed certification agencies in assessing the genetic purity of a variety/parental line/hybrid. As registration system for any new material is likely to come up in the future, this information would be of great help to develop seed producing and seed certifying agencies. Further, if plant breeder's rights are enacted, detailed and precise information would obviously be essential for undertaking registration granting rights and to deal with the likely disputes regarding ownership in the court of law and outside. Likewise, the information on recommended crop production and protection technologies needs to be managed in a way that all concerned can retrieve the same without loss of time.

## Seed Production

After the notification of a variety, quality seed production from nucleus through breeder, foundation and certified seed stages are undertaken. This is of major importance as seed is considered as the basic, critical and most vital input for enhancing and stabilising productivity, and harnessing higher net monetary returns, per unit area, input and time. In fact, seed is the single well-recognised carrier of production technology facilitating quest for higher and better crop yields. The farmers always recognise seed as the basic input for making other agro-inputs productive and cost effective (Fig. 5.2).

The Crops Division of the council has a specific responsibility of organising and managing breeder seed production programmes of different crops undertaken in its constituent institutes, directorates and centres of various agricultural universities. The job involves formulation, execution, monitoring and reporting of breeder seed production of different crops and their varieties each year. Allocation of reported production of seed and their timely lifting by foundation seed producing organisations are required to be monitored much more efficiently within a very limited time span each season to ensure the effective conversion of valuable breeder seed. The breeder seed production programme is monitored by the ICAR while the Department of Agriculture and Co-operation (DAC) in Government of India, further monitors the use of breeder seed in foundation and certified seed production. The latter is ultimately used by the farmers for their cultivation of crop. Thus, there is a link up between DAC and ICAR, and the whole chain of seed production, from breeder foundation to certified seed production is managed by the two departments. For undertaking this programme effectively, a calendar of operation is finalised jointly. A perusal of the calendar of operations indicates, that a number of steps need to be followed under strict time schedule if the breeder seed produced by the ICAR is to be properly utilised for production of foundation seed. As many as seven proformae have been standardised for allocation, production, reporting, monitoring and utilisation of breeder seed of various crops and their varieties. Obviously then, the need for proper information management and flow is a necessity. Without an appropriate computerisation of the system, the whole chain of programmes could be disrupted.

As many as 48 exclusive breeder seed production units, meant for both field crops and vegetable, crops, are located in different state agricultural universities and ICAR institutes. The number gets further increased as each university/institute may be producing seed at its different centres. In some of the universities, breeder seed is produced at over 10 locations. The magnitude of information and limited time available makes it virtually impossible to manage the programme by sending the proformae as also other information through post, and compiling and communicating the same manually. A streamlining of this particular system through proper information management is a must if inter-commodity, inter-regional disparities in production and productivity of crops are to be reduced, seed being the most vital input for agriculture on which 70 per cent of our population is dependent.

**Benefits**

Undoubtedly, the size and complexity of information in the three areas of germplasm management, varietal development and seed production management makes it difficult to comprehend a complete computerisation of the system. A general idea of the kind of requirements for these three areas has been presented, though a better understanding would require a detailed study of the overall working to tackle these aspects. Only then specific requirements of hardware, software, networking, etc., could be appreciated. What is essentially needed is a holistic system's approach to help streamline the overall system? There is need to develop such a design of the system that there could be a dynamic dialogue between the system and the users. The personnel to undertake these jobs do not obviously have basic training in computer science and technology. This particularly makes it essential that a simplified system with ready acceptability by novices in the use of computers is evolved.

The benefits likely to emerge are obvious. Three points are mentioned:

(a) Germplasm management could be done more effectively, consequently resulting in better utilisation of the germplasm in the developing better varieties and hybrids for enhancing productivity and production of different crops;

(b) Management of co-ordinated programmes and, in turn, documentation of information related to crop varieties and crop production/protection technology can lead to effective dissemination of information and also effective utilisation of the technology resulting in much needed enhanced and stabilised production;

(c) Management of breeder seed production programme would provide a system capable of yielding perceptible dividends in the form of increased production of improved foundation and certified seed, and, in turn, would ensure adequate availability of the right kind of seed to the farmers to enhance his production and farm income.

## Conclusion

In conclusion, computerisation is the necessity of the day and efficient, workable and cost effective information system for the development of crops, varieties and their quality seeds is of prime concern, which is required to be paid much needed attention.

6

# RURAL ELECTRONICS

DR. VINAY DHARMADHIKARI*

## Introduction

As a first reaction, many people in our vast country, especially those working at the grass-root level in over six lakh villages of India, would find it rather perplexing that the so-called elitist and western technology of electronics, which brings us sophisticated computers, medical equipment and automation, could have much relevance to the villagers' life and in rural development!

## Relevance of Electronics

Before getting into specific examples, let us note that there are those who believed that India is a rich country, where we find too many people are poor, which is not necessary ! This poverty is avoidable, through intelligent use of our natural resources such as land and water, efficient use of energy and creative harnessing of the native Intelligence (IQ), especially among the villagers. Electronics and computers are believed to be intelligence-aids and knowledge-processing machines, and hence, they are fundamentally very relevant for changing from poverty into richness.

When a friend who was denoting his life for rural development was asked why he believed that technology such as electronics would be useful for the poor in rural India, he answered by observing that the wrist-watches and radios became accessible to the poor, only when electronics made them cheaper ! In fact, it must be noted that electronics is the only field where prices keep declining and the

---

* Department of Electronics, Government of India.

performance keeps improving by an order of magnitude every five years! So why should electronics not play a major role in the rural development and make our resources more wealth-generative?

But if this is true, why has this not occurred in a massive way, till date? Could it be because of our bureaucratic and precedence-bound ways in which our government officials, our politicians and our big businesses work? Towards the end of this paper, certain directions and observations are shown, which can provoke our officers, politicians and industry/education people, to appropriate actions.

**Capitalistic Economics vs Ecology-minded Economics**

Let us take an example. There is Rs. 6,000 worth (6,000 kWh) of solar energy incident on every 10,000 sq.ft of India's land surface per day, most of which is left unused, leading to desertification of our land and deterioration of our cities. However, through proper use of science and technology (S&T) techniques including electronics, and the use of the best of our ancient village-culture, we can capture this energy and put it to use for food production, shelter and other wealth generation activities, without use of fertilisers, pesticides and diesel-guzzling marketing practices. Our current pricing structures for electricity, water fertilisers and diesel are, in fact, causing us to be poorer and wasteful of our energy and our natural resources through the use of capitalist market-economics, based on cash-transactions instead of the more suitable, ecology-minded economics, based on calorie balances! Later in the paper, experiments attempting to do this using IT will be mentioned.

**Illustrations on Computer-use**

Let us turn to actual rural uses of computers and electronics:

– One of the earliest demonstrations of a computer being used for rural planning was in the late 70's in Dharmapur Taluk, in preparation of a tribal sub-plan, where it was possible to design a road network of connect 45 growth centres to a state highway system at one-third of the cost of the usual PWD plan, prepared without the computer. Another computer model was used in deciding the locations of service centres to provide five basic services at selected villages within a cost-limit of Rs. 14.00 lakhs.

The computer model was able to minimise the maximum distance of any of the 237 villages from the nearest service centre, to 6.5 km. In both of these cases, the results of the computer model were, in fact, actually implemented in the field with slight modifications, thus establishing that computers can provide field-usable solutions.

- Another example is the work of a Deputy Commissioner for IRDP in a Karnataka District, where he acquired a small 8-bit desk computer for IRDP monitoring and in identifying the appropriate families for effective benefits. For example, it is of no use to give loans for milch-cattle in villages where the ratio of grazing land-to-cattle is very low and the distance to veterinary doctor is large. With the assistance of the computer, this Deputy Commissioner was able to increase the performance of the IRDP schemes to much above the national norm and interestingly, it allowed him to release some staff from office paper work, to send them out in the field.
- In Surendranagar district, Gujarat, a micro-computer in the district collectorate was used to develop 10 applications over 18 months, which were being used on a regular basis and the computer was being used for monitoring various tasks at the district level.

Apart from the above examples which involved support and funding from the State or Central Government, there are other examples of computer and electronics usage in voluntary agencies, such as, SRI-Ranchi, a computer training centre in Howrah District, West Bengal, a low-cost geodesic shelter construction and estimation software in Ankoli, Maharashtra, and computer software for lift-irrigation planning with over 30 different variables by an irrigation consultant in Karhad. In addition, there are various electronics product assembly operations undertaken by electronics corporations of the various States (such as, KELTRON, KEONICS) and by KVIC/voluntary institutions such as Gandhigram (Tamil Nadu) and SWRC (Rajasthan), where employment is given to rural women and others.

**Necessity of Integrating Electronics in Rural Habitat**

These and many such other examples, however, remain more as

"exceptions to the rule"; and are seen by many as "islands" of electronics and computer use, within the ocean of general ignorance or distrust about the computers and electronics technology. What can be learnt from such experiences is that any effort to introduce the use of electronics and computers in villages needs to be well-integrated into the rural environment; and needs to address most of the basic needs of the villagers such as income generation, nutritious food, shelter and education and entertainment without cash expenditure, etc. In fact, the major disturbing trend of massive migration and brain-drain from rural areas into the urban slums is an evidence for the pervasive need of our rural people to look for some of qualities of the urban life style; which, when and if, made available in rural areas, will prevent this unhealthy brain-drain from our villages.

Although electronics has been quite evident in the urban life-style through its devices such as the telephone, FAX, television, video-player and cable television, there is nothing inherently against taking these devices to the rural areas in a cost-effective manner by designing a new kind of rural environment! In fact, beginning in this direction is already being made in a wasteland portion of Maharashtra (near Solapur) in an experiment called RURBANISATION/FOTOTRON. In this area, at village Ankoli, village Muramba and Shri Anna Hazare's Ralegan-Siddhi, computers are being installed to be run by villagers, interacting in Marathi — and these computers can be made to run without airconditioners in a properly designed low-cost housing structure, which makes use of the bio-mass and efficient solar energy conversion.

Jointly with an academic institution and other voluntary agencies, a novel scheme called SURYA (Synthesis of the best of Urban & Rural Lifestyles through informatics applications) is being implemented for electronics-aided rural development, with the technical guidance and co-ordination from C-DAC, Pune (Centre for Development of Advanced Computing) which is a society under the Department of Electronics. It is yet to be seen how such novel efforts which integrate electronics with agriculture, housing and socio-economic interventions, are evaluated and replicated by the governments, both at the Centre and the States, where such projects will first be met with natural suspicion and with questions of jurisdiction and "qualifications". But only such integrated projects, can make sustainable and viable contributions in converting our *potentially* rich rural areas into *actually* rich rural areas, as was remarked by Hon'ble Shri Pranab Mukerjee, Deputy Chairman, Planning Commission.

**Video-Tutorials**

It may be worthwhile for those of us who are concerned about using electronics for the benefit of our toiling masses and the under-privileged, to think creatively and with a bold vision to ensure how such novel and (grandiose-sounding schemes) such as the ones mentioned earlier, can be supported and, more importantly, replicated rapidly in parallel, in rural India. Successful and path-breaking agricultural and land-water management practices in the experiments, such as, FOTOTRON by Shri Arun Deshpande, over-land drip-irrigation multi-cropping by Padmashri Anna Hazare, the repertoire of agri-yield increasing experiments from Prayog-Parivar of Prof. Shripad Dabholkar and so on, need to be video-taped and computerised for Indian-language interactive tutorials with all farmers, in a cost-effective way. Such applications are to be regarded as an equally important mission of the Department of Electronics, along with the traditionally emphasised one about electronics production promotion and R&D for industrial clients.

In fact, in his book *The Third Parent*, former Chairman of Electronics Commission and Media Advisor to the Prime Minister, Shri P.S. Deodhar has proposed a financially viable scheme (NETSS) for education through a Ku Band Satellite with 24 channels, of which six channels for entertainment are shown to earn enough revenue to support all 15 educational channels in Indian languages. This is currently being evaluated by the Department of Electronics, in association with I&B Ministry and Education Departments.

**Funds and other Assistance from DoE**

The Department of Electronics (DoE), Regional Development and Employment (RD&E) Division, held two national workshops at Pune and Ranchi, where over 52 rural electronics product-ideas were identified. Models for rural employment generation were evolved and implementation funds are being made available from DoE, DST, NABARD etc. RD&E Division, DoE is very much interested in working with private sector electronic industries and rural marketers of farm-machinery, fertilisers, etc., in taking up these products either for R&D, marketing or for R&D *plus* marketing *plus* rural production. DoE has already started providing government funds in the form of seed-capital, for private companies and voluntary agencies which hitherto had mainly gone to public sector.

Similarly, DoE and CSIR laboratories have several projects which have developed electronic products, applications and computer software, having relevance to rural areas. We would welcome a frank examination of their claims in terms of field usability and commercial viability of these products, and proposals for undertaking actual implementation of the products in the areas of agriculture, health, income generation, etc. In both these aspects, the RD&E Division within DoE would be happy to receive inquiries and provide finances.

Certain pilot-applications and demonstration projects have been funded in spreading computer and electronics use for rural areas, to such diverse agencies as SWRC-Tilonia (by Bunker Roy), All India Association for Educational Technology (Prof. M. Mukhopadhyay), Society for Rural Industrialisation (Dr. A.K. Basu, Ranchi), Soft-Edge Data-Services centre near Lonavala, etc.

**Four Challenges for Indian S&T**

It may be felt in our IITs/RECs and our Industry that rural technology and rural applications of electronics are problems of rather low-level technology and low-level intellectual challenge. The reality, is the contrary of it. From the recent experiences with many rurally oriented S&T projects, it can be observed that the problems of designing Hi-Tech applications for rural areas in cost-effective and commercialisable manner, are much more technically difficult and intellectually challenging; but we as a society have failed to highlight this to the IIT graduating classes, a large proportion of which keeps going abroad to find challenges and not just for money.

What the rural applications may lack is the glamour and the extraneous rewards of international publications and foreign trips to seminars and conferences in US and Europe ! We the scientists, technologists and industrialists, need to seriously address the important community related problems of the villagers, because that is where India's unique strength lies.

Few of us realise that India has the same quantum of rain-fall available as the USA, but 1/3rd the area of USA. But India's utilisation of water resources is only 15 per cent of that by USA, which means in India we not only let most of the torrential rain-fall go unutilised for irrigation and for hydel power, but we also allow the erosion of our most fertile soil and the resultant silting of our large reservoirs and rivers.

However, this does not have to be so. As already shown by the shining Rishi's of today, such as, Dr. A.K. Basu of Ranchi and Anna Hazare of Maharashtra, applications of science-techniques can prevent both problems and yield abundant agro-yields and social development, to boot !

Thus, the four challenges for electronics and other S&T experts are as follows:

(1) Efficient use of our land and the incident solar energy;
(2) Rain and ground water conservation and utilisation;
(3) Avoidance of our unhealthy addiction to petro-chemical based fertilisers/pesticides; and
(4) Improving the inefficient consumption of electricity and fossil-fuels.

Unless we can commit to achieve massive progress in the above four areas, there would be no escape from the triple crisis of foreign-exchange drain, rupee resource crunch and environmental degradation, which we perennially face through successive governments.

The above can be complemented by enumerating certain recent pronouncements of eminent thinkers and statement, on the subject of how information technology (IT) and S&T can be seen for its contribution to social-rural upliftment.

### Comments of Alvin Toffler in his Book *Powershift*

"The less developed countries will take a completely fresh look at the role of Agriculture, regarding it not necessarily as a backward sector, but as a sector that potentially, with the help of computers, genetics, satellites and other information technologies, could someday be more advanced, more progressive than all the smokestacks, steel mills, and mines in the world. 'KNOWLEDGE-BASED AGRICULTURE' may be the cutting edge of economic advance tomorrow. Agriculture will not limit itself to growing food, but will increasingly grow Energy-crops and Feedstocks for new materials".

**Comments of Shri Chandra Shekhar former Prime Minister, April, 1991**

(i) Even after forty years of independence, the rural population in over six lakh villages has basically remained un-helped from benefits of crores of S&T expenditure and effort;

(ii) Our land being fertile and the natural resources being available in abundance, makes it all the more puzzling why we can not attack our poverty and pitiful conditions, such as, lack of drinking water and low agricultural productivity and employment;

(iii) Electronics has played a great role in the overall national development. We have so many national laboratories of excellence and eminently successfully experts and researchers in the field of electronics. However, they have not been successful in carrying fruits of this technology to the rural poor;

(iv) So many of the government departments and public sector companies are undertaking high-technology efforts; but these are not well-coordinated. The reasons for this lack of co-ordination and the lack of visible results in rural poverty alleviation is not lack of resources (which we have plenty) but, instead, the lack of will-power and a lack of commitment on the part of people in decision-making positions;

(v) When epidemics and social calamities get started, why is there no immediate investigation taking place, using information technology, to prevent the spread of the epidemic especially among the poor and to take curative actions?

(vi) We have computers in every district but they are being used less than an hour a day — I am told. Crores of rupees worth of investment in high-teach area is lying idle or underutilised and out of order;

(vii) Electronic industry and Department of Electronics should evolve a Five-Year Action Plan to deliver the benefits of electronic investment of the country, to rural areas. If a practical plan is presented, then the government will provide adequate resources.

**Comments of Shri T.N. Seshan, former Cabinet Secretary, February and May 1990**

(1) A better use of our satellite and Doordarshan transmission capability should involve demonstrations of the practical scientific farming tutorials instead of transmitting Chitrahaar programme. The electronic tools of satellite and computers must be used to collect the locally-relevant and local-made micro-plans, combined with NIC information resources, sort these wisely and make them available to the wise people in the villages – enabling them to make their own decisions. With the micro-planning ability through the use of computers, we can avoid unwise plans or schemes which, for example, propose to graze cows in Andamans.

(2) The information technology, which can be made extremely user-friendly, should be used to prevent monopolisation of facilities and resources, such as, water, electricity, land and government funds, etc., in the hands of a few powerful and well-connected individuals especially in rural areas, who will appropriate these for their self-use. If our information technology cannot do this, then, I would say, it has not been used properly.

(3) Our foreign exchange resources being scarce, we must prevent import of non-essential electronic equipment, which does not contribute in removing the stress of the poor or which does not provide income generation opportunities or make the use of natural resources more efficient.

**Conclusion**

It is hoped that thoughts such as above can contribute by inspiring the creative minds within us to think in non-traditional terms. Our villagers, though not very literate, are as wise and resourceful as any other people in using the right technological tools and devices, if they are clearly shown to be cost-effective. Perhaps other electronic industry leaders and community-minded technocrats can be provoked into debating the ideas into translating these into specific actions and projects.

# 7

# WATER RESOURCES

A.D. MOHILE*

## Introduction

Water Resources Management is a multifaceted sector covering water resources assessment, planning, design and development of water resources for conservational (irrigation, water supply, hydro-power etc.) and non-conservational (flood control) uses through surface and groundwater developments, operation of water systems including reservoir regulation, operation of water distribution system, flood and drought forecasting, and field management of irrigation.

Water Resources Management, particularly for irrigation, has been accorded a high priority in India. Out of the available resources of about 1800 $km^3/yr$, about 300 $km^3/yr$ is being consumptivity utilised through a large number of major, medium and minor surface projects and though public and private groundwater development. A live storage of about 143 $km^3$ through major and medium projects has been created. In the minor sector, about 0.23 million tanks, 0.14 million surface diversions, 0.5 million lifts, 9 million dugwells, 4 million shallow tubewells and 0.1 million deep tubewells have been constructed. With 76 million ha of irrigation potential created, a very large portion of the country's population is directly involved in water sector.

The largeness of the sector, the large geographic canvas of the development and the complex organisational structure involving multiple control and decision-making is a special feature of this sector. This makes the use of modern information technology complex but beneficial. CWC has sponsored a national seminar on

---

* Chief Engineer, Central Water Commission.

use of computers in hydrology and water resources. The papers being presented in this seminar (CWC, 1991)[1] have provided a considerable information about the status in regard to use of IT in water sector. Using this and other sources, the present paper reviews the progress already made in this regard and brings out the possibilities of accelerated development.

The purpose of this paper is to discuss the strengths, limitations and shortcomings of the developments, and to present a plan of action for accelerated use of IT in water sector. Such a plan needs to be deliberated, analysed and acted upon.

**Classification of the Uses of Information Technology for Water**

The use of modern information technology applications for water resources would have to be developed as a complete package comprising all aspects of water resource management. As would be discussed later, the present developments have been piecemeal and require many man-machine inter-faces during the various phases of data collection, data processing and storage, analyses of information and decision-making.

However, the various types of uses of information technology in water resources management can be conveniently classified as follows:

1. Data collection and database management;
2. Analyses of information for planning, design and construction;
3. Real time analyses of information for operation including automation in management;
4. Management information system for water sector.

This classification is not exclusive. For example, real time and automated management of water systems may involve automatic collection of data, data processing and database management, information analyses through models etc.

**Data Collection and Database Management**

The water sector has enormous data needs. It needs both the time-invariant or slow-moving data to be stored for very occasional replacement, and time-variant data to be stored and continuously updated as a time series. These data needs are depicted in Fig. 7.1. The different types of data as described below:

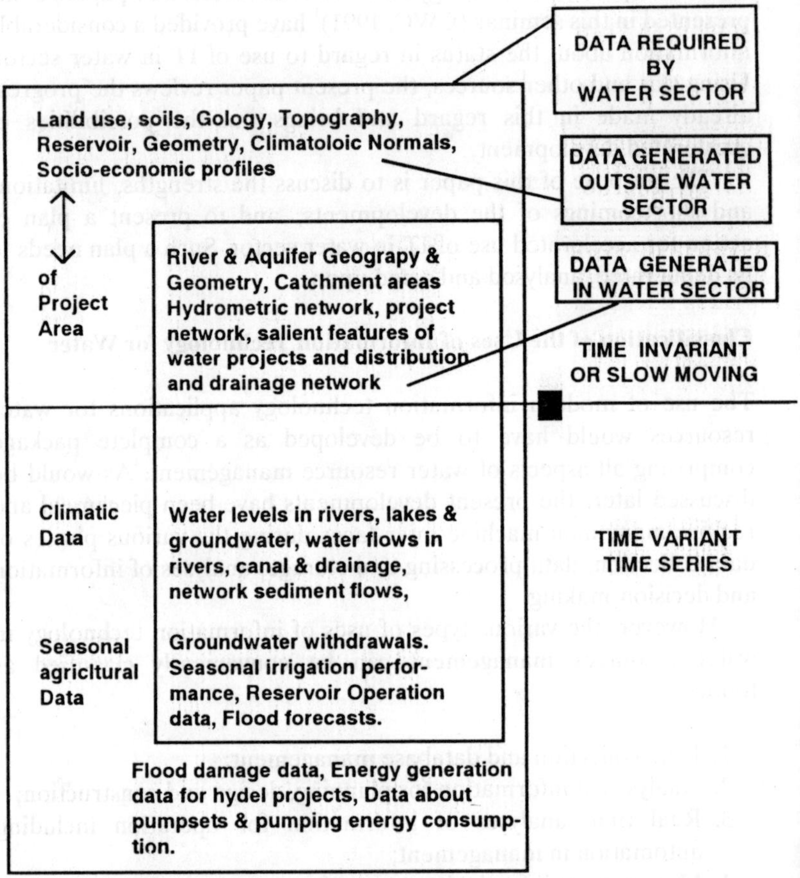


FIG. 7.1: Main Data Requirements of Water Sector

*Hydrological Data*

This consists of time series of river water levels, river discharges, sediment flow concentrations, groundwater levels, lake and reservoir water levels. Hydrometeorological data such as time series of rainfall, evaporation, dew point and climatological data also form an adjunct to the hydrological data although this may be generated in a separated meteorological network.

*Water Utilisation Data*

Water utilisation data can be either projectwise or basinwise or by administrative divisions. This would consist of time-series of water diversions and reservoir release, flows at salient points in canal networks, groundwater withdrawals, flows in drainage network, etc.

Data on irrigated agriculture like cropping pattern, crop calendar, crop yields, farm economic data, etc. would be required as an adjunct to the utilisation data. Project-related data for completed projects, operational data, reservoir water balance and release, water allocations, etc., would also have relevance to water utilisations.

*Time Invariant or Slow Moving Data*

Project data, data about geology foundations soils, agricultural soil survey, topographical data etc. may have to be generated. Also, data about the geometry of the river network, catchment area and various salient points, the general landuse soils and slopes in catchment, salient features of the various projects, design capacity data about water distribution networks, planned cropping pattern and calendar, etc., would have to be stored.

## Information Technology in Water Data Management

We will now describe the state of IT use in water data management.

### (a) *Management of Hydrological Data*

In regard to the hydrological data considerable attempts at computerisation have been made. Parashar and Gupta[1] describe the network classification and coding system as well as the hydrological data processing, storing and reviewing system as being used in CWC. Shastri and Bhatia as also Reddy *et. al*[1] describe another data storage and retrieval system being used in CWC. These have been developed for use on computers like NEC 1000. Gurumurthy and Krishna Veni[1] describe hydrological data management system based on dBase III developed for micro-computer application. Samusundaran and Srinivasan[1] describe data storage and retrieval system which seems to be particularly useful for rainfall data or flow data of intermittent rivers since storage volume is conserved by storing non-zero values only. Rao and Manoheran[1] describe another IBM PC compatible data management system using a dBase type software.

Thus, a large number of database management systems for hydrological data have been developed in India. However, there is need for further improvement. Instead of developing a large number of systems independently, it is necessary to develop a national hydrological database management system with some components designed for PCs and some for mainframe computers. Apart from the data storage and retrieval programmes for different types of uses, integration of various regional and organisational data banks in a single national system is essential. A number of plans made for this purpose particularly under the National Hydrological project[9] developed by CWC and NIH are not making any headway.

Development of packages of appropriate retrieval programme is essential from the users point of view. For example, the rainfall data would have to be retrieved as time series of, say, monthly or annual rainfall for a few stations for one purpose, whereas for another purpose like storm analyses the rainfall of all stations within the geographical boundary only for, say, 7th to 10th September 1913 would have to be retrieved and plotted. Today, no programmes are available for the latter type of retrieval.

Most database management software being used in India are limited to storage, simple processing like periodical total or averages and publication of data. Statistical quality control checks, if any, are being made before inputting the data and this is an inefficient procedure. Software for various internal and external quality checks has to form an integral part of the data management system, since such checks can be done for more efficiently in the computer. For hydrologic data, WHO[2] describes simple methods of quality control through machine processing.

(b) *Project Management, Utilisation and Water Economic Data*

Gupta and Mehta[1] present the software developed for storing salient information about the very large number of minor irrigation structures in the country which include dugwells, shallow tubewells, surface lift and surface flow schemes including minor tanks. This system is already partially operational. Thirumurugan et al[1] have described data management system for storing and retrieving salient features of all large dams in the country. Khanna and Char describe database management system for flood damage data. For water utilisation data, perhaps information technology has not been used much.

(c) *Discussions on Data Management*

For specific discussions about problems in hydrologic data managements, see the above paragraphs.

A common difficulty in developing a national database management system is in regard to the restricted nature of the data, the inhibitions of agencies to share the data and information, and the complex administrative and bureaucratic procedures involved in data retrieval. Users in water sector face considerable difficulty in obtaining rainfall data from the climatological data bank of India Meteorological Department (IMD). Exchange of hydrological data amongst state also has considerable difficulty. Water utilisation data, in particular, is hardly being made available at a centralised place and unless this forms part of water data bank, it, would be difficult to make proper water assessments.

Water data management cannot be improved by use of computerised system of collection, processing, storage, transmission and retrieval alone. The use of Information Technology will have to start with a good design for a water information system and a water data bank. For both, preliminary concepts and models are available. The NNMRS working group[3] prepared a structure as shown in Fig. 7.2. The Water Data Bank structure as proposed in the National Hydrology project[9] is given in Fig. 7.3. In both structures, there is an emphasis on regional centres as the focal points. However, since the data are distributed not only geographically but also organisation-wise (State, Centre) and subject-wise (rainfall, surface water, groundwater, water quality, water use), considerable organisational re-arrangements would be required before implementing such models. Detailed descriptions of hydrological data banks in 14 countries is published by WHO.[4]

With more and more use of remote sensing for data collection, much of the natural resource data are now being stored conveniently as overlays in Geographical Information System (GIS). The main advantage of this is in making the various data like population, land use and forestry, soils physiography, topography and slopes, rainfall and climatic data, etc., available gridwise exactly in the same format to make retrieval, analyses, tabulation and plotting every easy. Except for the SHE software being used in the National Institute of Hydrology and software for groundwater data management presented by Ganapati, Subramaniam and Vasudevan. GIS type methods of data management are uncommon in India. One difficulty in water sector in using GIS is that much of the data like river discharges, water projects, water distribution network, etc., are not distributed a really but appear as point or linearly transposed phenomena. Even then GIS-based data management systems need to be developed for hydrology and water sector, with necessary retrieval and analysis packages.

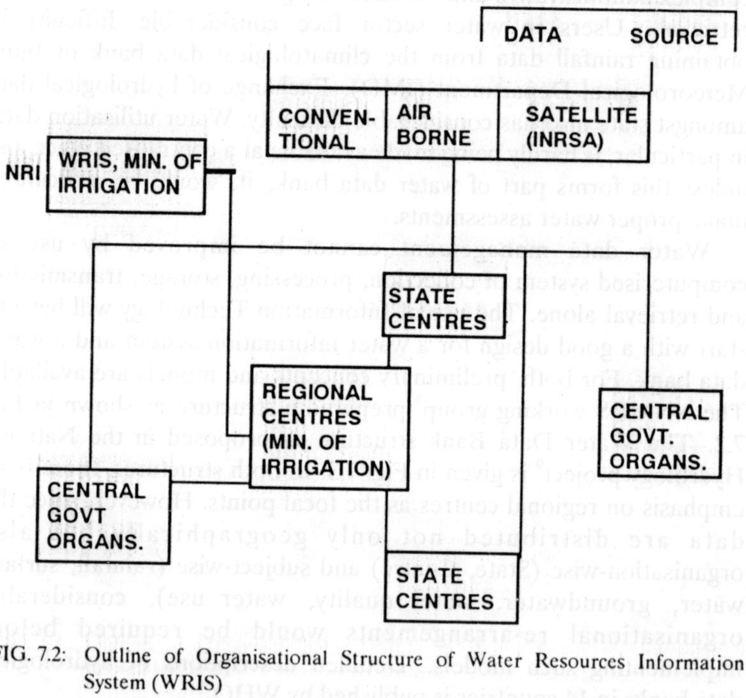


FIG. 7.2: Outline of Organisational Structure of Water Resources Information System (WRIS)

## Analysis for Planning Design and Construction

### *General*

These constitute the 'non-real time' uses in water sector. The larger time availability for analysis allows sophisticated model building and simulation activities, and also allows decision-making after considering various alternatives studies. Thus, these are ideal for elaborate computer-based analysis, and data and information communication problems are not severe.

We will discuss the status of computer use in the following classes of problems:

(i) Hydrological analysis including water assessment;
(ii) Irrigation water management;
(iii) Water resources systems analysis; amd
(iv) Design and estimating of water development structures for construction management.

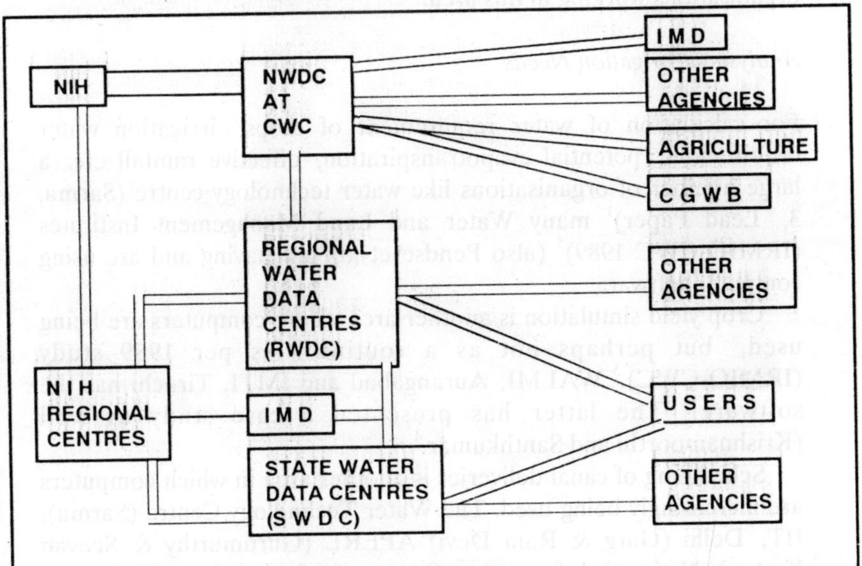


FIG. 7.3: Proposed National Data System (NWDS)

*Hydrologic Analysis*

A very large number of computer programs have been developed worldwide. In India, programs developed elsewhere have been utilised and also a large number of programs have been developed.

HOMS is an international technology exchange programme of the World Meteorological Organisation which encourages transfer of many good software programmes. The Hydrological Engineering Centre (HEC) of US Army Corps has also brought out very useful general purpose software.

The CHWR Seminar proceedings[1] incorporate at least 40 papers discussing cases of use of computers in this area. The applications range from rainfall runoff relations, yield studies for reservoirs, sediment transport, reservoir sedimentation, river hydraulics, water balance, groundwater models and balances, storm analysis, unit hydrography determination, flood analyses, flood routing methods, dam break studies, etc. Thus, this is an area in which a large number of scattered softwares are available. In the experience of the author, computer use has become a norm and a routine in almost all Indian organisations working in this area.

### *Analysis of Irrigation Needs*

For calculation of water requirement of crops, irrigation water requirement, potential evapotranspiration, effective rainfall etc. a large number of organisations like water technology centre (Sarma, 3, Lead Paper)[1] many Water and Land Management Institutes (IRMIO-CWC 1989)[5] (also Pendse et al,[1] are having and are using computer software.

Crop yield simulation is another area where computers are being used, but perhaps not as a routine. As per 1989 study (IRMIO-CWC).[5] WALMI, Aurangabad and IMTI, Tiruchi has the software. The latter has presented a case study as well (Krishnamoorthi and Santhkumar.[1]

Scheduling of canal deliveries is another area in which computers are increasingly being used. The Water Technology Centre (Sarma), IIT, Delhi (Garg & Ram Devi) APERL (Gurumurthy & Seevan Kumar) National Informatics Centre (Mehta), Anna University (Vennugopal & Patnaik), WALMI, Aurangabad (Pendse), CWPRS (Ramkripal)[1] etc. are using computers for this purpose. The author has seen that at least in some medium projects in Gujarat, this use has reached the farmers in the field.

### *Water Resources Systems Analyses*

The development of water resources systems analysis are directly related to development of information technology and use of computer is almost essential.

Both mathematical optimisation and simulation are used in water resources planning, although simulation methods are the mainstray or the planning process (Mohile, 8, Lead Paper).[1] The CHWR seminar proceedings report the use of these techniques for reservoir systems (numerous authors), cropping pattern optimisation (Chinni, Krishnan & Mohan[1] water distribution systems (Venugopal et al).[1] An earlier review (Mohile & Jagannathan)[6] indicates the coverage of these techniques, internationally as also in India.

*Design, Estimation and Construction Management*

The design problems in the realm of water engineering involve solution of higher order partial differential equations such as the equations of theory elasticity (structural problems), St. Venant equations (open channel hydraulics), unsteady pipeflow equations (surge problems), Laplace equation (groundwater hydraulics, etc.), appropriate initial and boundary conditions. These problems are extremely well suited to computer analysis using finite element methods, finite difference methods, etc., Various design and research offices in India are, therefore, using computers as a routine. The recent developments such as use of computer aided design, computerised estimation procedures, computer graphics and plotting, etc., allow transferring the mathematical analysis directly into design office practices. These extensions are not yet used as a routine. However, for earth dam designs, CWC has development a package ERDAM, which is an interactive slip circle analysis package capable of handling any earth dam design with numerous zones and material properties. It calculates the phreatic line, decides the critical slip circle and factor of safety and allows changes in the profiles and recomputation, leading to an acceptable design.

CWC is also using two large finite element packages for complex analysis problems. SESAM 80 is a Norwegian package available with NIC and is a general purpose one: ABACUS, developed, in U.K. and U.S.A. is especially suited for structural analysis of water related structures. Both incorporate elaborate graphics similar to CAD, which allow 3D representation of the structure or of the results.

Computers have been used for preparing design and estimates for Sardar Sarovar Canal (Kanatwalia, also Bhadake, as well as Baxi.[1] Back water profiles have been plotted by computers (Krishna and

Satyanarayana Murthy).[1] Design of cross drainage structures have been prepared directly (Modi and Shah)[1] WALMI, Aurangabad has programs which can prepare hydraulic design of field channels, estimate earthwork quantities, prepare contour plans, design and levelling for on-farm development and check the quality of land levelling as done on computers (IRMIO-CWC, 1989).[3] These efforts of linking analysis with design and designs with estimates are few, and this represents an area where much faster development is required.

Use of computers for project monitoring has not become very common in India. CWC along with NIC has developed a software COMP-MON based on FOXBASE/FOXPRO working in DOS environment. This is a DBMS package capable of retrieval of data in different formats. So far, computer graphics have not been linked with this. The system is under proving storage. In the States, similar attempts have been made in Gujarat in particular. For monitoring of Sardar Sarovar, computers are being used.

Information Technology is used in water resource construction mainly in two ways. Inventory management for machinery spares is being done by CWC through a DBMS type software similar to those discussed for data management, project monitoring, etc. More important use is in the use of control system and robots. This use is not common but has started in India. For example, computerized laser-aided guidance system for directional control in tunnel and trench construction is being manufactured and used in India. In Maharashtra, for accurate and quick land levelling for on-farm development, grade control system using sonic and laser censors have been used in areas near Aurangabad. To reduce the safety hazards to workers, robotic equipment has been used for "shotcreting" the roof of the power house cavity in the river bed power house of Sardar Sarovar Project. Robots are proposed to be used for tunnel rock bolting of the Ranga Nadi hydro-electric project in the North East. Laser-controlled trenching machines are likely to be used for installation of sub-surface drainages in Punjab and Haryana. Micro processor-based batching plant for obtaining an accurate control on the concrete is being used by the contractor for Sardar Sarovar Project. Robotics has other applications such as sub-marine bulldozers for under-water work, remote control boring machines, laser control bulldozers for accurate control of earth-work machinery for hazardous work, etc. These, however, have not been used in water resource-related construction work in India. Development of robotics is now receiving the attention of Ministry of Water Resources and Central Water Commission.

**Real-Time Water Management**

Real-time water management requires a good data storing and transmission network (preferably of telemetric type), simple and robust analyses models which do not require large data and which can cope with partial failure in data storage and transmission systems, and a quick decision-making process, either manual or computerized. In addition, in the automated mode, the decision commands are passed back and executed as part of the system.

In regard to flood forecasting methodology, computer-based models having facilities for updating parameters, which are common abroad[10] are not being used sufficiently in India. In general, however, while theoretical and model-building work has progressed, field implementation experience in such system in India is somewhat limited. Even after years of computerisation, flood forecasting service of CWC is mainly based on manual data collection, HF/VHF transmission and manual analysis to decide forecasts.

Although a large number of computerised models are being used (Sudhindra 6, Lead paper)[1] the pilot application for real-time use has been tried only in Upper Yamuna and is going to be used in DVC and Godavari. The Narmada Control Authority also has plans for computerized real-time system for data collection and reservoir operation. Real-time automatic flash flood warning systems for eastern rivers are sought to be developed by CWC with external aid. Real-time operation of water distribution through automation is being thought of for the Sardar Sarovar Canal. Tungabhadra Project, Jayakwadi Project (Majelgaon dam), etc. However, a workable mix of centralised, computerised, automated management, semi-automatic devices, and ungated proportionate distributors etc. suitable to Indian conditions need to be developed through trials. A conceptualization of such a system, at the inception stage, for Tungabhadra, is shown in Fig. 7.4.

Use of reliable sensors, and choice of appropriate data transmission (telemetry) system are of utmost importance to real time management of water systems. As stated, the VHF/HF voice transmission is the normal method for flood forecasting in India.

Satellite telemetry has been tried in Yamuna with a mixed success, whereas NICNET seems to operate satisfactorily via satellite. Much thought has been given to the advantages of Meteorburst systems, but high costs of imports seem to have prevented its acquisition. A detailed documentation of world-wide experience of telemetry in hydrologic data are available in the Toulouse workshops published by WHO (1987).[8] It is important that a proper design of a national water data transmission system is evolved and unplanned overlaps in different agencies adopting separate underutilised networks is available.

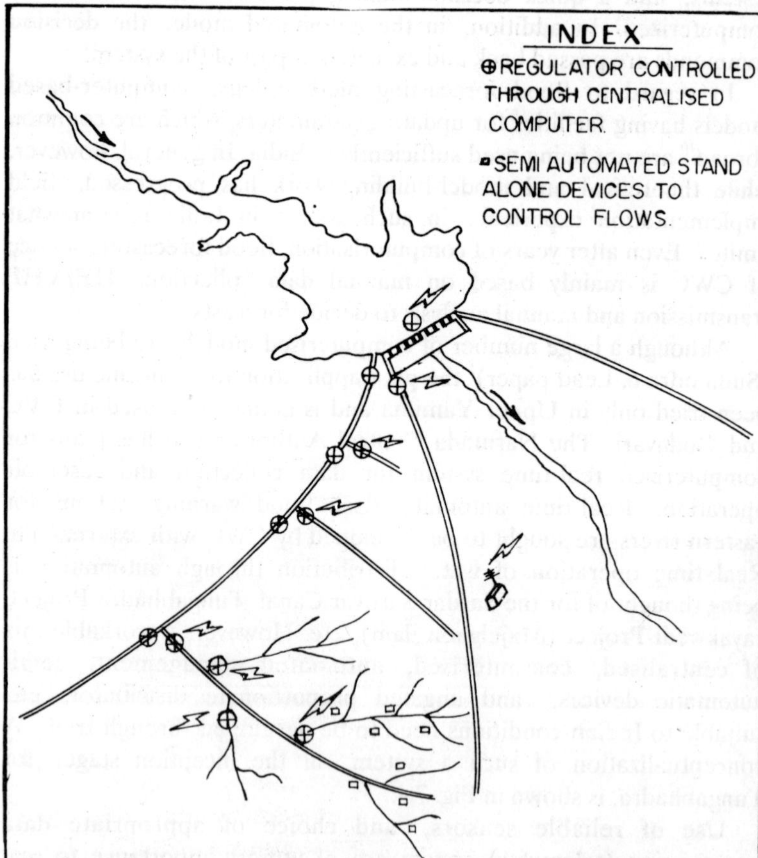


FIG. 7.4: Schematic Diagram of Pilot Project for Automation on Tungabhadra RBHLC

**Expert Systems in Water Sector**

The human decision-making process cannot be replicated by mathematical models and algorithms along. In deciding the models to be used at each branching point or in reviewing the overall acceptability, a somewhat intuitive process based on the mass of experience is often used. For allowing non-experts to take similar decisions, expert systems (ES) need to be developed.

In India, there seems to be little experience in either using or developing ESs in water sector. Raman (Lead paper 5)[1] gives a review and pleads for developing a knowledge-based expert system (KBES) for flood and drought management. Pavuluri et al[1] mention that a KBES for food preparedness is under development. A large number of problems in water sector like hydrologic planning, determination of design storm and floods, forecasting and flood fighting decisions, water allocation among users or states, irrigation scheduling structural designs, etc., require considerable skills and experience which need to be captured in expert systems. Since a generation of experts who could apparently take good decisions with limited analysed information would soon be replaced, development of expert systems for water-related problems assumes some urgency.

**MIS for Water Sector**

Management Information Systems (MIS) working on a computerised, data and information base, represents an area where computers directly aid tactical and strategic decisions by higher management. The purpose of this sector is such a well designed MIS for water sector, as distinct from the general attributes of any MIS in government.

An MIS for water sector does not exist. An attempt to list requirement of an MIS for project data has been presented by Garg and Ramadevi.[1] Similarly, IRMIO-CWC (1989)[7] presented a proposal for MIS and for a pilot MIS development for Rajasthan Irrigation department. However, both these attempts seem to discuss the IT problem of data base, structuring of MIS, etc., rather than fixing goals for the MIS from a Water Manager's view point.

Although, as we said, MIS water does not exist, notable stray attempts have been made. Berkins and Reddy[1] have described the use of NICNET for monitoring reservoir levels. Mehta has described the use of NICNET for monitoring of flood forecasts. Kukreja, et al[1] describe an information system FFWNPAS operated by CWC which can give tabulated or graphical information of current events and forecasts as also the appraisal of forecast performances. All theses have elements which can be used in an MIS. Another information system WAPIS, operational in India, allows information transfer and retrieval. Its operating is limited to technical documents and does not have the large data as required by an MIS.

In the author's view, a comprehensive MIS for water sector needs to be designed. It should be capable of generating the following reports:

(1) *On line Reports about Catastrophes which have Occurred or are Imminent*

This will cover unusually high and usage water levels in reservoirs or rivers, very high levels coupled with storm situation, unusual changes in the shapes of water bodies (monitored by satellite, analysed by image processing) which may indicate failure of reservoirs or flood embankments, landslides blocking natural rivers, etc. Heavy flood damages, accidents related to water sector, law and order problems affecting water sector, etc., also need to be reported.

(2) *Periodical Reports of Unusual Events*

High floods, droughts, unexpected problems or delays in construction or operation of projects, large deviations between, planned/expected and actual cropping pattern, unusually high or low reservoir water levels or river flows or groundwater levels (as compared to planned working tables, or as compared to earlier experience), information about earthquakes in vicinity or projects, etc., should be included in this report. Unexpected breakthrough, important achievements, etc., also need to be included.

(3) *Periodical Report of Performance and Assessments*

These reports would be more informative but less frequent (say, monthly, six monthly or annual). These would include hydrological assessment (including river flows, reservoir levels, groundwater situation) assessment of water diversions and utilisation, assessment of irrigated crop production, groundwater withdrawals, flood damages, water balance of river basins, progress of projects under construction, progress of development of irrigation potential, progress of research, development and training activities, etc.

Apart from these three types of report reaching the top management, many more detailed report would have to be generated for the middle management level.

Such an MIS cannot be constructed without a strong database and information transfer facilities. However, planning and design of such MIS for water sector needs to be initiated.

## Conclusion

The water sector has very considerable use of information technology. New disciplines like space technology or operations research which grew in the past three decades have a better chance of integrating and adjusting to growth in information technology. However, even while utilising established techniques, the water sector has shown considerable resilience in adjusting to information technology. Water sector personnel are using IT to a large extent in R&D, training, planning and design, operation and management (and, to some extent, construction) are reasonably familiar with using IT for water. The computer usage in the sector has now become operational rather than experimental.

However, in the past three decades, the use of IT in water sector has been fragmented, and a large number of scattered software has been developed. Similarly, scattered attempts have been made for linkage of sensors, data transmission and computers. With the experience already gathered, the stress in the last decade of twentieth century can be on synthesis, in coordinating, chaining together of available DBMS, available software, etc., as also in developing and implementing larger systems like national water DBMS, water MIS, expert systems for water planning, an integrated system for analysis and design, drafting and estimating, automated project management systems, etc. Larger use of control systems and robotics in constructions is also necessary.

Considering the developments which have already taken place in the use of IT and their strengths and weaknesses as also the sectoral needs and potentials for IT, following plan for actions suggested:

(A) *Data bank management*:

Establishing a national DBMS for Water

(i) Standardizing formats of water data for computer storage, for different data types and hardware, for use by all agencies in India;
(ii) Preparing standard data retrieval programmes after considering user requirement so that processed data and information is available in standard formats;
(iii) Preparing standardized statistical quality control software for checking internal and external collection of data, data corrections, gap billing, etc., as a part of the DBMS-water;
(iv) Interlinking organisational and regional databases networks for water;
(v) Organisational and policy changes to facilitate free exchange of data.

(B) *Analysis of data*:

(i) Classification and cataloguing of available software;
(ii) Changing software formats, in such a way that input and outputs formats are standardized;
(iii) Linking small software programmes into sequences so that output of one programme can be used directly as input to another; providing options of assembly of such sequences;
(iv) Developing expert systems from sequences, by systematic debriefing of experts; and
(v) Developing interactive packages to link analysis with designs, designs to drafting software and drafting with estimate preparation.

(C) *Real-time Operation of Water Systems*:

(i) Development of better sensors;
(ii) Establishing one or a few national water data transmission systems, after considering their reliability under adverse weather, maintainability, costs, etc. (separate unplanned overlaps in transmissions systems by different agencies need to be avoided);

(iii) Development of designs of canal cross regulators, gates and hoists etc, to suit canal automation. The design is to be somewhat tamper proof so that tampering may involve closure of supplies; and

(iv) Design of micro-processor based stand along flood warning system which would sense catchment rainfall and cloud cover and directly warn downstream population.

(D) *A National Management Information System – Water*

Finalising, designing and implementing a water MIS, having attributes as discussed earlier. Design and implementation activities can start ahead of establishing either a national Water DBMS or a national water data transmission system (see A&C above mentioned) by using available network and conventional transmission. When the pilot DBMS – water for one basin is available, this will be linked to water – MIS.

(E) *Organisational and Education and Training Aspects*

(i) Establishing a standing machinery such as a national committee for use of information technology in water sector to periodically review progress and give policy directions;

(ii) Undertaking a large training programme for upgrading capabilities of personnel. This should not be limited to senior or central office staff, but should involve field workers and users; and

(iii) The training needs of water sector personal would be of two types:

(a) General training in use of computers,

(b) Training in use of computers for problems of water sector.

Since training faculty for (b) above-mentioned would be extremely short, training of type (a) should, as far as possible, be conducted by persons not in water sector, so that experts in IT use for water sector can be utilised as trainees for type (b) use.

(iv) Developing water-related overlays for a national geographic Information system, covering both the time invariant and time variant date.

(F) *Action Plan for Pilot Projects*

Immediately starting pilot projects in some areas, such as:

(a) Developing and starting pilot projects in some areas,
(b) Installing and operation of a computerized water database management system in one basin of about 50000 km$^2$, covering all subsectors and data types;
(c) Automated water distribution and scheduling for one major project;
(d) Saturation computerization of one planning and design office in water sector; and
(e) A pilot project can be taken up for logging of dam instrumentation data to a micro processor, and for conducting real-time preliminary analysis at the dam site. Periodic detailed analysis may be carried out by further analysis of the logged data in a larger computer centre. However, the in-situ processing, should detect unusual behaviour and give early warning.

## REFERENCES

1. "Proceedings of the National Seminar on use of Hydrology and Water Resources" sponsored by Central Water Commission, New Delhi, 1991.
2. World Meteorologic Organisation "Machine processing of hydrometeorological data" Technical Report No. 115, WHO Vol. 275, Geneva, Switzerland, 1971.
3. "Report of the Force on Water Resources" National Resources Management System (NNMRS) ISRO Headquarters, Bangalore, February 1985.
4. World Meteorological Organisation "case studies of National Hydrologic organisation Data Bank" operational hydrology report No. 17, WHO No. 576, Geneva Switzerland.
5. IRMIO-CWC "State Training Institute profile on Micro computer Training" LBIT/WAPCOS Technical Report 24-A, January 1989.
6. Mohile A.D. and Jagannathan E.V. "Water Resources Systems Engineering — Status and Indian Perspective" Status Report No. 8, Research Scheme applied to RVP, CBI&P, New Delhi, March 1984.
7. IRMIO-CWC, WRM&T Project "Management Information System and Pilot MIS Development for Rajasthan Irrigation Project" Technical Report No. 37, LBII & WAPCOS, November 1989.

8. World Meteorologic Organisation and others "Telemetry and data transmission for Hydrology" proceedings of the International Workshop, Toulouse, France, March 1987.
9. National Institute of Hydrology "Proposal for National Hydrology Project (Surface Water)" March 1987.
10. International Association of Scientific Hydrology "Hydrological Forecasting Symposium" proceedings of the Oxford Symposium, April 1980.

# 8

# RURAL DEVELOPMENT-I (General)

A. RAMAKRISHNAN*

## Introduction

Rural development and poverty alleviation have been the major thrust of the government policies since the Seventh Five-Year Plan. There has been a significant shift from areas-oriented programmes to specific employment-oriented individually targeted programmes. Particular mention is made of the IRDP where the credit and subsidy are provided to targeted individuals in order to generate income earning assets. Similarly, wage employment programmes (*Jawahar Rojgar Yojana* – JRY) have the twin objectives of creating an asset base in the rural areas in order to fulfil infrastructural gaps and provide employment and wage opportunities to the rural poor seeking work and wage. Slowly the objective of providing wage employment is shifting to employment guarantee and right to work. During the Eighth Plan, rural development is likely to take share of 50 per cent of the Plan funds for investment.

## Need for Computer-based Information System

The need for reliable and timely information for decision-making requires pooling of data obtained at the district level and converting them into a database at the national level. The information has to be validated and consolidated at the State and Central levels. The Department of Rural Development has evolved a comprehensive system of monitoring and concurrent evaluation of major rural

---

* Ministry of Agriculture, Government of India.

development programmes like IRDP, JRY, DPAP and Rural Drinking Water Supply Programmes. The emphasis is on strong databases and subsequent feedback on the implementation of the programme. To build up effective measures, computers have been installed in all the District Rural Development Agencies (DRDAs) in the country using the software developed for computerised rural information system project (CRISP). So far, computers have been installed in 80 per cent of the DRDAs of the country.

The information flows from the districts to the State and the Centre *via* NICNET. This information enables the policy-makers to monitor and analyse the plan schemes, programmes and other related activities.

**Application Areas**

The main programmes amenable to computerised management informatics system are: (1) Integrated Rural Development Programme, (2) Jawahar Rojgar Yojana and (3) Rural Water Supply Programme. These are large programmes with annual outlays exceeding Rs. 2000 crores and implemented in far-flung areas in the country. The poverty alleviation programmes benefit about 10 million people and the Rural Water Supply programme covers villages with total population exceeding 17 million.

The computer software needed for this Department is developed by the Rural Development Informatics System Division of the NIC. Through discussions with the senior officers of the Department, areas of computerisation are identified and software developed to generate reports and monitor the status of different projects operating in the various divisions of this department. At present the following computer-based MIS is in operation in the Department:

(1) A query-based interactive system to generate all the information relating to Integrated Rural Development Programme operating in all the States and Union Territories. Reports are generated and analysed for the asset productivity schedule under the IRDP. Concurrent evaluation of the programmes is done and the reports are generated to monitor the total population benefited under the programme;

(2) State-wise profiles of the programmes have been developed

to generate the updated status of all the schemes under the IRDP, RWS and JRY operating in the States;

(3) In the Land Reforms Division, a petitioner inventory system is developed to handle the petitions received in the Department from across the country. The petitions deal with the grievances reported by the petitioners who included VIPs like MPs, MLAs, etc. The system enables the division to send the grievances to the States and also to follow up the matter. The system is useful, given the sheer magnitude and volume of the petition received in the division;

(4) A quarterly monitoring system has been developed for the monitoring of land-ceiling laws and related programmes in the Land Reforms Division;

(5) A software for the dictionary of land is operational in the States and is under development in Union Territories;

(6) A query-based MIS has been developed for the DPAP/DDP programmes to monitor the status of the projects under these schemes in the various States;

(7) A foodgrain situation information system has been developed to report on the foodgrain production, marketable surplus, storage capacity and godown stocking throughout the country for various foodgrains like rice, wheat, etc. This report is analysed and supplemented by charts;

(8) This department has also developed software for application in routine areas like payroll, inventory system, VIP references and daily engagement schedule and so on;

(9) For the Rural Water Supply and Sanitation Division, three software have been developed. These are:

    (i) Programme monitoring system (PMS)
    (ii) Programme reporting tool; and
    (iii) Rig monitoring system.

These systems generate report on the financial and physical achievements. In the PMS, data are collected from the public health engineering department in the district and sent to the State headquarters where these are consolidated and sent to Delhi via Delhi NICNET. This gives us critical database of planning, location and impact of the Water Supply Scheme already implemented. The rig monitoring system monitors the movement of rigs and its activities. Twelve reports and 47 charts are generated quarterly and reminders are sent to concerned authorities. Other systems under development in the division pertain to the creation of software for the National Drinking Water Mission for eradication of guinea-worm, etc. Areas to be tackled for the future are the library information system for the departmental library, development of standards for quality control, market planning and designing, 20-point programme, etc.

**Computerisation of Land Record in the Country**

The survey and settlement records in the country are very old. Due to negligence and ineffective maintenance and also plethora of land laws, the land records do not reflect the correct position on the field. The land records at the village level are at present maintained manually as per the provisions of local land laws. The objectives of the computerisation of land records management are:

(1) To reduce the inordinate delay in giving copies of the record of rights of the land holding to the landowners: By preparing a database of the basic land record data and updating them on a regular basis, every landholder can be given the copy of land record instantaneously.

(2) To reduce the workload of *patwari*: Today, the *patwari* at village level is burdened with drudgery of paper work which affects his fieldwork. This is expected to be reduced with computerisation.

(3) Minimising tempering of revenue records: Revenue records have always been of critical importance to the rural masses. Records are tampered with the from time to time to by pass the land reform legislations. By introducing proper security measures, it is expected that computerisation of land records would protect the legitimate rights of the landholder and minimise the unauthorised manipulation of the records.

(4) To create land management information system: The land records are the sources of rich data base pertaining to availability and use of land. Today, reports are generated manually at the village level for use in the areas of agriculture, land utilisation, irrigation projects, rural

development programmes etc. By having an updated database, it is expected that decisions could be made on all the relevant projects using timely and reliable data.

As a first step towards the computerisation of land records, the Department of Rural Development has started pilot projects in 15 States. One district has been taken in each State and Rs. 25 lakhs have been sanctioned per district. Each of the pilot district has been given the freedom to choose their own software. The NIC is acting as a modal agency in clearing the projects at Delhi on behalf of the department.

Standardised hardware configuration has been sanctioned in all the districts. At the district headquarters, PC AT with IBM RAM and 40MB hard disk have been taken. At the tahsil level, PCs with lower configuration are given. The data entry work is done at the district headquarters using the department staff. It is expected that the computers will be first kept at the district headaddquarters and subsequently to be moved at the tahsil level. The basic land record data are stored in cartridge tapes and updated on a regular basis. Copies of land records are proposed to be given free to the landholders in the first stage to ensure correctness of the data entered. Subsequent updating of all the transactions of any land will be made at the tahsil level.

It is expected that in the second phase this computer network will be extended to areas of land registration, mapping by digitization, consolidation of land holdings, etc. At present, data entry is made and outputs are taken in local languages, moving on to GIST cards in the future. Land record management is one of the most promising areas of computerisation. In the Eighth Five-Year Plan, this department has proposed that land records in all districts in the country should be computerised. Progress will depend upon the success in the pilot projects.

**Problems in Computerisation**

Some of the typical problems faced in the matter of computerisation in the government departments are:

(i) Training and updating of manpower on a regular basis to develop a positive attitude towards the usage of computers in day to day working;

(ii) Timely updating and discontinuation of manual system are delayed due to the inherent fear of the failure of computerised system and breakdown; and

(iii) Maintenance of hardware in the field. There are problems in getting uninterrupted power supply at the district and tahsil level which interferes with the smooth functioning of the computerised system.

**Conclusion**

In dealing with computerisation of land records, there is a major behavioural problem encountered in breaking down the mental blocks in the revenue system. The present revenue manual system has been in vogue for hundreds of years and there is a lot of personal power associated with the revenue functionaries due to their highly personalised knowledge of records. This obviously gives a clout in the working of the revenue department and the interface with the public. The introduction of computerised system would obviously mean that this power will get reduced and to that extent there is a resistance to the change-over from the manual to the computerised system.

9

# RURAL DEVELOPMENT II (CRISP)

K. RANI RATNA, T.T. PRASAD and D.C. MISRA*

## Introduction

This paper restricts itself to an analysis of the very nature of rural development programme's planning, monitoring and role and scope of Information Technology (IT) to streamline and improve the information flow and analysis. It also addresses itself to the problems in design and implementation phase of an Information System (IS) specially in the context of rural development programmes. The Computerised Rural Information Systems Project (CRISP) was launched in 1986 by Government of India to assist District Rural Development Agencies (DRDA) on Information Processing (IP) related to poverty alleviation schemes at district level. This agency, i.e., DRDA is entrusted with the responsibilities to implement poverty alleviation programmes sponsored by Government of India and State/UT Governments.

## Rural Development Logistics

Rural development is a planned process of resource inputs into rural areas in developing countries. In developing countries where majority of population live in rural areas, the task of rural development is a major challenge comprising demand and supply of inputs, management of available resources, infrastructure and utilisation of these in various development sectors at different levels of administration. The

---

* Planning Commission, National Informatics Centre (NIC), Government of India.

question is how to study and analyse these parameters so that a definite trend emerges to help in working out the planning strategies.

The infrastructure to manage the information related to rural development sector or any other area does exist in the form of administrative departments in all countries. What, then, is the need and advantage of introducing the IT? There are time-tested laws and ways to check and manage the information. In India, some of the departments are still working on the rules and concepts evolved by Great Moghuls, Mauryan and British rulers. Even work culture has crystallised which shapes the attitude of officials of each department and also sets the pace of work. The introduction of IT into this kind of scenario, where attitude and pace are two major barriers, enhances the degree of complexity.

The rural development programmes in India are of two kinds. The aim is to assist individual family and the individual below poverty line by (a) offering subsidy and institutional credits and (b) also providing wage employment to the people. The objective is to assist the poor people with the help of above schemes to bring them above poverty line. This involves lot of financial inputs from Government of India and State Governments. The management of financial information is another aspect which could be addressed effectively.

Decentralised Administration (DA) with greater emphasis on Panchayati Raj where people are vested with proper "Authority and Responsibility" shared with elected representatives could bring sea-change in total management with the help of proper utilisation of IT/IS to meet planning and monitoring needs of all quarters of development.

A characteristic of our administrative setup is unidirectional flow of information, i.e., upward. The information flows from panchayat to block to district to State to centre. It is never distributed horizontally or downward which often leads to "Information Duplicacy and also Gap". This monopoly could be broken with the help of application of the Networked MIS in Decentralised Administration. The existing system in our country often tends to mould the way of application/utilisation of any new management tool into their age-old habits and customs instead of changing the very nature of itself. Hence, very often success of application of IT depends on how far it meets traditional interest of bureaucracy in managing total affairs. Any systems designer/developer has to be cautioned about this feature.

Another aspect for systems developer/designer is to incorporate the practical logistics of field level operations/conditions. Most of the time district officers evolve their own workable model for scheme implementation than what is suggested to them by higher authorities. Any system design which does not meet user's practical requirements will lead to chaos irrespective of its technical standing. User's acceptance is the priority issue in system design with minimum overhauling of the age-old registers and data collection procedures in first phase itself.

The achievement of targets is one of the important duties of development administration which often leads to low quality implementation of schemes. Very often, economic viability and feasibility test of a scheme with respect to beneficiary's background is not done properly by institutions engaged in financing which often leads to low loan-repayment and the subject suffers from continuous poverty. These practical aspects must be taken care of during systems design phase.

The systems design also should be very flexible to meet the geographical and, administrative set-up, planning and monitoring technique's diversity. Hence, basic design (core module) should be developed at central level for the whole country and development of peripheral software layers should be left to the programmer assisting the end-user to meet local requirements.

**Reversible Development**

This is another feature of developing countries. This means very often reversible development takes place after development cycle is completed and all information related to it recorded/stored into MIS. Hence, MIS should be regularly updated to take note of this kind of phenomenon. System should also automatically be able to inform/alert the planning /monitoring authorities to take the corrective measures against indicators forcing reversible process.

The selection of hardware and software for the district level in view of prevailing management condition and also field condition should be done on the basis of the following parameters:

- Needs of the user
- User's adoptability and learning
- Projected load of data processing

- Available maintenance support
- Future upgradation adoptability
- Cost and benefit analysis
- Availability of computer manpower
- Availability of training institutions
- Availability of other system related infrastructure, its status and maintenance (i.e. power supply, air-conditioning, etc.)

These parameters may not be standard but in view of field conditions prevailing in India, above conditions would be suitable to increase acceptance of introduction of IT.

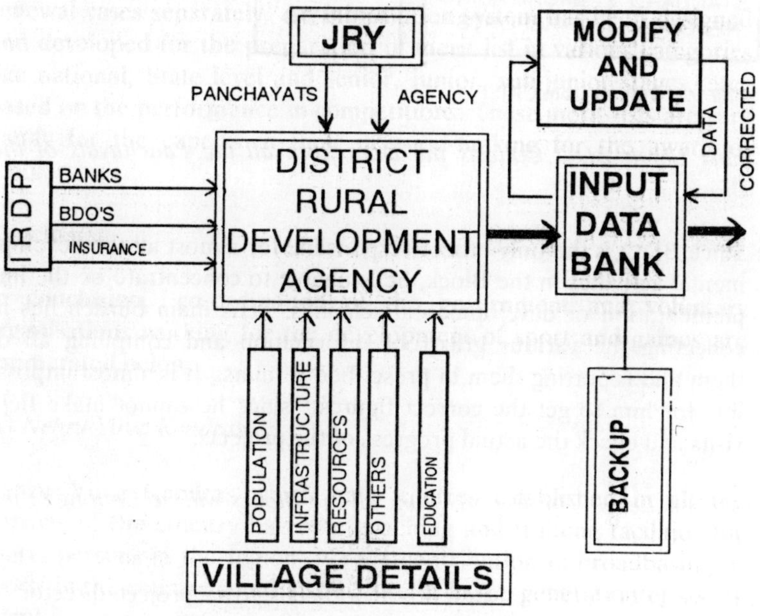


FIG. 9.1: Organisation Structure of CRISP

**Implementation Logistics and Information Flow**

District Rural Development Agency (DRDA) is the nodal agency involved in implementation of Rural Development Schemes. In some states like Karnataka, Zilla Parishad (ZP) looks after these schemes implementation. In the entire process of implementation of these poverty alleviation schemes, the Block Development Officer (BDO) plays very important role. He implements these schemes at field level and collects the data and sends various reports to the Districts. There are two levels of data collection in the districts:

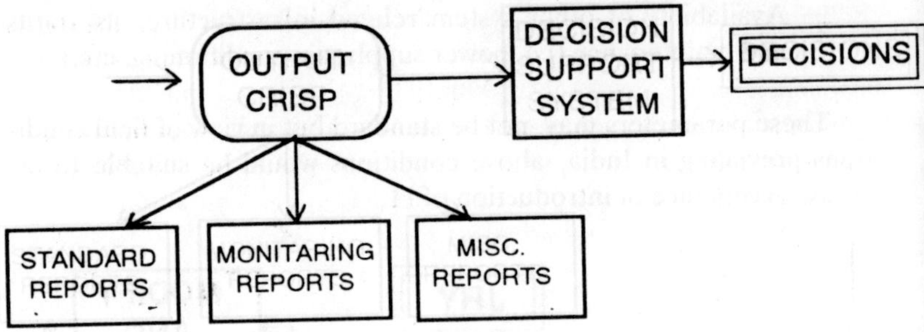


FIG. 9.2: Outputs from CRISP

*First Level: BDO Collects the Data from all the Panchayats of the Block*

Since BDO is the only officer responsible for almost all the developmental activities in the Block, he is unable to concentrate on the implementation of developmental schemes. His main burden lies in collecting the various grassroot information and compiling all of them and reporting them in prescribed formats. It is almost impossible for him to get the correct figures, since he cannot make field visits and check the actual progress of the projects.

*Second Level: The Reports from all the Blocks will be Coming to the DRDA/ZP*

Every DRDA/ZP is staffed with officials from project director to lower division clerk. It also has (i) accountant (ii) assistant project officer (APO) (iii) investigator. The main job of the accountant is to maintain the accounts, APO to administer the smooth implementation of the schemes and the investigator to compile various reports and required analysis for monitoring. But presently all of them are deeply involved in compilation of the data. They compile the various progress reports received from all the BDOs to arrive at district figures.

The district report is sent to the State/Central Government. Here they do not have any mechanism to cross-check the information provided by BDOs. They are fully dependent on the figures received from BDOs. Unfortunately, the schemes have become target-oriented and the quality of the implementation is suffering. This is quite visible if one sees the implementation process of various schemes. For example, let us take Integrated Rural Development Programme (IRDP). In the first quarter, the coverage of beneficiaries will be ranging from 200-400. But if one sees the last quarter, especially in March; the number of beneficiaries covered will be in thousands.

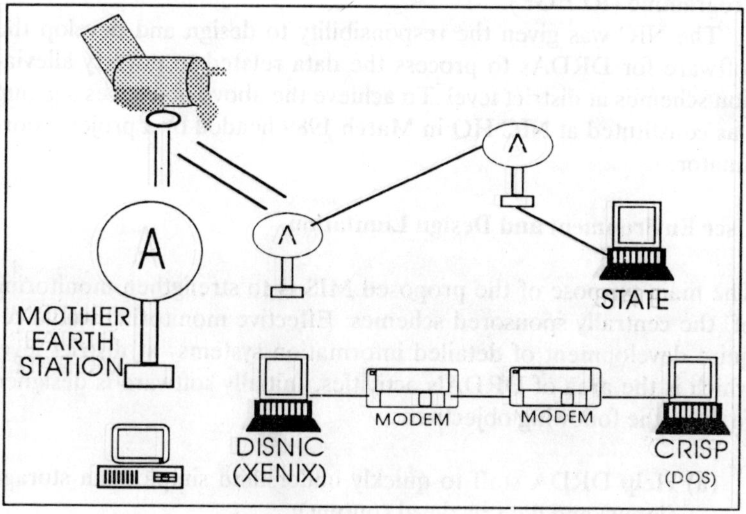


FIG. 9.3: Connecting DRDA Machines in NICNET

Most of the time the DRDA staff are worrying about meeting the targets. The actual assessment of the schemes is done by concurrent evaluation. This is just a post-mortem and finding the disease rather than curing the disease in time. The concept of concurrent evaluation is to find out the impact of schemes and bottlelnecks in the implementation. It is an analytical exercise which often does not take place because of target-meeting exercise.

**An Effort to Improve the Situation: CRISP**

In this context, the Department of Rural Development (DRD),

Government of India, launched a project on pilot basis in ten districts of the country in March 1986. The NIC was given the responsibility to support implementation of the project. During pilot phase, NIC also provided hardware to ten pilot districts (Udaipur, Patiala, Kanpur, Betul, Hazaribagh, 24-Pargana, Cuttack, Chittoor, Quilon and Thane). A pilot system for DRDAs was developed in consultation with these districts on anti-poverty schemes covering mainly IRDP, Development of Women and Children in Rural Areas (DWCRA), Training of Rural Youth for Self-Employment (TRYSEM) and Wage employment schemes like National Rural Employment Programme (NREP) and Rural Landless Employment Guarantee Programme (RLEGP).

The NIC was given the responsibility to design and develop the software for DRDAs to process the data related to poverty alleviation schemes at district level. To achieve the above objectives a group was constituted at NIC HQ in March 1989 headed by a project coordinator.

**User Environment and Design Limitation**

The main purpose of the proposed MIS is to strengthen monitoring of the centrally sponsored schemes. Effective monitoring would require development of detailed information systems at district level which is the area of DRDA's activities. Initially software is designed to serve the following objectives:

(a) Help DRDA staff to quickly understand simple data storage (input) and data retrieval (output);
(b) Create basic records of beneficiaries and works under rural development programme;
(c) Provide an easy method of generating various reports prescribed by the State and the Centre; and
(d) Gather basic information about villages to support planning activity for anti-poverty schemes.

To achieve the above objectives, like in any sector, the choices for software and hardware in rural development are an outcome of the systems design. NIC installed PC/AT machine (286-based) with all peripherals in pilot DRDA's across the country. The pilot systems (CRISP ver 1.0) was installed before March 1987. While designing the software for CRISP; the first question, in terms of design, was the quantum of change we wanted to introduce.

The formats for data entry at DRDA level were designed after a series of workshops, meetings and training programmes with district development officials. These workshops, seminars and training programmes were organised at NIC HQ and in the districts. In the context of rural development computerization, the following of system design considerations would be necessary:

(a) The users are going to be non-professional first-timers;
(b) Primary focus on databases requires to be established;
(c) A moderate degree of change should be attempted in the first phase and the process could begin to gain momentum; and
(d) An overlay on the existing manual system would probably pay off much faster than totally new management system;

**Feedback from Pilot DRDAs**

The pilot system was installed in all pilot DRDAs by NIC. The onsite training programme was conducted. Initially data collection was a big problem which was solved by employing volunteers on incentives basis. Udaipur, Cuttak, Hazaribag, Patiala, Chittoor, Betul and Kanpur could show remarkable success during pilot phase. The post of programmer, operator and data/entry assistant were also sanctioned to pilot DRDAs. NIC suggested guidelines for their recruitment. It was also felt by CRISP group that uniformity in data collection would be of great help before expanding the project to all DRDAs. In general, pilot phase was great success which gave DRDAs an exposure of modern technology and its application to solve the problems.

**Project Expansion**

After successful implementation of pilot phase, Department of Rural Development (DRD) and NIC evaluated the impact of new technology in processing data related to poverty alleviation schemes and degree of acceptance by DRDA. The feedback received was good. Hence it was desired to expand the project to all DRDAs of the country. In mid 87, DRD, Government of India issued an order expanding CRISP project to all the DRDAs of the country. Also they suggested that CRISP package should initially focus on important schemes like IRDP, NREP, RLEGP, Rural Water Supply (RWS) and village database only.

During project expansion phase, the DRD also suggested to the State governments to identify an agency to support CRISP implementation. These agencies were asked to provide support to the DRDAs by posting a programmer at district level who will develop the required local reports on CRISP platforms and also conduct training programme for DRDA staff. UPTRON, HARTRON, ESPL, APTS, KELTRON, OCAC, PTCS, etc., were identified as state level nodal agency to support CRISP implementation in various states. These institutions were trained on the design and methodology of CRISP software by CRISP group, NIC, so that any future modification could be done without any problems to meet the state DRD or DRDA requirements.

### Selection of Hardware

The IBM PC/AT compatible systems with DOS as operating system was decided upon, which would permit both standardisation as well as access to a wide range of popular software. However, under CRISP (expansion Phase), the States were allowed to purchase the systems according to the configuration suggested by NIC. The States/DRDAs were advised to purchase a system with all peripherals at the ceiling cost of Rs. 1.10 lakhs. This gave very good benefit in terms of involvement of user in the entire process.

### Software Environment

The CRISP package has been developed in dBase III Plus environment with utilisation of power of clipper. Foxplus has been used in XENIX environment which is available in each district on DISNIC machine (80386-based). These packages are user-friendly and easy for modification to meet local needs.

CRISP version 2.0 is more user-friendly and very flexible in design. Many modules on other poverty-alleviation programmes like DWCRA and TRYSEM have been included. The free query system was also added to village database and IRDP.

As mentioned earlier, the foundation of information systems for rural development lies in establishing large databases which meet certain initial requirements. The basic focus of CRISP is on establishing a database for every single area of activity of District Rural Development Agency (DRDA). Thus, there are databases on village resources, house holds, beneficiaries and works taken up by different agencies under various employment programmes.

Initialisation is the core and mandatory exercise of CRISP package. The user has to fill the district hierarchy in this option. Option would ask for block, panchayat and village names under each sub-division according to our existing administrative structure of blocks and panchayats. After entering all these details, the control can go to programme's modules. The idea of having this kind of option is that all the information which does not change for a period of time may be stored here and, later on, may be displayed as and when user requires it in programme's module through windows. It saves lot of data-entry time and, at the same time, does not require any validation checks.

The most frequently required reports for monitoring are made available under output option of the package. Some of the typical reports are given below :

*IRDP:*

1. Key indicator report
2. Monthly physical/fianancial performance (district/block)
3. Cumulative physical/financial performance (district)
4. Conditional beneficiary listing
5. Bank physical/financial performance for a given block/sector (primary/secondary/tertiary), etc.

*JRY:*

1. Quarterly progress report (QPR)
2. Summarised MPR (telex form)
3. Detailed MPR with block level break-up.
4. Money allocation to panchayat, etc.

Similarly, many other reports in village database, TRYSEM and DWCRA provide detailed information required for programme's planning and monitoring.

## Training

Once the basic system design and software package has been developed and field-tested, training for users has to be initiated.

In pilot phase, the training to ten DRDAs were imparted by central CRISP team on site as well as at NIC headquarters, Delhi. Normally, the duration of training programme is one week in which participants get good exposure of package and different other logistics regarding data collection and periodic updation. But once the project expanded to all DRDAs of the country, it was realised that five members (two systems analysts, three programming assistants) of central CRISP team would not be able to tackle it conveniently. Hence, it was decided to engage the best professional institutions in the country which were already giving computer training, both in the public and private sector. Many reputed institutions were engaged to conduct training at State and district level.

The first part was to impart training to the trainers. These training institutions were explained in minute details the objectives of the programme as well as the kind of effort that was required to be made. Subsequently, in each State, these training institutions organized workshops for district-level users. Each DRDA was represented by project director and a statistical investigator level officer. The training workshops at the State level was followed up by hands on training at each and every districts site. This follow-up action did not occur in some of the States and, as a result, there was considerable delay in starting CRISP in these States.

A simple CRISP hand book was prepared which would be used in every DRDA to handle the CRISP programme. In the software package itself, one of the options on the menu "self learning" has been provided for users to work on tutorials which will give them knowledge of word processing, spread-sheet and database management. By involving various training institutions on a commercial basis, an element of competition was introduced. The central CRISP team evaluated the impact of training given by the institutions through a direct feedback from the districts.

## Current Status

The CRISP hardware has been installed in at least 80 per cent of DRDAs. Also at least they have been given twice training on CRISP and general topics related to computerisation. Now DRD is taking keen interest in monitoring the statewise utilisation of PC/AT and CRISP software. Some of the States like Haryana, AP, MP partially UP, have shown good progress and require more attention in terms of training.

The XENIX version of CRISP software 2.0 is also ready. Some of the states (W.B., Arunachal Pradesh., Karnataka, etc.) could not purchase h/w due to lack of funds or other reasons. However they are ready to utilise the DISNIC machine (80386-based) with XENIX environment.

NIC is supporting project implementation in most of the States. The State level MIS for DRD has been developed in most of the States in which data are received from district with the help of NICNET. After required analysis is done at State level, the relevant reports are sent to DRD using NICNET. Currently CRISP systems (DOS environment) at district level are not connected to NICNET. Steps are being taken to connect above machine to NIC district systems (XENIX environment), which are already connected to NICNET, using telephone line so that the NICNET facility could be extended to DRDAs also. This has been achieved with active cooperation of DRD.

**Conclusion**

If any information system meets users requirements with simple operational logistics, it can be called a successful one. It should have the flexibility for future adoptations in terms of either technology or scheme logistics. We are happy to say that information system developed for DRDAs (CRISP) by NIC has got these characteristics. It is a complete MIS for DRDA to monitor the poverty alleviation programmes (IRDP, JRY, TRYSEM and DWCRA).

The district-level users were also very reluctant and had doubts about the whole approach and motive. This could be removed with the help of repetitive training programmes, organising workshop/seminars and personal interaction. The district informatics officer (DIO) and district informatics assistant (DIA) of NIC are extending support to DRDAs on any issue related to computerisation. The effective maintenance of equipments and irregular power supply at district level are major problems.

The CRISP group, NIC headquarter, is now responsible for

project coordination, implementation, training and monitoring. Each NIC State Centre or identified State level agency has been given design and methodology of CRISP, so that any changes required by respective state DRD could be incorporated locally. This group also concentrates on the software development for new schemes in area of rural development and distributes the same to NIC state and district units.

# 10

# DECENTRALISED PLANNING (DISNIC)

ASHWANI SAPRA, SATISH SHARMA and MADASWAMY MONI*

## Introduction

Information is a vital resource and is for use like the other conventional factors such as land, labour, capital and organisation. "Informatisation of economy" is changing the role of economy as an "information movement and management (IM&M)" economy. Information systems (IS) are assuming an ever increasing importance in the developmental process of a nation and becoming an integral part of every sector: economic, cultural, educational, social or political. Developmental process in a country needs a sophisticated information flow from the lowest level of administration to the highest national decision making level and also information access to various agencies (both governmental and non-governmental) who are involved in developmental activities for upliftment of the society with or without financial assistance from government sources.

Information technology (IT) facilitates the development process by applying various IT tools in planning, administration, monitoring and evaluation, coordination and policy making not only in government but also in non-governmental organisations. Even though information collection and process have been identified as a concurrent activity in India, and also through various statistical legislations in the country, the development of informatics in government took a forward jump with the formation of National Informatics Centre (NIC) in 1977 and the establishment of NICNET in the country during 1980-90.

---

* National Informatics Centre, Planning Commission, Government of India.

Rural development, community development, and social development have been given due importance and the development planning process in the country is carried out through successive Five-Year Plans, and also through decentralisation by establishing local government bodies (panchayats and nagarpalikas). Socio-economic planning and plan management requires the availability of an extensive information system based on reliable data to facilitate the development and to analyse policy options by employing modelling and forecasting techniques. Informatics network plays an important role in the information flow from the implementation level to the planners at macro (national), meso (state), and micro (district, block, and village) levels.

Distributed Data Bases (DDB) are today the most promising area and a much needed tool for informatics professionals, IS experts and administrators. DDBs are the converging point of networking and data base technologies, respectively representative of distribution and integration. This is due to fast and often explosive evolution of these two domains over the decade. The concept of Distributed Processing (DP) has emerged as a result of technological, economical and organisational factors. The evolutionary watch-word of the distributed processing movement is "power to the people". DDB establishment approach can be viewed as follows:

(i) Top-down where local databases do not pre-exist but result from partitioning and the Global Database Administrator is free to select any partitioning strategy even if the final allocation is more or less dependent on the distributed DBMS (e.g., GISTNIC) and

(ii) Bottom-up where local databases are already implemented on local DBMS and then are integrated in order to constitute a global database, meeting the application requirements (e.g., DISNIC).

**Distributed Sectoral Databases for Decentralised Planning**

Since India has different types of terrain, resources, climate, socio-economic levels and distinct problems, preparation of a comprehensive micro-level plan either for a village, or cluster of villages, requires a strong spatially area/region oriented geo-integrated socio-economic-cum-natural resources database for planning, management and decision-making at grassroot level. Over the years, increasing emphasis has been placed on multi-level planning, from the national level to the state and to the district level and to the small area (development block) which was considered as a "suitable and manageable geographical unit area" for planned development within the frame of district planning and other levels in the multi-level planning structure. Rural development represents the major component of decentralised planning.

Decentralised planning calls for an immense amount of data and information specially to meet the new orientations in planning that have emerged in the recent years. Decentralised planning presupposes availability of relevant information at different levels in a desegregated form at as many of these levels as possible. Hence development of distributed information systems and databases at national, State, district and block level (grassroot level) is essential for the effective socio-economic planning for social transformation in the country and also to bridge the information gap for planning at these levels, and has got its evolutionary approach depending upon the data usage and comprehensive understanding of information requirement for planning purposes.

The micro-level planning approach is essentially to meet the objectives of: (i) optimum utilisation of human as well as natural resources available in the area, (ii) improvement in income and employment opportunities for rural masses, and (iii) integration of area development with the development of people residing therein, and also to address itselt to the problems of the rural poor and formulate realistic targets for reducing: (i) poverty, (ii) unemployment, and (iii) inequality.

Data requirements for micro-level planning at block level may be grouped as follows:

A. Plan Formulation: (i) Assessment of the available resources and additional resources required for the development, (ii) To consider the need of the people with particular reference to the weaker section of the society, (iii) Formulation of schemes/programmes with specific objectives on the basis of the above details; here national priorities should be given utmost importance and wherever it is necessary linkage between local programmes and special programmes should be established, and (iv) Setting physical and financial targets to be achieved within the specific time-frame under each scheme/programme.

B. Plan implementation which is a sensitive aspect of the planning process, involves the issues such as: (i) to find out suitable agencies for assigning the responsibility for implementation of the scheme/programmes; (ii) to provide suitable infrastructure to ensure a timely and healthy progress; and (iii) monitoring the progress and timely solution of the problem arisen.

C. Evaluation is a systematic and proper assessment of a programme with reference to the objectives of the schemes/programmes; the data generated at the implementation and evaluation stages should be input data for future plan formulation.

**Infrastructure for Government Informatics Development**

Government organisations use and produce information. Information is the essence of their existence. It is a fact that many government ministries/departments and organisations are not so careful about the collection, storage and retrieval of information as they are about money. The realities are: (i) Information collected by government organisations imposes a heavy cost on business; (ii) Information that is not available may cost a great deal of money; (iii) Information that is not used may lose a great deal of money; (iv) Information systems are today and for the foreseeable future a pre-requisite for effective national development; and (v) development within the government administration can be used as a lever for technical development in society as a whole [UN090].

National Informatics Centre (NIC) is the nodal S&T organisation of Government of India, under the Planning Commission, to introduce information technology (IT) tools for management support (MS), development of databases (DB), model-bases (MB) and knowledge-bases (KB), decision support systems (DSS), Geographic Information System (GISNIC), fileless-office concept, electronic mail services (NICMAIL), and tele-informatics services in the Government at the Central, State and district level in the country. NICNET which is a satellite based computer communication network, established during the Seventh Five-Year Plan period (1985-90) provides informatics network facilities to the government administrations for IT implementation. NICNET is expected to be enhanced during the Eighth Five-Year Plan period (1990-85) to cover about 5300 Blocks/Tehsils through out the country to facilitate grassroot level development planning and administration which has been emphasised during this plan period. NICNET comprises the following:

(a) Very large Computers (NEC-S1000) at the NIC Regional Centres (Delhi, Pune, Bhubaneshwar and Hyderabad);
(b) ND-550 or equivalent super mini-computers at State capitals, for providing informatics service to the States;
(c) Super PC-AT computer systems at each district, to provide services to the district administration;
(d) PC-AT computer systems at each block development office to provide informatics services to the block level administration (to be implemented during eighth Five-Year Plan period);
(e) Master earth station at NIC headquarters, Delhi and a Micro earth station at each of NIC State units and district informatics centres, for exchange of information via INSAT-1D satellite.

While NICNET makes use of the satellite communication (INSAT-1D) for long distance links, terrestrial communication is used for short distance intra-city network through leased telephone lines or dial-up lines using Public-Switched Telephone Network (PSTN) for integration to NICNET.

In general, NICNET facilitates the Central Government as well as the State Governments for: (i) Monitoring of vital socio-economic products, (ii) On-line retrieval of data, (iii) Optimum utilisation of expensive computer resources, (iv) Emergency communication systems, (v) Sharing latest software tools, (vi) Dissemination of information, and (vii) Exchange of messages and information between Central Government, State Governments and districts.

Application of IT for rural development was given the top priority by the government by launching various government informatics development programmes of NIC such as DISNIC, GRID (grass-root level informatics development programme during the Eighth Five-Year Plan period), CRISP (sponsored project of the Central Rural Development Department for implementation by NIC at DRDA level), sectoral informatics programme (AGRIS, ARISE,

ENVIS, education, industry, etc.), public informatics programme (GISTNIC, NNRMS of DOS and NRDMS of DST, etc.). Multi-functional use of IT facilities for rural upliftment at village level is expected to pave the way for the use of IT for community use and rural development in a broader perspective. Informatics development programme at district and sub-district level are explained in brief in the following sections.

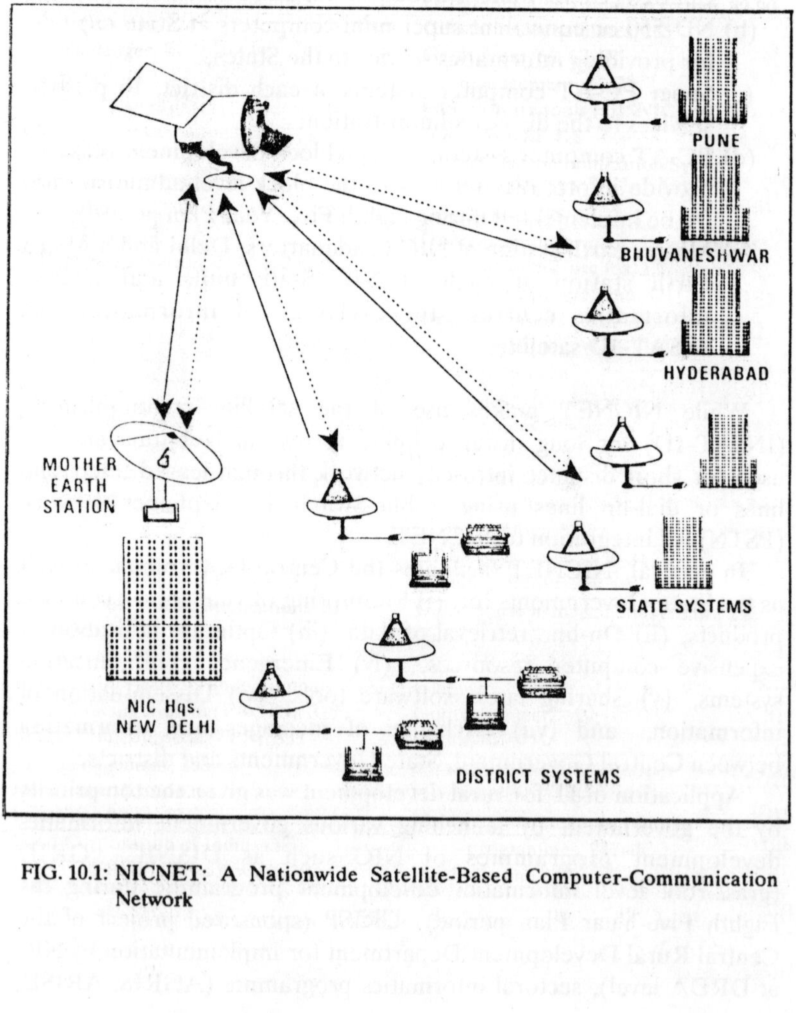


FIG. 10.1: NICNET: A Nationwide Satellite-Based Computer-Communication Network

(A) *DISNIC Informatics Development Programme at District Level*

DISNIC programme was launched in 1987 with the specific objective of bringing in IT standards for the government district administration and hence envisaged to: (i) develop the necessary information/databases (both spatial and non-spatial) in various sectors of the economy for planning and decision-making at the district level, (ii) promote informatics culture at the district level through appropriate training programmes, (iii) facilitate information standardisation and discipline, wherever required, (iv) improve the analysis capacity and the presentation of the statistics utilised for national, regional and district planning, (v) develop modelling and forecasting techniques that are required for decision-making for socio-economic development, and (vi) promote GIS techniques for planning and also remote sensing data applications for natural resources management at grassroot level.

With the establishment of NICNET, the implementation of the DISNIC Programme has facilitated the development of DDB on NICNET as a bottom-up approach where local DISNIC sectoral databases are already implemented on local DBMS at the district level and then to integrate them in order to constitute a Global Database meeting the End-Users' application requirements at state/national levels, using the distributed database management system (UDMS) of NICNET.

B. *DISNIC-PLAN Programme for Facilitating Micro-Level Planning*

As per the recommendations of the committee of "Study Group on Information Gap" of the Planning Commission, proformae for information collection for micro-level planning at district, block, and village level were designed and distributed to the State governments, under the DISNIC-PLAN programme. The DISNIC-PLAN programme aims at: (i) creation and maintenance of district, block and village level databases in respect of socio-economic, agro-economic and natural resources, etc., (ii) expert systems development, and (iii) also integration of GIS Techniques for micro-level planning, using NICNET facilities at the district level. Voluntary agencies can look into the data for its utility with respect to their requirements. Many State governments are in the process of information collection to create the database. Agencies like

NABARD would like to use the village data for their credit plans.

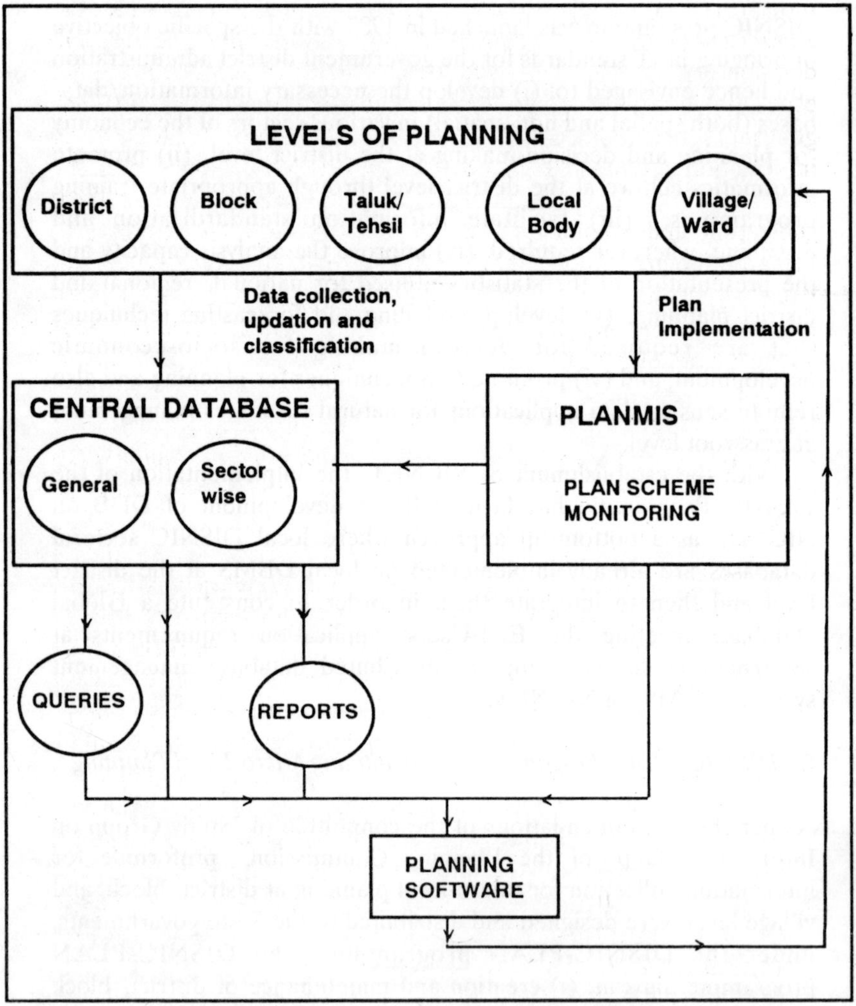


FIG. 10.2: District Planning Information System

(C) *GRID Programme at Block Level*

With the implementation of DISNIC programme, NIC has initiated information revolution at district level through its various databases to provide demographic, socio-economic and development indicators. With the quick availability of information, the administrators can now devote more time to the actual planning and decision-making. As the block is the smallest developmental unit, especially in implementing development programmes and the block generates basic information, the development of block level information system is expected to go a long way in increasing the availability of information for decision-making, monitoring, evaluation and planning. The GRID programme is expected to facilitate the grass-root level development planning and administration which has been emphasised during this Plan period. Implementation of GRID programme will take place during the enhancement of NICNET facilities.

The Working Group on block level planning under the Chairmanship of Prof. M.L. Dantwala has also recommended the desirability of maintenance of data at village level in various areas mentioned below for block level planning. GRID programme is expected to cater to the following areas:

(a) Tehsil/Block level Database Project on Development sectors, e.g., (Rural Labour, Agriculture Development, Animal Husbandry Development, Dairy Development, Minor Irrigation, Soil Conservation, Industry (SSI, Rural, Agro-based), Social Forestry, Wasteland Development, Wetland Development, Fisheries Development, Community Development, Rural Development), Social Services (Health and Nutrition, Education, Drinking Water Supply, Housing, Sanitation, Welfare Programmes, Local Transport), Cooperation, Banking and Financial Institutions for credit facilities, etc.;
(b) Land Records Informatics;
(c) Panchayati Raj Institutions Informatics;
(d) Nagarpalika Informatics;
(e) Employment and Training;
(f) Information System on Women in Agriculture, Women and Rural Development, Women and Environment, Legal Provisions protecting women, Employment opportunities for women, Science and Technology component assisting Women, Women and Education, Women and Health, etc.

(D) *Involvement of Voluntary Agencies for Government Informatics Development Programme*

Voluntary agencies (VAs) supplement government efforts in the implementation of poverty-alleviation programmes and minimum needs programme, and more and more grass-root level voluntary agencies are getting identified for associating in the implementation of such programmes in the country. VAs play the crucial role of being the "eyes and ears" of the people in the field. Voluntary agencies working for rural development at the village level require access to the information collected by various government agencies at the village level. Information collection at the village level involves: (i) manpower, (ii) money and (iii) time. This can be saved to a great extent, if voluntary agencies have access to the information collected by the government agencies; and also the cooperation among the government agencies, non-governmental agencies and the private agencies, etc. in this regard.

Voluntary agencies assist the district planners in deciding what sorts of assets should be provided to the beneficiary in a particular region depending upon the available infrastructure and resources. VAs are involved in collecting such information by door-to-door canvassing in the rural areas for the identification of IRDP beneficiaries on the basis of annual income. Voluntary agencies have expertise to conduct evaluation studies on programmes run by: (i) grass root level agencies, (ii) social action groups and (iii) activists, and they have systematic orientation and realistic terms of reference of assessing "people and programme".

(E) *Information Access to Voluntary Agencies who are involved in Rural Upliftment/Advancement*

Information is no longer going to be the bottleneck for the social development, as the entire government administration has access to the informatics network (NICNET) and involved in the government informatics development programme at national, State, and district level. The Government Informatics Development Programme by NIC is governed by institutional arrangements, such as, NSCC (NIC-State Coordination Committee), NDCC (NIC-District Coordination Committee) and NMCC (NIC-Ministerial Coordination Committee). NIC has signed MOU with all States and UTs for effective implementation of this programme.

Voluntary agencies may like to assess their information needs from NICNET databases, such as, DISNIC, CRISP, GISTNIC and other sectoral databases for utility in rural upliftment, and also for the development of GRID at the block level. VAs can have grants-in-aid from the information technology development programme of NIC for IS-related projects for rural upliftment/advancement. Problems due to non-availability of proper facilities for information exchange and also information access felt in the planning process by VAs are expected to be eased out by rallying around NICNET.

**Conclusion**

DISNIC-PLAN project is under implementation in various district nodes of NICNET under the DISNIC programme. State government departments and district level authorities are actively involved in the implementation of the project. Many State Governments have identified pilot districts for the preparation of a comprehensive micro-level plan (decentralised planning) either for a village or cluster of villages using the DISNIC-PLAN project facilities.

# 11

# WEATHER AND ENVIRONMENT

B.M. CHHABRA*

## Introduction

Meteorology is helping man to harness the forces of the atmosphere for social and economic benefits to man kind. The spectrum of its applications in different fields of human activity is growing wider and richer everyday. The meteorological know-how has become essential in almost all fields of economic development, viz., agriculture, water management, industry, transportation, housing, environment control and the utilisation of natural resources. The application of Information Technology (IT) and other modern equipments including satellites have given a new outlook to the science of weather forecasting.

## Application Areas

Meteorology has applications in almost every field which concerns human beings. Computers are being utilised in meteorology starting from observations, preparation of weather forecast and to the point of providing end-product to the user. Various steps involved in this process are given below.

### (A) *Observing System*

Observations form the basis of meteorological studies. A precise weather forecast for any area demands precise facts collected in millions from all over the world at fixed synoptic hours. On fixed hours, large number of land stations, merchant ships and aircrafts

* India Meteorological Department, Government of India.

record meteorological observations, such as, pressure, temperature, wind, clouds, humidity, rainfall, fog, haze, visibility, etc. Upper air observations are also recorded by releasing balloons with attached Radio-Sonde equipment which are followed by RADARS from the ground. Personal computers are used to make the computations within short time. But still the gap remains over oceans, forests and mountainous regions for understanding and prediction of weather. Satellites have provided a new observing system to cover this gap.

(B) *Satellites – The New Tools*

The artificial earth-orbitting satellite is a new means of observing the weather; it presents two important advantages over all other known techniques as indicated below:

(i) It provides a means of observing the weather from outside the atmosphere; and
(ii) It provides a means of prompt weather information on a truly global scale.

Meteorological satellites are of two types: (i) polar orbitting satellites and (ii) geostationary satellites. Polar orbitting satellites provide instantaneous pictures of an area around their path while geostationary satellites provide pictures of the same area continuously. Satellites are equipped to take pictures and measure radiations. These observations are used to estimate temperatures, cloud cover, snow cover, areas of dust haze, fog and winds in the various layers of the atmosphere. Pictures help in the detection of cyclonic storms while they are deep into the sea area and also other significant weather systems. Thus satellites help the meteorologist to collect useful meteorological information from otherwise data sparse regions. India was continuously using American and Russian meteorological satellites from 1960 onwards for meteorological information. On 30th August, 1983, INSAT-1B was launched. It became operational on 15th October, 1983. INSAT-1B was placed into the geostationary orbit over the equator at 74°E at an altitude of approximately 36,000 km. The meteorological instrument on board were: (i) very high resolution radiometer (VHRR), and (ii) The data collection transponder. INSAT-1D was launched on 12th June, 1990 and is located at 83.0°E at an altitude of 36,000 km. It is being presently used. Its resolution is 2.75 km. in the visible and 11 km. in the infra-red channel.

All data from satellite is received first at Delhi earth station of Department of Telecommunication from where it is transmitted over microwave link to the meteorological data utilisation centre (MDUC) at Lodi Road, New Delhi. Here data is processed round the clock with the help of fast computers. INSAT-II with improved resolution will be launched in the late 1991*. For this purpose new computers to process the data are being installed. A sample picture of a cyclonic storm in the Bay of Bengal at 0430 UTC on 7th May, 1990 is shown in Fig. 11.1. Meteorological satellites thus have really helped in the modernisation of meteorology. Credit for this goes to the development of fast computers and computerised communication system.

### (C) *Radars*

Electronics are having more and more applications in modern Meteorology. Second World War saw the development of RADAR in which ultra-short wireless waves were used to detect high flying enemy aircrafts. These ultra-short waves are reflected not only by metallic bodies, but also by the water droplets in the clouds and the areas of rain in the sky. The reflected intensity increases with the size of the droplets. Areas where large drops are numerous show themselves as bright patches on the Radar screen. Severe cyclonic storms also reveals itself as a bright converging spiral on the Radar screen when it is within the range of the Radar set. X-band radars have been provided at almost all important aerodromes and S-band at important coastal stations to detect cyclones. Range of cyclone detecting radars is 400 Km. Radars have really helped meteorologists to improve their service to aviation and in storm warning of the coastal areas. Computers are being used to process radars data and incorporate the same in computerised weather forecasting.

### (D) *Computerised Telecommunication*

An efficient communication system is a backbone of an efficient meteorological service. All meteorological data collected by various means is required to be exchanged among the user countries. Global

---

* Since launched in July, 1992.

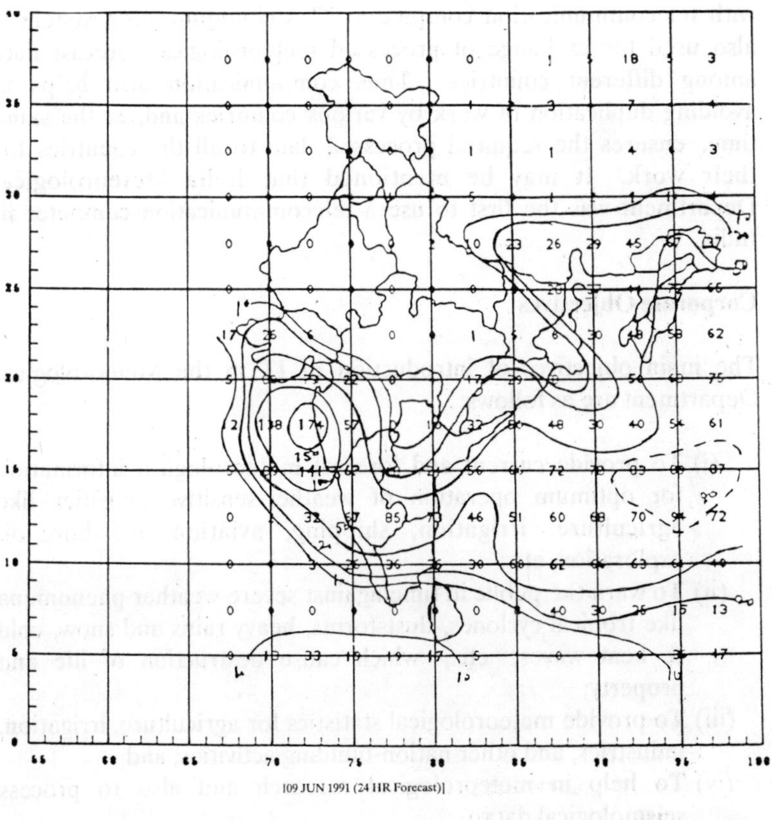

FIG. 11.1: **Rainfall (mm) over India with NCMRWF Improved Model Physics**

exchange of such voluminous data (estimated at 5 million five figures groups per day) on real time basis has become possible only with computerisation of telecommunication facilities. World Meteorological Organisation (WMO) has provided a scheme of Global Telecommunication System (GTS) for quick exchange of data between different countries. India is connected to Moscow, Melbourne, Tokyo, Cairo and various other international circuits for global reception and transmission of data. In Delhi, VAX-11/750 telecommunication computers are being used for this purpose. Thus Delhi is an important centre for the exchange of international meteorological data. India has also an efficient national telecommunication system. All major airports have been equipped with telecommunication computers. This communication system is also used for exchange of processed meteorological forecast data among different countries. Thus communication also helps in avoiding duplication of work by various countries and, at the same time, ensures the required processed data to all the countries for their work. It may be mentioned that India Meteorological Department was the first to use a telecommunication computer in India.

**Corporate Objectives**

The main objectives of introduction of IT in the Meteorological Department are as follows:

(i) To provide current and forecast meteorological information for optimum operation of weather-sensitive activities like agriculture, irrigation, shipping, aviation, off-shore oil exploration, etc.;
(ii) To warn the public in time against severe weather phenomena like tropical cyclones, duststorms, heavy rains and snow, cold & heat waves, etc., which cause destruction of life and property;
(iii) To provide meteorological statistics for agriculture, irrigation, industries, and other nation-building activities; and
(iv) To help in meteorological research and also to process seismological data.

**Computer-Based Methodology**

(a) *Objective Analysis*

The data received from the telecommunication computer is decoded by a scientific computer. It is subjected to various quality control checks. The data so received are at irregularly spaced observational stations. The solution of hydrodynamical equations governing the flow of the atmosphere require the values of the meteorological parameters at regularly-spaced grid points. This is necessary because these equations are non-linear and do not have analytical solutions. Their approximate solutions are obtained by numerical methods using finite difference and other numerical schemes. The technique by which the data are obtained at a large number of equally-spaced grid points from irregularly-distributed observations is known as objective analysis. This is being carried out daily in India Meteorological Department using a scientific computer.

(b) *Numerical Weather Prediction*

Forecast of the pressure fields by numerical solution of the equations of motion using initially observed state of the atmosphere generally with the aid of an electronic computer using numerical techniques is called Numerical Weather Prediction (NWP). This is being carried out in India using simple 5 level models. In other advanced countries more sophisticated models are being used.

(c) *Computerised Cyclone Prediction*

About 90 years of cyclonic storm data in the Bay of Bengal and Arabian Sea have been analysed with respect to time and location of its formation, direction, and speed of movement, etc. This database is used along with the characteristics of the current storm by an expert system developed for the purpose to predict 24, 48 & 72 hours positions of the cyclonic storm. Mathematical models and computer programmes have also been developed to predict the storm-surges. The prediction of storm-surges are of immense benefit to the villagers in the coastal areas.

(d) *Climatology*

Climatology of a place is the average weather of that area. In India, Meteorological Department database for more than 100 years have been created. This data is a valuable asset and is being used to find out future trends of weather and climatic changes. It may be mentioned that in India no definite trends have been found in rainfall.

(e) *Monsoon Forecast*

General weather forecasts are issued for 24 hours to 48 hours and in some areas an outlook is issued for a week. But monsoon, which is very important for Indian economy, constitutes about 70 to 80 per cent of the annual rainfall of the country. Special Seasonal Forecast for the period June to September are given. Methods with different parameters have been developed using regression techniques for this purpose. Such forecasts are very useful to the government for planning purpose.

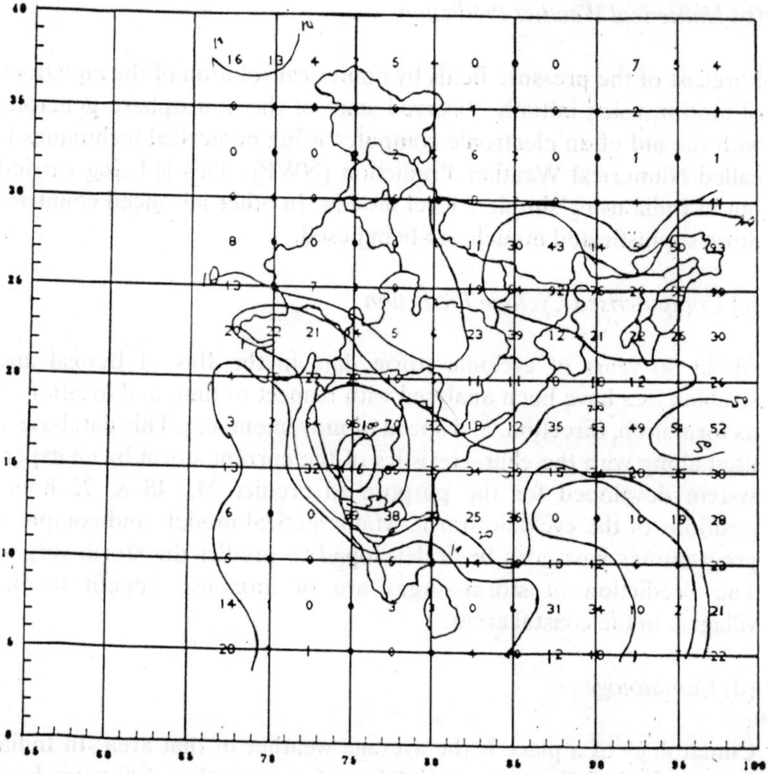

[10 JUN 1991 (48 HR Forecast)]

**FIG. 11.2: Rainfall (mm) Over India with NCMRWF Improved Model Physics**

## (f) *Crop Yield Models*

Statistical models have also been developed in India to estimate the principal crops of the country based on long-term weather and technological inputs using computers. The total food production of the country estimated by these models is generally in good agreement with the actual figures.

(g) *Air Pollution*

Computerised models have also been developed to estimate the pollutions created by the industry and its effect on human beings and agriculture in the area. These models will help in the future town and industrial planning in such a way that the environment pollution will remain under control. For the present state, mankind is responsible by cutting of forests, eliminating some of the animals/birds, construction of large scale concrete jungles in the cities and creating large scale industrial areas. Computerised statistics may help to control this activity by keeping proper records.

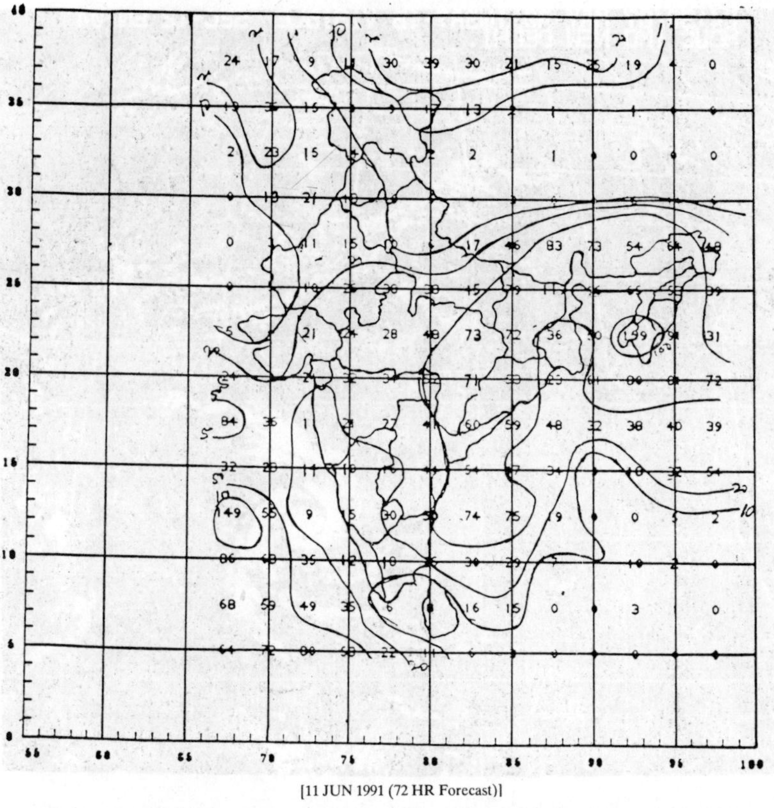

[11 JUN 1991 (72 HR Forecast)]

FIG. 11.3: Rainfall (mm) Over India with NCMRWF Improved Model Physics

**Benefits Derived**

Computerised information technology has helped the meteorologists to improve the weather forecast for aviation, shipping and agriculture. It has also helped in the improvement of cyclonic storm prediction for coastal areas. It has resulted in enormous saving of human life and property. Environment models developed with the help of computers will also help in keeping the air pollution under control in the existing cities using different preventive measures and also help in the planning of new pollution-free cities. Thus, use of computers has given a new outlook to the science of weather forecasting and we look forward for further improvement in this respect.

FIG. 11.4: Cyclonic Storm in the Bay of Bengal at 04.30 UTC of 7th May, 1990

**Conclusion**

In India, introduction of computerised Information Technology (IT) in meteorology did not pose any problem. In fact, India Meteorological Department introduced Hollerith machines in 1945 and first computer in 1963. A modern scientific computer was acquired in 1973. India Meteorological Department was also first to use a communication computer in 1976. The first super computer CRAY XMP-14 is also being used for medium range weather forecast in meteorology. It is being managed by Department of Science and Technology.

# 12

# ENVIRONMENT

HARJIT SINGH*

## Introduction

It is universally recognised that information, particularly scientific and technological including environmental information, is one of the basic resources for the socio-economic development of the country. As a resource, information is like electric energy and the impact of reliable, fast and inexpensive information on the national economy will be as great as that of electricity. Some specialists even go as far as to say that information is the resource of resources, i.e., on which depends all other resources because it is information which premits other resources to be identified, evaluated and utilised. Information is an essential ingredient of change and change is nothing but a transformation resulting from a new contribution of data or different treatment of existing data. Information is the only resource which grows as it is sub-divided and spreads. Under development, in the final analysis is a consequence of the lack of capacity to generate information, to handle it properly, to store it, to perform it regularly and to disseminate it equitably.

The flow of fresh and reliable information is the parameter of progress. It is a form of modern currency, an investment for the future. The newly emerging high-tech disciplines such as super computers, telecommunications, micro-electronics, new sources of energy, bio-diversity, environment, etc., are valued more in terms of information generated than anything else. Many advanced countries are said to have entered into a state called "post-industrial society" in which rise of the GNP depends not so much on the production and distribution of goods and commodities but on the generation, dis-

---

* Ministry of Environment and Forestry, Government of India.

tribution and application of scientific knowledge and information. In some of these advanced countries, more and more people are working in information-based service sectors than in all other employment sectors put together.

In meeting the information needs of various user groups, it is necessary to distinguish the uses of information and users of information. There are several types of users of information including those engaged in fundamental scientific research, applied scientists working on R&D, technologists, teachers, writers, industrialists, library personnel, business faculty and so on. Each category of these users has different use of information for different purposes.

**Corporate Objectives**

The information clientele forms a broad spectrum of various sectors. They could be from R&D discipline or entrepreneurs or students or business personnel or others. A scientist may require information for general need to keep himself informed of the latest development over the field of science and technology, an environmentalist may require information to appraise himself the latest environmental development, a business magnet may be in need of information only from business angle. But, whatever may be the need, the user group requires information with a particular objective. Therefore, each information-seeker has a particular path in which his information needs to travel. So according to the diversity of the clientele, the information needs also become diverse. It differs from a researcher, to a policy maker or to an engineer or to an industrialist or even to the general public. Information is required in all parts of public administration system, e.g., in government departments like Agriculture, Industry or Social Welfare, departmental agencies incharge of commercial operations, Railways, P&T or government corporations like Food Corporation of India or public companies such as, Coal India, Steel Authority of India Ltd. and its subsidiaries. What is most important is to develop a management information system (MIS) to meet the objectives of different clientele.

A comprehensive MIS should have the following characteristics:

(a) It should cover all the salient aspects of the programme with reference to the principles, goals and objectives in view;
(b) It must be selective;

(c) It should be transparent and not opaque, i.e., it should clearly bring out the relationship between the input and output, effort and the result, the money spent and the result derived;
(d) It should bring out outstanding success as well as outstanding failures; and
(e) It should be periodic so that there is a systematic and sustained monitoring over a period of time.

## Computer Based Methodology

We are experiencing now what may be termed as the "push of technology" and its impact on every facet of information handling. The advent of digital computer and the advancement in the telecommunication and audio-visual technology have opened up a new possibilities in dealing with problems arising from collecting, organising, disseminating a vast amount of scientific and technical information. Computer and communication technologies are not only merging but are also converging with related technologies such as printing and photography. When all these elements are fully integrated the resultant capability for information transfer and exchange would create a form of material information inter-dependence. Even, one can say that the merger of the computer and the communications with other technologies would result in the development of a total new information infrastructure for the society.

It has been government's endeavour now to provide benefits of computerisation to all nooks and corners in India for accessing all information needs. With the development of various databases, it has become possible to search and sort large quantities of required data rapidly.

In the initial stages, the information networks operated in a batch processing mode which was not a very satisfactory arrangement for information access and retrieval. However, with the development of the packet switching technology during the 1970s', "on line information network" permitting an attractive man-machine interface has become popular and is being widely used. Improvisation of productivity has resulted in government operations through streamlining of information base, systems analysis of the organisational structure, quantitative studies feeding the planning process and, in general, evolving an effective managing information system for each government department with exchange of information among them. This has been catalysed by National Informatics Centre (NIC) which was conceived in 1973 and nucleated in 1975 to develop methodologies for implementing a governmental information System and to demonstrate to the government departments the benefits that accrue from computerisation. NIC has also developed, distributed and decentralised informatics and computer network for government management information system. Computer Maintenance Corporation (CMC) has also introduced a commercial computer network INDONET incorporating an integrated information management and distributed data processing facilities spanning the entire country.

**Benefits Derived**

The NIC has launched its District Information System (DISNIC) under which selected information from the districts can be transmitted to the State computers. Similar information from all the districts will be transferred to the computer at State Capitals under the supervision of the State Governments before passing it on to the regional centre and the national centre. The national centre will be able to query the databases in the States and vice-versa. The relevant decision support information from the districts, thus readily available with the State Governments and with the Central Government DISNIC through NICNET, will fill the long-felt information gap for the planning agencies and will facilitate the decision-making at various levels of Government of India.

National Information System of Science and Technology (NISSAT) set up in the Ministry of Science and Technology, Government of India, has been functioning to meet the scientific and technological information needs through its sectoral information centres.

**Environmental Information System**

An Environmental Information System (ENVIS) has been set-up by the Ministry of Environment and Forests with a chain of distributed information centres on the priority subject areas of environment and located in the various professional organisations throughout the country to meet the environmental information needs of the users.

Bio-technological Information System (BTIS) has been established in the Department of bio-technology for meeting the information requirements in the field of bio-technology of the user community.

Besides, various network of information as given below have been launched/being launched to make information available to the user community:

1. RAILNET: computer network for the Railways,
2. OILNET: computer network for oil sector,
3. EDUNET: computer network for educational institutions,
4. BANKNET: computer network for banking applications and electronic fund transfer,
5. TRANSNET: a computer network for transport sector,
6. POLICENET: a computer network for the police, and
7. COALNET: a computer network for coal.

**Problems Encountered and their Solutions**

India, despite its having third largest scientific man power in the world, still is not so well placed in the matter of generating storage, transmission and retrieval of scientific and technical information for the benefit of the scientific community. In spite of the advanced communication systems, a large segment of the science and technology community does not have ready access to current and other information. This is practically impossible for the researchers in the remote location.

There is a serious lack of adequate number of libraries and information centres in the country. There is no adequate bibliographic control of Indian scientific publications and papers, publication of governmental agencies, publications of academies and societies, etc. Even in the area of scientific publications, we lack not only the quantity of the scientific journals but also the quality of production. Still, there is a heavy dependence on foreign information source. It is a common experience that international journals reject publications from developing countries due to their lack of comprehensiveness which, in turn, is due to lack of latest information and incomplete references. By setting up several information systems in the country, the S&T information needs have been partially met.

**Conclusion**

S&T information can be further improved upon as follow:

– The on-line access to international databases available on many

network should be made possible;
- Important databases should be procured and provided to selected information centres for use by our scientists;
- The existing communication facilities should be upgraded to facilitate quick and easy information transfer;
- Training of personnel in information handling should be provided on priority basis;
- A nation-wide campaign should be organised to promote use of the information and its access at various points;
- A National Science Trust should be set-up to increase the facilities for document delivery for the benefit of the scientific community in the common areas; and
- Linkages of the various national information systems should be made immediately to interact the information needs.

Information systems on the other areas should be set-up to meet the information requirements on the S&T community in particular and the people in general.

# 13

# DESKTOP MAPPING

PROF. J.G. KRISHNAYYA*

## Introduction

Desktop mapping combines the properties of thematic maps with those of computers: Properties of thematic maps are integrative; wholistic; location-specific; spatial distribution; density; access. Properties of computers are speed; repeatability; precision; neatness; compact storage. Properties of computer storage are portability; copyability; compactness; updateability. Correctly designed thematic mapping software packages can make easy the task of viewing data and finding unusual cases, or locations where norms have not been met. Such identification and selection is the key to effective administrative management as well as ensuring that increasingly scarce state funds are optimally utilised to improve the conditions of the people.

## Thematic Maps

Thematic maps are produced by projecting tabular data onto a set of regions (or alternatively a set of locations or a set of routes) on a map. Regions can be filled with a choropleth hatching; points can have different markers, or symbols of different sizes, or barcharts or even piecharts. Sometimes piecharts can be projected over a choropleth background, providing an extra dimension information.

The choropleth itself can be many different types — equal interval; user-selected intervals; percentile; or even mean/standard deviation. One can also represent the flows between regions (of persons, money, grain, coal, etc.) by lines of different thickness, or thick and

---

* System Research Institute.

thin directed arrows. A great variety of thematic techniques are available with desktop mapping.

Desktop thematic maps can both be viewed on the screen (in black and white or in colour), or examined on paper in user-selected sizes (up to A1). The usual mode of use is to generate, store and view on the screen a number of alternatives, making changes in the techniques and symbols used, and editing for aesthetics, before obtaining a high quality printout. In Query Mode, when information about one particular place (or many locations) is required, this can merely be viewed (*in colour?*) without taking a hard copy.

We introduce below and illustrate a few of the possible applications of desktop mapping -- first at State headquarters, then at district level, and finally at taluk level. This is by no means to be taken as a complete listing of possible applications, for many others too have come up in detailed discussions with various officials. We offer this introduction as a contribution to finding ways to improve the effectiveness and efficiency of State Government with a minimum of additional investment or training.

**Applications in the State**

Let us look at the applications at the level of departments of government at State headquarters. They are of four main types:

(i) Monitoring performance
(ii) Policy analyses
(iii) Planning and budgeting
(iv) "What if...?" analysis

Desktop mapping can make possible significant easing of the workload at State headquarters in respect of these four activities which concern the officials at that level. This means that more cases can be examined more carefully, that more thought can be given to critical issues, and that more alternatives can be taken up when necessary even within time limitations.

Some of the departments which have some or all of these applications are:

Planning Department
Finance Department

Education Department
Health Department
Agriculture Department
Social Forestry Department
Electricity Department (and State Electricity Board)
Public Works Department (and Area Development Authorities)
  Buildings
  Irrigation (and the Water and Sewerage Boards)
  Roads and Bridges
Tribal Development Department.

Taking first applications in the Planning Department, we have:

(a) District-wise and taluka-wise reports sector-wise for printing in annual reports and answers to assembly questions;
(b) Policy analytic support for Annual Plan and Five-Year Plan allocations, sector-wise and district-wise;
(c) Evaluation of the minimum needs status of different talukas and districts and their progress sector-wise, quarterly and annually;
(d) Identification of scarcity-endemic and drought affected talukas;
(e) Evaluation of EGS and similar State-wise programmes on the basis of monthly or seasonal data; and
(f) Evaluation of the 20-point programme results, on a multi-dimensional basis.

In the Finance Department, we can map sales tax collections by taluka. Cash flows in state treasuries is an important area where net inward and outward flows can be seasonally mapped, grouped and analysed. With suitable base maps accompanying the proposals, it will be possible for the Finance Department to examine the spatial aspects of major schemes coming to it for cost benefit analysis. This will lend strength to the social dimension of such analyses. Spatial analysis of treasury challans will provide valuable policy insights.

The Education Department has direct responsibility for high schools and above, but receives much useful information on primary and middle schooling. The simplest mapping of boys' and girls' enrolment rates, of the average size of class and of examination results will provide many leads for further detailed study at local level. What is important is that the problem-areas be identified and separated from those that are doing alright. Per-student budgets for teacher salaries, for repairs, for equipment, etc., can be compared spatially to throw up areas needing attention. Because desktop mapping is fast, it can be used to compare school attendance in different months and seasons. Instead of taking two weeks to prepare, a taluka-wise education map can be prepared in 15 minutes and be xeroxed for distribution the same day, thus providing feedback to the concerned regional (district?) officers responsible. Transfers and postings are yet another area where mapping can clarify the situation.

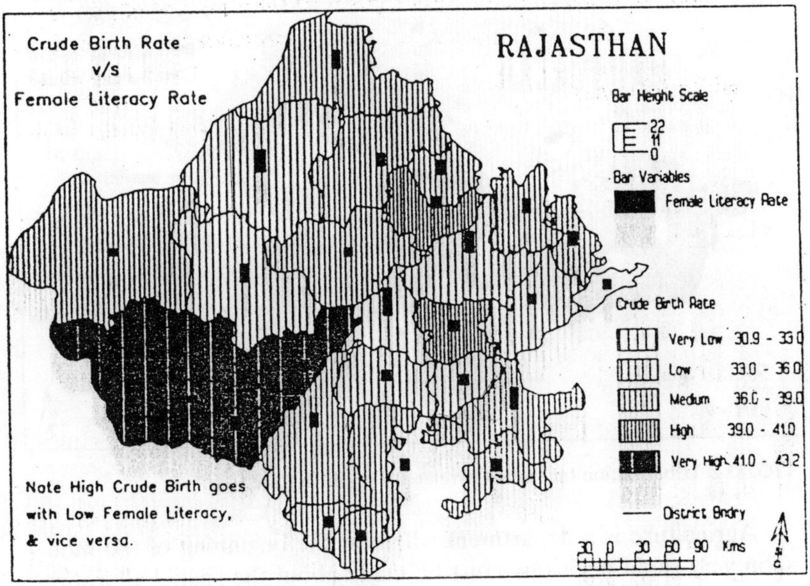


FIG. 13.1: Policy Analysis: Female Literacy vs Birth Rate

Health is a field requiring very rapid response to information because of the short shelf-life of medicines and the speed of epidemics. With child health, maternal care, and preventive medicine assuming greater importance, there is need to monitor performance closely, to map out areas where drinking water is unsafe in future months and to use this as an input to medical programming. Likewise, areas with poor drainage (when and if it rains) become centres of other types of infection. These, too, can be mapped in real time. There is equal need to keep an up-to-date map of all reported infectious cases, so as to help determine the vectors and to keep them under control. Desktop mapping can play a big role in medical administration by helping focus attention on needy areas. Mapping will also offer a lot of help in the tasks related to personnel assignments.

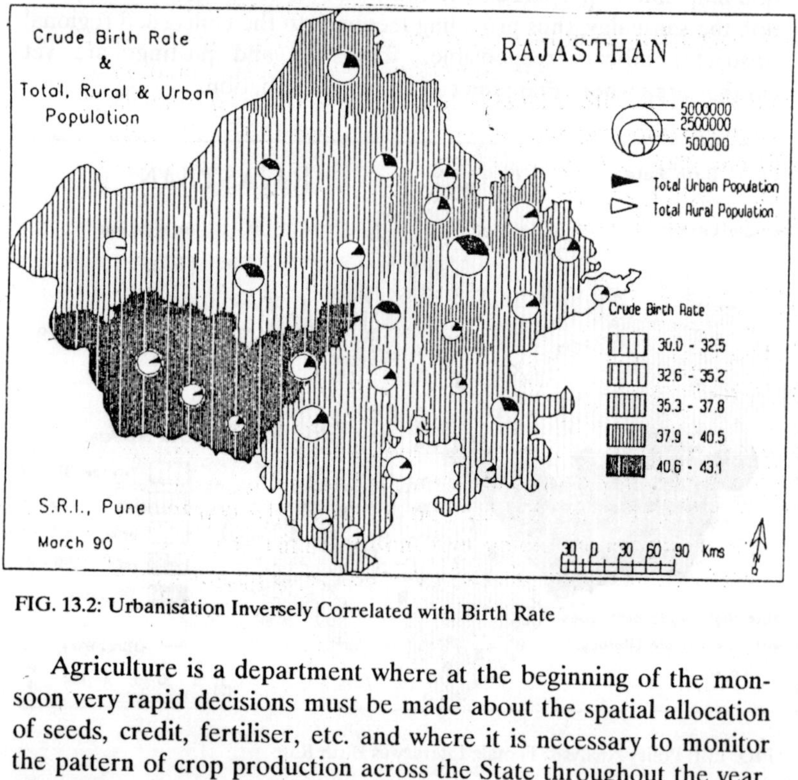


FIG. 13.2: Urbanisation Inversely Correlated with Birth Rate

Agriculture is a department where at the beginning of the monsoon very rapid decisions must be made about the spatial allocation of seeds, credit, fertiliser, etc. and where it is necessary to monitor the pattern of crop production across the State throughout the year. The ability to plot and to view several variables together will be of special value in relating crop amounts and value to credit, fertiliser usage, etc., spatially. These are all analyses that need to be conducted at aggregate level using taluk or district-wise data. Other related analyses concern irrigation project impacts, the effect of major and minor regulated markets and warehouses on production and prices, and the spatial pattern of prices of agricultural commodities over time. The periodic movement of technical personnel can be rationalised and needy areas identified using maps.

For Social forestry, desktop mapping can be used in project planning and strategic cost benefit analysis, as well as to compare the display of the programmes in different districts and talukas and the relative unit costs of different components of the programme, which would reveal any problems.

The Electricity Department and the State Electricity Board have a tremendous amount of spatial information on generation, but more importantly on transmission and distribution. In fact, special-purpose modules can be added to THEMAPS to help identify places where the transmission network requires change. Merely monitoring the condition of the State-wide network, which is being continuously upgraded, is a significant step. THEMAPS would also be used to provide a real-time picture of the electricity scene if it were connected on-line to the Electricity Board database. Control and monitoring of extension works on the distribution network across the State can be also effectively done with the help of maps.

The Public Works Department has a unique problem of having to readjust its budget location-wise and responsibility-wise in January, after it is known exactly how much money will be available till March-end. Making these decisions can be eased by using a spatial picture of the needs and of the progress of various types of work till then. Forward budgeting for equipment, re-positioning of special equipment and allocation of personnel are other major functions that could be served.

Tribal Development has activities in many more of the talukas than is commonly recognised. Thematic maps will make it possible to monitor the different dimensions of the T.D. Department's work, and also to compare the effectiveness of programmes in different regions. Since it is difficult to travel throughout the State, thematic maps depicting the maning, facilities and the academic and other results, e.g., of Ashram shalas, location-wise, will be useful in evaluating their performance. Such maps can uniquely be used to communicate with tribal leaders and communities about the programme of the T.D. Department.

We have discussed these State Headquarters-level applications at some length partly to indicate how much can be done with – how much value can be obtained from – just ONE digital base map of the state, that includes the taluka boundaries, the districts, the divisions and the 300 to 350 important towns plus rivers and the road (and rail) network. These elements are digitised on different layers, and appear only as needed. It can have a tremendous impact on the rapid recognition of problems, on the clarity of analysis and on the quickness with which solutions are defined.

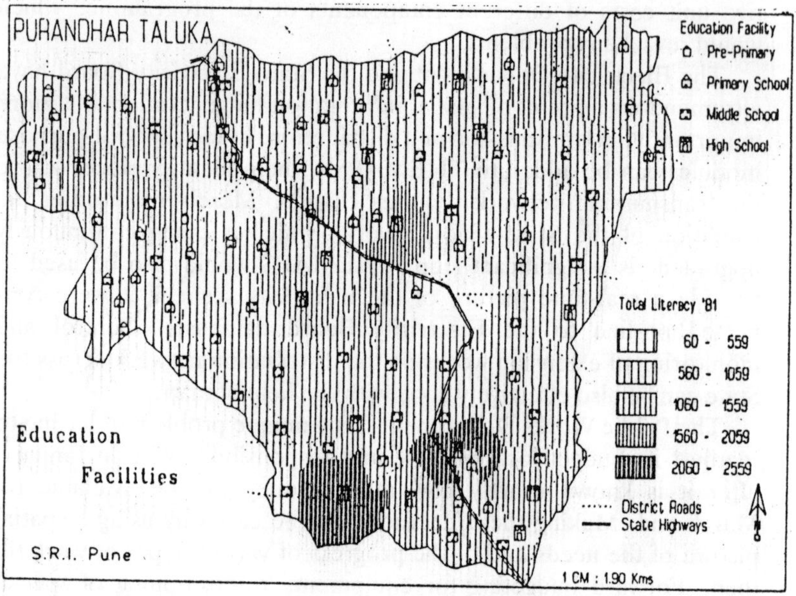


FIG. 13.3: The Map to Locate New High Schools

## Applications of Desktop Mapping at the District Level

For most of the service departments like Health, Education, P.W.D., etc., the district is where the actual planning and later execution is done, and this is where the detailed planning database resides. Nasik district, with the help of NIRD, Hyderabad, has prepared a two-volume Integrated District Plan document which has been much appreciated and commended by the Multi-level Planning Group in the Planning Commission. This is supported by extensive use of maps. Low-cost replication of this methodology through all the districts in the State can be achieved by using a set of district digital base maps with taluka boundaries, locations of villages, with road and rail networks, rivers, canals, with some indication of forest areas (if any) and, in hilly regions, of contours.

One of the most important applications is the ranking of villages and the identification of the Growth Centre hierarchy, so that the location of the next set of services can be logically, economically and most beneficially decided. THEMAPS and its associated relational DBMS, STAT, can be used very efficiently with information about the existing layout of facilities in villages to help plot the Growth Centres and Service Centres, and to indicate the future pattern of growth.

Special attention can be given to the planning and monitoring and analysis of the Minimum Needs Programme — Water Supply, Rural electrification, and so on. Since Zilla Parishads and Collectors are responsible for reporting on achievements under the 20-point programme, this can be effectively planned, monitored, analysed and evaluated by using maps.

Thematic maps of the districts, in the hands of the collectorate planning officer and statistics officer can become a powerful tool for:

(a) Highlighting the problems,
(b) Achieving a consensus on priority areas requiring attention,
(c) Illustrating through "what if" maps the results of various alternative allocation strategies at the ZP among talukas and villages, and
(d) Producing theme-wise pictures of the district for exhibitions and general public education, and for communication to the press about district programmes and progress.

All departments of State Government will find it useful to picture their activity spatially, once this has been adopted by the State Government as the normal means of "viewing" the district. It will also enable the district officials to more easily motivate their village and taluka-level staff, since their areas of responsibility will be clearly seen on the map, they can be classified according to performance, and thematic maps prepared showing the achievement of the areas each person is responsible for. Such maps can also help to identify areas where additional personnel, or training, are required.

In summary, with 1000-1500 village locations depicted on the base map, along with the arteries of communication, supported by the attribute data in the database, it will become possible at district level to conduct all kinds of analyses, e.g. of the marketting of agriculture produce, of the movement from village to markets and the seasons therefor (suggesting possible new roads), and so on. Detailed planning, as in the Nasik document, for multi-sectoral development, can also be done. More important, since the information is in the computer, it becomes readily possible first to view various alternatives, and later even to adjust the programme rationally, according to the budget available, without making arbitrary, across-the-board reductions.

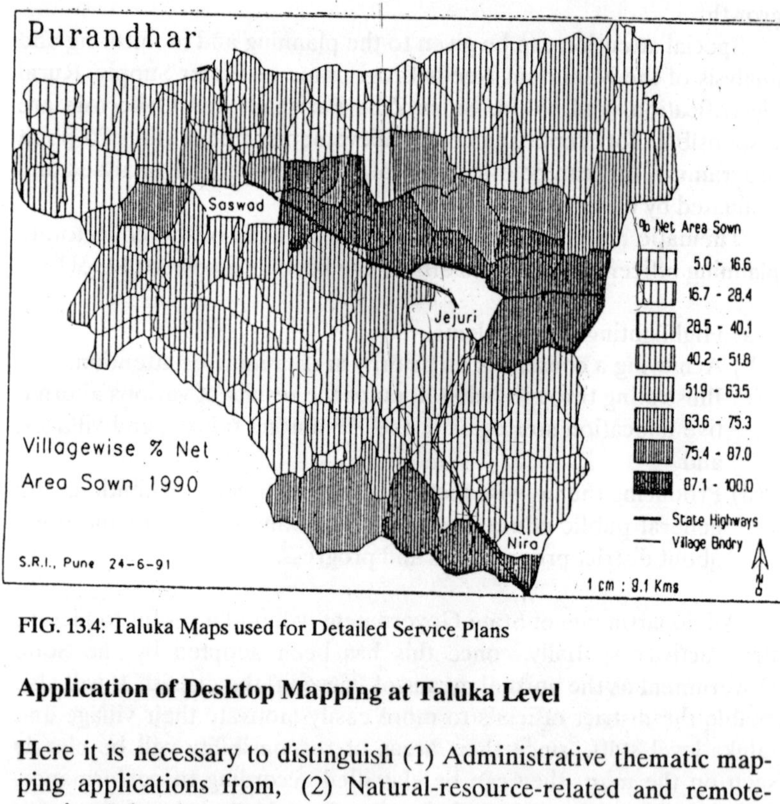


FIG. 13.4: Taluka Maps used for Detailed Service Plans

**Application of Desktop Mapping at Taluka Level**

Here it is necessary to distinguish (1) Administrative thematic mapping applications from, (2) Natural-resource-related and remote-sensing-related applications.

Desktop mapping by and of itself will fully meet the first set of applications which are concerned with displaying facts about the taluka on what is essentially an administrative/political map of the area. While settlements, village boundaries, forest area boundaries, rivers, roads, railway links, electricity lines, etc., are recorded, only rudimentary geological (soil or contour, information is held in such administrative maps. This makes them easier and quicker to digitise, which is an important consideration when there are 200-400 talukas in the State.

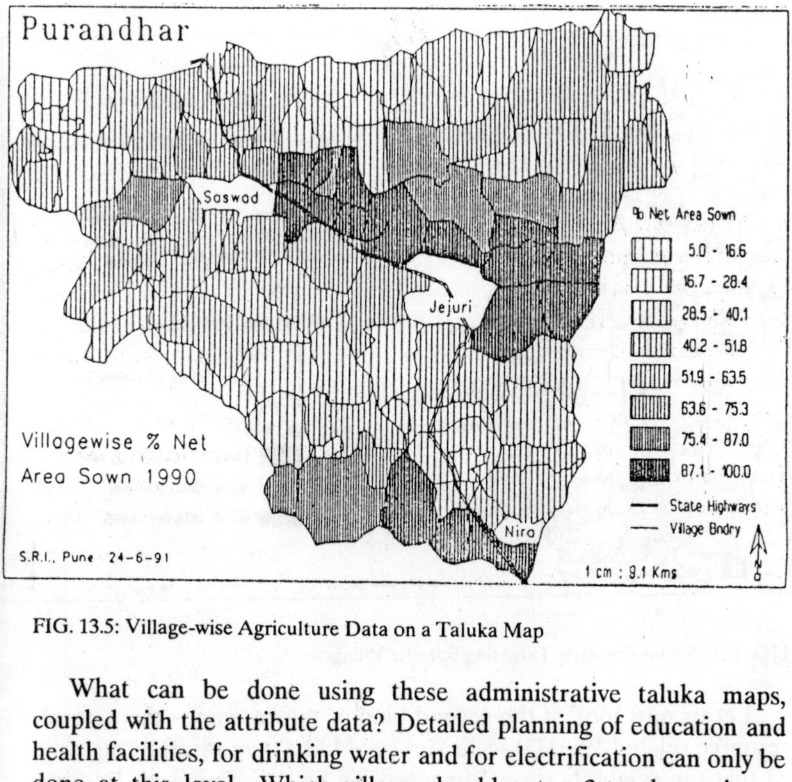


FIG. 13.5: Village-wise Agriculture Data on a Taluka Map

What can be done using these administrative taluka maps, coupled with the attribute data? Detailed planning of education and health facilities, for drinking water and for electrification can only be done at this level. Which village should get a 3-teacher primary school and which should expand into a middle school? Where should the next High School be located? Which road should be upgraded from ODR to MDR? Where should the next health station be located? Which village should get a telephone and which the protected water supply. These decisions can only be made by viewing the situation in full context, which means the demography, patterns of work, the land use in each village should all be available in the database.

Thus while the district is the correct level for controlling and sanctioning programmes, most people-oriented programmes should be initiated using village-wise data in a taluka horizon. This can effectively be done with the administrative map. Thus the Minimum Needs Programme, Social Forestry Programme, 20-point programme, are all best planned using this map and data.

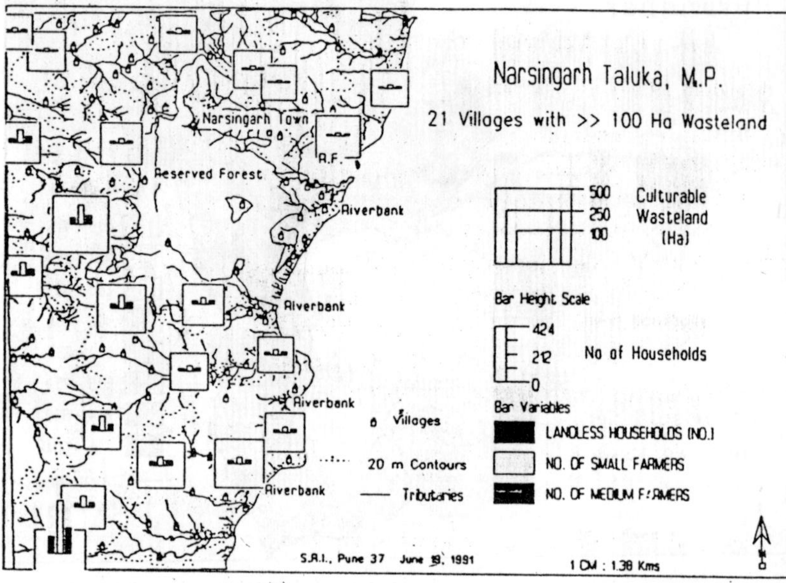


FIG. 13.6: Social Forestry: Targeting Specific Villages

Let us now look at the second kind of taluka map – the natural-resource related 1:50,000 scale Survey of India map carefully digitised so that the remotely sensed imagery can be superimposed. Because of the need for greater accuracy, and the requirement to add layers corresponding to a soil map and a contour map, this map may quite difficult to produce. Once it is available, however, some interesting possibilities do open up.

This high-precision taluka map, which has a soil-type layer, can also be used by the Agriculture Department and Irrigation Department for detailed crop recommendations. If the contours are highly accurate, it is possible that the PWD could use an automated road-routing algorithm for first-cut solutions as well.

Here the increased accuracy of the map enables us to use it for more and more technical purposes which formerly were done by experts or by trial and error. Information about regions which are both digitised, and derived from imagery, can be used to tell about current forest cover, cropping patterns, etc. There is a much higher "initial cost", of course, here both in the digital map and in the additional software modules. The payoff may also be considerable. We do recommend that this type of map be also tried.

Another application of detailed maps, especially useful in agriculture planning, relates to watershed planning and the superposition of survey numbers to watershed maps. Because of the need for contour information, watershed outlines are usually made from 1:25,000 or 1:50,000 sheets. However, the survey number information is generally available only on 1:2000 or 1:4000 sheets. Bringing this information together is easiest done through a digitising process, since the final output maps can be at almost any desired scale. This is an excellent self-sufficient, self-justifying and cost-effective introductory application of desktop mapping for most Agriculture Departments.

**Conclusion**

In this paper, we have introduced a few State headquarters applications, District-level applications and Taluka-level applications of Desktop Mapping. This has had necessarily to be brief, and we have not been able fully to explain each application.

Implementation of Desktop Mapping in a State Government department will require a close cooperation of design specialists in the subject with decision-makers, and with the officers who have to maintain the databases and keep them up-to-date. The Systems Research Institute, which has over 10 years experience in this field, and a multi-disciplinary team of professional staff, makes its resources available for design, for digital map-making, for custom software development, and also publishes a newsletter and runs regular training courses.

# PART IV

## SECONDARY SECTOR

(Focus on Material)

# 14

# MANUFACTURING

M. SRINIVASAN*

## Introduction

Information system has traditionally been under accounts department in Indian companies, due to the early exclusive usage of computers for payroll and accounting applications. This has resulted in many standalone applications on computers, such as, share accounting, material accounting, purchase handling, payroll, financial accounting, etc. This is understandable in a technological environment of centralised computing.

However, this trend of keeping applications as islands continues, in spite of many technological solutions, both in hardware and system software, supporting an integrated approach. The reason is mainly due to the fear in the mind of the traditional EDP person added with the lack of integrated application software. Integrated information systems, both for office and factory, can be implemented only by concerted effort, by end-users and EDP staff. This is more so for factory applications, since integration at factory, whether off-line or on-line, is many times more sophisticated than in an office.

An integrated information system is shown in Fig. 14.1, with application software, system software, computers and workstations shown in separate layers.

An integrated information system in manufacturing should take care of all functions in a manufacturing setup, starting from tendering, load simulation with and without work-in-process, product costing, design and manufacturing bill-of-material, order processing, production scheduling (both macro and micro), shop documents handling, shop progress reporting, part and material requirement

* Knowledge Engineering and Consultancy Services Pvt. Ltd.

planning, purchases, capacity planning, delivery and despatch, billing etc. It should provide integration for these functions, both for operational and management level.

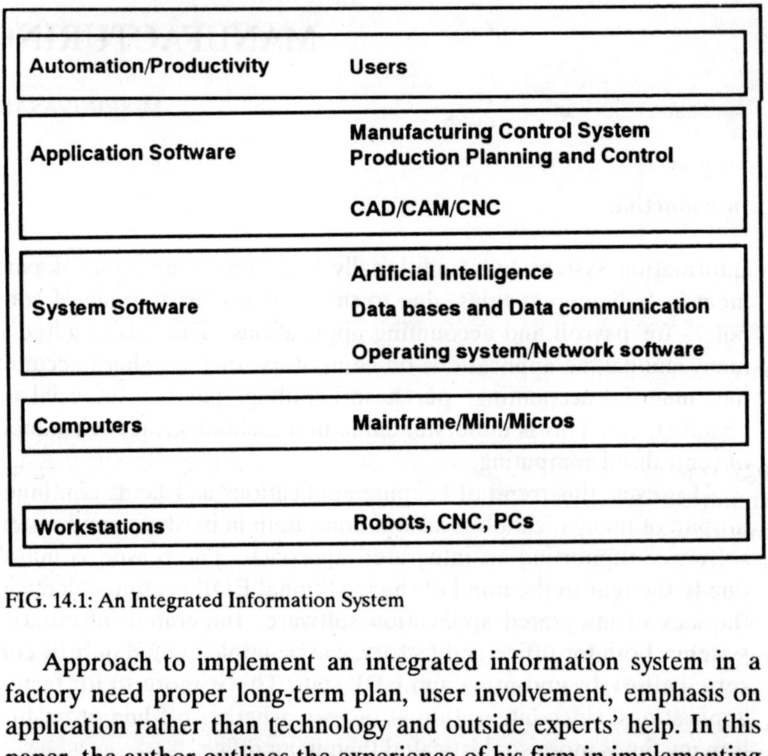


FIG. 14.1: An Integrated Information System

Approach to implement an integrated information system in a factory need proper long-term plan, user involvement, emphasis on application rather than technology and outside experts' help. In this paper, the author outlines the experience of his firm in implementing integrated information systems in a few companies in India and suggests ways for successful implementation of such systems, since failure will cost the company more in user morale than in hardware and software cost.

**Integrated vs Stand-alone Applications**

The difference between stand-alone and integrated applications in information system is given in Fig. 14.2. AT&T has found in its survey of information system users that successful systems have demanded investment of $1000 in application, $100 in training and $10 in software for every $ spent on hardware. This is true in a developed country where technology cost is very low compared to manpower cost.

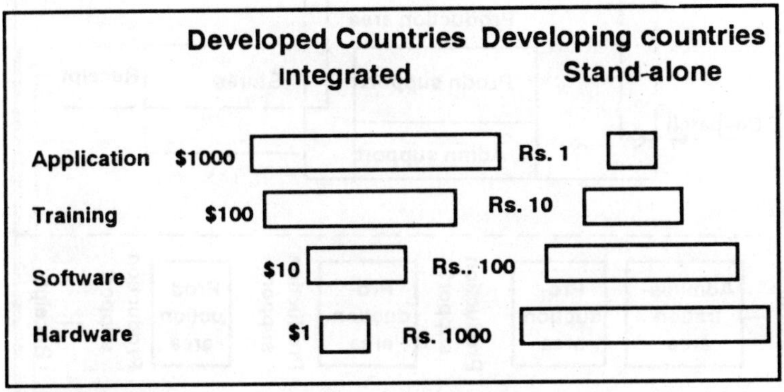


FIG. 14.2: Difference between Integrated and Stand-alone Applications

The situation is the reverse in developing countries. The technology cost is very high compared to manpower cost in developing countries. Hence it is likely, that companies in India developing information system spends Re. 1 for application, Rs. 10 for training and Rs. 100 for software for every Rs. 1000 spent on hardware.

This may be alright for stand-alone applications, even in a developed country. But attempting this kind of budget for integrated information system is inviting disaster. Integrated information system warrants a pattern of investment as shown for developed countries, even though the investment in software, training and application may not be direct cost. This cost in software, training and application will most probably be people-involvement cost.

### Manufacturing set-up and Information Systems

Information systems have been implemented successfully in many manufacturing units in India in the past, but mostly in islands. Applications, such as, payroll, share accounting, financial accounting, material accounting, purchase handling, production planning, etc. have been done for large companies on large computers. Either the applications have been so huge or the computers so batch-oriented, that integration of all related information applications have not taken off in many cases. The main reason would be the lack of understanding of the demand in budget for integrated systems as given in Fig. 14.3.

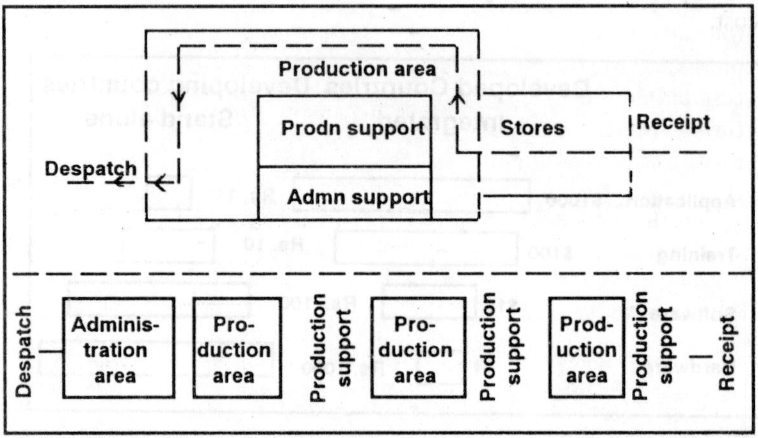


FIG. 14.3: Integrated Systems

It would be wise to understand the manufacturing mechanics in order to appreciate the implications of Fig. 14.3. The integrated information system can be evolved by starting from the factory. Figure 14.3 indicates two of many possible combinations in a manufacturing setup. Any manufacturing area can be divided as the production area, where actual manufacturing process takes place, production support area, normally near production area to support with tools, raw materials, etc. and administrative area, where administrative functions such as accounting, security, welfare, etc., are taken care of. The information system has been traditionally kept in the administrative area far away from the production area, a reason enough for failure of integrated information system.

However, with the advent of mini-computers and later personal computers, the hardware portion of information system got distributed, with software, training and application mostly centralised through EDP department. This is still alright for stand-alone applications, because they get developed centrally and then planted on the distributed hardware, with training and software coming from a central department. User involvement is growing, but not reached a critical stage for taking up integrated information systems.

**Emphasis on Application, not Technology**

Investment, either direct or indirect, for a successful integrated information system, as given in Fig. 14.2 can come only by giving emphasis to applications and users. Hence the starting point for a successful integrated information system is the workflow in a manufacturing set-up and not bits, bytes or MIPS. A typical workflow for a manufacturing set-up is shown in Fig. 14.4. The information flow and the integration need can be understood better once an expert understands the workflow.

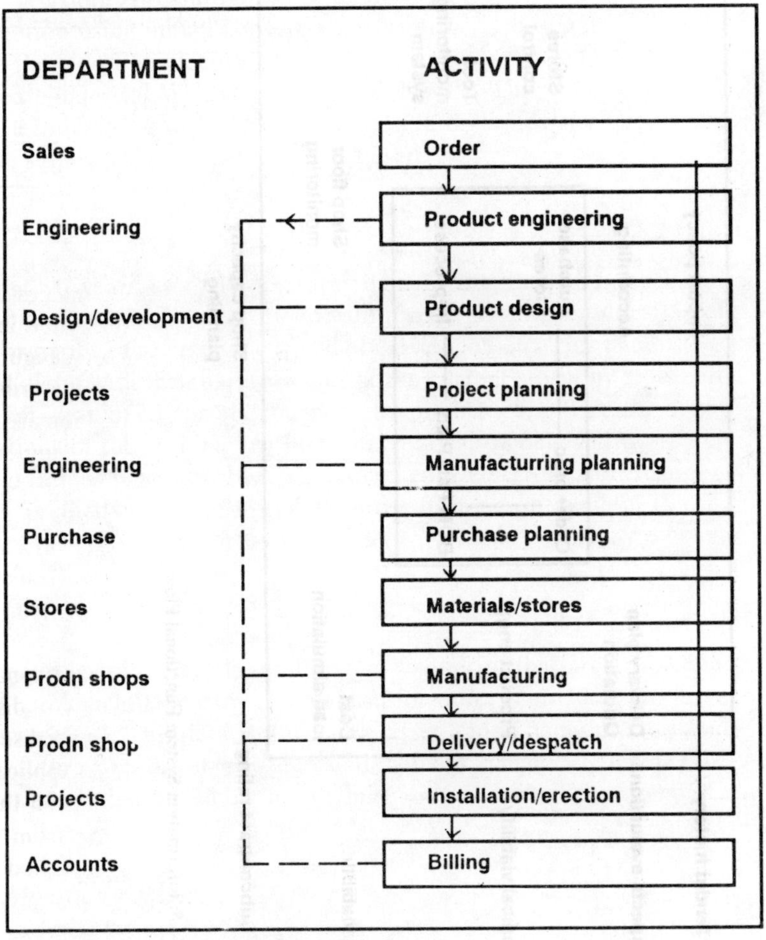


FIG. 14.4: Work-flow in a Manufacturing set-up

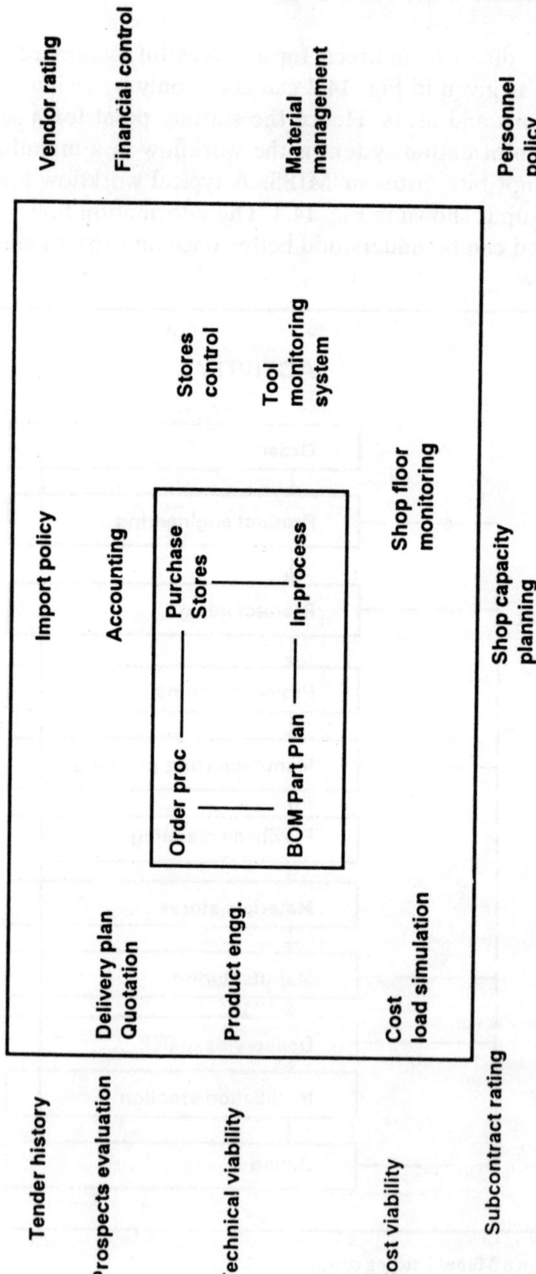


FIG. 14.5: Information System Functional Flow

This workflow is a general flow applicable for project engineering type, job type engineering or repeat job manufacturing. For job type engineering and not project type, eliminate the two activities of project planning and installation in the above Figure 14.4. For repeat job manufacturing and not job type engineering, eliminate one activity of product design.

An expert should normally be able to arrive at an information system functional flow as shown in Fig. 14.5, with major software modules identified for all the functional requirements for a manufacturing set-up. It would be advisable to organise the software needs in three layers, namely production-related, control-related and management-related.

The plan for integrated information system should then look for methods of linking the information system to the work-flow. This has to be done by two means, one by physical access to the information system by a user, namely, an information workstation (or node) and two by proper methoding (method of access).

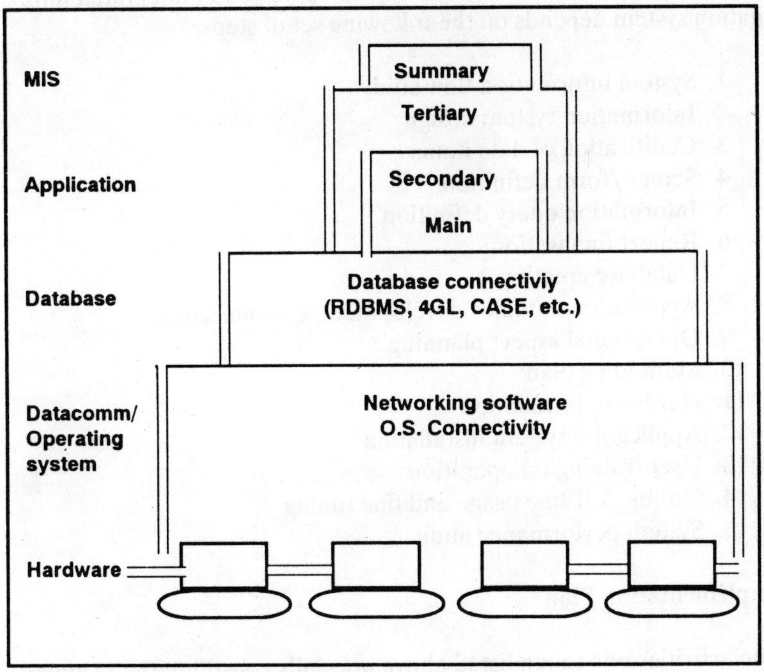


FIG. 14.6: A Typically Integrated Information System

An information work-station in today's technology scenario could be a DTMF telephone, a VDU terminal, a personal computer or a computer workstation. The number and type is determined by both the rate of interaction of users and location of interaction of users with the information system. The number and type of user work-station will then determine the connectivity of them together and to the database. A typically integrated information system will thus be like in Fig. 14.6. The planned system will be in layers with the work-stations forming the base, interacting with the users. A hardware, such as, a mini or LAN, provides the hardware connectivity, permitting users to interact with each other. The system software, such as, operating system databases and network software sits on top of this hardware providing the base for linking application software modules, such as, order processing, purchase, materials, shop planning, work-in-process, etc. These modules will interact on user's request creating a production database which can be used by managers for controlling the production. The management can get overall production reports for them to make strategic decisions.

The implementation and successful operation of integrated information system depends on the following set of steps:

1. System information flow study
2. Information system design
3. Codification of data items
4. Screen/form definition
5. Information query definition
6. Report finalisation
7. Database creation
8. Application modules development/customisation
9. Operational aspect planning
10. Methoding plan
11. Hardware installation
12. Application system installation
13. User training on operation
14. On-line/off-line usage and fine tuning
15. System performance audit.

**Implementation Plan**

The activities one to ten listed above normally constitute the planning of an integrated information system. This is neither an exhaustive list nor in the proper order for all manufacturing organisation, but a recommendation that has worked in many organisations.

In this planning stage, a detailed information system flow need to be designed after understanding the user's workflow and existing information system flow. This should give the expert an idea as to whether to opt for an application package or to develop them totally. In the current scenario, it is highly favourable to go for a package for the following reasons.

*Package Advantages*

- Packages are developed in RDBMS and 4GL, so highly flexible;
- Functions, parameters and data are well delineated.

*Development disadvantages*

- Development cycle being long, likely disinterest of users;
- Possibility of getting into perpetual system design.

The input method and their contents can be finalised along with the kind of information needed by users on the screen frequently and in reports periodically. The report formats and periodicity also are planned at this stage. The RDBMS/4GL options nowadays provides a lot of flexibility in query and report building, provided, the data has been captured.

In most organisations going for integrated information systems, the one-time data required, such as, design and manufacturing bill of materials and master data such as staff list, work centre list, cost centre list, machine list, material code, etc., would be available, but possibly in different computers and even in non-computer forms. These need to be collected and created as a database suitable for the integrated application modules.

Normally, in parallel with the database creation will be the customisation or development of the application modules. The number of computer programmes to cater to a typical manufacturing information system would range from 500 to 1000.

The operational aspects of the integrated information system need to be planned at this stage, so that the method of linking the work-stations to the users and their respective data input, information query and reporting are well understood. This should normally result in a methoding manual, describing normal and exceptional procedures for all the staff in the manufacturing setup, as to how to interact with the integrated information system to get maximum benefit out of it for the organisation.

**Operational Plan**

Getting this planned system to operational stage starts with the hardware and software installation. The application developer would also install the application software and the database to test the system. Users will be trained in the operational aspects to conform to the plan in the methoding manual. The hardware, software and application staff need to be around all the time during the initial phase of operation to provide handholding to the users and remove operational irritants that are bound to arise in the early stages of usage.

The system needs fine tuning by hardware, software and application suppliers to suit user's requirement. The most important aspect during this stage should be training of users to use the system as well as to train other users themselves. Training in overall planning, hardware, software and basic concepts of manufacturing systems, etc., may have to be taken up much before operational stage, in quantities depending on the organisational need.

Operating the system for a few months will give the users confidence to interact with hardware, software and application vendors, in order to fine tune the system. But what is more important is for the users to feel confident about the performance of the information system in terms of direct (monetary) and indirect (intangible) benefits to the organisation. An outside expert may be of help in this benefit identification.

**On-line or Off-line**

The decision whether to operate the application and work-stations on-line or off-line is a major one entirely depending on the workflow and information flow of the organisation. However, once the decision is made to operate the application in on-line mode, the workstation could be operated partially on-line and off-line. Figure 14.7 indicates these on-line/off-line application and work-station possibilities for the workflow seen earlier.

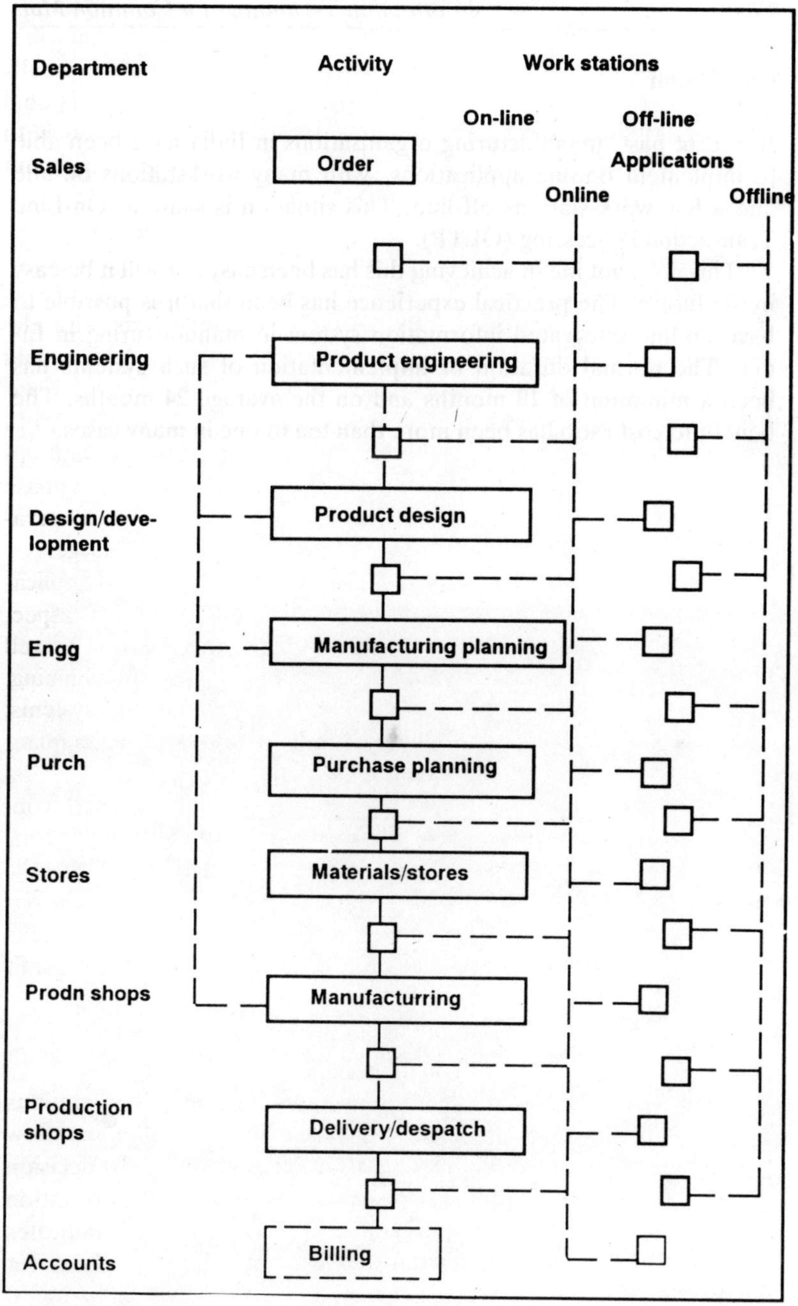


FIG. 14.7: On-line and off-line Applications

## Conclusion

In recent past, manufacturing organisations in India have been able to implement on-line applications, with many workstations on-line and a few work-stations off-line. This situation is same as On-Line Transaction Processing (OLTP).

This does not mean achieving this has been easy nor will it be easy in the future. The practical experience has been that it is possible to have on-line integrated information system in manufacturing in India. The normal duration of implementation of such systems has been a minimum of 18 months and on the average 24 months. The benefit to cost ratio has been more than ten to one in many cases.

# 15

# STEEL
# (SAIL Experience)

DR. A.K. JAIN*

## Introduction

'Information Revolution', the force behind the changing socio-economic patterns of the world since last decade, has equally provoked Indian steel industry as any other and perhaps more significantly in Steel Authority of India Ltd. (SAIL). Consequent to the emergence of computers as a powerful tool, SAIL is on a move towards a 'computer culture'. Proliferation of personal computers at the shop level in its plants during the last 3 years, supported by steady growth of state-of-the-art communication facilities and automation of process control, has ushered in a new environment of information age. This has also resulted in a positive impact on the informatics industry in India as well as an onset for socio-economic changes. Information upsurge in SAIL with all its ups and downs has been moving steadily towards achieving its corporate objectives, i.e., to utilise the power of informatics through decision support systems in all key application areas to improve productivity, quality and profitability.

SAIL with its corporate office at New Delhi, its plants located at Bhilai, Bokaro, Rourkela, Durgapur (Durgapur Steel Plant and Alloy Steel Plant), Burnpur and Salem, Central Marketing Organisation (CMO) at Calcutta with its regional offices at Delhi, Madras and Bombay, R&D Centre (RDCIS) at Ranchi, Central Coal and Supply Organisation (CCSO) at Dhanbad and captive iron ore mines in the Bonai Range (near Rourkela) form the backbone structure of steel industry in India. In addition there are around 250 other offices of

---

* Steal Authority of India, Ltd.

SAIL, covering branch offices and stockyard spread all over the country. Such a vast and spread out organisation needed a massive informatics infrastructure to provide inter-connectivity of various plants and units and the modernisation of the same to improve efficiency.

**Advent of Computerisation in SAIL**

Computerisation started in SAIL in the 60's with its centralised data processing centres at various plants and units, but these centres were involved in conventional financial accounting, payroll, inventory management, etc., by a few select computer professionals in batch mode. Hence for years data processing was carried on in an isolated manner. There was practically no on-line information management and decision support systems. This led to a general lack of awareness among users about computers and use of information technology to create any visible socio-economic impact on production aspects. On the communication front, SAIL was in dire straits which can be illustrated as:

- There was no communication facilities between plants/units;
- Voice communication between HQ/CMO and plants was through manual boards and was only 25 per cent utilised; and
- Practically no communication facilities existed within mines and between mines and plants/rest of SAIL. For example, in some of the mines, the only means of communication was through jeeps which used to be a very slow and expensive.

This was the scenario when SAIL management visualised an integrated approach to modernise its plants, to bring all plants and units closer on communication networks and spread a computer culture. The strategies and methodologies to implement its ambitious plans were carefully chosen in tune with the above mentioned environment. Role of electronics, viz., communication, computerisation and process control in steel industry has been visualised as :

- Automation and process control techniques need to be adopted to increase efficiency in major process areas, such as, blast furnaces, coke ovens, sintering plants, steel melting shop, soaking pits, reheating furnaces, boiler and power plants, etc.;
- On-line communication and real-time information transfer for

decision making to mobilise resources and cut down waiting time between processes;
- Effective monitoring of power, gas, steam, etc., using supervisory control and data acquisition (SCADA) systems to optimise energy distribution;
- Increased reliability/availability of furnaces by improved methods of maintenance based on condition-monitoring of equipment through micro-processor based computer compatible instruments;
- On-line quality monitoring and control thereby minimising rejection;
- Manpower training on simulated computer control system to use modern techniques;
- Computer as a tool to be introduced at shop level; and
- Launching of computer awareness drives and exposure seminars to educate common users of the SAIL plants and units.

SAIL adopted a bottom-up approach to implement its objectives, considering the imminent resistance against changes. A step-by-step method was selected to introduce computers and communication media.To bring about the massive information upsurge, SAIL concentrated mainly on two most essential aspects as follows:

(a) Providing the media and connectivity for information exchange (both on voice and data) between its plants and units together by establishing suitable communication networks; and

(b) Bringing in the desired reorientation of SAIL personnel (both EDP and users) for adopting to the new information technology-based environment.

**Telecommunication Support**

In the area of communication SAIL worked on a simple but nonconventional, cost-effective and practical approach with support from DOT, NIC and WPC and has set an example by establishing its communication network to link SAIL's wide spread plants and units across the country on voic and data. SAIL's Voice Communication Network (SVCN), established in December, 1989 worked on the concept of networking EPABX's specially got designed to link clusters of users at plants and units of SAIL located geographically apart. On date, 350 subscribers located at 4 offices in Delhi, 5 offices in Calcutta, Bhilai, Bokaro, Rourkela, Durgapur, Burnpur (IISCO) and Dhanbad have been regularly utilising SVCN facilities on direct dialing basis. The network supports more than 2000 long-distance calls/day. SVCN has brought about a sea-change in the functioning of the top management personnel. Consultation between top managers on real time has helped quick decision and expeditious implementation. Plants and units have now been brought closer to share information. SAIL has also worked out its plan for extending SVCN to more than 30 important CMO branch offices using DOT-leased lines. Branch offices of CMO shall be linked to stockyard on VHF duplex voice/data links as described in Fig. 15.1.

To support data communication exclusively, SAIL has made use of the national network 'NICNET' of NIC. It has already set up 12 Micro Earth Stations (MES) with 1.2 m roof top antenna at Delhi, Calcutta, Bhilai, Bokaro, Rourkela. DSP and ASP, IISCO, Salem, VISL and Bolani Ore Mines and is in the process of setting up 8 more MES at remote locations of mines (Fig. 15.2). Information relating to day-to-day production, marketing, industrial relation and others is homogeneously exchanged between plants, units and corporate office through PC linked to MES. SAIL has also developed and tested improved software to be used for transmission of large data files of CMO.

To extend the voice and data communication facilities to remote iron ore mines of SAIL on Orissa and Bihar border, SAIL configured and designed a special digital UHF network using state-of-the-art Time Division Multiple Access (TDMA) and DAMA techniques. 200 lines EPABX at 9 location in Bonai-range mines are now linked through the Base station at Kiriburu and remote stations at other mines on 2 megabit data-stream providing allocation out of 30 channels on demand assignment basis. The system specially configured, designed and indigenously manufactured has been established in the mines and shall be soon linked with the SVCN through gateway at Rourkela Steel Plant.

To connect the distant coal and limestone mines of SAIL, 18 sites spread over 700 Kms. in Bihar, Orissa, MP and West Bengal, including plants and the Raw Material Directorate at Calcutta, SAIL has established HF-network providing duplex voice. The network is now being established on ISB mode to provide simultaneously telex facilities. Fig. 15.3 shows the communication facilities provided in mines.

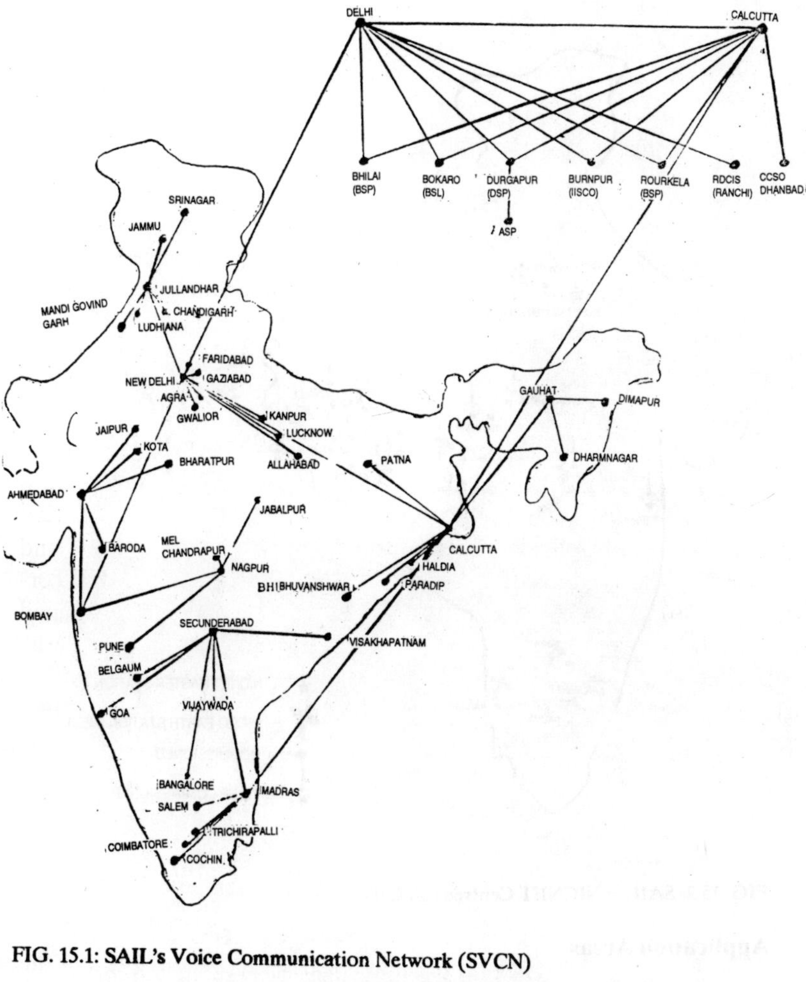


**FIG. 15.1: SAIL's Voice Communication Network (SVCN)**

Table 15.1 shows the consolidated facilities now available at various plants and units of SAIL. With the above communication system, all implemented indigenously, SAIL possesses one of the largest and most effective private communication network (Table 15.1). This has provided the basic media required for SAIL to step into an era of information age for meeting the challenges.

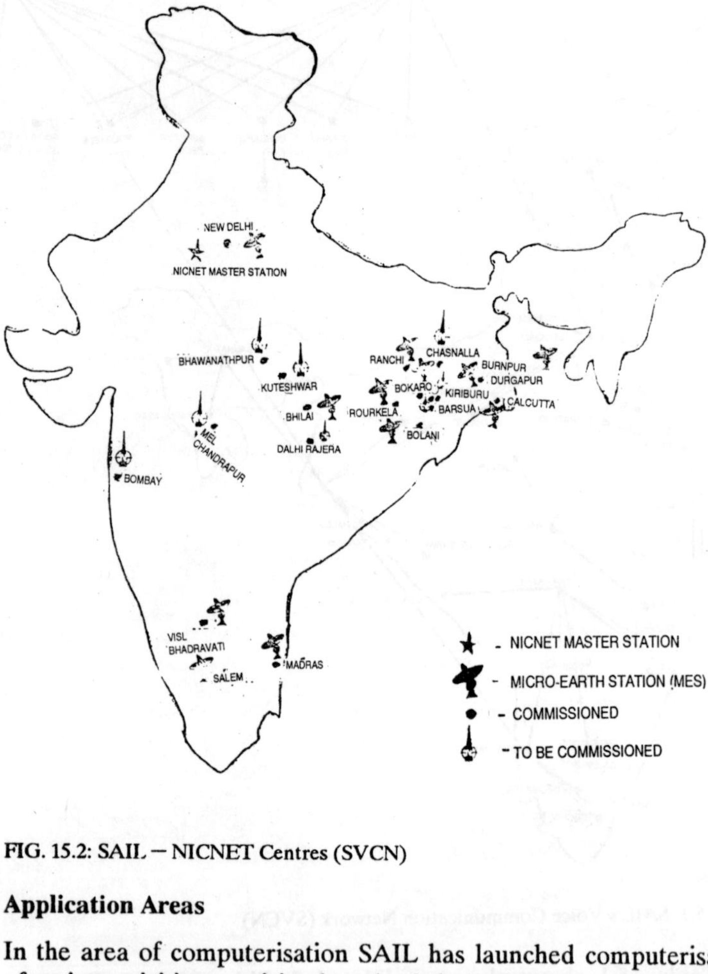


FIG. 15.2: SAIL – NICNET Centres (SVCN)

## Application Areas

In the area of computerisation SAIL has launched computerisation of major activities requiring long lead-time of 2-3 years involving the following projects:

- Computerised Maintenance Management System (CMMS). This includes preventive maintenance, materials module, shop scheduling and condition based maintenance system. The first phase of this project is already implemented at Rourkela;

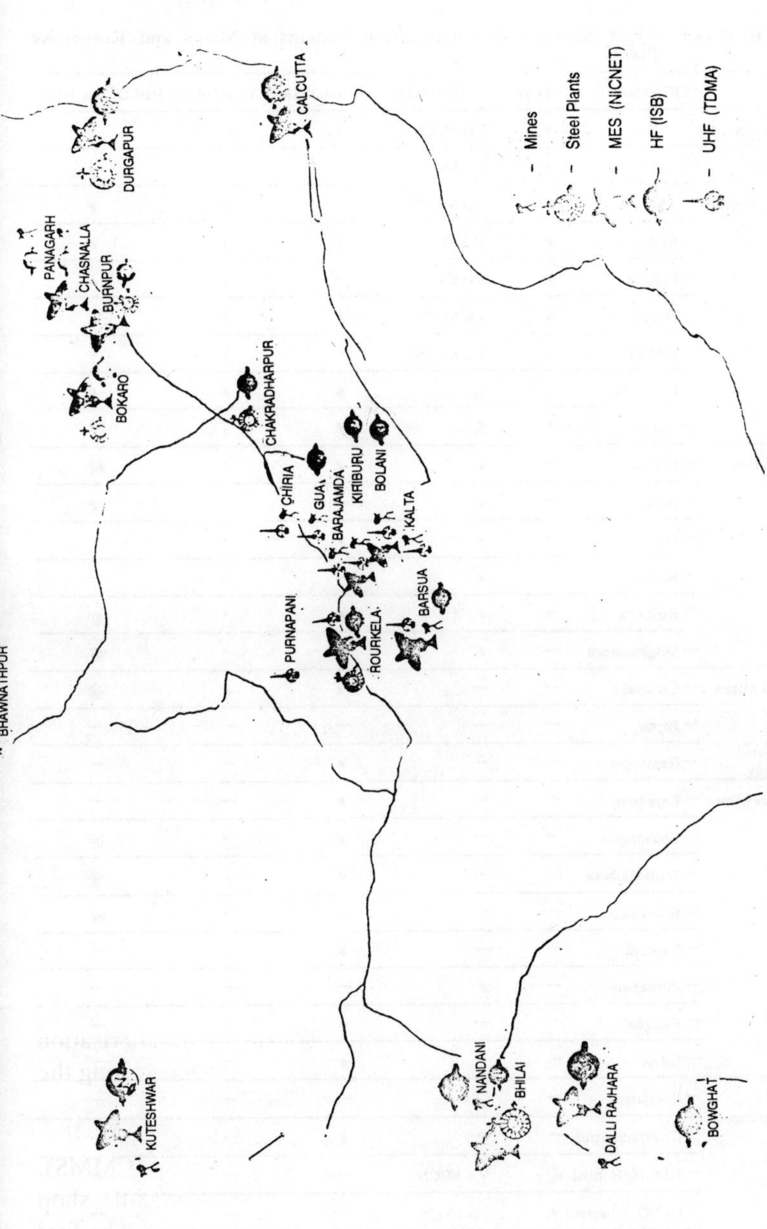


**FIG. 15.3: Communication Systems for SAIL Mines and Steel Plants**

TABLE 15.1: Chart Showing Communication Systems at Mines and Respective Plants

| | LOCATION | SVCN | UHF-TDMA | HF-ISB/SSB | VHF HAND-HELD | NICNET |
|---|---|---|---|---|---|---|
| Calcutta | | # | Via SVCN | # | — | # |
| Delhi | | # | Vis SVCN | — | — | # |
| Steel Plants | — ASP | # | Via SVCN | — | # | # |
| | — Bhilai | # | Via SVCN | # | # | # |
| | — Bokaro | # | Via SVCN | — | # | # |
| | — Durgapur | # | Vis SVCN | —# | # | |
| | — TISCO | # | Via SVCN | — | # | # |
| | — Rourkela | # | @ | # | # | # |
| | — Salem | # | @ | # | # | # |
| Iron Ore Mines | — Bersua | — | # | # | * | @ |
| | — Bolani | — | # | # | # | # |
| | — Gua | — | # | # | * | — |
| | — Kalta | — | # | — | * | — |
| | — Kiriburu | — | # | # | * | @ |
| | — Maghataburu | — | # | # | * | @ |
| Coal Mines | — Chasnalla | — | — | # | # | @ |
| | — Jitpur | — | — | — | — | — |
| | — Ramnagar | — | — | # | — | — |
| Other Mines | — Baraduar | — | — | # | — | — |
| | — Bhavnatpur | — | — | # | * | @ |
| | — Dalli-Rajhera | — | — | # | # | @ |
| | — Kuteshwar | — | — | # | * | @ |
| | — Nandini | — | — | # | # | — |
| | — Purnapani | — | # | — | — | — |
| | — Ranghal | — | — | # | * | — |
| | — Satna | — | — | # | — | — |
| Other Locations | — Barajamda | — | @ | — | — | — |
| | — Chakradharpur | — | — | # | — | — |
| | — RDCIS, Ranchi | @ | Via SVCN | — | — | # |
| | — CCSO, Dhanbad | # | Vis SVCN | — | — | — |
| | — MEL, Chandrapur | — | — | — | — | — |
| | — VISL, Bhadravati | — | — | — | — | — |

INDEX # IMPLEMENTED @ UNDER IMPLEMENTATION
— NIL * PROPOSED THROUGH RATE CONTRACT

- Material management system;
- Computerisation of Production Planning and Control (PPC).
- Supervisory Load Control Centre (SLCC) at Plants and Calcutta to on-line monitor the power scenario above SAIL plants to support decision taking in respect of power consumption/scheduling etc.;
- Materials tracking system covering ingots, blooms, billets, etc.
- Public Deposit Scheme (PDS);
- MIS with networking of process control computers and management systems.
- Marketing information system –

  (a) CMO Calcutta and regional offices,
  (b) Plants;

- Automation of blast furnaces;
- Traffic movement system;
- Automation of sintering plants;
- Automation of LD converters;
- Automation of coke ovens;
- Revamp existing EDP application, viz., payroll, financial accounting based on distributed database processing using RDBMS, client-server techniques to down size the computing hardware.

Establishing a lead in process automation, blast furnace-7 of Bhilai Steel Plant was the first one to be computerised in 1987. Encouraged by the improvements in productivity-enhanced experience gained, other plants have also taken active interest in computerising their blast furnaces.

**Standardisation of Hardware and Software**

Having launched such major programmes and having taken a lead in establishing communication links, it would have been meaningless if a total awareness drive was not spread at the workers level and usage of micro computers not started at working level where information is generated. The processing power has been now taken to the users through proliferation of PC's and mini-computers. For this purpose, SAIL has systematically emphasised on standardisation of hardware and software through rate contract procurement approach of PC's and mini-computers. The benefits realised are enormous, for example :

(1) Standardisation of hardware and software has enabled uniformity and interpretability of application;
(2) Bulk procurement of hardware and software from limited approved vendors has given price advantage of 15 to 25 per cent;
(3) This process has also resulted in better after-sale service by vendors. Software piracy and virus menace has been curbed through corporate licensing of software and procurement of other licensed software packages through rate contract;
(4) Procurement time of hardware and software got reduced drastically from 6 to 8 months to only 30 days because time consumed in floating tenders and cooperative evaluation of tenders was not required.

Standardisation and rate contract procurement of PCs in SAIL had visible impact on the computer industry also. Healthy and open competition for supply of quality approved (by STQC Cell of DOE) PC systems and peripherals compelled PC manufacturers to reduce their costs of production and improve quality to meet STQC laid down standards. The practice initiated by SAIL is now understood to have been adopted by other large organisations also.

**Conclusion**

SAIL is now well-set on its path to accelerate the use of information technology. The impact is visible from plants to townships. The whole SAIL community has come closer and even the remotest parts of SAIL is aware of the latest happenings in the steel industry and the world. Computers have penetrated not only every remote unit of SAIL including mines but also homes and schools of SAIL townships, where computer sources make a necessary part of the curriculum. There is an ever-growing consciousness of the power of information technology in SAIL families.

# 16

# OIL

B.N. TALUKDAR*

## Introduction

Oil India Limited (a Government of India enterprise) is actively engaged in exploration as well as exploitation of hydrocarbon (oil and gas) and transportation of crude to various refineries. Apart from that, it also produces LPG from available natural gas. OIL operates in areas of Assam and Arunachal, onshore/offshore Orissa, western part of Rajasthan, part of Gangetic basin and Saurashtra offshore. The task of company is well-diversified and so are the corporate objectives of the company.

OIL has adapted well-established technologies for each of its operations. The amount of information generated by most of the operations are enormous and need extensive computer support for analysis and management of data. The data generated and processed at various locations form a complete set of information for interpretation and facilitate decision-making process. OIL uses the latest information technology for close and increased monitoring of each activity that leads to a better understanding of relationship between organisation's actions and its outcome. Information technology has provided easy way for information gathering, analysis and its interpretation to provide information support in decision-making.

## Present Scenario — Computer Resources

OIL's course of journey towards computerisation started in the year 1980 when it commissioned a computer system, MEGASEIS (SELS

---

* Oil India Limited.

32/75 with RTM 6.75 OS) to cater to the need of seismic data processing and reservoir simulation studies. MEGASEIS is equipped with seismic data processing software and reservoir simulation software. It has been extensively used for the above said purpose and a total of 45587 standard line-kms (SLKMs) of seismic data have been processed during the period from 1980 to 1990. The system has provided all processed seismic informations for interpretation without any delay and thus reduced time-gap between seismic data acquisition and releasing of the well-locations. It has also provided adequate system support in carrying out reservoir simulation studies to predict reservoir and well-behaviour and to plan optimal field development strategies.

OIL procured HCL system IV (in 1982) and HCL system Horizon III (in 1987 replacing system IV) to meet its need of financial and inventory management.

An integrated approach towards computerisation of OIL's activities started when OIL planned and procured a wide range of hardware keeping in view of its information system requirements at various levels within the organisation as follows:

(a) CYBER 930 mainframe — for development and implementation of an integrated information system, reservoir studies and various other engineering applications;
(b) CYBER 830 mainframe — for seismic data processing;
(c) Micro VAX workstation (7 Nos.) — for interactive interpretation of seismic data, well-log data and for reservoir studies; and
(d) PC's, PC/AT's PC/XT's — to facilitate office automation and to carry out data processing jobs at various locations (departments) within the organisation in a distributed manner.

The list of hardware and software resources available with OIL are given in Tables 16.1 and 16.2.

**Present Scenario — Information System Development**

OIL has already installed 7 Nos. of Micro Vax work-stations and is in the process of installing mainframes CYBER 930 and CYBER 830. OIL has plans to network all the systems via CDC network. This will adequately fulfil all of the computer requirements for the development of an integrated information system, apart from providing facilities for seismic data processing, seismic and well-log interpretation and other engineering applications. The networking diagram is illustrated in Fig. 16.1.

TABLE 16.1: Hardware available within Organisation

| System description | Operating system | Main area of application | Commis-sioning yr | Stat |
|---|---|---|---|---|
| MEGASEIS SEL 32/75 | RTM 6.75 | Seismic data processing<br>Reservoir studies | 1980 | in use |
| HCL HORIZON III | UNIX | Financial management | 1987 | in use |
| MICRO VAX Work-station | VMS | Seismic interpretation<br>Well-log interpretation<br>Reservoir studies | 1988-1 No<br>1991-6 No | in use |
| PC, PC/XT, PC/AT | DOS 4.0, UNIX | Office automation<br>Data processing<br>Data analysis | 1987-<br>1991 | in use |
| Cyber 930 | NOS/VE | MIS, reservoir studies<br>Project management<br>Engineering application | 1991 | Comm. |
| Cyber 830 | NOS | Seismic data processing | 1991 | Comm. |

TABLE 16.2: Software available within Organisation

| Office auto-mation tools | Programming language | DBMS | Application package | Others |
|---|---|---|---|---|
| Wordstar | FORTRAN | dBASE III | Seismic data processing | Per/Time |
| Wordperfect | BASIC | dBASE IV | Seismic data interpretation | Survey package |
| Framework III | COBOL | Unify | Well log interpretation | Timetable |
| Lotus 123 | C | Oracle | Reservoir studies | |
| HG | PASCAL<br>Cybil | IM/DM | | Project management system |

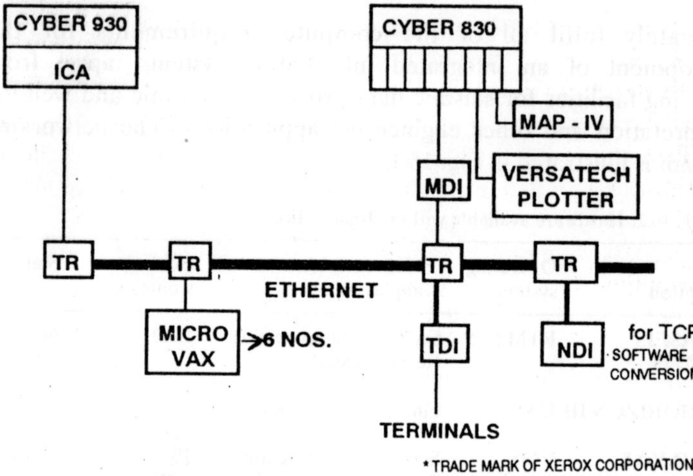


FIG. 16.1: Basic Network Connection

For its day-to-day operation, OIL has started using available information technology in office automation, database management and in data analysis. Many software packages have been developed in house as well as by external agencies using available database management software to meet the information requirement at various levels. Some of the software developed in-house are listed in Table 16.3. The process is still on to fulfil the growing demands of information system support in new areas. This has generated an awareness about the impact of information technology in day-to-day operations and also in decision-making.

TABLE 16.3: Software developed within Organisation

| Application package | DBMS/ Language used | User |
|---|---|---|
| Production database | Clipper | Geological department |
| Seismic information system | dBASE IV | GDAP department |
| Personnel information system (For OIL executives) | -- do -- | Personnel department |
| Analysis and tracking of Oil Movement | -- do -- | Pipeline department |
| Budgeting and planning | -- do -- | All concerned |
| Training information system | -- do -- | Training & Development |
| Drugstores information system | -- do -- | Medical department |
| Pathology information system | -- do -- | -- do -- |

With the availability of computer resources within the organisation, the general awareness regarding computer among the OIL personnel has gone up multi-fold. The various in-house as well as external computer training courses attended by OIL's personnel has supplemented to this. The awareness has motivated them to identify the information-needs at their level and to develop distributed information system with the help of OIL's own technical support. In this process, various areas of activities are getting computerised and contributing towards the development of an integrated information system. As the process till today is spontaneous and are meeting only specific needs of user in specific areas, there have been redundancy of information and duplication of efforts. A systematic approach to develop an integrated information system is the need of today.

OIL has plans to computerise most of its activities and to develop an integrated information system with the following general objectives:

- Implementation of MIS to support the decision-making;
- Improvement of the flow and availability of information for management;
- Effective monitoring of activities to meet the set targets; and
- Providing information support to meet the corporate objectives.

**Future Perspective**

With the available technology of software and hardware and the state of awareness within OIL's personnel, OIL is all set to meet its goal to have an integrated information system for information support at operation level as well as for management. The present need is to organise all the information generated by various activities in a centralised database (Fig. 16.2).

All the informations pertaining to exploration activities, viz., geological, geophysical, well logging, etc., are to be organised is an Exploration database (EDB). Similarly, information generated by drilling as well as production activities are to be managed by Drilling and Production database (DDB and PDB). All of these together will form a Petroleum database (PDB).

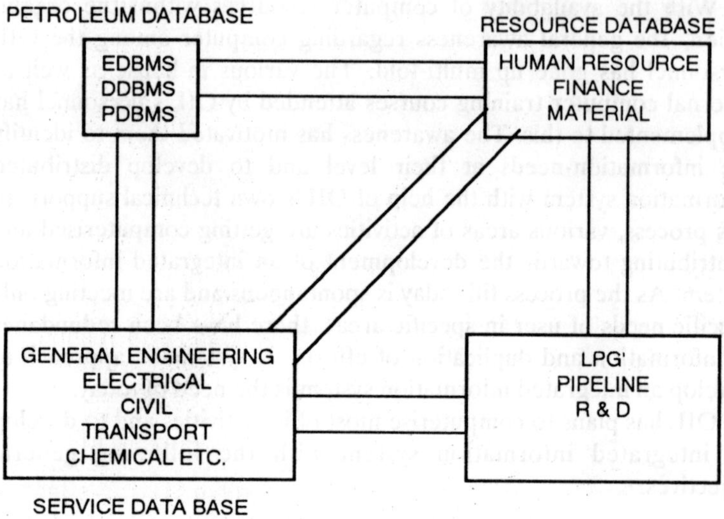


**FIG. 16.2: Database management in OIL**

The service departments play an important role in meeting the corporate objectives of OIL. Upgrading of technology and adequate service support at proper time and place are major concern to the management. Because of increase in demand for technical services, it is necessary to develop services database (SDB) for adequate services support.

Effective management of resources, viz., human resource, finance, material, etc., are critical in achieving the corporate goals. There is a need for developing a resource database (RDB) for effective planning, monitoring and availability of resources at appropriate time and place. This will also cater to the need of information support for human resource development.

Informations generated at other areas of operation of OIL such as LPG, R & D and pipeline are to be maintained in a separate database, in order to provide information support to these operations.

The activities of OIL are geographically distributed in far-flung areas, where adaptation of recent information technology for data communication are essential and critical. With the recent developments in data communication technology, there is immense scope for introducing real-time information processing systems. OIL is already in the process of installing a supervisory control and data acquisition system (SCADA) in its Naharkatiya oil field. The system will acquire real-time information from various oil collecting stations (OCS) and will communicate this information to the centrally located computer system. The computer will build up information database with complete production log of the producing wells. In a similar way, real-time processing system technology can be adapted in other high-technology, arena including exploration drilling, seismic data acquisition, etc.

**Conclusion**

With the implementation of information system for information support at operational level as well as for management, OIL can plan to implement a Decision Support System (DSS). As OIL will continue to update itself with the latest information technology including artificial intelligence, the same will continue to play an important role in all the areas of OIL's activities in years to come.

# 17

# OIL AND NATURAL GAS

P.K. MITTAL*

## Introduction

Exploration and exploitation for oil and natural gas is a challenging task involving a variety of activities like geoscientific surveys, interpretation to delineate the field, reservoir assessment and drilling and development of the field for production. Currently the basic data acquired from different surveys, such as, gravity, magnetic, seismic, well logs, etc., exceeds a trillion bytes of information for prospect. Decision-making would be prohibitively delayed without computer-aided analysis and synergic interpretation of the data. Fast access to various types of data is essential in reducing the turn-around time involved in processing and interpretation of data for exploration and development of hydrocarbon reservoirs.

Continuous monitoring and processing of data collected during drilling helps in proper selection of drilling parameters. Ensuring safety and prevention of blowouts depend on the immediate access to the correct control information, which is provided by microprocessor based mud-logging units. With proper reservoir evaluation and choice of production parameters, the life of the oilfield can be prolonged and optimum recovery of hydrocarbon reserves in place can be achieved. It is worthwhile to mention here that in spite of best efforts, only about 30 to 60 per cent of the total in-place hydrocarbon reserves can be recovered with the present state of art.

## Necessity of Computers

To cope up with the increasing loads of data processing and inter-

---

* Geodata Processing and Interpretation Centre, Oil and Natural Gas Commission.

pretation, the oil industry has been adapting the latest technological advancements in the field of computer hardware and software. Array Processors (AP) (IBM 2938, IBM 3838, ST-100, etc.) have been developed and designed primarily to cater to the needs of seismic data processing in oil industry. Vector processing capabilities of CRAY and IBM systems have already been utilised for the exploration data processing. The latest trends in parallel processing are being studied in the industry in India and abroad to utilise the new emerging technology for highly compute-bound applications such as prestack migration of seismic data in areas involving steep dips of subsurface strata.

Though there is a decrease in the hardware costs of computing power, the programming costs are increasing. In oil exploration, software costs are the most significant part of an effective computerised application. The computer applications in exploration range right from the quality control in the initial stage of data acquisition to processing of data through complex algorithms for time series analysis and the integrated interpretation of the multi-disciplinary geoscientific data by the use of Interactive Interpretation Work Stations (IIWS).

Large and easy to find reservoirs of oil and gas have already been discovered. What is in store for future has to come from small, geologically complex and hitherto inaccessible areas including deep waters. The number of new discoveries will increase but the size grows smaller. To find and produce oil from these reservoirs at viable costs, the quality of data acquisition, processing and interpretation has to be better than ever before. Reduction in exploration and production costs is possible through the use of computers at various stages.

## High Volume of Data

A typical survey vessel can collect about 100-120 line kms of seismic data in offshore areas. Each km will have about 20 'shot points' in a typical situation. Each shot point may record at least 48 channels for a duration of 5 seconds or more. If a sampling interval of 4 milliseconds is selected, the amount of information per km. would amount to 960,000. Thus more than 96 million words of data is collected by the ship every single day.

The increase in the production of oil and natural gas and the innumerable number of petroleum products generated will have an immediate effect on the socio-economic growth and overall development of the country. The increased production of oil and natural gas in India, year after year, has enabled the expansion of the transport network, power generation, fertiliser production and vast number of petroleum products leading to the growth of industry in general. Increased use of petroleum products has helped the domestic sector in attaining improved standards of living. The production of fertilisers and pesticides has resulted in agricultural growth. Valuable foreign exchange to the tune of 3500 million US dollars saved by indigenous production of oil and gas has been used in other developmental projects. The production of oil has been steadily increasing, being 90.03 million tonnes (MMT) in the Sixth Plan and 144.53 MMT in the Seventh Plan. The LPG production was 6.71 lakh tonnes in the Sixth Plan, which increased to a staggering 26.79 lakh tonnes in Seventh Plan. In spite of a steady increase in the rate of production, it is estimated that only one out of twenty families in India currently use LPG for domestic cooking purposes.

Oil and Natural Gas Commission, the pioneering organisation in India, has always been in the forefront in updating its computer resources. Computer facilities are provided in every region to meet the processing and interpretation needs. ONGC has achieved self-sufficiency in the fields of seismic data processing and interpretation through interactive work stations. All the seismic data acquired by various field crews of ONGC are processed in one of its five computer centres. Even the data acquired by foreign contractors are processed here. Only in exceptional cases is the data allowed to be processed by agencies outside India. With the general increase in data volumes and use of special processing techniques, and increased use of 3D seismic data for reservoir evaluation and development, the existing facilities are becoming inadequate. The process of upgrading the existing computer systems in under progress. Table 17.1 shows the computer resources for processing of various types of data and Table 17.2 shows the various interactive interpretation work stations installed in ONGC.

**Personal Computers for Quality Control**

The advancements in personal computers have now allowed the explorationist to take PCs to the data acquisition sites. Performance of

TABLE 17.1: Main Frame Computers Installed at Different Work Centres of ONGC

| WORK CENTRE | SYSTEM | SOFTWARE | CPU RATING | ARRAY PROCESSOR | MEMORY | DISK STORAGE | TAPE DRIVES |
|---|---|---|---|---|---|---|---|
| GEOPIC DEHRADUN | IBM 3083 | WGC | 7 MIPS | 4 (30 MFLOPS) | 32 MB | 40 GB | 16 RTD + 32 CTD |
| RCC BOMBAY | TATA ELXSI | DISCO | 6 MIPS | 1 (30 MFLOPS) | 16 MB | 5 GB | 8 RTD |
| RCC MADRAS | ND 570 | GECO | 4 MIPS | 1 (12 MFLOPS) | 16 MB | 4.2 GB | 6 RTD |
| RCC CALCUTTA | EC 1061 | SDS-3 | 0.5 MIPS | 1 (30 MFLOPS) | 8 MB | 4.6 GB | 8 RTD |
| RCC BARODA | EC 1061 | SDS-3 | 0.5 MIPS | 1 (30 MFLOPS) | 8 MB | 4.6 GB | 8 RTD |

GEOPIC = Geodata Processing and Interpretation Centre
RCC = Regional Computer Centre
RTD = Round Tape Drive
CTD = Cartridge Tape Drive

TABLE 17.2: Work Stations Installed at Various Work Centres of ONGC

| COMPUTER CENTRE | NAME | HARDWARE | SOFTWARE | DISK CAPACITY | MEMORY |
|---|---|---|---|---|---|
| GEOQUEST (3 Nos) | | MICROVAX II, I TAPE DRIVE | I E S, ZYCOR | 950 MB | 5 MB |
| GEOPIC | OFF-LINE | 2 GRAPHIC TERMINALS, 1 RASTER CONTROLLER | | | |
| DEHRADUN | CRYSTAL (1 No) | HOST IBM 3083, I DIGIPAD, RAMTEK CNTRLR | W G C, CPS | SHARES WITH HOST | SHARES WITH HOST |
| | ON-LINE | 2 GRAPHIC MONITORS, 1 CAMERA | | | |
| RCC | EXPLODER-3 (2 No) | MICROVAX-II, NETWORKED WITH ELXSI-6400 | IES, DISCO | 689 MB | 9 MB |
| BOMBAY | EXPLODER-4 (2No) | MICROVAX-II, NETWORKED WITH ELXSI-6400 | IES, DISCO | 689 MB | 9 MB |
| | ON-LINE | | | | |
| RCC | CHARISHMA (2 Nos) | ND 570/CX, VICOM MICROPROCESSOR | GECO, GMS | 348 MB | SHARES WITH HOST |
| MADRAS | ON-LINE | 1 GRAPHIC MONITOR EACH | | | |
| RCC | INGOS-IM (1 No) | CM-1420 | INGOS, RAFOS | 20 MB | 256 KB |
| CALCUTTA | OFF-LINE | | | | |
| RCC | INGOS-1 M (1 No) | CM-1420 | INGOS, RAFOS | 20 MB | 256 MB |
| BARODA | OFF-LINE | | | | |

geophysical instruments can now be monitored under field conditions. Software is available in the industry to perform impulse response tests, check against cross-feed between adjacent recording channels, perform dynamic range analysis and ensure identical behaviour of all recording channels. While the seismic data is being generated, noise analysis can be carried out so as to determine the best spacings between geophones and similar recording parameters such as spread length, shot interval and group interval. PCs are used in the Western countries to generate first hand 'brute stack' plots of seismic data for a quick look at the sub-surface information being recorded in the field. If the quality is found to be unsatisfactory, the data can be re-acquired with modified parameters immediately by the same crew without loss of time and money.

Dedicated microcomputer systems such as RDS-550, HP-1000 and HP-85 are used for well-logging operations at the drill-site. Microcomputers are also used in geochemical laboratories during quantitative analysis of core samples. For reservoir-modelling and estimation of potential of reservoirs, ONGC has many computers, such as, HP-9000, HP-1000, COMMODORE-64, HP-85, besides VAX 11/780. These are used to study the petrophysical properties of the reservoir, like particle size, porosity, permeability, viscosity of the crude oil and pressure-studies.

Small computers are used aboard offshore survey vessels for recording, processing and storing satellite navigation data for location fixing. The survey ships M/V ANWESHAK and SAGAR SANDHANI of ONGC are fitted with such integrated navigation systems as well as the microprocessor-based systems for recording gravity and magnetic observations after regular intervals of 10 seconds or less. The data is directly recorded on digital tapes which are subsequently sent to computer centres for further processing. Computerised information systems are used in process platforms for real-time control as well as data communications to land based stations for monitoring and control of operations.

**Application of Computers in Seismic Data Processing**

The mainframe computers support the processing of the large amounts of seismic data both from 2D and 3D surveys. The processed seismic data enables the interpreter to directly visualise the earth's sub-surface and is ultimately used to provide an estimate of the reserves of oil and gas.

In a seismic experiment, an impulse of energy is injected into the earth through the use of dynamite, airgun or other sources of energy, and the reflected energy from the sub-surface layers is recorded by the response of the transducers planted at regular distances from the source of energy. A multi-channel cable carries the data (one channel for one set of transducers called geophones on land and hydrophones in offshore) to the recording equipment where the data is sampled and multiplexed in time and digitally recorded on a magnetic tape. This experiment is repeated by exciting sources at regular intervals along a profile, simultaneously moving the receivers following the source. Basic processing of this data in preparing a seismic section depicting the earth's cross section along the profile involves the following major steps:

(1) *Demultiplexing:* It is the rearrangement of the data samples recorded in chronological sequence to trace sequential order. (A trace is a set of samples recorded by a single set of geophones/hydrophones).

(2) *Gain Recovery:* The loss of amplitudes of the reflected energy due to the spherical divergence of the input impulse and absorption due to rocks are compensated to make the trace a stationary time-sequence.

(3) *Geometry and Sort:* The individual traces are given the actual coordinates of the source and receiver positions along the profile and traces having same midpoint locations [corresponding to the reflected energy from Common Depth Point (CDP) for horizontal reflectors] are collected together.

(4) *Deconvolution:* The input impulse is elongated due to the earth's filtering action before it is recorded due to selective absorption of high frequencies. In deconvolution, the earth's filtering action is statistically estimated and inverse filters are designed and applied to increase temporal resolution.

(5) *Velocity analysis:* The multifold data collected in CDP technique provides a means of estimating the velocity as a function of reflection time within the earth by the use of coherency measures. The velocities from a very important part of the final stack and migration processes for properly imaging the dipping layers to the appropriate positions in space and time.

(6) *Stack of CDP Traces and Display:* The differential time shifts

for different source-receiver configurations are made and the traces of the same midpoint are summed together to increase signal to noise ratio. The display of many such traces from consecutive midpoints along a profile constitutes a seismic section depicting the earth's section for interpretation.

Advanced processing includes enhancing the signal in the frequency and space domain, imaging the dipping reflectors to their correct positions through migration algorithms, attribute analysis based on Hilbert transformations to obtain instantaneous properties of phase, frequency and amplitude, angle-dependent reflection energy analysis and many other such steps, all involving high amounts of CPU time as well as voluminous input/output operations.

**Computer-Aided Interpretation**

With the increase in data acquisition to find new oil and gas reserves and the increasing use of 3D seismic data for reservoir studies and development, the manual interpretation of data has become virtually impossible. The interpretation is an iterative process in which the data are analysed, an initial geologic model is developed and then tested against all available data. The model is successively modified and improved until there is a good agreement between all available data and the hypothesis. With the small microcomputers packed with the power of the mainframes of yesteryears, the computer aided interpretation systems have become a reality to assist the explorationist. The interpretation software is specifically designed to support the compilation, display and manipulation of the massive amounts of seismic, geological and well-log data. Automatic tracking of reflection layers, preparation of contour maps, generation of 3D perspective views, overlaying of well-logs on seismic sections for correlation, etc., help the interpreter in formulating the geological model. Facilities for integrating the information and checking new alternatives quickly significantly improve the quality of interpretation.

The current interactive workstations are providing multiple software packages on one system. However, the integrated exploration system will be complete only when the data and information are shared between the different packages transparently to the user. The need to develop such systems is increasingly felt by the oil industry. Efforts are being made in a big way to develop open systems and facilitate compatibility between software from different vendors.

With the growth in size and experience, the data within an oil company grows to unmanageable proportions. Then the need is felt to have a centralised pool of data which can be accessed and shared by all concerned scientists involved in interpreting and evaluating prospect or developing a field. Unfortunately, the computer industry has not yet been able to evolve a standard Exploration Data Base system. Individual oil companies in the developed countries are using their own proprietary systems and no system is commercially available. In ONGC, considerable work has been carried out for developing databases for seismics, gravity magnetics, location map data and work is in progress for log database also. After the integration of the above data into a single database, significant advantage will be available to the explorationist.

**Indigenous Software Development**

The software to process the gravity, magnetic data and well-log analysis are developed by the ONGC scientists. From raw gravity and magnetic observations recorded on the ship, corrected Bouguer and magnetic anomaly maps can be generated after correcting for changes in water depth, ship movements and diurnal magnetic variations, etc.

Data pertaining to electrologs, neutron logs, gamma ray logs, sonic logs and various other types of logs can now be processed by inhouse computers. Software is available for formation evaluation. Software has been developed for graphic display of seismogeological sections, geochemical data processing, lithofacies map generation, volumetric estimation of hydrocarbon reserves, automatic log zonation and many more geoscientific applications to meet indigenous requirements.

Several software packages have been developed for quality processing of seismic data. Programs for interactive editing of raw seismic records, interactive velocity analysis, wavelet extraction, seismic attribute analysis, interactive spectral analysis are but a few to mention in the area of seismic software.

New areas in which software has been developed include heavy mineral analysis, simulation of multiphase pressure-drop conditions, pipeline design for the transport of crude oil and gas and other applications involving optimisation of drilling and productions operations.

## Problem of Computer Purchase

Under the present system, it takes around three years to import a computer system specific to the needs of the oil industry. There are delays in obtaining clearances both from Indian as well as foreign governments. In the past there have been well known delays in obtaining CRAY supercomputer for the India Meteorological Department as also in obtaining clearance for the array processor (IBM 3838) for ONGC. The present system envisages the specifications to be firmed up by the user department, followed by global tendering and evaluation through bench marking. The concerned ministries are also involved for sanctioning the expenditure since the funds involved are enormous. The net result is a lead-time of around 2 to 4 years and by the time the order is finalised and computer system is installed, it is already obsolete, thanks to the fast growth rate of information technology industry. Better systems with more current software are available at lesser price on the day a new computer installed.

What is needed is an innovation in the purchasing policy so far as the computer systems are concerned. Concepts such as board purchase and spot purchase (of Crude Oil) which also involve astronomical sums of money have to be combined together. With the joint efforts of ONGC, the computer manufacturers and their representatives in India, Department of Electronics and the concerned ministries, a workable purchase system can certainly be evolved with the objective of ensuring that the most suitable computer system may be imported and installed in an organisation within a period of six to eight months of the requirements being finalised and approved.

## Conclusion

With the increase in data volumes and also the advent of new compute-intensive signal processing techniques such as dip move out stack and pre-stack depth migration, the oil industry will definitely need supercomputing capability. Vector processors with speeds exceeding 200 MFlops and parallel processing systems are needed in the immediate future. While vector processing has already come of age and software for the same is commercially available today, parallel processing systems are still under development. Centre for Development of Advanced Computing (C-DAC), under the Department of Electronics, Government of India, has already done considerable work in the line, with the release of their parallel processing machine (PARAM) heralding the advent of this technology in India. Development of suitable application software so as to utilise the supercomputing power of parallel machines is the challenge to be undertaken by the oil industry in India.

Networking of various remote computer systems in the oil sector is another essential task which has to be undertaken and completed in the immediate future. The power of networked computer systems is too well-known to emphasise here. Suffice it to say that a user in one work centre can have timely and convenient access to the data he needs to complete his interpretation and evaluation of possibilities, irrespective of where data actually resides. This capability is bound to ultimately result in more oil and gas for the country.

# 18

# COAL

S.K. CHAND*

## Introduction

Coal India, as a major public sector enterprise, has introduced computerisation for resource management in a variety of areas. These include material management, sales and marketing, personnel and administration, equipment, power, project planning, design and monitoring, accounts and finance, and social welfare and medical facilities.

## Application Areas

(1) *Material Management*

- Inventory control
- Stores management
- Vendor evaluation
- Equipment supply-ordering.

In view of increasing production and large volume of materials management activities to be monitored, an integrated online MM system covering inventory control, stores and purchase management has been developed for implementation in all the subsidiaries. The system will generate accurate and timely MIS for proper monitoring and controlling inventory of about Rs. 570 crores blocked in several lakhs of items of stores and spares held at various central and regional stores scattered all over the country. Central database at CIL and subsidiaries is being used for vendor evaluation and

---

* Coal India Limited.

monitoring of orders for large equipments.

(2) *Sales and Marketing*

- Consumer dossier
- Demand supply availability
- Transportation

Computerisation of marketing information system for consumer satisfaction, quality control and proper billing and realisation of outstandings has been taken up and is under way. To serve the consumer effectively and efficiently in terms of linkage, financial coverage system, programming and despatch in time, minimisation of backlog, reconciliation of outstandings and refund/adjustment, quality control, etc., and accordingly to generate reports to act as an aid to planning and control mechanism, computerisation has been considered necessary in all the companies in a phased manner.

On priority basis, in the first phase during 1991-92, road sales operation at all the companies has been envisaged to be brought under computerisation. In 1988-89 computers have been installed at regional sales offices for their day-to-day jobs and for generation of MIS reports for better control at CIL level. Quality of coal supplied to power sector is being centrally monitored at Delhi office.

(3) *Personnel and Administration*

- Biodata and personal files
- Training needs
- Manpower planning
- Succession planning
- Performance assessment of senior executives.

Coal India today has about 17,000 executives of which a large number are in senior executives grades. Their biodata and personal files are maintained at corporate level. There is a programme for development of software which will get integrated with various parameters in ACR so that the assessment of performance of executives can be objectively judged. The program will also generate training needs in addition to fulfilling the needs for manpower planning and succession planning.

(4) *Equipment*

- Ordering, supply, erection
- Maintenance management
- Availability and utilisation
- Deployment

CIL has developed in-house software on maintenance management system and has implemented it in some specific opencast projects. During 1989-90, maintenance management system was implemented in five projects and it is under implementation in seventeen other projects. Plans have been made for integrating maintenance management system with on-line MMS to achieve better monitoring and control. Extension of this project for breakdown analysis and proper warning system is under process of development.

CIL has taken up two projects on total integrated mine management system (TIMMS). TIMMS is based on On-line data capture at the source and integration of different functional modules to suggest the best line of action to fulfil the required objective. At the core of the system is the on-line truck monitoring module consisting of complex arrays of sensors, transmitters/receivers and central processing unit.

The first of the two sites is in Gevra OCP at SECL. All the computers and transmission hardwares have already been installed. Testing and trial run will commence soon.

The second system is planned to be installed in Rajmahal OCP of ECL. A computer hardware has been finalised for computer by METCHEM of Canada. The software has been selected. Training of systems professional to operate to this system has started from early 1991.

(5) *Power*

- Availability
- Generation and transmission
- Load management
- Planning

There is a large gap between the demand and supply of power in the country. This affects coal production. A strict vigil has to be kept on the generation of different supplying agencies and future projections for requirement of power has to be made which can dovetail with the corporate plan of the company. This includes setting up of captive power plants and a better load management both by supplying agencies and Coal India. This area is still virgin.

(6) *Project Planning, Design and Monitoring*

- Bore hole data/geological data
- Planning/design of OC mines
- Monitoring
- Network
- Investment

For mine planning and design a VAX 11/780 computer system with sophisticated software has been installed. MINEX software will help in automating the open-cast mine planning taking raw data from bore-hole surveys. The software is already in operation and extensive training has been conducted. DISCO software will help in interpreting seismic survey data. GTSTRUDL will help in better structural design. In Parallel, the regional institutes are gearing themselves up for automating design and drafting through computers. The VAX centre at CMPDIL has already started generating mine plan through computers.

CIL has developed a software named "COALPROM" which can generate information on the slipping projects, slipping activities, cost overrun of projects and action required to be taken to keep the projects within cost and time. This system is being introduced through PC in all projects costing Rs. 100 crores and above in the first phase and in projects between Rs. 20 to Rs. 100 crores in the second phase. 'COALPROM' is an ongoing project. It was implemented in ten such mines and 250 officials were exposed to this programme.

(7) *Accounts and Finance*

- Investment planning
- Budgeting
- Resource allocation

(8) *Social Welfare and Medical Facilities*

- Periodic Medical Examination (PME)
- Hospital management
- Housing and water supply
- Education and manpower

To record medical history of workers, a plan has been drawn to computerise periodic medical examination centres. A study to develop the system has been completed with the help of doctors. Some PME centres, totalling about 30, will be covered under this plan. The software is ready and installation is underway.

**Conclusion**

Coal industry, as it stands now, is an agglomeration of various cultures. This is primarily because of the historical reasons. The industry is continuously making efforts to evolve a unified culture taking in the best of the Government, the private and the public sector. In such a situation, development of management information system at one go is very difficult. Though Coal India is geared for the development of integrated management system for the entire industry, the development over the years have been in bits and pieces and in spurts. In fact, the MIS has been developing both ways, that is, bottom upwards and top downwards.

Coal India is spread over eight States and many of the coal producing units are in remote areas. The prospecting and boring sites are situated mostly in deep jungles away from any kind of communication. The data collection and transmission to area headquarter is a serious problem.

Establishment of data communication links with the subsidiary companies and the units had been identified as the major thrust area long back. A plan was drawn to connect units, areas, subsidiaries and headquarters under COALNET. All the companies have been connected to Coal India and some of the major projects are in the process of getting connected.

Alongwith this, computer installations are in progress in subsidiary headquarters and a network of PC/XTs and ATs have been established. Total number of PC/XTs and ATs installed so far is 421. In the year 1990-91 alone, 100 computers were installed.

Several studies have been conducted to standardise the data reporting formats and the codes.

Training of personnel for operating and use of computers has been an area of concern for CIL. Large numbers have been trained during the last few years and in the year 1990-91, about 100 persons underwent the training for use of computers.

# 19

# POWER

M.I. BEG*

## Introduction

In the development of power, the nation has spent over Rs. 77,000 crores since independence. This constitutes 19 to 20 per cent of the public sector outlays. There have been sustained efforts right from the beginning of planned economic development to improve power position in the country, since it was fully realised that the electrical energy is a vital and key input for the industrial and agriculture sectors. Consequently, the power sector expanded at an average rate of redoubling every seven years. The installed generating capacity in India which was about 1,300 MW at the time of independence has now increased to over 66,000 MW. The generation of electricity has increased from about 5 BUs (billion units) to over 264 BUs during the same period and the per capita consumption of electricity, which is said to be a good indicator of the development of a country, has gone up from 13 units to about 236 units. The progress made in the rural and agricultural sector has been phenomenal since independence. The consumption of electricity in this sector which was insignificant at the time of independence now stands at about 25 per cent of the total consumption. About 87.7 lakh pumpsets stand energised and 82.4 per cent of the villages have been electrified.

Though the installed generating capacity has increased manyfold since independence, consequent to heavy investment and tremendous efforts put in by the power sector, the demand of electricity has all along been out-stripping its supply. The quality and reliability of power supply has not improved to the desired extent. We are facing a situation of wide fluctuation in supply voltage and frequency,

---

* Central Electricity Authority.

frequent interruptions and low voltage conditions. The country faced a power shortage of about 7,000 MW during the last year i.e. 1990-91.

The 12th Power Survey Committee projected a peak demand of 78,438 MW and energy requirement of 4,28,613 Gwh by the end of Eighth Five-Year Plan. Accordingly, the Central Electricity Authority in its Perspective Power Plan (1987) had suggested an incremental capacity addition of the order of 48,000 MW to meet this demand. However, the Working Group on Power (1989) recommended a reduced capacity addition programme of installation of 38,369 MW (comprising 7434 MW of hydel, 30,230 MW thermal and 705 MW nuclear) during the Eighth Plan keeping in view the status of various projects. The load generation balance study, with this capacity addition revealed that while on the all-India basis, the country may face peaking shortage of about 16 per cent, the energy availability position may be rather comfortable. The power programme may, however, have to be further scaled down due to various constraints.

According to present assessment, it may not be possible to add more than about 27,000 MW capacity. Thus the available energy may be much lower than envisaged by the Working Group. It may be worth mentioning here that demand projections of the 14th Power Survey Committee are now available, according to which the peak demand by the end of the Eighth Plan is estimated to be 63,760 MW, which is much lower than the previous projections. In spite of this, the gap between the demand and supply may continue to be substantial, may be around 16 per cent in peak demand and around 3 per cent in energy.

**Sources of Power Generation**

The traditional main resources of power generation in India have been hydro and coal. Since 1959 Nuclear resources have also been brought in. Gas-based power generation has also been started in a big way in the recent past as a result of large-scale exploration and transportation of natural gas. The total estimate of various resources of power in the country is as under:

Hydro : Approximately 600 Gwh of firm annual energy equivalent to 84,000 MW (at 60% load factor) of installed capacity. Out of this, only about 20 per

| | | |
|---|---|---|
| | | cent potential including benefits from the on-going projects stand exploited so far; |
| Coal | : | Total coal reserves are estimated at 1,86,000 million tonnes out of which substantial share can be used for power generation; |
| Nuclear | : | Uranium and thorium reserves are estimated to be 67,000 tonnes and 363,000 tonnes respectively. When used in breeder reactors, thorium resources would be equivalent to about 600,0000 million tonnes of coal; and |
| Oil & Gas | : | The present balance of recoverable reserves of oil are about 728 million tonnes and about $686 \times 10^9$ $m^3$ of gas. A large part of the gas reserves (more than 65%) comprises free off-shore gas on west coast. |

Besides traditional main resources of power, non-conventional renewable sources of energy, such as, solar, bio-gas, wind, tides, sea-waves, ocean thermal energy conversion etc. are also foreseeable available sources of energy. The traditional sources of power cost about Rs. 3 to 4 crores per MW including its transmission and distribution. The non-traditional sources, however, are likely to cost much more. The cost of commercial fuels such as coal, lignite, petroleum products and natural gas is becoming more and more. It would, therefore, be necessary to look for various options which could help in bridging the gap between supply and demand.

**Demand and Supply Management**

In this context, it becomes extremely important to look for the options of demand-side management, identify strategies to get more generation from existing power stations, and also transmit them efficiently in order that consumers get the desired power as per the correct parameters. This would mean adopting effective load management measures such as staggering of load, extending life of existing power plants by renovation and modernisation, reducing T and D losses, effective regional grid operations, etc. The electricity pricing can be used as a tool to develop a better relationship between supply and demand which can help to reduce the capital requirement. In this connection, the example of cheap supply of energy to farmers for the growth in food production could be cited. The difference between the cost of production and sale of energy to farmers is now growing out of proportion. Similarly, the pattern and consumption of electricity in the domestic sector is also undergoing dramatic change due to extensive and intensive usages of domestic appliances using electricity for improving the quality and way of life.

The availability of cheap energy has, it is said, lead to inefficient utilisation of energy. The tariff or the pricing of electricity, therefore, needs to be used as a tool for better and more efficient energy utilisation and thus evolve better relationship between supply and demand. The potential for time-of-day pricing and other innovative options could be considered to manage the peak demand. Serious considerations could also be given to offer incentives to those consumers who wish to increase their consumption during off-peak hours and thus help in reducing overall peak-time demand.

**Energy Conservation**

In view of the fact that conventional resources of energy are limited and huge investments are required to meet our energy demand, effective measures for conserving energy have to be taken. Energy conservation does not imply curtailment of economic activities, but it simply means reduction in the amount of energy required to accomplish a given task. It has often been touted as an additional source of energy because of its potential to meet energy demand through effective energy efficient strategies. In India, while per capita energy consumption has been one of the lowest, the energy consumption per unit of GDP is one of the highest even in comparison with other developing countries. This means use of more energy for a given amount of output. It may be due to inefficient equipment, inefficient production process, present tariff structure and lack of awareness about the values to the notion of energy conservation.

Most of the industrially advanced countries have adopted appropriate energy conservation measures since the oil crisis of seventies. However, in India the need to conserve energy has not yet permeated in our social consciousness. On the one hand, there is a total conceptual appreciation of the problem whereas, on the other, there is a characteristic lack of enthusiasm in implementing measures for energy conservation. This suggests that our approach to conservation of energy on the national scale is not enough and something more needs to be done. The experience of other countries gives us a direction and shows that the ideals of conservation can be translated into reality only if they are backed by appropriate administrative, legal and financial inputs. The productive processes both in the industrial and agricultural sectors need a careful re-look in order to reduce energy consumption per unit of production. Highest priority is being given in this field by conducting energy audit of industries and by introduction of energy-efficient equipment, especially the induction motors and other technologies in industrial and agricultural sectors. With these measures, savings of energy of about 25 per cent in these sectors could be possible. To implement urgently the energy conservation measures so as to reduce the future generation capacity requirement by about 5,000 MW during the 8th Plan period, the government has earmarked Rs. 1,000 crores for energy conservation methods.

**T&D Losses**

Power losses in transmission and distribution system are high. The pilferage of energy in some areas makes the problem more acute. The national average for transmission and distribution losses is 21 to 22 per cent. The urban area distribution due to paucity of funds have not developed on optimum lines and constitute a significant component of T&D losses. Urban development will be the highest in the next 20 years. Control over distribution and transmission losses, therefore, assume considerable importance. These losses can be brought down to 15 per cent through system-operating checks. From purely economic considerations in the present state of our power systems, investments on reduction of T&D losses offer a very attractive proposition, since the cost of adding one MW of power to the grid through reduction of T&D losses is expected to be more economical than adding one MW by setting up a new hydro or thermal station.

**R&M of Power Stations**

Financial resources being limited, it is felt that maximum generation from existing power plants is imperative. A mere one per cent increase in the plant load factor can yield an additional output of 500

MW from the already installed capacities whereas for a 500 MW capacity to be installed, the cost would be Rs. 1,000 to Rs. 1,100 crores. Power plants, both thermal and hydel, have been identified for renovation and modernisation during Eighth Plan period. In essence, however, this policy will be the continuation of efforts made in this direction in the Seventh Plan. The Seventh Plan R&M programme has given good dividends as the thermal plants have given additional output of 7,000 MU during 1989-90.

**Integrated Operation**

In spite of the good progress shown in the power transmission system, it has failed to keep pace with the requirement on account of increase in generation capacity. At present, the country is witnessing shortage of power in some areas also on account of transmission constraint. This has been on account of inadequate investments in transmission and distribution, lack of required degree of integration amongst the different regional power systems and poor operational discipline. All these factors have contributed to comparatively low reliability and poor quality of power supply to consumers and, in some degree, to the prevailing power shortages in the country. Constant efforts are being made to achieve the optimum utilisation of generation facilities through establishment of inter-State and inter-regional grids.

**New and Renewable Energy Resources**

In the present circumstances when there is resource crunch, conventional energy sources are also depleting and environmental degradation from power projects is assuming greater emphasis, increased effort on harnessing of new and renewable energy resources like bio-gas, solar energy, wind power, micro-hydel, Geothermal and tidal, etc., appears logical and essential. The total tidal energy resources in India are assessed to the extent of 9,000 MW. Investigations of a tidal power project in the Gulf of Kutch with a capacity of 900 MW are in progress. It is estimated that it may be possible to generate 6,000 MW of power through bio-gas and 2,000 MW from sugar based agricultural waste. In addition, about 20,000 MW wind power is also estimated. Today in the country, we have got wind power generators of a total capacity of 30 MW only. Solar stations up to 30 MW are also being contemplated.

### Small/Mini/Micro Hydro Schemes

Development of small/mini/micro schemes needs to be encouraged for power supply especially to remote areas. Economic sites on existing canal drops as well as small dams also need to be taken up for development of small hydro potential. Small hydro can play an important role in rural electrification. There are thousands of villages in the hilly areas where extension of transmission lines is rather difficult and costly. Harnessing small streams for power can usher an era of fast economic development in these areas. Considering the advantages of small hydro, Government of India has accorded high priority to development of these schemes.

### Computer Application in the Development of Power

The CEA at the national level and other organisations including power utilities at the regional and State levels have been conscious of the importance of computer, the most versatile tool for management, in the development of power sector from the early years. The use of computers in the CEA started as early as in 1965 by hiring computer time at various computer centres of ICAR, Planning Commission, Delhi University, IIT, IMD, etc. Its application was mainly limited to solutions of power system studies. With the installation of CYBER system at NIC, computerisation in CEA increased exponentially. Subsequently, with the installation of its own in-house NORD 32/70 super-mini computer in the year 1987 on one hand and a number of PCs and PC/ATs on the other, no area of CEA activities has escaped the influence and use of computers.

A few important applications worth mentioning are as follows:

— Besides offline studies and generation of various power data, the need for introduction of on-line computers for real-time monitoring of our power grid was felt during the Fifth Five-Year Plan. Accordingly, the schemes were formulated by CEA for establishment of computer based regional load despatch centres comprising sophisticated computer systems with standard peripherals, colour videos, mimic board and software for Supervisory Control and Data Acquisition

(SCDA) and automatic generation control. This scheme took off towards the end of Sixth Five-Year Plan and major portion of these have been completed during the Seventh Five-Year Plan.

— In the area of generation and expansion planning studies, CEA interacted with several power utilities abroad and acquired WASP – III package from IAEA, Vienna, EGEAS package from EPRI, U.S.A. and ISPLAN package from IDEA, U.S.A. These packages were implemented on various computers, such as, IBM/360, CYBER/170, VAX-11/750, NECS-1000 and ND 32/70 by the CEA. These packages were used for formulation of the 1st and 2nd perspective National Power Plans and for determining the major contours of power flows in various regions of the country and are presently being used for carrying out techno-economic appraisal of various projects and reliability evaluation of the Eighth and Ninth Five-Year Plan power development programmes.

— In the field of power system transmission planning studies, power flow analysis. Short circuit analysis, transient stability analysis, reliability analysis, economic analysis, etc., are being carried out on in-house NORD system of CEA using PSAP and EMTP — VPA packages.

— Among the large list of reports computerised with software developed in CEA, a few worth mentioning are:

(i) Daily generation report
(ii) Energy performance status report
(iii) Energy overview
(iv) Monthly thermal and hydel review
(v) Annual thermal review
(vi) Monthly generation, availability, planned maintenance and forced outage report
(vii) Group-wise status performance reports
(viii) Action plan
(ix) General review
(x) Power supply position during Eighth and Ninth Five-Year Plans
(xi) Load forecast analysis
(xii) Designing and analysing transmission line support and transmission towers

(xiii) Power data

(xiv) Requirement of key inputs such as coal, cement, steel, etc.

(xv) Analysis in respect of requirement of funds for power projects

(xvi) Data base in respect of techno-economic parameters and status of power projects being considered for benefits during Eighth and Ninth Plan periods.

The other very important area where of late we have been feeling the need for computer application is the management of the power sector database as part of the overall Management Information System (MIS). The power sector like all other important sectors of national economy is being geared up to have adequate hardware and software facilities to support the ultimate information system which would also be a part of inter-sectoral database for assisting decision making at the national level. The facilities in this area which are already available with National Informatics Centre (NIC) at the national level would be made use of for the purpose.

## Conclusion

While inferring from the past and looking ahead into the future perspective of power development in the country, it becomes very clear that in spite of impressive growth in the power sector, the situation we are presently facing is that of the conditions of power shortages. Challenges before the power sector are many. With the resources crunch, balance of payment problems, depleting resources of conventional, non-renewable sources of energy, new alternatives for energy may have to be explored. The new and renewable sources of energy carry great importance in the Indian power scene. Their development best suited to Indian techno-economy is to be expedited for the betterment of future of power industry. The analysis also clearly indicates that a long-term strategy for development of power in the country based on effective demand management and energy conservation measures would have to be formulated so that both demand and the supply-side options are addressed simultaneously. On the supply side, keeping in view the highly capital-intensive nature of the power supply industry, efficiencies of the electricity supply as well as consuming sectors are to be improved to maximise their outputs.

More momentum is required to be given to energy conservation by intensifying mass education through electronic media right upto the level of small consumers. There is urgency to design special programmes to attract bulk and large consumers for making them to join the national task of energy conservation. Life extension programmes of existing power plants would also have to be given due attention in years to come. It would be important to accelerate the process of investigation and the harnessing of various resources for power generation including non-conventional sources of energy for meeting the projected electricity demand. Mini/Micro/Small H.E. schemes could also be useful for meeting needs of remote and isolated areas. Power Sector is fully conscious of future challenges and with the adoption of these strategies along with extensive computer application, it hopes to render the best of its services to the nation in the years to come.

# PART V

## SERVICE SECTOR

(Focus on Community)

# 20

# BANKING

B.B. SAXENA*

## Introduction

The Indian banking industry has been making significant efforts at technology upgradation at various levels as recommended in the Report of the Committee on Mechanisation in Banking Industry (1984) headed by Dr. C. Rangarajan, Deputy Governor, Reserve Bank of India.

The Committee made the following main recommendations:

(i) Mainframe computer systems should be installed in head offices of banks and made fully operational. These systems should support accounts and reconciliation, management information on credit and deposits, administrative services named earlier and database management;

(ii) Zonal and regional offices controlling about 200 branches should be equipped with micro processor systems supported by adequate configuration of off-line data-entry terminals. These systems should take over transcription, editing of all data-flows emerging from branches under their jurisdiction and should transmit all the information to head office on computer tapes/floppy discs only;

(iii) Clearing houses in Bombay, Madras, New Delhi and Calcutta should be equipped with MICR equipment and national clearing should be introduced. Computerisation of settlements in clearing houses in other cities managed by the Reserve Bank of India should also be introduced. All banks should establish service offices in the top 100 centres; and

---

* State Bank of India (SBI).

(iv) In regard to the mechanisation of banks branches, branches in metropolitan centres and other urban areas, having a workload of about 1,000 vouchers per day should be equipped with Advanced Ledger Posting Machines (ALPMs) with attached memory. A few branches could also have Model II machines, i.e., Electronic Accounting Machines (EAMs) for handling back-office operations.

The programme of mechanisation/computerisation in banks as envisaged in the above Report has come to a close. By the end of June 1990, banks had installed about 6 mainframes, 250 minicomputers and 5007 ALPMs at over 1300 branches. MICR equipment and two-way national clearing have been introduced at the four metropolitan centres. One-way national clearing has been introduced at Hyderabad, Ahmedabad, Bangalore and Nagpur.

As far as SBI is concerned, it installed 5 mainframes (which were recently replaced by 2 more powerful mainframes), 82 minicomputers and about 450 personal computers at its administrative offices by the end of June 1990. In addition, it mechanised back-office operations at 287 branches. SBI preferred initially to mechanise the back-office operations as against the front-office computerisation undertaken by other banks for the following reasons:

(i) Ease of implementation;
(ii) Lower cost;
(iii) More security;
(iv) Lack of skilled manpower; and
(v) Possibility of frequent power and/or system failure at large number of centres.

**Dr. Rangarajan Committee's Second Report**

Based on the experience gained during the period 1984-1989, the Committee on Computerisation in Banks set up by Government of India under the Chairmanship of Dr. C. Rangarajan has submitted a more ambitious plan for branch computerisation for the period 1990-94. The focus of the report is improvement of services to the customer. The salient findings and recommendations in the report are as under: –

(i) A survey of opinion conducted amongst banks and other institutions revealed that computerisation has considerably helped banks in house-keeping, provided slightly better service to customers and had been seen to be useful by bank employees;

(ii) The purposes of computerisation have been identified as improvement in customer service, house-keeping, decision-making and productivity/profitability;

(iii) Considering the need to show demonstrable impact on customer service and also taking into account the infrastructural constraints relating to power supply, computer support and maintenance and the state of telecommunication links, the thrust of bank computerisation for next 5 years should be to fully computerise 2000 to 2500 large branches at the top 30 centres, having a workload of 750 vouchers per day or more;

(iv) At the branch level, the attempt should be to provide customer service by giving a choice to the customer to go to any free counter convenient to him unlike the present system of dedicated counters/machines. Further, connectivity between branches should also be established to effect instantaneous transfer of funds and facilitate effective monitoring and control;

(v) Computerisation at branch level can be through one of the following 3 alternatives: –

(a) Each of the selected branches can be a super-micro, mini or super-mini with required number of on-line terminals at the counters and back-office. The system at the branch would be linked over BANKNET (RBI's communication network) datacom lines to its own central computer (mini/super-mini/mainframe) in the same centres which would serve as a back-up. Connectivity would be provided through BANKNET and/or through public data network;

(b) Each of the selected branches may have PCs operating under LAN, with a mini-computer as server. Branches will be connected with each other and the nodal point or RBI, through BANKNET, directly or through concentrators. The computer system of a proximate branch would serve as bank-up to another branch. It would then be possible to avoid separate host systems for each bank; and

(c) On-line terminals or PCs at the counter and back-office at each branch could be hooked on to one central system for that bank, which may have suitable safeguards against failure (fully fault-tolerant system). Leased lines can be used, backed up by dial-up lines. This alternative subsumes availability of reliable telecom lines. Alternative (a) has been recommended as a preferred solution;

(vi) Some of the housekeeping functions, such as, periodical reports to management, statutory returns, interest calculations, etc., for the remaining about 37,000 branches spread over thousands of centres can be done using the computers installed at the nearest regional/zonal offices;

(vii) *Phased Implementation*

(a) In the first two to three years, banks may take up about 500 large branches with daily voucher load of 1,500 and above for total computerisation;

(b) The remaining about 1,500 to 2,000 branches, with daily voucher load between 750 to 1,500 vouchers could be taken up in the second phase. Meanwhile, back-office operations at these branches should be computerised and later extend the scope to front-office activities in a modular fashion;

(viii) After the branches are fully computerised, banks may gradually connect them within a centre and between centres as may be dictated by operational needs and availability of reliable DoT lines;

(ix) All the ROs/ZOs (and local head offices of SBI) numbering about 920 should be taken up for computerisation during the period;

(x) BANKNET should be used for several intra-bank and inter-bank applications;

(xi) Small networks of ATMs may be tried out, to begin with in Bombay, by installing cash dispensers and ATMs at strategic locations such as airports, railway stations, etc.;

(xii) Signature storage/retrieval systems, on-line terminals at corporate customer sites, customer authentication through laminated, tamper-proof machine readable cards, other ancillary equipment such as word-processors, copying machines, facsimile machines, etc., should be provided; and

(xiii) The objective of mechanisation in India is not to replace man with machines. Rather the objective is to make work-life more meaningful. The programme of computerisation will not result in any reduction of labour. Of course, there has to be some reallocation of work. In fact, computerisation in banking industry is expected to reduce the drudgery involved in routine work.

**Present Status of Computerisation**

There has been no significant progress in implementation of the above recommendations as it has not been possible for the Indian Banks' Association, in spite of best efforts, to arrive at an Industry level settlement with the staff federation. Meanwhile, SBI has entered into a bipartite settlement with its staff in 1989 which enables it to implement a substantial portion of the recommendations. Recently, the Indian Overseas Bank has also been able to finalise a settlement with its staff for the purpose. It is expected that the other banks will soon follow suit.

As per the IBA Agreement dated 10.4.89 with the Staff Federation, all the banks were permitted to take up one branch for total mechanisation. Accordingly, most of the banks are in the process of fully computerising one of their branches. Some of them, viz., Bank of India, Dena Bank, etc., already have a fully computerised branch. ATMs have also been installed by Bank of India at Bombay and Indian Bank at Madras.

Computerisation in SBI dates back to 1966 when it computerised the reconciliation of inter-office transactions. Subsequently, computers were introduced for handling several tasks at the Bank's Central Office and Local Head Offices as under:

| *Central Office* | *Local Head Offices* |
|---|---|
| (i) Settlement of government transactions | (i) Weekly abstract |
| (ii) Drafts reconciliation | (ii) Analysis of charges |

| | | | |
|---|---|---|---|
| (iii) | Reconciliation of agency transactions | (iii) | Performance budgeting |
| (iv) | Rupee travellers cheques reconciliation | (iv) | Analysis of large advances. |
| (v) | Management information system | (v) | Analysis of term advances. |

(vi) Personnel skills record
(vii) Investment information system
(viii) Foreign exchange dealing
(ix) Reconciliation of nostro accounts
(x) Staff provident fund and pension fund
(xi) Stationery management
(xii) Computerised payroll

Computerisation/mechanisation of operations at the branch level was conceived by an in-house task force constituted in May 1982 and, as recommended by it, mechanisation of back-office operations was introduced in the bank. So far, about 300 branches have been mechanised and another 300 branches have been identified for the purpose. The main objectives of computerisation/mechanisation in SBI is to improve the house-keeping, customer service, decision-making, MIS and productivity/profitability, as also improve the working environment for the employees. With this end in view, the Bank has introduced a number of office automation equipments, such as, facsimile machine, PC-based telexes, zerox copying machines, etc. Arrangements are also in hand to introduce automatic note and coin counting machines, automatic teller machines, signature storage and retrieval systems, microfilming of records etc.

The main problems faced by SBI are lack of skilled manpower and unsatisfactory hardware and software support from the vendors. SBI has still not been able to introduce all the modules of the back-office mechanisation package mainly because the vendors have not been able to complete the necessary software even after a period of 2-3 years. Power failures/fluctuations also create problems at some of the branches. Restrictions on the memory of the back-office systems is also proving as an handicap to standardise the hardware and software being used by us.

Notwithstanding the problems, following projects have been taken up by us for urgent implementation:

(i) On-line real-time transaction processing in 25 major branches having a concentration of corporate customers located in different parts of the country with networking thereof;

(ii) Total computerisation and networking of 23 branches in South Bombay;

(iii) Total computerisation of 5 selected branches (of which one branch, viz., NRI branch, is completed); and

(iv) Back-office mechanisation of about 600 branches.

It may be mentioned here that a number of foreign banks like Citibank, ANZ Grindlays Bank, Hong Kong Bank, etc. have fully computerised their operations and are, therefore, competitively better placed vis-a-vis the nationalised banks at metropolitan centres. It is, therefore, extremely important for the Indian banks to computerise expeditiously their operations to be able to provide premium service to the public.

**Progress in Communication Networks**

In view of the importance of faster medium of communication in a service industry like banking, the Reserve Bank of India has set up a communication network called BANKNET for the use of member banks. The network has become partially operational and efforts are being made to operationalise all the lines as soon as possible. Arrangements are also in hand to develop suitable application packages for use of the member banks.

Many banks have established their own "store and forward" networks. State Bank of India has a voice network called SBINET which connects 64 cities and 134 offices. It has also the following :

(i) Message Switch Network working on teleprinter lines (MSN).

(ii) Remote Area Business Message Network (RABMN).

**Conclusion**

Against the above background, the following issues are needed to be considered:

(i) The relative advantages/disadvantages of central processing vs. distributed processing and guidelines for decision-making;

(ii) Manning of computer policy and planning departments of Banks. Estimated manpower requirements — who should head the department, a bank executive or a technical expert?

(iii) Estimated investment on computers and communication during the next 5 years;

(iv) Industrial relations climate in our banks does not sound to be conducive for aggressive mechanisation. Mechanisation/computerisation cannot be meaningfully undertaken without such climate. What needs to be done?

(v) What should be the organisational restructuring to ensure that the requisite momentum is imparted to the process of computerisation of bank's offices; and

(vi) The need or otherwise for setting up a subsidiary exclusively for development of banking application software for the banking Industry. Also the need for standardisation in accounting, banking produces and procedures.

# 21

# GENERAL INSURANCE

V.S. DHRUV*

## Introduction

General Insurance Industry has completed 18 years of service to the nation as a public sector organisation. Prior to its nationalisation in 1973, general insurance was by and large city-oriented in its culture, catering mainly to the needs of the organised trade and industry. Consequent upon take-over by the government, 107 companies including branches of foreign companies operating in the country were merged and grouped into four companies:

(i) National Insurance Co. Ltd., Calcutta;
(ii) The New India Assurance Co. Ltd., Bombay;
(iii) The Oriental Insurance Co. Ltd., Delhi;
(iv) United India Insurance Co Ltd., Madras.

The General Insurance Corporation was incorporated in November 1972 as a holding company and the above four companies were formed as its subsidiaries from January 1, 1973. All the four companies operate on an all-India basis in competition with one another through a three-tier marketing network of regional, divisional and branch Offices spread throughout the country.

During the last 18 years of operation, the industry has undergone a virtual revolution in various facets of its working. While continuing to be responsive to the needs of the traditional sectors of commerce and industry, new avenues have been explored to serve other sectors of society, particularly in rural areas.

---

* General Insurance Corporation of India (GIC).

While the world non-life insurance industry has been experiencing fluctuating fortunes, the general insurance industry in India has steadily scaled new heights. The total gross direct premium income in India of the general insurance industry has increased more than thirteen times since 1973 to stand at Rs. 2788 crores at the end of 1990-91. This represents an average annual compound growth rate of 15.5 per cent. At this rate-by the end of the century the gross direct premium income is expected to exceed Rs. 10,000 crores per annum.

Organisational Network (Number of offices)

| | 1975 | 1981 | 1986 | 1990-91 | 2000-01 |
|---|---|---|---|---|---|
| Regional | 20 | 28 | 53 | 71 | 100 |
| Divisional | 240 | 399 | 844 | 1072 | 1500 |
| Branch | 529 | 919 | 2192 | 3041 | 4000 |
| Total | 789 | 1346 | 3089 | 4184 | 5600 |

Manpower

| | | | | | |
|---|---|---|---|---|---|
| Officers | 3306 | 5735 | 9227 | 14145 | 21000 |
| Marketing | 4294 | 9330 | 12841 | 14038 | 21000 |
| Clerical | 15303 | 21708 | 27464 | 39953 | 60000 |
| Supporting | 4103 | 4048 | 6195 | 10878 | 15000 |
| Total | 27033 | 40821 | 55727 | 79014 | 117000 |

The general insurance industry which had traditionally catered to trade, industry and commerce has during the last 18 years made conscious efforts to spread out to the semi-urban and rural areas. In the process, the industry which had 789 offices and 27000 employees in 1975 has today 4184 offices and 79000 employees spread all over the country. Projecting the above rate of growth, the industry is expected to have more than 5600 offices and 117000 employees by the turn of the century.

**Industrial Relations Scenario in Early 1980's**

The two public sector industries in the service sector viz., banking and Insurance have been regarded so far as employment-generating industries for the educated unemployed. In the early 1980's, the industrial relations scene in these industries was strained. Between 1980 and 1984, there was a stalemate and the disputes between the management and the employees' unions were subjected to litigation at the Supreme Court level. The resultant low morale and resentment in them made it difficult to bring the unions to the negotiating table.

In the agreement entered into between Indian Banks Association and All India Bank Employees Association in September 1983, the inhibitions and apprehensions of the employees' unions, about the computerisation, were more manifest in their insisting for restrictions in selection of the computers/microprocessors and their areas of applications. This thereby limited the scope of computerisation to dedicated and stand-alone systems for specified purposes ("Electronic Ledger Posting/Accounting Machines"). Further, use of the computers for improving the customer service and locating the computer systems at semi-urban and rural areas were excluded from the scope of the mechanisation activity.

In 1985, after the new government assuming office. There set in a mood of give-and-take, and in the process, the introduction of modern technology in the office working environment was agreed to by the unions. The impact of the changing attitudes of the unions was evident from the different understanding reached with regard to computerisation.

**Organisational/Corporate Objectives**

The primary objective for introduction of computerised systems in the working of the offices in the general insurance industry has been improvement in "Customer Service". However, this could not be insisted upon at the time of signing the MoU with the employees' unions mainly because the computer culture had not caught up in the industry and for such a project commitment and cooperation of the employees was absolutely essential. As a matter of compromise, the objective was limited to the improvement in house-keeping operations to be carried out in the back-office.

In the ensuing next round of discussions with the employees' associations, it would be possible to bring home the point and make them realise the need and urgency for giving primary importance to the cause of customer service. This should then lead to a good decision support system and improvement in productivity and profitability of our operations.

### Memorandum of Understanding (MoU) with Employees' Associations

The industrial relations scenario in the general insurance industry was not much different. After various rounds of discussions, a Memorandum of Understanding (MoU) was signed in November 1986 on the introduction of computerised systems in the offices of the general insurance companies. The MoU allowed wider scope in terms of selection of computers and their use.

Besides the eased industrial relations another, relevant factor influencing the terms of the MoU was the technological advances and the entry of the personal computers in the Indian market. It was envisaged in the MoU that the current technology, viz., general purpose personal computers would be used in the offices. However, this agreement also restricted the use of computer systems to data processing rather than for raising the level of customer satisfaction. The jobs specified to be done manually included the customer interaction and thus the major objective of improved customer service could not be taken up on the computerised systems.

In the MoU, the employees' unions were assured that introduction of computers/microprocessors and the computerised systems would neither be allowed to result in a ban on recruitment nor would there be curtailment in promotional opportunities for the employees. It was agreed that except for the initial recruitment of a small number of systems personnel (10 each for the four subsidiaries and GIC), no person would be recruited even on temporary basis, and employees from within would be trained to work on the computerised systems and would be given skill/functional allowance. There could, however, be redeployment of such employees but there would not be any compulsive transfers outside city/town of posting. External arrangements for data processing was agreed to be gradually discontinued and taken over on in-house systems.

### Operational Constraints Imposed by MoU

Exclusion of the branch offices (then numbering 2192) from the purview of the computerisation project truncated the programme. The branch offices from where the transactions originated situated in the cities/towns across the country were left out of the scope. By restricting the computerisation only up to divisional offices, the capture of data at its origin was denied and thereby the pace of implementation was retarded.

The inadequacies of the manual working to cope with customer requirements, in terms of quality and the increasing volume of work, was instrumental in planning for the introduction of computerised systems in our offices. The provision in the MoU that customer service-related activities such as issuing of policy documents, notices for renewal of insurances, premium rating, acceptance of proposals as well as claims processing be carried out manually denied the benefit of computerisation to the customers.

Having accepted that the existing employees should be trained to enable them to shoulder new types of responsibilities, there cannot be any dispute over the restriction on the number of systems personnel. However, the fact remains that the restricted number of these personnel required was inadequate to attend to developing standard software for all insurance applications as well as to operate the UNIX-based minicomputer systems installed at 70 regional offices, and the microprocessor-based systems at 1000 divisional offices. Neither could the personnel administrative machinery cope up with the requirements of deployment of suitably trained employees in adequate numbers from the existing cadres, nor could they make any alternative arrangements in consultation with the employees' unions.

**Computerisation Methodology**

(a) *Distributed Data Processing*

Decentralisation of computers and computerised systems was best suited to the geographically spread organisational set-up of the insurance industry with the large number of offices performing identical/similar functions. As insurance business is being transacted from our divisional and branch offices, centralised data processing was considered unsuitable for this purpose.

With a view to harness the advantages of distributed data processing and, at the same time, ensure integration of data/information, standardisation of hardware and system software, uniform and standardised application software for similarly placed offices like divisional and regional offices were adopted as the basic principles while drafting the methodology for introduction and implementation of computerisation programme.

(b) *Technical and Approval Committees (Steering Committees)*

For the purpose of systematic planning and implementation of the computerisation project, two committees were set-up at the industry level for the purpose of evaluation and selection of computer hardware and software, working out the details for implementation and ensuring performance according to a given time schedule.

Both the committees have been functioning jointly for the last six years and decisions on standardisation of hardware, systems software and centralised development of uniform software for common application areas. Other procedural and operational guidelines have also been drawn up by these committees. Common decisions were taken on all aspects of the computerisation programme so that the pace of implementation is similar and uniform in all the companies.

(c) *Selection and Standardisation of Hardware and Software*

Emergence of personal computers with capabilities of voluminous data processing capacity facilitated our approach in standardisation. As IBM compatible systems with more or less standard configurations were available with a number of computer suppliers, it was easily possible to achieve a high level of standardisation. It was also possible to capture and process data at the divisional offices and only summarised data/information was required to be maintained at the regional and head offices.

The configurations of the Hardware for Divisional offices consisted of IBM compatible personal computers (PC-AT + 2 PCs and Dot matrix printer). In addition, the Cartridge Tape Drive(CTD) (conforming to QIC 100 standard) was provided in every divisional Office to function as a back-up and data storage device. This CTD had the facility of functioning as a hard disk to a limited extent and so could be used in case the hard disk in the PC-AT became non-functional.

At the regional and head offices, MC 68020 processor based Mini computers with on-line storage, dot matrix printer, line printer, streamer tape drive and CTD with PCs as intelligent terminals have been provided. The systems software chosen for the mini-computers was the Unix environment.

As no single supplier of equipment was found to possess infrastructural resources to supply and service the entire requirements of our industry, a multi-vendor environment was opted for. This ensured that the programme did not depend on one supplier alone. By standardising on the processor, the bus structure and peripherals as well as hardware independent Unix system environment, we could develop and implement common software for regional and head offices regardless of different hardware systems from a number of vendors.

Mention should also be made here of the important decision to standardise on a single relational data base management system for the mini computer systems (UNIFY RDBMS). It was visualised that the development of integrated management information system required for the controlling and decision-making at the top management level would be served better if a uniform RDBMS is used. All application software developed uses UNIFY RDBMS for reports and queries.

(d) *Implementation Plan*

The computerisation was taken up in a phased manner as follows:

(i) *Phase I* covered the GIC, head offices one regional office and two divisional offices of each subsidiary company (total number of offices-17) (Period : June 1986 to June 1987);

(ii) *Phase II* covered Regional and Divisional Offices at four Metro Centres, viz., Madras, Bombay, Calcutta and Delhi and one divisional office under each of the remaining regional centres of the subsidiary companies. (total number of offices — 1251) (Period : June 1987 to March 1988);

(iii) *Phase III(A)* covered the regional and divisional offices of major cities/towns. (total number of offices — 264) (Period : June 1988 to December 1988); and

(iv) *Phase III(B)* covered the balance regional and divisional offices (total number of offices — 487) (Period : December 1988 to March 1989).

(e) *Application Software*

(i) *Core group methodology*: Software development activity was taken up by the nucleus of systems personnel recruited in 1986. A 'Core Group' concept was adopted where a group of systems as well as user department personnel was formed for each application area. Main consideration while adopting this methodology was to avoid duplication of efforts and at the same time adhere to the time schedule drawn up for effective usage of all the systems installed.

Teams consisting of systems personnel and a manager of the user department as co-ordinator of the software development group were formed. It was envisaged that the teams would finalise user requirements based on their study and circulate the specifications to other companies. Once final and common specifications were drawn up, the software development and testing would be taken up by the systems personnel at the head office of the company where the system study was undertaken. Once the programmes developed are tested at the head offices and found acceptable, the software could be ported and implemented at other locations.

With this approach between 1987 and 1989, we could develop and test comprehensive software for all the application areas mentioned in the beginning. The implementation of the software was taken up by the individual companies with the help of the systems personnel at their offices.

(ii) *Application Areas*: In view of the constraints accepted at the time of signing the MoU, it was imperative to restrict the computer application areas to the following back-office activities:

| Offices | Software developed for | Software implementation environment |
|---|---|---|
| DOs | 1. Underwriting | 1. MS DOS. Ver 2.0 . . . 4.01 |
| | 2. Accounts | 2. MS COBOL Ver 3.0 |
| | 3. Motor loss control | |
| | 4. Claims | |
| | 5. Bank guarantee control | |
| | 6. Statistics | |

| | | | |
|---|---|---|---|
| ROs | 1. | Personnel information | 1. UNIX SYSTEM 5.2.2...5.3.2 |
| | 2. | Estate and establishment | 2. MF COBOL LEVEL II ET |
| | 3. | Financial accounting | 3. UNIFY RDBMS Ver 3.2 . . . 4.0 |
| | 4. | Development (inspector performance analysis) | |
| | 5. | Budgetary control | |
| HOs | 1. | Personnel information management system | 1. UNIX SYSTEM 5.2.2 . . . 5.3.2 |
| | 2. | Estate and establishment | 2. MF COBOL LEVEL II ET |
| | 3. | Financial accounting | 3. UNIFY RDBMS Ver 3.2 . . . 4.0 |
| | 4. | Re-insurance | |
| | 5. | Investment | |
| | 6. | Corporate planning | |
| | 7. | Budgetary control | |
| | 8. | Foreign operations | |

(iii) *Standardisation of Input and Output Forms and Procedures*: Prior to nationalisation of general insurance companies, there were more than 100 odd companies (Indian and foreign) operating in the country. These companies had different practices and procedures. The nationalised general insurance industry inherited these non-standard procedures and practices. The standardisation of the procedures, input formats and other forms being used in the offices of the companies was a very arduous task. After the formative years of the merger, steps were initiated to have a complete study of the varying practices prevalent and evolve a standard working procedure. It was considered prudent to identify commonalities in the different practices/procedures and then develop working software for the common base and allow customisation to a certain extent till such time standard systems and practices evolve over a period of time. Even where standard procedures were available, the customisation was becoming unavoidable as the computerised system had to be implemented and integrated into the working environment without interrupting the present operations.

(f) *Manpower and Training*

Considering the situation that the Industry did not have any computer culture at all, it was agreed that all the requisite manpower would be developed from within by suitable training. However, to begin with, a nucleus of systems personnel were recruited for taking up the immediate task of development of working software for the application areas identified. They were also assigned the work of training the operational staff and users on the software developed and assist them in the implementation of the same. Building up skills and expertise from scratch for the project of such a vast spread of offices was an immense task and could not be achieved in a short period. The training efforts have been initiated and are now passing through a gestation period.

(g) *Status of computerisation programme*

Table 21.1 shows the installation of computer systems in the Divisional Offices and Table 21.2 shows the position in the Regional Offices. Approximately 90 per cent of the offices have been provided with computer systems. Only in 5 per cent of the Offices covered, systems are yet to be installed and made operational.

**Benefits Derived**

The achievements of the General Insurance Industry in the Computerisation programme and the benefits derived thereof must be looked at with the backdrop of the scope of computerisation being limited to house-keeping and back-office operations. Having deferred the computerisation of areas related to customer satisfaction, the broad based efforts made so far has resulted in building up of infrastructural, skills and above all the cultural and environmental changes required for the purpose.

The computerisation efforts made so far, have given the industry an entirely different environment from the one that was prevailing in 1986. With computer systems in every office/department, it has been realised by all that the future growth and profitability of the organisation depends on the optimal and effective use of modern technological aids. The stage is now set for the organisation to involve all resources — manpower and computer systems — for improvements in the services to the customer and better decision-making.

Constitution of a management services department at regional and head offices has given the initial momentum required for the programme as follow:

TABLE 21.1: Computer Systems in Divisional Offices

| | Summary of all Companies | | | |
|---|---|---|---|---|
| | Phase I and II 1987-88 | Phase III A 1988 | Phase III B 1989 | Total |
| Total No. of DOs | 245 | 231 | 598 | 1074 |
| Divisional offices covered | 245 | 231 | 476 | 952 |
| DO systems operational | 244 | 218 | 382 | 844 |
| DO systems installed but not operational | NIL | 11 | 44 | 55 |
| DO systems not installed | 1 | 2 | 45 | 48 |
| Systems not procured | NIL | NIL | 122 | 122 |

TABLE 21.2: Computer Systems in Regional Offices

| | Summary of all Companies | | | |
|---|---|---|---|---|
| | Phase I and II 1987-88 | Phase III A 1988 | Phase III B 1989 | Total |
| Total No. of ROs. | 18 | 33 | 20 | 71 |
| Regional offices covered | 18 | 33 | 11 | 62 |
| RO systems operational | 18 | 32 | 9 | 59 |
| RO systems installed but not operational | NIL | NIL | 1 | 1 |
| RO systems not installed | NIL | 1 | 1 | 2 |
| Systems not procured | NIL | NIL | 9 | 9 |

### (a) *Awareness and spread of Computer culture*

Installation of computer systems in almost all the offices within a short span of 3-4 years has created an environment conducive to successful implementation of computerisation. Stand-alone PC based systems and standard utility packages have spread computer skills.

Providing of terminals to user departments at the regional and head offices has paved the way for acceptance of computer systems as an integral part of the day-to-day operations. It has also facilitated introduction of the latest trends,viz., end-user computing.

### (b) *Decentralised Data Processing*

The divisional offices would now be in a position to handle more volume of business — both in terms of premium income and insurance documents — with same or a marginal increase in manpower resources. With the skills available at all the divisional offices, the stage is set for spreading the culture/skills to branch offices facilitating branch computerisation.

Development of common software (to the extent possible) has enabled standardisation of systems. This standardisation of software enabled divisional offices at remote locations to render mutual assistance in problem solving, thus overcoming the paucity of skilled personnel at these locations.

### (c) *Employees Relieved of Monotony and Drudgery of Routine Jobs*

The main beneficiary so far in the efforts of back-office computerisation has been the employees who have been relieved of monotonous and voluminous jobs of a repetitive nature.

Further, both successful development and implementation of computerised systems and the taking over of the data processing work earlier contracted to an external agency on the in-house systems created confidence and ready acceptance of computerisation.

### (d) *System Improvements*

The development of minimum working software based on the common specifications has brought to focus the need for systems improvement. Steps have also been initiated for improvements in the working procedures. Close coordination between user departments and MSD during software development has set the stage for standardisation and improvement of input documents and working procedures.

Further, in a number of departments the employees who acquired sufficient skills/expertise could develop ad hoc software for their work areas and thus systematise their working to a considerable extent. This would enable further integration of the systems into the total environment.

(e) *Better House-Keeping*

With the capture of transactions at divisional offices, i.e., nearer the originating office, it has been possible for these offices to maintain up-to-date records. They are also in a position to quickly finalise operational results — trial balance.

The computerisation of divisional offices has made the divisional managers realise the importance of House-keeping also, as against business growth which had always been of top priority.

(f) *Savings in Cost and Efforts*

Termination of external arrangements for data processing has resulted in cost savings. The core group methodology adopted has brought savings in software development efforts, by avoiding multiplication of efforts.

(g) *Infrastructure Built up for Higher Levels of Computerisation*

It has been possible to build up basic infrastructure required for introducing communications and data/information transfer through computer network. This would also result in considerable saving both in cost of (and efforts for) communications, data storage and data retrieval.

**Problems Encountered and Their Solutions**

(a) *Paucity of Skilled Personnel for Computer Operations*

All the skills and expertise required for computerisation has been agreed to be developed from existing resources by adequate training. The training, reorientation and redeployment of our existing employees for implementation of computerised systems is inescapable. This is an ongoing activity and has a certain gestation period.

In the initial stages, the resistance to change and new culture, coupled with ambiguity in career prospects, inhibited employees from coming forward to take up training and new assignments related to computer operations.

(b) *Lack of Adequate Training Infrastructure*

The computerisation project was started from scratch and computer culture/literacy was non-existent among our employees.

The vast scope of the computerisation programme covering almost 1,000 offices in the length and breadth of the country called for huge training efforts for imparting skills of computer operations in all regions simultaneously.

The day-to-day operations on the in-house software required specific training and the personnel who developed the software were best suited for this purpose. The group of 10 officers for each company could not handle this huge task of training, in addition to development, customisation, and assistance in implementation at various offices.

Professional training agencies could at best be utilised for the computer awareness and other courses of a general nature.

(c) *Frequent Changes to System Specifications*

The user department officials could not visualise in one go all the input and output requirements. This is mainly due to the fact that no one was fully conversant with the entire requirements for an application area. In addition, there have been varying practices prevalent and evolving a common system applicable to all these similarly placed offices/departments was difficult. Further, they were not aware of how to put down specifications for computerised systems. Thus, the software development activity was prolonged and by the time the software was completed, there arose a situation where customisation was needed to user requirements prevailing at the time of implementation.

(d) *Role of User Departments in the Implementation*

There has been some misunderstanding as to the role of the user department has to play in the computerisation programme. There have been instances where the earlier concept of data processing was being stressed by the user departments. They expected MSD to function as a data-processing centre and give all the reports/outputs to them. This situation continues in most of the regional offices. The active role of the User in the 'end-user computing' and data-processing has not been fully realised.

At present, there is no single or uniform source document for capture of input data. This has resulted in the intermediate transcription of data on to a specific format for data capture. Thus, instead of reducing the work, the manual work of transcription was additional.

(e) *Poor Vendor-Support for Hardware and Software Maintenance*

The multi-vendor strategy adopted by us has been an achievement in that our programme was not dependent on one vendor alone and the purchase and installation of systems could be completed as planned.

Problems of after-sales support from vendors started when the programme for installation of computer systems for mofussil centres was in progress. The inadequate vendor infrastructure at these locations led to poor hardware maintenance support from them.

When the hardware defects are not rectified promptly, considerable time is lost and the employee confidence and morale is affected.

(f) *Non-Availability of Power*

Critical power supply position in certain parts of the country makes it difficult to get power supply for a reasonable period of time in a day for computer operations. In addition, power fluctuations affect operations directly leading to data corruption.

**Solutions Adopted**

(a) *Selection, Training and Deployment of Skilled Personnel from within*

Employees with the right aptitude were selected by means of an aptitude test and interview for the functional posts of data entry operators and programmers (senior operators). The employees selected for the post of senior operators were also given financial incentive by way of reimbursement of tuition fees for COBOL programming course done by them.

With the help of a group of system personnel, in-house training programmes were organised for volunteer employees on computer concepts and programming skills. Emphasis was also laid on operational efficiency of the system already installed. As part of the contract for supply of systems to every office, the suppliers of equipments were required to give operational and machine familiarisation training to the user personnel. This was to ensure that minimum computer awareness is created as soon as the systems are installed in the respective offices.

Certain professional training organisation were also engaged for conducting tailor-made courses on specific application software developed in house for divisional offices. On-the-job training programmes were organised on the divisional office software. Special intensive training programmes have also been organised for hardware diagnostics and first level maintenance as well as for Software system design, programming and implementation.

As the efforts are made in isolation and not in an integrated manner, the need for a separate training institute exclusively for computer training has also been felt and a beginning has been made in this regard. However, the regular induction and refresher courses in the training colleges include lectures/modules on computerisation.

We are also contemplating development of computer-based training materials and video-training cassettes on the application software for insurance operations.

It has been realised that only by a combination of all the techniques of training listed above will enable us to meet our requirements for skilled personnel and conscious steps are being taken in this direction.

### (b) *System Improvement, Software Development and Implementation by User Departments*

Isolated efforts are being made in the area of systems improvements and software customisation to tune the same to the existing working environment. The delay in development of software and the frequent changes to specifications contributed to the customisation of the software at each company level.

A lot of work remains to be done in the area of standardisation of procedures as also in the integration of computerised systems in offices in the same organisational tier and facilitate vertical integration.

System study groups have been formed in the GIC and the companies for review of the systems and their improvements. As an ongoing activity, the fruits of such exercises would be made available to all companies from time to time.

(c) *Hardware Maintenance and Support*

Since we have a large number of PC-based systems which are relatively simple to maintain, we have adopted a three-pronged approach for this problem as follow:

(i) Annual maintenance contract with suppliers;
(ii) Third-party maintenance arrangements; and
(iii) Self-dependence on diagnostics and first-level maintenance and diagnostics.

Hardware maintenance training programmes are being organised to train MSD officials at regional and head offices for identifying the problem and trouble-shooting to a limited extent. The correct diagnosis helps the maintenance personnel to come with the required spare parts and set right the same in a single visit.

Posting of trained hardware engineers at Metro cities to take care of contiguous states is also being contemplated. Maintenance of spare parts and other inventories are also being planned at specified centres. In the case of mini-computer systems installed at regional and head offices, the support is required from the original supplier of equipments and the support cannot be substituted in the near future. Our experience gained so far shows that the problems of hardware and software related to PC-based systems can be overcome by training adequate number of personnel on the first level of maintenance. Third-party maintenance for this area is now becoming popular.

As against this, the problems faced in respect of Unix-based systems are more serious. The requirement of trained personnel to maintain and operate the hardware and software on the Unix systems cannot be easily developed. There is a general scarcity of expertise in this area in the country.

Systems engineers are also required to be trained in the details of the architecture and diagnostics of first-level maintenance for the Unix systems. This would improve the effectiveness of the visits of the representatives of the suppliers of equipments for maintenance and reduce their repeated visits for the same problem.

Alternatives like uninterrupted power supply systems in addition to diesel generator sets have been experimented with. We have also provided software solutions.

### Extending the Computerisation in the Insurance Industry beyond Data Processing

The unfinished tasks of the programme on hand and the need to enlarge its scope to cover areas relating to customer satisfaction is the first priority.

Extension of the programme to the branch offices, issue of policy and other documents, on-line servicing and answering queries, integration of the systems, etc., are some of the vital requirements. These are to be attended to and completed before we raise our computerisation beyond of data processing.

Computer systems no longer remain restricted to the areas of data processing. They have already diversified in the following fields:

(i) Communications and networking,
(ii) Desktop publishing,
(iii) Electronic mail,
(iv) Decision support systems, and
(v) Expert systems.

Future office would be using integrated systems for voice and data communications. The future office would also utilise image processing systems for data storage and retrieval.

Our industry is keenly observing these technological advances and is ready to experiment with these emerging trends in office automation.

### Conclusion

In view of the fact that the benefits derived from this phased computerisation programme are isolated in individual pockets, the full impact would be felt in course of time. This broad base would enable the successful integration of various systems across application-areas at the industry level.

It is also envisaged that the computer literacy and training programmes would help in the implementation of the system in mofussil and remote areas.

# 22

# HEALTH

DR. SUJOY K. GUHA*

## Introduction

Within the human body, there is a complex system of information generation, storage, transfer and processing and this activity is vital for survival and well being. It is, therefore, not surprising that information technology in the world external to the living system has emerged from a study of the living system. But after the initiation, information technology developed with little communication with health sciences. The divide became so wide that information sciences and computers, except for the narrow application area of statistics and epidemiology, came to be considered as esoteric and of little relevance to the health field. But, as often happens in science, the pendulum swung and over the past 15 years there has been a rush to derive all possible benefits from information technology and areas like expert systems have received a special thrust on account of the demands of the health sciences. Today, information technology with computers as the base is an integral part of health research as well as the practical delivery of health care.

## Health Research

In the finding of new knowledge and developing new techniques, the capability of handling large amounts of data arising out of the complexities of the biological system was extremely limited in the past. Extreme simplification and approximations had to be brought in, even to make small problems tractable. Consequently, the results

---

* Centre for Biomedical Engineering, Indian Institute of Technology and All India Institute of Medical Sciences.

were almost trivial. With increasing capabilities of information science a number of problems have been tackled in a more realistic way. The current knowledge of DNA structure and its implications in life processes is to a large extent on account of the computer simulation and modelling which helped investigators to select the appropriate experiments out of the myriads of combinations and permutations possible. Similarly, most of our understanding of the mechanisms underlying control of blood-flow comes from computer models of complex vascular structures. Even in routine tissue histological research, the methodologies of pattern recognition have helped scientists to examine large tissue specimens and to identify subtle comparative variations which would have been missed in the manual methods of examination. Data of this kind has lead to a perspective of tissue formation as well as tissue pathology.

Time-varying dynamics is another feature which has come into biological research as an outcome of the computer power in information handling. There are now numerous examples. One of the aspects on which research is underway here is muscle dynamics. A computer-based dynamic activation modelling of muscle fibre activation not only gives better physiological data of the control functions in muscle contraction but also helps in diagnosis of muscle disorders and in the design of aids for the disabled. The domain of use in the neural field is fast expanding. Various neural analogs can now be analysed, thus bringing new perception of learning and may help in clarifying the roles of two mechanisms that is new pathway formation and chemical changes in the learning process. The integration of all activities within the human body has always been intuitively assumed. Now the interactions can be modelled with powerful information handling systems. It seems likely that many of the present-day views arising out of the research on isolated subsystems of the body will undergo a change. There are indications that some of the concepts projected in the Ayurvedas and forming the base of Ayurvedic medicine may be shown to be a good description of life.

A somewhat unexpected development has come about in the pharmaceutical research. Traditionally, the approach to finding new drugs has been an empirical one with time-consuming and expensive *trial and error* type of animal and at times human trials. Scientists seldom thought of designing a drug for a specific purpose. Molecular design, which requires large computing facility, has changed the situation. It is quite possible to design molecular structures for a particular purpose and then experimentally verify the efficacy. Thus more specific drugs are being marketed and at the same time the approach makes humans less of a 'guinea pig' in the exercise of drug development research.

**Diagnosis**

Probably diagnosis is the largest application area of information technology today and it is in this area that there is already substantial commercial returns. The entire field of *Imaging* as we know it now is an outcome of information processing. X-ray imaging was known from long. Now with computerised tomography, a revolution has come in. Not only the X-ray exposure level has come down making the procedure safe at the same time, the data generated has increased manyfold. Furthermore, the data reconstruction methods enables presentation of the large body of data in a form readily perceived by the physician and even paramedical staff. Hence, now a large part of the work load is being taken over by paramedical staff giving the doctors more time to deal with vital patient management decisions. Three-dimensional data reconstruction brings forth abnormalities which would have been completely missed earlier. Moreover, the precise localisation of the pathology allows for target-specific manipulation. It is no wonder that today imaging of various kinds is the highest financial return area in medical practice.

The unaided human mind has difficulty in judging trends when the time course is long or the amount of data is large. Therefore, for very long diagnosis has been based on data obtained at a point in time. At the early stages of pathology, the data as a point in time is usually normal but subtle changes in the trends have already taken place. Trend analysis methods as well as data superimposition by computation makes the trend apparent and thereby indicate the onset of pathology very early while it is in a correctable stage. In respect of the heart activity, trend analysis has brought out alterations in the rhythm which occur very early in heart disease. A comprehensive risk-index model formulated at the IIT and AIIMS seems to be useful in identifying transition to high-risk domain for individuals while they are still quite asymptomatic. There is also research underway in a different body organ, the teeth, where computer-based graphic data presentation helps to assess trends in dental deformities and suggest means for correction. A software known as DIG-CEPH, short for digital cephalometrics, is now available for wide usage.

In the science and practise of laboratory investigations for diagnosis as, for example, determination of blood chemical constituent levels, there is always the problem of artifacts. Previously, the validity of the result depended entirely on the skill and care taken by the person carrying out the tests. Very often, the results were unreliable because the skill or attention was missing. In any case, it has never been possible to have the ideal conditions. On-line computer analysis methods which can be in-built into clinical laboratory equipment with the help of microprocessors can pinpoint errors and at times compensate for errors, thereby minimising artifacts. In this manner, laboratory data has become very much more reliable and doctors can base their judgement on the data. There are some situations where information processing can help in interpretation of the data, too. Automated electrocardiogram analysis is an example. Computerised ECG analysis is rapidly coming to a stage where the accuracy is close to that of an average physician. As yet the artifact rejection capability does not match that of the human mind. In this respect, too, the past few years has brought significant achievements.

A most exciting development in the clinical horizon is the formulation of Expert Systems to aid in diagnosis. Some of this is already in the domain of practicality. With the large number of poisonous agents now in industrial use, the diagnosis of poisoning in the clinical situation is a nightmare for the doctor. Poison diagnosis software gives valuable assistance. Computer-based data banks for poisons are now being established. In India, a poison diagnosis information base has been developed here and implementation is expected. In general medical practice, psychiatric illnesses are missed as often to the extent of seventy per cent or sometimes even more. This is because the general practitioner seldom has adequate grounding in psychiatry and more so the time available for identifying psychiatric illnesses is limited on account of the hèavy patient load. A computer method has been developed here for assisting the general physician in this respect. The time-requirement is within reason and the diagnostic accuracy for common psychiatric illnesses comes close to that of the trained psychiatrist. The approach can be implemented on a PC and, therefore, could be made available to many general practitioners.

In India, the large number of people residing in rural areas pose a challenge to health care delivery. Effective care can be given only if the medical histories of each individual is recorded and can be easily accessed by the health worker. Clearly, recording the history on registers is not feasible because the health worker has to go from house to house usually on foot. To meet the need here, a small hand-held medical data-recording microprocessor based 'computer' has been designed and tried. This device is soon to go into our national health care programme.

**Therapeutics**

Information technology is gradually making an impact in therapy, too. Especially in management of acute illness where several interventions have to be made in a coordinated manner, computer help is quite effective. An example is the management of a patient in diabetic coma. The rate of infusion of various drugs needs to take into account the present state, past state as well as the characteristics of the individual patient. Programming a computer to simulate the patient dynamics and on-line feeding in the parametric status gives the instant-to-instant optimal infusion rates and an infusion pump can be controlled. The survival rate is far from possible without this help. Similar mode leads to marked improvement in survival in cases of severe burns.

In case of moderate illnesses also, a well-recorded history presented in time-trend form by information management methods aids in arriving at the optimal therapeutic regimen. Drugs which have produced adverse reactions in the particular patient can be avoided and also drugs which in the past have not been effective need no longer be tried. In this manner, the treatment time is reduced. With the large number of drugs now available, each under varied trade names, it is not unusual for a doctor to commit mistakes in prescribing the dosages. A computer data-recording system can alert the physician.

New therapeutic modalities are coming up which depend on computer data processing for effectiveness. The linear accelerator system for treatment of cancer is an example. In fact, the whole exercise of therapy planning using radionucleides in cancer management can best be done with computer analysis. It is significant that in both the cases of linear accelerator as well as radioisotope treatment planning, Indian scientists and engineers have given the 'latest' in the field. It is very essential that proper support be given so that the lead is maintained.

### Rehabilitation

After therapy, the patient is sustained and brought into the mainstream of life by means of rehabilitation medicine. Information technology is vital for successful rehabilitation. A person becoming blind has to be given access to written word and diagrams. A novel concept formulated here allows the blind to 'read' letter-text and diagrams from a computer monitor by presenting the illumination of the screen in tactile form. A system of this kind for classroom teaching will soon be manufactured in India and will be the first of its kind internationally. The spastics have very little motor control and verbal as well as written communication is difficult, if not impossible. The computer can be of help here, too. A system developed here enables a spastic to control a computer by minimal residual motions, such as, touch, blowing or possibly even eye, movement. A special equivalent of a graphic shorthand allows for fairly fast communication, although the movements are small.

For orthopaedically handicapped, there are special computer applications. An analysis of electrical field distribution patterns in the human limb carried out here indicates that paralysed muscles can be stimulated by external electrical sources so as to restore function. Since limb movement involves well-controlled graded activity, the stimulus pattern must also be varied under computer control during movement itself. Where muscle power is normal but limbs have been amputated, the current generation of artificial limbs designed in USA has in-built information processing so that instant-to-instant data regarding the speed of movement, nature of terrain and direction changes are integrated to set the artificial limb dynamics to an optimal level. With these means, even a bilateral above-knee amputee is able to play tennis.

Probably, the most exciting developments are taking place in respect of sensory deficits. Artificial vision with on-line data processing now appears to be a realisable goal within the coming decade or so. Already artificial cochlea is giving to the total deaf a perception of sound as well as pattern variation. Here a new approach of an extra-cochlear prosthesis has been taken up to provide hearing to the deaf without having to implant electrodes, a procedure beset with clinical hazards. Information processing will enable the deaf to recognise sounds.

**Conclusion**

Information technology is an integral part of modern health research and health care. The scope is immense and has far-reaching implications for human welfare. Progress has been less than what the potential justifies because the support is limited. Health is taken as an expenditure and not revenue-earning. There are now indications that realisation is coming that good health itself is a resource and therefore greater attention is being given. Advances in this area can come only if experts from different disciplines join hands and pool their knowledge. It is not necessary that every specialist should work exclusively in this field. The need of the time is that while working in their own disciplines, they spare some time to give the benefit of their special knowledge to advance health sciences.

# 23

# EDUCATION (CLASS Project*)

DR. R.P. GUPTA**

## Introduction

This paper presents CLASS project activities in five sections, viz., application areas, organisational objectives, computer methodology, benefits derived and problems and issues. The application areas confine to the initial planning made before launching the project. The organisational objectives cover the organisational and implementation issues of the project. The computer methodology discusses students' activities and teacher training strategy in the light of the objectives of the project. The last section draws attention on some of the problems faced during the execution of the project and reports on action taken to resolve them.

## Application Areas

Education is preparation for the future and a nation's future prosperity depends on the quality of the present education of those who will become tomorrow's work force. Children, who are today in primary and secondary schools, will be the bearers of this computer-based industrial and social revolution in the country from which no individual household, business or occupation would have been left untouched. The patterns of employment are changing rapidly and today's children will need to be trained for jobs which such tech-

---

* CLASS (Computer aided Literacy and Studies in School) Project.

** CLASS Resource Centre, National Council of Educational Research and Training (NCERT).

nological advances will generate. If these opportunities are to be accepted, an essential part of the spectrum of educational skills will be familiarity with the uses and applications of computers. With this in mind, Department of Electronics, with close cooperation of Ministry of Education, launched the CLASS project, as a pilot project, in the final year of the Sixth Five-Year Plan, i.e., 1984-85 on a national scale. Department of Electronics, (DOE) in collaboration with Ministry of Education constituted a committee consisting of members drawn from Indian Institute of Technology (IIT), National Council of Educational Research and Training (NCERT), Central Board of Secondary Education and Kendriya Vidyalaya Sangathan. The committee was assigned to work out details of the teacher training programme, curriculum for students and the other academic activities proposed to be undertaken.

The committee held its first meeting on February 20, 1984 and decided that NCERT would hold the National Workshop in collaboration with Department of Electronics, Ministry of Education and Culture and Indian Institute of Technology, Delhi for considering the basic framework of the project, drawn up by Department of Electronics and elaborated through discussions between the Ministry of Education and NCERT. The workshop was held on March 26-27, 1984. In this workshop nearly 100 representatives from more than 40 institutions and agencies participated. In addition to these, a nine-member team of computer education experts from U.K. participated in the workshop. The experts shared their experiences in the implementation of the computer literacy programme in the U.K. The workshop deliberated on curricula, evaluation, monitoring and management of the project.

**Organisational Objectives**

The administrative requirements for implementation, maintenance and the monitoring of the project are looked into jointly by the Ministry of Human Resource Development (MHRD) and DOE. For this propose, Government of India constituted two committees, viz., Steering and Implementation committees, which have been reviewing the implementation and providing policy directions from time to time.

Selection of schools under the project is being carried out by MHRD from the list of schools recommended by each State Government and Union Territory Administration. Number of schools covered under the project is decided on yearly basis depending upon the availability of the funds for the project. At present, more than 2500 schools from 25 States and 7 Union Territories are covered under the project.

CMC Ltd. has been shouldering the responsibility of procurement of computer hardware including their distribution and installation. Maintenance of hardware and distribution of software to schools and resource centres are also undertaken by CMC.

NCERT is assigned the responsibility of academic planning which includes curriculum development, teacher training, development/ selection of instructional material and software for the project. NCERT also looks after monitoring of the project, coordination of activities of Resource Centres, and planning of teacher training and other logistic support at the national level.

Implementation and monitoring of the project at the school level is being carried out through 60 resource centres which are located in institutions that possess trained personnel to organise teacher training and also provide directions to schools. Functions of the resource centres as identified are as follows:

- support/consultancy assistance to teachers of selected schools;
- monitoring the implementation of the programme with a view to particularly identifying problems and their solutions;
- training of teachers of schools covered both in the experimental phase and the wider expansion phase;
- maintenance of computers and attending to some urgent replacement of parts for which purpose the resource centres would have to maintain spares;
- interaction among themselves and also with other educational training institutions;
- development of curriculum and teaching strategies;
- software development, both for computer literacy as well as computer assisted instruction/learning; and
- promotional activities with a view to popularise the programme.

For performing the above-listed functions, each resource centre has a coordinator. The coordinator performs the above-listed duties in addition to his normal work in his department. The coordinator is assisted by a full-time project fellow appointed on year-to-year basis at a consolidated salary of Rs 1500 p.m.

Besides the resource centres, in order that there exists a proper co-ordination between the resource centres and State governments and the CLASS Project schools, each State/Union Territory government has named a senior-level officer as the nodal officer for the project who devotes time for the project over and above his normal duties. These nodal officers are responsible to disburse funds for the recurring expenses of the schools which they get from Government of India through NCERT.

**Computer Methodology**

The curriculum development aims at achieving the objectives of the CLASS Project which are given below :

- to provide students with a broad understanding of computers and their use;
- to provide hands-on experience
- to familiarise the students with the range of computer applications in all walks of human activity and the computer's potential use as a controlling and information processing tool; and
- to demystify computers and to develop a degree of ease and familiarity with computers which would be conducive to developing individual creativity in identifying and developing applications relevant to their immediate environment.

To attain the above objectives, the emphasis in this programme is on manipulative skills rather than on teaching the principles of computer science. It is regarded only as a first step in promoting the use of computers in a variety of situations. This strategy was considered to have liberalising influence in schools, by making teachers sensitive to and ultimately capable of utilising the computer for improving the effectiveness of instruction.

Although the number of schools, i.e., 250 included in the first phase was felt to be rather small, considering the large number of senior secondary schools in the country, it was agreed that at the initial stage it would be desirable to make a modest beginning. From that point of view, 250 schools could be regarded as a reasonable number where the experimental phase of the programme could be introduced in a variety of educational situations.

Further, experience gained in this phase were considered of immense importance and would be utilised in the following:

(i) determining the feasibility of expanding the coverage of the programme in the Seventh and subsequent Five-Year Plans;
(ii) identifying problems which would require to be attended to, particularly when the coverage of the programme would be expanded;
(iii) identifying the change that would be required in educational management structures with a view to incorporating the computer as an essential tool for education; and
(vi) identification for the modifications that would require to be made in the implementation strategy.

Two computers and one printer of the following configuration were supplied to each selected school under the project:

| *Item* | *Quantity* |
|---|---|
| BBC microcomputer Model B | 2 |
| Colour monitor 14" | 2 |
| 5 1/4" disc drive | 2 |
| Dot matrix printer | 1 |

Five computers and one printer with two additional back up systems were recommended to be supplied to each resource centre set-up under the project. Later on, one VCR and one television were also supplied to these resource centres.

(a) *Curriculum Structure*

The curriculum is so designed that while the generic or multipurpose software packages could be used for open learning exercises irrespective of the special area of interest of a student, the computer-based learning (CBL) packages can be more profitably used for acquiring both generalisable and specific cognitive abilities in science, social science and mathematics. Generally, a CBL package goes beyond the boundary of a specific topic around which it has been developed. In fact, the packages selected under the project highlight the basic structure of natural and social sciences and in that sense they are independent of the curriculum.

The general philosophy inherent in the CBL packages is to promote learning through parametric representation of observations and problem-solving. The system facility available for generating graphics in different colours and sound enables a child to give shape and form to his ideas and in the process enriches his imagination and creativity. These aspects of personality of a student can hardly be developed through the traditional non-interactive technology and textbooks. However, it is important to note that the computer will not replace the teacher or the laboratory. On the contrary, the computer will enable the teacher to extend his role much beyond his existing instructional materials and practices. It needs to be emphasised that the objective of the project in the pilot phase is not to teach programming. A general acquaintance with the commands used in the different packages may generate interest in programming in some students. However, the machine could be more profitably used for educational computing in a wide area as stated above rather than routine programming. These considerations led to develop the following schedule for the student activities in the project follows:

Phase I

1. WELCOME package
2. MICROPRIMER
3. DART (Turtle graphics package )
4. MATHLAND (another Turtle graphic package)
5. Computer based learning (CBL) packages

Phase II

6. QUEST (database management)
7. SAMHITA (another database package)
8. EDWORD (word processor)
9. NCERT WORD PROCESSOR (another word processor package)
10. Computer based learning (CBL) packages

Phase III

11. EDFAX (teletext emulator)
12. Computer applications
13. Computer-based learning (CBL) packages

14. SPREADLORD (spreadsheet package)
15. Project Work

(b) *Curriculum Methodology*

To execute the programme, it was considered necessary to arrange one-week orientation of faculty of the resource centres so that the three-week teacher training programme (Table 23.1) is executed uniformly in all the resource centres. The teacher training programme laid emphasis on developing sufficient acquaintance with the commands of each package and develop adequate understanding of the application areas of the software. In addition to this, student curriculum execution and procedure of monitoring of the project were given ample importance.

TABLE 23.1: Teacher Training Programme

| Lecture | Total Time (hr.) | Practice | Time |
|---|---|---|---|
| *Orientation*<br>—Objectives of the program<br>—Role of teachers<br>—Tool to work with | 2 | | |
| *Getting Started*<br>—Identify parts of the computer system (monitor, keyboard, diskette, cassette recorder, etc.)<br>—Explain their functions and usages | | Turn the system ON/OFF. Load and run some interactive programmes. | 4 |
| *Curriculum*<br>—Outline the student curriculum | 2 | | |
| *Word Processing*<br>—Creating, editing, formating and printing documents. Familiarity with concepts of inserting, deleting and formating of text EDWORD/NCERT WORD PROCESSOR | 6 | 1. Create and print a letter.<br>2. Create and print a report.<br>3. Prepare and print a table. | 12 |

*Contd.*

| Lecture | Total Time (hr) | Practice | Time |
|---|---|---|---|
| *Logo/Graphics* | | | |
| — Basic commands, defining and manipulating objects, sequencing of operations building complex graphics patterns from simpler forms (DART AND MATHLAND) | 4 | Exercises of increasing sophistication to develop skills in man-machine interaction | 12 |
| CBL Packages on various subjects — Rekha, ABO Blood Groups, 4 semiconductors, interference titration, question banking, etc. | | Demonstration of these packages according to interest of teachers | 10 |
| *Database/Spreadsheet* | | | |
| — Explain in very simple terms the concept and use of a database, queries report generation; demonstrate use of spreadsheet Packages in planning and simulation (QUEST, SPREADLORD and SAMHITA) | 6 | 1. Create a simple database for school library design and use queries for their databases<br>2. Develop and use spread-sheet for a business problem | 12 |
| *Basic Programming* | | | |
| — Introduce simple elements of BASIC | 4 | Write 2 or 3 simple programs in BASIC | 8 |
| *Computer Organisation* | | | |
| — Identify and explain elementary parts of a computer system. Retake these to the classroom situation | 4 | Go through a package that simulates certain aspects of computer operation. | 6 |
| *History of Computers* | | | |
| — CAI Packages to be used in schools packages | 1 | Run some of the CAI | 4 |

*Contd.*

| Lecture | Total Time (hr.) | Practice | Time |
|---|---|---|---|
| *Maintenance*<br>—Putting the system together<br>—Basic trouble shooting<br>—Interfacing with maintenance organisation | 2 | Go through the exercise of bringing system up from a disconnected state. Execute simple diagnostic programs. | 4 |
| *Monitoring and evaluation*<br>—Evaluation plan<br>—What is to be monitored<br>—Interfacing with Resource Centre. | 2 | —Examples:<br>—Developing a small database for a problem drawn from classroom/personal context<br>—Some problem solving in physics, mathematics finance, etc. using spreadsheet.<br>—Time tabling for the school. | 8 |
| | Total 40 | | 80 |

TABLE 23.2: Advance Level Teachers Training Programme

| Lecture-cum-demonstration | Time (hr.) | Tropic | Practice session Time (hr.) |
|---|---|---|---|
| *Orientation*<br>—Objectives of the programme<br>—Role of teachers<br>—Tools to work with | 1 | — | — |
| *History of Computers*<br>—Computers of different generation<br>—Computers jargons (bits, bytes, etc.) | 2 | — | — |

*Contd.*

| Lecture-cum-demonstration | Time (hr.) | Tropic | Practice session Time (hr.) |
|---|---|---|---|
| *Relevant Information About BBC Micro/SCL Unicorn* | | | |
| — Connectors at the rear of the micro<br>— Connectors underneath the micro<br>— Memory usage in the micro<br>— About RAM and ROM | 1 | — | 2 |
| *Curriculum* | | | |
| — Computing and programming in BASIC | 1 | Step-by step programming in BASIC | |
| *Structured Programming* | | | |
| — Introduction<br>— Counting FOR/NEXT/STEP<br>— Iteration REPEAT/UNTIL<br>— Functions and procedures<br>— Conditions IF/THEN/ELSE<br>— Subroutines | 4 | Designing and making use of structured programming | 10 |
| *Top Down Analysis* | | | |
| — Breaking into simple problems<br>— Making flowcharts | 2 | Solving problems by topdown analysis | 2 |
| *Disc Filing System and Utilities* | 3 | | 4 |
| — * FORM40, *VERIFY<br>— * SAVE, *LOAD, *RUN, *DUMP<br>— * SPOOL, *EXEC,*LIST<br>— * COPY, *ENABLE, *BACKUP<br>— * BUILD, *TYPE<br>— * ACCESS<br>— * COMPACT,*DRIVE, *DIR,*LIB<br>— * CAT, *INFO<br>— * TITLE, *RENAME, *OPT and<br>— * HELP | | Using different commands to DFS for<br>— Preparing disc for use<br>— Saving and loading blocks of memory<br>— Converting program files to text files and vice-versa, dumping program files to the screen<br>— Various ways of copying files and discs | |

*Contd.*

| Lecture-cum-demonstration | Time (hr.) | Practice session Tropic | Time (hr.) |
|---|---|---|---|
| | | – Creating text files from keyboard and dumping them to the screen or printer<br>– Protecting files from damage<br>– Examining free space on the disc<br>– Changing drives, directories and libraries<br>– Getting information about the files on a disc<br>– General utilities | |
| *Graphic Programming Modes 0,1,2,4,5*<br>– Colour facilities<br>– Line drawing and colour filling<br>– Palette changes<br>– Redefining characters<br>– Windowing<br>– Simple animation | 2 | Computer operations for graphics designs | 6 |
| *Sound Facilities* | 1 | | 2 |
| – Define envelopes<br>– Using more than one sound channels simultaneously | | Developing music/tuning on computer<br>Creating different softs of sound | |
| *Teletext Programming Mode 7* | 2 | | 6 |
| – Incorporating teletext control codes in a program<br>– Designing teletext screens | | Operating mode 7 for teletext | |
| *File Handling* | 4 | | 10 |
| – Principles of filing<br>– Serial files<br>– Filing commands | | Making different type of files and their operations | |

*Contd.*

| Lecture-cum-demonstration | Time (hr.) | Tropic | Practice session Time (hr.) |
|---|---|---|---|
| – OPENUP, PRINT, INPUT/ CLOSE<br>– Writing a structured program to create, read and update serial files.<br>– Random access files<br>– Writing a structured program to create, read and update a random access file | | | |
| *Programming Some Keys* | 2 | | 2 |
| – Programming function keys and cursor control keys.<br>– Controlling printer within a program | | | |
| *Useful *FX Calls* | 1 | | 2 |
| – Disabling ESCAPE, cursor editing and other keys<br>– Clearing the key-board buffer<br>– Altering flash and auto-repeat rate | | Making use of different *FX calls | |
| *Machine code* | | | |
| – Introduction to machine code | 1 | | |
| *Basic Assembler* | 2 | | |
| – Introduction | | | |

The curriculum model to be used by students under CLASS project in schools will be the same as those used in the teacher training programe. As in the teacher training programme, the methodologies followed in the school will be lecture-cum-demonstration, group-discussions, practice-sessions, briefing and debriefing sessions for each module, project work and independent self-study. The teacher will not be required to deliver formal lectures on computers. Resource centres will be responsible for deputing resource persons to the school for delivering such lectures.

Approximately, 60 periods may be needed for individual/group hands-on experience for an effective utilisation of the software. The activities under the course may be divided into three phases spread over 30 weeks in the first year. Each student, in a group of 3 or 4, should get an access to the machine at least once a week for one full period. The full period of the CLASS will be considered as two consecutive school periods on similar lines as is followed for physics/chemistry/biology practical classes. The pilot school is expected to rearrange its time-table for the students selected from a given class in such a way that these students, who opt for the computer literacy, are exempted from attending the periods meant for socially useful productive work, etc. The computer literacy teacher should also be able to conduct demonstration lessons but freeing them from other workload. The participating students should be encouraged to take innovative/creative projects with the computer.

Any rigid criterion for selecting the students for the course on the basis of academic achievements alone should be avoided. In fact, a mixed ability group will enable the teacher and the school to assess the role of the microcomputers in enhancing self-learning ability of students with widely different competencies.

(c) *Operational Design*

One demonstration lecture may be initially adequate for introducing a package for practice by a group of students. The demonstration sessions may be used mainly for introducing the commands for software to be used in practice session. Demonstration sessions may also be organised by the school to create a general awareness among students and teachers of the school who are not participants of the first course.

Group discussions and briefing sessions may be organised around the following topics:

(i) Getting to know the hardware:
   (a) Monitor, printer, keyboard, tape and disc drive,
   (b) Taking care of the equipment: DO'S and DONT'S;

(ii) Introduction to the commands of DART and MATHLAND;
(iii) (a) Introduction to the commands of QUEST and SAMHITA,

(b) Guidelines for the identification of the subjects and fields for preparing the databases;

(iv) Introduction to the commands of EDWORD and NCERT WORD PROCESSOR and the features of editing of texts;

(v) Introduction to the commands and scope of EDFAX;

(vi) Computer applications with special reference to India (to be arranged by the resource centres);

(vii) Showing of video films on computer organisation and computer applications; and

(viii) CBL packages to be interspersed over the total course duration, highlighting the interacting nature of learning concepts with applications.

The general features of CBL packages have significant instructional value. The teacher need not unduly emphasise the importance of such packages from the point of view of teaching academic subjects as such. It is desirable that students are enabled to participate in practice sessions outside school hours. This may be either in the working days or on sundays/holidays.

Occasionally, the school may hold lecture-cum-demonstration for students from neighbouring schools and also for parents and members of the neighbouring community for creating general awareness about computers and their educational, social and technological implications in a wider sense.

**Benefits Derived**

As discussed in the preceding section, the pilot project was to provide valuable information required for the planning and expansion of the coverage of the computer literacy and use of computers in teaching and learning. The pilot phase of the project did attain its objectives. It provided varieties of information necessary for implementing the computer education throughout the country in a planned way. Government of India has made use of the same for preparing the plan for introduction of computer education in the country.

Each school covered under the CLASS Project is expected to train about 40 to 60 students during one year in computer awareness and three teachers from each of the selected schools are exposed to use computers in teaching and learning. The students undertake activities as per student curriculum. How far the activities have been effective was studied by Space Application Centre (SAC) at the instance of Department of Electronics. The evaluation study had the following two main objectives:

- to determine the extent to which the goals of demystification were met; and
- to evaluate various aspects of the CLASS pilot project so as to provide guidelines for proposed expansion plan.

The evaluation study revealed that:

- Demystification objective of the project was partially achieved: 15.6 per cent of the students were de-mystified as per the criterion developed for the evaluation;
- The project was implemented best in Kendriya Vidyalaya followed by State Government schools and aided/private schools in that order; and
- In most of the schools "welcome package" was the most widely used package. All the packages supplied were not used in most of the schools.

This was the position during the initial stage of the pilot phase. Now, teachers' competence in use of computers is being enhanced by conducting advance-level training programmes so as to enable teachers in the software development and evaluation of the same.

In addition to this, the period of the implementation of the pilot phase encouraged the development of educational software in the country. Besides NCERT and CMC Ltd., several software houses in private sector have initiated work in this area. As a result, 14 such packages have been developed and supplied to schools so far. The CMC has developed key boards and EPROMs in 11 regional languages, namely, Assamese, Bengali, Gujarati, Hindi, Kannada, Malayalam, Marathi, Oriya, Punjabi, Tamil and Telugu.

Further, the CLASS project has paved the way for experimentations in the area of computer-aided instruction/learning. Several studies are being conducted by teachers/students of M.Ed/M.Phil to study the efficacy of computer-aided instruction and integrating the educational software to the conventional teaching/learning activities. Besides these studies, teachers trained under the CLASS Project use software in their teaching as and when required. The project as such has created the environment for launching computer aided instruction/teaching in a systematic way.

**Problems and Issues**

As already indicated, the pilot project was launched by using hardware and software imported from U.K. Because of the late arrival of the hardware and software, the programme could be implemented late during 1984-85. The pilot project was then extended up to 1985-86 by adding another 500 schools. Consequently, training on another 1500 teachers was organised. The programme was similarly extended by adding 500 more schools during 1986-87 and 700 schools during 1987-88.

The evaluation entrusted to the Space Application Centre was completed in June, 1986. This evaluation report was helpful in indicating the weaknesses of the project at the initial stage. In addition to this, the regular monitoring system, field visits to schools, experiences of nodal officers and coordinators of the resource centres were the main sources in identifying the problems. Some important ones are discussed below:

(a) Most teachers are deputed to the training without ascertaining the proper attitude they have towards learning this new technology. Some criteria need to be developed for selection of teachers to be trained;
(b) During teachers training, three teachers are allotted one computer for hands-on experience which remains insufficient. As they have to implement the CLASS activities independently, they need more hands-on experience to attain full understanding of the activities. To ensure adequate hands-on experience to teachers during training, each resource centre has to have more systems and other physical facilities;
(c) The teachers are likely to forget what they have learnt because of non-availability of computers in schools immediately after training programme is over. There is, therefore, a need to install the computers in schools before the training is over and reduce the gap between the training and commencement of the teaching in schools. There was a long time-lag in the sanction and installation of systems in the schools;
(d) There are more than 16 distinct languages in the country

through which instruction is imparted to children. The coursewares so far available are in English language. English language posed a problem for both students and teachers in a large number of schools. This problem was tackled in a limited way. Regional language-script generating software on BBC/SCL UNICORN microcomputer has been attempted by CMC Ltd. The problem of using regional language still remain unresolved, because the RAM of the BBC/SCL UNICORN microcomputer, i.e., 32 K, is grossly insufficient to develop software in regional languages;

(e) The software packages supplied to schools are mostly in the subjects of science and mathematics, whereas the policy has been to train teachers from all the disciplines. Therefore, there is a greater need to develop software packages in languages, social sciences, commerce, etc., so that the teachers from these disciplines are also attracted and motivated to adopt the technology in their routine teaching;

(f) Most of the resource centres, set-up under the project, are from the engineering colleges and universities having Computer science as one of the department. Experience has shown the diminishing interest of some resource centres and weak support provided by them to the schools under the project. This is because these institutions are not in direct touch with schools and are heavily loaded with their own teaching and research activities. These Centres can be more fruitfully utilised for organising advanced level training programmes and for development of educational softwares;

(g) The average age of a teacher coming for training is 40+ years. Naturally, the methodology to be adopted for the training has to be different than training the younger teachers. Experience shows that activity-based training material seems to be more suitable; and

(h) The size of the monitor available for the training is 14". This screen size is too small for a group of 30 teachers to be trained at a time. Though wide-screen television, available at the resource centre, was used for demonstration of the programmes, but the resolution became poor.

The above-listed problems were discussed in the meetings of the Coordinators, Implementation and Executive Committees. Some of the problems were resolved and it was felt that an overall review of the programme became imperative for proper directions and planned expansion.

## Conclusion

In conclusion, it may be mentioned that an expert committee was constituted in 1986 under the Chairmanship of the Education Secretary to recommend the programme objectives, the hardware and software choice and management system for implementation of CLASS Programme. The committee worked in two expert groups to study the listed issues and submit their recommendations to the committee. One of the group headed by Dr. Utpal K. Banerjee worked on software and logistic support aspects whereas the other group headed by Prof. H.V. Sahasrabudhe worked on the hardware aspects. These reports have made a series of recommendations for the implementation of the programme, keeping in view the provisions in the NPE, the experience gained in implementation of the programme since 1984-85 and the evaluation of the programme done by the Space Application Centre, Ahmedabad. Keeping this in view, a scheme for regular implementation of the programme has been prepared. The salient features of this scheme are as follows:

- Coverage of all senior secondary schools by 1990;
- Supply of at least five systems in each school to ensure coverage of all students at +2 level in the school. Transaction of the programme at + 2 level and integration of the programme with the curriculum; and
- Resource support to schools through regional and district level resource centres.

This programme would have some significant improvements over the pilot phase. Some of these are as follows:

(a) Literacy would remain the immediate objective of the programme gradually leading to educational computing for students, individually and in groups;

(b) Instead of 2 microcomputers, 5 to 8 microcomputers would be given to a school to allow all the students at +2 stage in the school to be covered by the programme;

(c) A large programme of software generation would be taken up with emphasis on Indian languages; and
(d) Resource centre support would be provided to schools at district and regional levels.

# 24

# TELECOMMUNICATIONS

GOPAL DASS*

## Introduction

Information is data (for example, raw facts or observations) that have been put into a meaningful and useful context. This gives information value for specific persons and meets their particular information needs. Thus, information is a basic resource which is very essential for individuals and organisations to survive and succeed in society. In developing countries of the so-called third world, people live in an agro-industrial society composed primarily of farmers and industrial workers. In India, 80 per cent of its 850 million people live in villages. They earn their living mainly through agriculture. Only a small percentage of total workforce in the country is engaged in industrial activities.

In the developed and advanced countries of the West and the far East, people no longer live in an agriculture society or an industrial society. Instead, they are living in an information society where a majority of workforce consists of *knowledge workers* engaged in service occupations. They spend most of their work time creating, using, processing and distributing information. The category of knowledge workers includes executives, managers, professionals, such as, engineers, scientists, accountants and teachers; and office staff, such as, secretaries and clerks. All these people earn their living using information technology to create, manage and distribute information resources which are then used to help them manage the human, material, financial and other resources involved in their work responsibilities. Information thus is the most valuable commodity for knowledge workers, their organisation and for the society. Their so-

---

* Mahanagar Telephone Nigam Limited (MTNL).

cial, cultural and economic progress is heavily dependent on efficient management of information resources.

**Information as a Resource**

The organisations are faced with continual changes in environment and scope of their operations. Information is an important and valuable organisational resource that must be properly and efficiently managed for an organisation to survive and succeed. The organisation rely on information technology and information system to provide appropriate information for their efficient operations and effective management. This information must not only be reasonably accurate, it must also be timely. If accurate and timely information is not provided to the end-users, the organisation will suffer strategic disadvantage against its competitors. An information system and the adopted information technology which do not properly support an organisation to achieve its strategic objectives, corporate goals and do not lead to its overall progress may seriously damage that organisation's prospects for survival and success in a competitive business environment. Thus information technology plays a vital role in our everyday life and in our society, dependent as we are on the effective use and efficient management of information resources.

The field of information technology is constantly changing and expanding, as dramatic technological development and research findings in human behaviour are opening new possibilities. Sociology, psychology and economics are the disciplines that contribute towards behavioural aspects while science, engineering, computers and telecommunications contribute towards technological aspect of the information system technology. The convergence of information processing technology (computers) and telecommunications has revolutionised the whole concept of information management. The direction of the computer technology today is toward increased connectivity where any computer in an organisation can communicate with any other one. This connectivity is provided by telecommunication links. A major challenge for the information society is to manage its information resources to benefit all its members. This, for example, means using information technology for efficient management of limited material and energy resources.

**Telecommunications**

Telecommunication is the sending of information in any form (e.g., voice, data, text and images) from one place to another using electronic or optical media. Transmission of voice is achieved through telephone network. Data communications is the term that describes the transmission and receiving of data over telecommunication links between one or more computer systems and a variety of input/output terminals. All forms of modern telecommunications now rely heavily on computers and computerised devices. However, in most developing countries including India, the telecommunications even today overwhelmingly mean voice transmission, i.e., telephone. Data communications is relatively at a very low key.

The importance of telecommunications as an essential infrastructure for the social and economic development of the society was realised in this country only in mid-eighties when it was declared as an essential infrastructure and included in the core sector. Since then the scenario has been changing rather rapidly. Today, the telecommunications is playing more important role in support of rural development, maintenance of law and order, defending the frontiers and in economic development of the country. The corporate sector depends heavily on telecommunications for vital support in its operations, management and strategic objectives.

The telecommunications have become an integral part of all human activities may be social, cultural or economic. It is impossible to conceive of a modern society without efficient and reliable telecommunication services. Today, the level of development of a society is measured by the status of telecommunications services. Worldwide, there are about 560 million telephones for the total population of 5.6 billion. The advanced countries of the West and the far East with less than 15 per cent of total world population have more than 80 per cent of the total number of telephones in the world.

While in the USA the telephone density is over 500 telephones per one thousand population, in India there are less than 6 telephones per 1000 population. Within the country also, there is wide disparity in telephone density among various States and also, between urban and rural sectors. Metro cities of Delhi, Bombay, Calcutta and Madras, and also other major cities like Ahmedabad, Bangalore and Hyderabad have telephone densities ranging from 40 to 50 telephones per 1000 population. The whole of rural India have less than one telephone per 1000 population. This is clearly reflected in economic disparities between advanced and developing countries and also between rural and urban areas of a developing country like India. Modern, reliable and efficient telecommunication facilities are essential for efficient operation and management of corporate activities. Also, to accelerate growth of rural economy and to improve standard of living of rural masses, it is essential to extend and expand telecommunications facilities in rural areas. The role, present status and the trend of telecommunications in the two primary application areas, i.e., corporate sector and rural development is discussed here.

## Applications of Telecommunications

### (A) *Telecommunication in the Corporate Sector*

To survive and succeed in a competitive environment, an organisation big or small depends heavily on information resources for its operations, management and strategic objectives. The telecommunications requirement of big organisations are no longer limited to office telephone system or long-distance calling arrangement over telephone such as trunk calls and STD/ISD calls. They also need more complex computer-based telecommunication facilities, such as, data communication, text and messaging communications, image transmission and information retrieval, etc.

A list of specific applications of telecommunications for organised sector, grouped into major categories such as voice communications, data communications etc., is indicated below:

| | |
|---|---|
| (i) Voice Communications | Standard telephone service,<br>Audio conferencing systems,<br>Voice mail systems,<br>Office intercommunication systems. |
| (ii) Data Communications | Online transaction processing,<br>Inquiry/response systems,<br>Hardware/software sharing,<br>File and database transfer. |
| (iii) Text and messaging Communications | Teletype systems (e.g. telex)<br>Electronic mail. |

| | |
|---|---|
| (iv) Image transmission | Facsimile,<br>Image processing,<br>Video conferencing. |
| (v) Information retrieval | Bibliographic search services,<br>Videotex. |

In India, services and systems other than voice communications, teletype (telex), data communications (very limited extent) and facsimile are yet to be developed and popularised.

Some of the important business objectives of telecommunications applications and the benefit derived therefrom are summarised in Table 24.1.

TABLE 24.1: Examples of Business Objectives of Telecommunications Applications

| Objectives | Examples | Benefits |
|---|---|---|
| Obtaining basic information about business transactions from remote locations. | Customer orders from remote sales offices to corporate data centre for order processing, billing and inventory control. | Reduces delay in filling orders and issue of bills, allows quick updation of inventory. |
| Supply of requested information to remote locations. | Credit authorisation at the point of sale by inquiry/response of corporate data base. | Credit inquiries and response can be made on-line, thereby reducing delay in credit authorisation. |
| Reduction in cost of traditional means of communications. | Audio and/or video teleconferencing. | Reduces business trips. |
| Strategic support | Electronic data interchange to and from suppliers and customers. | Fast and convenient service locks in customers and suppliers. |

Telecommunications is not only a method of electronic communications, but it is a means of organisational connectivity, a competitive weapon and a vital investment in technology for effective management of information resources. Managers can use telecommunications as follows:

(a) To compress the time taken to accomplish business activities;
(b) To expand firm's business activities geographically; and
(c) To restructure traditional business relationship with customers, suppliers, creditors, competitors and other organisations.

Managers can use telecommunications to improve operational efficiency, functional effectiveness and innovations. However, these values will not happen without clear objective and careful planning. The top management should have clear vision as to what extent the organisation's business strategy and business goals depend on the use of telecommunications. A business that chooses to remain a small local enterprise has less need of information technology than an organisation that has countrywide or worldwide operations.

(B) *Telecommunications for Rural Development*

India lives in villages where 80 per cent people of the country's total population reside. We can call our country developed and modern in its true sense only when our villages are also developed. The rural India is characterised by very low economic activity. In the absence of any kind of industrial activity, there is total dependence on agriculture. This is an example of typical agriculture society composed primarily of agriculture workers. The per capita income and standard of living are low. Lack of communications facilities has been one of the main reasons for the present poor condition of rural India. The gravity can be understood from the fact that there are only about 5 telephones per 10,000 of rural populace and only some 30,000 gram panchayats out of a total of 230,000 have telephone facility in the form of a long distance public telephone (LDPT). Further, these LDPTs are the only means of voice communication to nearby towns or revenue headquarters which the rural folks need to communicate for their day-to-day need. They suffer from poor reliability and low operational efficiency as a majority of these LDPTs are provided on conventional overhead telephone lines. These telephone lines are often snapped by climatic conditions, moving vehicles and also quite frequently by vandalism. The repairs are expensive and time-consuming. High investment, low rate of return and non-availability of indigenous technology and modern equipment had been the reasons for very slow progress. However, lately the importance of reliable telephone facilities in rural development has been recognised and following mile-stones have been set:

- Modernise rural telecommunications through use of electronic RAXs and multi access radio relay systems progressively;
- Cover all the remaining 200,000 gram panchayats by LDPTs by the end of the Eighth Plan.

As each LDPT costs on an average Rs. 150,000 an investment of over Rs. 3,000 crores will be required for this purpose.

**Impact of Information Technology on Telecommunications**

Development of digital techniques and convergence of information processing and telecommunications technologies have revolutionised the field of information management world wide. Telecommunications processors, such as, modems, multiplexers, concentrators, front end-processors, EPABXs and other similar devices perform a variety of support functions between the terminals and computers in a telecommunications network. The electronic exchanges are all central processor controlled switches. Also computers have simplified many vital support and control functions of operations and management of telecommunications services. Some of the important support functions which have been computerised are as follows:

- Billing functions for both telephone and telex,
- Online registration of new demand and management of commercial waiting list,
- Directory information service including updation of data,
- Customer information,
- Personal information and pay bills,
- Inventory controls,
- Project management and control,
- Fault repairs and Cable records.

Many new services have become technically feasible due to introduction of computers in the field of telecommunications. Some such services are indicated below:

- Voice mail,
- Electronic mail,
- Cellular radio mobile telephone system,
- Videotex,
- Interactive data communications systems, etc.

Department of Telecommunication under its scheme named "Communications Information System for Department of Telecom." (CIS DOT) has adopted an integrated computerisation plan for efficient management of information and various support functions, such as, finance and accounts, fault repair service, commercial waiting list, cable records, directory information, customer information, personal information, project monitoring and inventory control, etc.

**Areas of Weakness in Telecommunications Services**

- Long waiting time for new telephones;
- Large percentage of old and obsolete equipment in the network;
- Inadequate funding resulting slow development and modernisation;
- Low call completion rate for local and NSD calls;
- Heavy dependence on operator assisted services;
- High fault rate due to vulnerable outdoor plant;
- Frequent damage of U/G cable plants due to vandalism; and
- High initial as well as operational cost of rural telephone service and negligible return on the investment rendering rural network financially non-viable. The services are accordingly provided as social obligation and the programme suffers cuts whenever there are more pressing demands on resources.

**Thrust Areas for Over-all Improvement in Performance**

- Accelerated development to improve availability, accessibility and connectivity;
- Modernised network to improve reliability and operational efficiency;
- Improved quality of service and enhanced customer satisfaction;
- Improved productivity and reduced operational costs;

- Value-added and phone, plus services, such as, voice mail, electronic mail, videotex and audio/video conferencing for better exploitation of the network;
- New services, such as, radio pageing, cellular mobile radio telephones and RABN, etc.;
- Liberalised indigenous production of telecommunication equipment to meet growing demand; and
- Extended reliable and efficient telephone facility to all villages in the country using digital switches and radio relay system.

**Perspective Plan for Telecommunications Services during 1990s**

(a) *Improved availability*

| | Present | 1995 | 2000 AD |
|---|---|---|---|
| Switching Capacity (million lines) | 5.9 | 11.2 | 23.2 |
| Direct Exchange Lines (million lines) | 5.1 | 9.8 | 20.0 |
| Telephone Density (number of telephones per 1000 population) | 6.0 | 10.9 | 20.5 |

(b) *Improved accessibility*

- An LDPT in each of the remaining 200,000 gram panchayats by the year 1995 and cover all the 576,000 villages by the year 2000 AD;
- Increased urban PCOs to 8 lakhs by the year 2000 AD;
- Provision of telephone facility on highways (every 10 Kms) as public utility service.

(c) *Improved connectivity by the year 2000 AD*:

- Increased TAX lines to 449800 by 1995 and to 929800 by 2000 AD. (Presently 186800);
- All telephones in the country to have access to NSD.

(d) *Development of Business Network*

– Integrated services digital network with facilities, such as, voice, telex, data, facsimile, interactive computer communications, audio and video conferencing with national as well as international accessibility.

(e) *Expansion of Telex Network*:

| | |
|---|---|
| Present | 51670 |
| Year 1995 | 87270 |
| Year 2000 AD | 142270 |

(f) *Long Distance Transmission Media (thousand route KMs)*:

| | Present | 1995 | 2000 AD |
|---|---|---|---|
| Microwave systems | 36.0 | 50.3 | 53.3 |
| UHF systems | 16.5 | 49.0 | 87.5 |
| Optical fibre systems | 7.1 | 23.4 | 31.5 |
| Coaxial systems | 27.9 | 31.5 | |

(g) *Messaging Facility*:

– Modernised telegraph services through use of large size store and forward message switching systems (SFMS)

(h) *Improvement in Quality of Service*:

– Reduced telephone faults to a level of 5 faults per 100 stations per month.
– Improved call completion rate to 60 per cent in live traffic.

(i) *Improved Productivity (staff/telephone ratio)*:

| | |
|---|---|
| Present | 72 per 1000 telephones |
| 1995 | 47 per 1000 telephones |
| 2000 AD | 25 per 1000 telephones |

**Conclusion**

Efficient management of information resources is vital for economic development of the society. We can afford to neglect development of modern telecommunications services only if we choose to remain economically backward perpetually. The services are financially viable in the urban and most of the semi-urban areas. However, rural areas are to be covered as an essential social obligation. These objectives will be achieved by increasing investment, developing indigenous technology, liberalisation of equipment production and effective management of services. Availability will be improved to wipe out current waiting list and to provide telephones on demand. Accessibility and connectivity will also be improved to make the network flexible and more efficient to meet customer needs. To make optimum use of the network, new and value-added services, such as, voice mail, electronic mail, videotex, audio/video conferencing and cellular radio mobile telephone services, etc., will be introduced.

# 25

# INTELLIGENT BUILDING

DEEPIKA SAXENA*

## Introduction

Increased efficiency at reduced cost is the dream of all executives in the world of commerce and industry. The explosion of modern technology has provided the capability to achieve these results. The development of microprocessor-based control and monitoring technology has opened the door to building automation and energy cost control. Automation allows us to increase control and accuracy of systems. Increased speed allows reduced response time for critical systems and allows complex tasks to be completed virtually instantaneously. In addition, automated systems reduce life-cycle costs through reduced maintenance and energy costs.

Increased safety and security is a benefit of the reduced number of components in the systems and for a system that is self-monitoring. Automated systems also afford increased flexibility in building designs because changes are often easily implemented by simple software modification or simple addition of remote sensors. Building managers also have the appropriate information at their fingertips to help correctly manage the vast array of functions under their control.

Integrating different building functions, e.g., air-conditioning, fire detection and protection, energy management, lighting control, security, access control, etc., into a single automated system can result in such benefits as lower initial costs, lower operating costs and improved safety. The cost of an integrated system that requires a single central computer and communications network can be considerably less than the cost for a number of stand alone systems.

---

* CMC Limited.

**Components of an Intelligent Building**

Controls, communications and information processing are the three key components of the electronic infrastructure of a building. This paper gives a brief overview of how computer technology makes it possible to control the operations of building equipment and machinery, the consumption of energy and the comfort level for personnel, and to provide greater levels of safety and protection, by integrating the control, communication and information processing.

Broadly, an intelligent building has the following components:

(a) *Controls*

- Heating, Ventilation and air-conditioning
- Fire management
- Energy management and conservation
- Lighting control
- Parking management
- Equipment maintenance
- Cable management
- Elevator control

(b) *Communications*

- EPABX
- FAX
- Private networks
- Public networks
- Voice and data communications

(c) *Information Processing*

- Office automation
- Documentation and library management
- Conference management
- Guest house management
- Restaurant management

(i) *Heating, Ventilation and Air Conditioning*

The computer monitors the operation of the air-conditioning system to indicate how satisfactorily it is operating, provide status indication for set points and run times, and provide a wealth of information in report form, thus helping to provide better management.

(ii) *Fire Management*

Fire management involves fire protection, detection, alarm and suppression. When a fire is reported, the computerised fire management system performs a series of actions like taking control of air handling system to stop the fire from spreading, dialing fire department, returning the elevators to ground floor, sounding an alert and directing the occupants towards safe exits, and so on.

Such a response is possible if fire detection and alarm system is integrated with other systems, e.g., audio communication system, security system, HVAC, equipment monitoring, elevator control, etc. Various sensors send inputs to a central computer which controls all these facilities, and performs the above-mentioned functions to minimise loss of life and property.

(iii) *Energy Management*

An automated system for energy management provides optimised control, such as, load shedding, amplitude control and other controls that provide substantial energy savings.

(iv) *Lighting Control System*

The lighting control system controls the artificial lighting automatically if the natural light entering the building is sufficient to maintain the required lighting level. The system also controls the lighting that has been left ON, because the area is unoccupied/out of normal working hours, etc. The control is carried out in several different ways, viz.,

- on a preset time;
- on a preset day;
- after a preset period;

– by a preset value of daylight;
– by a manual override;
– on availability of natural light;
– on detection of occupancy;
– on detection of movement.

The system reads the daylight availability outside the building through suitable sensors and controls artificial lighting based on the light level.

(v) *Access Control*

For security reasons, access to various zones may be restricted to authorised persons only. In addition, there may be a need to allow persons in zones at specified timings only. For example, service personnel in the building may be allowed only in the mornings only.

Access control is achieved by means of installing card readers at the doors where access is to be restricted. Each person has a card that has to be inserted in the card reader, which conveys the information encoded on the card to the computer, that, in turn, checks whether the person is authorised entry in that zone at that particular time. The system provides an additional advantage of recording attendance and may also be used to keep track of a person's movement.

(vi) *Security System*

The main purpose of the security system is to protect the area from intrusion. The system detects intrusion and sends the corresponding signal to the central computer. The central computer then analyses the signal to initiate appropriate alarms at different places or to take other predetermined action. Different types of sensors are used for perimeter surveillance and peripheral surveillance. Close circuit televisions are used in crowded areas to monitor the area for any suspicious movements.

(vii) *Parking Management*

In addition to installing card readers at entrances and exits to allow only authorised persons to use the parking area, occupants may be directed to their slots using a sophisticated computerised parking management system. Moreover, the visitors can be charged by the time for which they used the parking area.

(viii) *Equipment Monitoring*

The system monitors different equipment in a building and keeps a record of the maintenance schedule of each of the equipment like computers, photocopiers, telexes, etc. The system keeps track of the number of switch ON/OFFs, running hours and certain health parameters of the equipment and informs the operator well in advance the maintenance programme of a particular equipment, thus increasing efficiency and higher availability of the equipment.

(ix) *Cable Management*

The modern buildings contain a maze of unidentified, often abandoned cable. This occurs because new cable is added and old cable is left to remain because of high cost of cable removal.

Cable management is the understanding of the need to plan requirements, design flexibly and manage communications for the life of the facilities. Computer-aided design techniques are of a great advantage for an efficient cable management system.

(x) *Communications*

The purpose of communication system is to increase the efficiency of communication between people. The communication system can provide facilities for both voice and data communication. The provision of electronics private automatic branch exchange (EPABX) enables a range of functionality and flexibility, not usually available on small PABX, like detailed billing information, teleconferencing, etc.

With the provision of a central computing facility, accessing data residing on any computer connected to a national or international network can be made possible. This helps in accessing the information faster. This reduces the costly delay and many times the loss of information. The components used are visual display units, printers, facsimile, telex, etc.

(xi) *Information Processing*

With the advent of low-cost computers in business data processing, information processing has become very attractive. It increases the efficiency of common shared facilities, the exchange of business data processing capabilities and office automation.

(xii) *Office Automation*

With the advance of technology, paperless office concept is becoming popular. Executives have a computer terminal on their tables. They communicate within office with the help of electronic mail. Electronic notice boards allow any person to see the latest notices while sitting on his seat. The total correspondence is maintained in files on the computer media. Electronic filing not only helps in fast retrieval and better organisation of documents, but also saves the effort of maintaining important documents. Electronic diary helps executives to maintain the list of appointments and things to do today on the computer. The computer reminds the executives of the actions to be taken. Desk-Top Publishing (DTP) is an additional facility to format and print the documents into more presentable fashion. Word processing is an essential facility without which no office can survive these days.

(xiii) *Library Management*

The functions of a library include acquisition of books, journals, binding, serialising, cataloging and maintaining record of books issued. Further, it involves collecting fine from members for delaying return of books beyond the due date. In a big library, these functions are difficult to handle using a manual system. Computerised library management system helps the library officials provide these functions efficiently, thus providing a better service to the members.

(xiv) *Restaurant Management*

Restaurant management system involves various services like online display of menu, servicing to orders received through computer, billing, inventory management, staff management and so on. A computerised system allows occupants to see the menu and place order from their terminals, thus saving time.

(xv) *Guest House Management*

Guest house management system involves reservation of rooms by guests, billing (room charges, laundry, meals, telephone and so on). A computerised guest house management system can serve both the guests as well as guest house staff.

(xvi) *Conference Management*

In most of the office complexes these days, conferences and cultural functions are a routine affair. For efficient management of these conferences, attended by VIPs, a computersed conference management system is necessary. Computerised conference management system assists both the organisers and the delegates for better management of a conference.

**Conclusion**

The integration of the various facilities explained above makes a building intelligent. The I.Q. of an intelligent building depends on the number of facilities the building contains.

An intelligent building is a powerful dynamic tool which can be used to create the personal, environmental and technological conditions necessary for building occupants to maximise their individual capabilities, productivity and satisfaction. Energy conservation and sharing various facilities/costs are two most important benefits of intelligent buildings that make them critical in national interest.

It is important to realise that the role of an intelligent building is to be a servant of human needs, and not be a example of technology for technology's sake.

# 26

# ROAD (DTC Experience)

R.K. JAIN*

## Introduction

One of the main objectives of the Delhi Transport Corporation (DTC) is to provide an efficient economic, adequate, well co-ordinated, punctual and safe transport service to the commuters of Union Territory of Delhi and its neighbouring states. Comfortable transport facility to the people adds to enrich the economy of the nation as it affects the efficiency to a great extent. Unhealthy transportation adversely affects the commuters as it creates hindrance to make them reach their working destinations. Thus it is evidenced that regularity, punctuality and accuracy in all respects are the main objectives of the organisation by way of creating atmosphere favourable to increase the efficiency of the working people.

## Application Areas

To achieve the above objectives DTC has a fleet of around 4400 buses and around 42,000 employees, scattered in 36 depots all over Delhi, including two central workshops, one stores and purchase department, one printing press, one statistical and planning department, etc.

To maintain the above fleet, DTC has a central inventory system to procure spare parts according to the consumption and future demand. The workshops are maintaining and servicing these buses.

---

* Delhi Transport Corporation (DTC).

Depots, from where buses are actually operated and maintained, are the key places of the transport organisation. In each of the depot, the following jobs are being undertaken: –

1. Financial accounting system
2. Online ticket accounting system
3. Buses and crew scheduling system
4. Vehicle performance system
5. Depot store system
6. Personnel management system.

At corporate level, the main sensitive, sophisticated and complicated job is the pay roll system, which is to be prepared every month for around 42,000 employees and is not a small task. Personnel management system, i.e., the recruitment, selection, placement, efficiency and the maintenance of various types of personnel records of each employee, is another important task.

To analyse the working efficiency of the organisation, the statistics is to be maintained properly and based on that planning must be done to improve the efficiency in future and the future requirements. The performance of each vehicle, i.e., the history of each bus is also to be maintained just after its procurement, e.g. time-to-time servicing details, parts replaced, kms. covered, etc.

**Computer-Based Methodology**

Computer-based methodology is adopted to ensure accuracy economy, efficiency and skilled manpower in order that DTC is able to achieve its goal in the fields mentioned hereunder:

(i) *Central Inventory System*

This system has been divided into two modules, viz.:

(i) Kardex section, and
(ii) Purchase orders and indents.

It has been planned to make the inventory control system on-line by taking issues and receipts through terminals and generating indents through computer and pursuing the purchase orders through the system.

(ii) *Depot Management System*

This has been divided into seven modules, which are as follows alongwith brief descriptions:

(a) *Online Ticket Accounting System:* This module covers the entire procedure in terms of revenue collection and accounting through sale of tickets, generation of way-bill and its analysis, cash collection and control generation of up-to-date reports of statutory, statistical and decision support values. The module also covers important aspects such as route-wise, trip-wise performance and the like.

(b) *Bus and Crew Scheduling System:* This module covers scheduling of bus and crew, route vs. crew operation, time-keeping and control, route planning and frequency changes, etc. Periodical reports on control and management information will be generated as part of the process.

(c) *Depot Stores System:* A system of stores accounting and inventory control for the depot form the basis of the design of this module. This module covers stock receipt from central stores, stock, issues, consumption, local purchases, inventory reporting, indenting, etc.

(d) *Vehicle Maintenance System:* This module as a part of the Depot management system covers aspects on vehicle maintenance requirement, docking, inspection requirement based on the performance of vehicle captured and monitored through well-defined maintenance and control procedures.

(e) *Financial Accounting System:* This module of financial management courses of collection and accounting of revenue from sale of tickets, bills accounting, and depot pay-roll supported by adequate and up-to-date reporting features.

(f) *Personnel Management System:* The design of this module will be based on the use of database of depot personnel for generation of information on functional and administrative activities of the depot.

(g) *Management Information System:* Each of the modules will be designed based on integration approach so as to offer viable, timely and meaningful management in the process of effective decision.

(iii) *Pay roll system*

(iv) *Personnel management system at corporate level*
(v) *Statistical and planning system at corporate level*
(vi) *Vehicle performance system at corporate level.*

**Benefits Derived**

Information outcome of computerisation is more economic in comparison to the information received through manpower as it may have certain lapses. Besides, this technology makes an easy access to achieve inter-organisational information and ensures its accuracy and finality with its correctness and wholesomeness expeditiously. Possibility of transmitting its benefits to the common man in its dexterity, depthness and clarity together with intelligibility is latent in it. The technology is extremely useful in collecting integrated informations with exact and accurate data from the multiple units of an extensive organisation like DTC.

**Conclusion**

The benefits of computer-based methodology are innumerable but certain problems are to be encountered in adoption of its application. Financial stringency needs to be eliminated from its way as the procedure is quite expensive. Non-availability of software persons in the organisation is another complication to be solved. Arrangement of software persons from outside agencies for developing software involves immense finance. Besides, the organisation is lacking in skilled manpower. Steps are being taken to solve this problem of scarcity by arranging in-house computer training of the officers and officials of the corporation through outside agencies.

# 27

# RAILWAYS
# (Passenger Reservation)

R.D. SAKLANI*

## Introduction

These are several areas of public services which have direct interface with the common man, where the existing systems need to and can be improved significantly with the help of the developments that have taken place in the field of information technology. Examples are the telephone services, electricity billing, banking system, tourist information services; railway enquiries, reservation systems, ticketing, parcels and freight bookings; land revenue records, etc. Inefficient functioning of these services and the resultant harassment suffered by the users have been responsible for tarnishing the image of the government. In recent years, the government has been emphasising the need to improve efficiency and quality of service specially in areas of mass public contact. Immense possibilities exist to do so. For instance, take the land record system that touches the lives of over half of our population. Recently, a few resourceful and enterprising district administrations have shown that with the help of just a PC, land record system can be made very efficient. The impact on the poor farmer has been immense. He need not, any longer, accept the inevitability of out-dated, wrong and missing records. Imagine the impact it would have on almost every second Indian if the entire land-holding records in the country were to be computerised.

In this paper, however, we are concerned with the relevance to common man of information technology in the railway. One of the

---

* Ministry of Railways

most impressive applications of computers in the country in recent times, has been the computerisation of passenger reservation system on Indian railways. The Railways passenger reservation system is an area of mass public interaction and immense visibility. Every day over 2 lakh passengers queue up at various reservation offices all over the country for their rail journey requirements. The image of railways depends in a large way upon the quality of service they receive at the reservation counters. A vast number of 2 lakh customers include farm and factory labour, construction workers, taxi drivers, milkmen, small and medium businessmen, office workers, etc., from all over the country including from the remotest areas of Uttar Pradesh, Bihar, Assam, Andhra Pradesh, Tamil Nadu, etc. They have derived immense benefits from the railways computerised reservation systems. The result is a boost to the image of Indian Railways.

Through this paper, we share the fascinating experience of the Indian Railways in using information technology effectively in the area of passenger reservation system.

**Organisational Objectives**

Over 300,000 berths and seats are available each day on over 800 inter-city and long distance mail and express trains run on the Indian Railways. Taking into account cancellations and waiting-list transactions, these account for over 400,000 reservation transactions per day. Further, with the introduction of new trains each year, the reservation work-load has been growing at an average rate of 6 per cent per annum and is expected to reach about 600,000 transactions per day by 1995. While this work-load was comparatively small upto the late 60s, it could be managed fairly efficiently through manual process. By mid-70s, however, it became almost impossible to handle the ever increasing work-load in this way. Procedures became cumbersome, records far too voluminous and services totally inefficient. The manual system involved each reservation clerk exclusively handling reservations of a particular class of travel on two to three trains. With the reservations being available two months in advance, each clerk was required to handle 10 to 12 voluminous registers where in he entered particulars of each transaction, viz., name of each passenger with age and sex (to protect against transfer of reserved tickets which on Indian Railways is considered illegal), particulars of reservation requested, viz., origin and destination of journey, details of train, class of travel date of journey as well as particulars of tickets issued alongwith status of reservation, i.e., whether the accommodation asked for has been blocked and, if so, the coach as well as berth/seat number allotted, or else, wait list position. Preparation of passenger manifests was tedious and prone to errors. Reservation offices were situated at different locations in the city for different trains and classes. The service was slow and inefficient, and often meant waiting on queues for as much as 3 to 4 hours in uncomfortable environment. The customers were dissatisfied, while staff grumbled and management was perplexed. Efforts to rationalise the system had failed to have significant impact on quality of service. It was realised that the only solution lay in computerising the reservation system. Accordingly, a pilot project was taken up to computerise the reservation system at Delhi in 1984.

It is significant to note that the project involved an area which was appropriate for computerisation and where computerisation had become unavoidable.

The overall organisational objectives of the project were:

- Improve efficiency of the passenger reservation service by reducing the time taken for service at reservation counters;
- Reduce waiting time on queues;
- Universalise the service so that each counter serves all trains, all classes and for all types of transactions;
- Improve staff productivity;
- Improve working environment of staff;
- Eliminate or reduce scope for manipulation of records that existed in the manual system; and
- Improve overall image of railways that was being tarnished by large number of complaints in public, press and Parliament.

## Computer-Based Methodology

Applications of the nature of computerised railway passenger reservation system belong to the category of on-line transaction processing, viz., OLTP systems. Even within this classification, passenger reservation system is a mission-critical application. Some of the important attributes of such applications are:

(i) A significant segment of the working of the organisation (Indian Railways in this case) is critically dependent on the functioning of the computer system;
(ii) A very large number of users (reservation clerks) execute similar pre-defined activities;
(iii) Up-time efficiency required is of the order of 99 per cent and above; and
(iv) Recovery from any failure should be completed with absolutely no loss of data.

For the passenger reservation system, it was necessary to choose a combination of hardware and software solutions to adequately support the above attributes. At the same time, the system also needed to be totally reliable.

*Software Options*

Decision was required to be taken whether the software should be developed indigenously or should a suitable reservation package operating on railways abroad (such as Europe or USA) be adopted and modified to suit Indian Railways requirements. There did not appear to be enough proven experience within the country in developing software for such sensitive on-line, real-time application. Indian Airlines had adopted the USAS software which had been in use on a number of airlines abroad. Should the Indian Railways also follow similar approach? The experience of customers on Indian Airlines had not been particularly happy and thereby, had immense teething troubles that lasted for too long.

After considerable deliberations, it was concluded that the requirements of Indian Railways as distinct from those of Indian Airlines were significantly different from those of the railway systems abroad and, as such, any of the existing software packages would not suit. Besides, even if it was decided to modify an already developed system, the effort involved in modification itself was likely to be enormous and result far less satisfying. Then why should one not pick up the challenge? Some degree of national pride was also involved.

Discussions with DOE led to the conclusion that while no indigenous manufacturer was in a position to offer the type of hardware required for the system, sufficient potential was available with indigenous software houses, such as CMC, to undertake developmental work of this nature. Accordingly, it was decided that while the hardware platform would be imported, software development would be undertaken by CMC.

The classical approach was adopted by beginning with analysis of users requirement.

### *Analysis of User Requirements*

In this phase the users requirements were drawn up in full details. Data-flow diagrams were used for capturing and understanding the exact user needs. Railways deputed a team of officers and staff to sit with experts from CMC to work out the detailed requirement analysis. Procedures not covered by rules were studied and actual field practices were analysed. Such practices were incorporated in the users requirements.

### *Hardware Choice*

CMC already had some Digital Equipment Corporation's VAX machines and their software personnel had considerable experience of working on these machines. They felt that it was possible to develop the required software on VAX machines which offered the necessary system calls required for developing a reliable and sturdy package. The DEC hardware also had well-established reputation for providing excellent up-time. DEC had also announced that they would be supporting cluster architecture in near future, thereby providing for excellent modular growth. This capability of architecture allowing growth of additional CPU power and expansion of database without having to replace the old machines was considered very desirable. A decision was accordingly taken to develop the package on VAX machines.

Initially, for the pilot project, two VAX 750s were installed along with 8 disk drives of 256 MB capacity each. However, after successful implementation of the pilot project, it was seen that these machines could support only half the workload of Delhi. The hardware was accordingly enhanced to two VAX 8600s machines each with 32 MB main memory along with 32 disk drives (RA 81, each with 456 MB memory).

*Software Development*

The software was developed using conventional time-sharing option as was the recommended practice for VAX machines. Extensive recovery procedure were built into the system for transaction recovery, media recovery and recovery from system failures. Backups of database were taken every night to ensure quick recovery from all types of failures. Software was written in Fortran 77, using available features of the language. The code was re-entrant and shared between all users and important static data was kept in the memory in the form of global sections. Response-time achieved was of the order of 3 to 5 secs. Ticket printing took 10-15 secs. Software written followed modular structure. Development was done within a time-frame of 15 months and software released for testing in October 1985. The software was further refined in the next phase of the project and complete version was released in 1987.

*Further Developments*

There have been a number of developments since implementation of Phase II of the project at Delhi. The system has been extended to cover as many as 22 cities as of now, including metropolitan cities such as Bombay, Calcutta and Madras. Stand-alone computer systems have been installed at Delhi, Calcutta, Bombay and Madras with VAX machines of 8000 and 6000 series. At Secunderabad, as an experimental effort, an indigenously manufactured hardware, viz., Medha 930-31 computer system manufactured by ECIL has been used and the software developed for VAX machines has been ported on to the Medha hardware. Computer systems at Delhi, Bombay, Calcutta and Madras have been enhanced to link more cities and take up the additional reservation load. Major software changes have been carried out to incorporate functionalities, such as, those required for handling remote locations. The current software is version 3 of the original software incorporating requirements of remote locations.

*Future Trend*

Further work is in progress both for expansion of terminal network as also for inter-linking the five stand-alone systems. The software is being re-engineered to conform to the relatively more efficient client-server architecture. This approach would give benefits in terms of incorporating indigenously manufactured machines as clients, thereby using imported resources only for back-end database access. A distributed environment is being developed whereby various components of software will reside in different pieces of hardware including PC-based terminals. Networking is proposed to be achieved with transaction routing to the appropriate database-server and presenting a picture of national passenger reservation system to the operation. Work is in progress to set-up a PRS network. This project is likely to be completed in three years' time. An important feature of the network would be that it will be a heterogeneous network involving VAX nodes as well as the Medha node at Secunderabad. Software is being developed in-house for this purpose.

The hardware configuration for Delhi is shown in Fig. 27.1 and the Passenger reservation network on Indian Railways in Fig. 27.2.

**Challenges of Technology Change**

*Problems involved with Change*

Railway passenger reservation system has always been under the constant gaze of the public, politicians and the press. Be it long queues, excessive service-time or any failure of the service, instant and vociferous criticism is lodged through public complaints, criticism on the floor of Parliament and in the press. As such, railway management cannot afford any failure that could throw the services in disarray, say, through total shut-down of the system due to faults, upsetting allocation of accommodation, calculation of fares and refunds, etc. With a very large number of customers, it is required to serve (over 60,000 passengers per day in Delhi alone), any of these situations could even result in a serious law and order situation at the reservation offices, at railway platforms and in trains, resulting in disruption of train services. As such, it is a very sensitive service. Computerisation of the system, on the other hand, meant introduction of entirely a new technology and the consequent changes involved in work-culture and work-environment. The challenges posed and problems faced related to designing the system to suit the staff who operate the system, to get them to accept the changes, to get the management to agree to change and modify the age-old rules and regulations that were being treated as sacrosanct, to allay the fears and apprehensions of staff and management, in short, to design and install a computerised system that would work efficiently.

Resistance to change is in-born in human nature. Change is resisted primarily because persons involved suffer from fear of the unknown, fear of the new skills and techniques they will be required to acquire and fear of losing their professional competence. They may not understand need and implications of the proposed change and honestly believe that the change does not make sense for the organisation. Resistance to change is not limited to the workers alone. It extends to all managerial levels. It threatens to destroy power equations. There is in-born resistance to change: age-old, well-tried out rules and regulations. The resistance to change becomes much stronger if it is also accompanied by a total transformation in the technology of operation as was the case in changing over from manual to computerised reservation system.

### *Fear and Apprehensions of Management and Staff*

The railways reservation system is quite complex. There are six types of train services, seven classes of travel, over 70 kinds of concessions, 25 different types of reservation quotas, and 66 types of coaches with different accommodation layouts; complicated rules with regard to break-journey, modification of earlier transactions, refunds on unused tickets, fare structure, routing of journeys, allocation of accommodation, etc.

Management and staff were not sure whether, with such complex system, appropriate software could be designed to take into account the plethora of rules and regulations that govern reservation procedures. They were also not sure whether such a system could function efficiently keeping in view the massive volumes of reservation workload handled and sensitivity of the service to consequences of failure. Typically, a single train passenger manifest contains 1000 to 1200 names. Failure of any part of the system, viz., CPU, disk drives, printers, communications system, software, air-conditioning or power supply could result in total chaos. It was to be an on-line real-time system and, with the queue lengths of as much as 20 to 25 at the counters during peak-demand hours, break-down of service even for a few minutes could not be tolerated. It could result in stampede and serious break-down of law and order.

*Pilot Project Approach*

Keeping the above considerations in view, it was decided as a first step to take up a pilot project in Delhi where users' specification were defined, hardware configured, software developed, appropriate infrastructure, viz., power, air-conditioning, communication links, etc., provided and the system installed and tested in live environment. The system developed needed to be accepted by all concerned, viz., management, operators and the customers before it could be extended. As things went, the pilot project in Delhi succeeded beyond expectation and resulted in acceptance of the system and made it possible for very quick extension thereafter to cover Bombay, Calcutta and Madras within one year.

It is quite conceivable that a perfect system could be designed with appropriate hardware and software, communication and infrastructure support and yet such a system would not work if it was not acceptable to the operators at the counters, to their supervisors and, to the accounts functionaries for whom the century-old tested accounting system was sacrosanct. For instance, in the old system for every pair of stations and for each class of accommodation there was a separate series of pre-printed card-tickets. Accountability at the ticket-dispensing end was based on concept of 'opening' and 'closing' numbers of printed card-tickets from which the number of tickets sold in each shift by each reservation clerk was derived. Similarly, at the destination end, collected tickets were arranged in series.

Effectiveness of ticket-checking at the terminal station was measured by the percentage of missing tickets from gate collections. Any collected ticket found out of series would signify a fraud committed either at the ticket-selling end or else it was counterfeit ticket. Both possibilities needed immediate investigation and action. The new system, on the other hand, does away with the 'series' concept altogether. The new concept was a major departure from existing practice and involved fundamental changes in accounting system. The new system had to be sold to and accepted by management and staff. Similar changes had to be made in several other rules and regulations.

*Participation of Staff and Management in the Project*

To ensure that the system developed met the requirements fully, was workable and efficient and that it was acceptable to the staff as well as the management, the project team included representatives of management at all levels, supervisors, operators and their supporting staff and CMC who were responsible for designing the system and developing the software. Care was also taken to include only those who were positive in their approach, displayed some degree of originality and creativity and, above all, were non-controversial, and whose opinion was expected to be respected by others. The team so constituted ensured that the changes required were tailored to the needs of, and acceptable to, management and staff and hastened the process of their formal acceptance. The user requirements were defined by the active participation of this entire group. If one most important action responsible for the success of this project was to be identified, it was the thoroughness with which the user requirements have been specified. This document of 250 pages is the result of the effort put in by 30 experts including 15 from the railways and 15 from CMC working for 14 to 15 hours a day for a period of 15 months. The thoroughness of this document is responsible for the smooth implementation during the pilot project and the speed with which the system was subsequently extended to cover the metropolitan cities.

*Change in Technology, Demystifying the Computer Mystique*

The project involved major change in technology, work environment and work culture. Computers were already being used in India, but not for such an application, to be operated by staff at this level. The Indian Airlines experience with computerised reservation system was not very relevant as it handled far less transactions, served altogether a different class of clientage and the counter operators were recruited with higher education background and selection criteria. No one believed that staff of the calibre that man the railways' reservation counters could at all learn to operate the computer terminals efficiently. The railway staff itself was highly apprehensive. Computers were something highly technical and beyond them to understand and much less to operate upon. It was decided to involve a few from amongst them in the development of the project at all stages. It helped in demystifying the computer phenomena. As a result of their participation in the project, the staff representative on the project team gradually learnt and understood that the CPU was a brain that did calculations and contained in its memory rules and regulations of the game just as the counter clerk does; the disk drives are registers which are being accessed either to read the records they contain or to write particulars of fresh reservation transactions. Thus, the mystery of computer disappeared!

When the system had been developed, it was subjected to intensive testing by the selected staff. They enjoyed the pleasure of detecting bugs. This gave them a feel of the system. They saw the bugs removed and the system gradually improve to ultimately give them the confidence that it was working according to the logic they themselves applied in the manual system. Further, unlike the manual system, when it made no errors. they spread their confidence among their colleagues and this resulted in widespread acceptance of the computerised system by the entire reservation staff. They were also convinced that the system provided enough security features and no one could enter transactions against their accounts. Their accountability for cash transactions was secure. They developed faith in the system.

### *The Man-Machine Interface*

The reservation system in Delhi under the manual system was manned by about 600 staff. Almost a third of these comprised those promoted from lowest grades for which formal education of even primary level had not earlier been essential qualification for entry into service. The system, for it to succeed, had to be designed keeping even such of the staff in view. In this context, the man-machine interface was of crucial importance.

The software developed is menu-driven. Great care has been taken to design the screens in such a manner that once an operator has gone through the first familiarity session on the training terminal, he can learn by himself. There are prompts at each field-level to assist the operator in learning process, to guide him to the next step he is required to take, to flash his mistakes and educate him, to provide him information and to build his confidence. As a result, the operators required just 6 days' training, at the end of which they are trained enough to operate on the reservation counters and a month's time thereafter, to reach the level of their own top efficiency. On an average, it takes 2-1/2 minutes to serve one customer. This includes time taken for money transactions. Individual performance of serving 200 customers over a six-hour period is quite common. The highly user-friendly system has been responsible for doubling staff productivity.

*Training and the Trainers*

By the time the system was developed, tested and proved, there was already available a nucleus of staff, which had been part of the project-team and had picked up enough expertise and proficiency as well as confidence in using the system. A few from among them were selected and trained to become trainers. Thus, the staff learnt to operate on the system from their own colleagues. This increased staff involvement in the project.

*Fear of Job Security*

Indian Railways have entered into an agreement with recognised unions that there will be no retrenchment of serving employees due to computerisation; surplus staff will be redeployed without transferring them to another station; and even with the reduction of cadre strength, promotional prospects of existing staff will be preserved. The commitment given to the staff has been fully honoured. The staff and the unions have supported the computerisation of passenger reservation system whole-heartedly.

*Learning Curve*

Staff were motivated to speed up learning process. A system of monetary awards along with issue of commendatory letters was introduced. Performance of each staff was monitored each day and individual performances were displayed on notice-boards giving names of those who had excelled as well as those who had not done well. This helped in improving the performance of the staff, their productivity having almost doubled.

*Capability to tolerate fault — Built in Redundancy against Failures*

Computerised passenger reservation system is an on-line real-time application involving public service on a massive scale not matched elsewhere. During peak periods on peak-days, there could be as many as one thousand customers queued in front of the counters as at the New Delhi reservation complex. Even 15 minutes' shut-down of the service, for whatever reasons, cannot be tolerated. Solution lay in providing fault-tolerant system with built-in total redundancy. This has been done. The three CPUs at Delhi, for instance, operate under cluster-mode and access common database. Similar redundancy has been provided with respect to disk drives, communication channels, air-conditioning, power-supply, etc. The DESU power supply is tapped from two different sources. In case of total power failure, diesel generating sets switch on automatically. For the intervening period, battery back-up takes over. The entire power-supply is through the UPS and floating battery bank. The UPS itself has a back-up. Similarly the entire communication system has built-in redundancy. Route as well as media-diversity has been provided with a combination of cable and UHF system (and even satellite for link-up with Bombay, Calcutta, etc.). All possible care has been taken to ensure a service free of break-downs. The experience with the system during the last five years has been very satisfactory.

**Benefits Derived**

Computerisation of passenger reservation system on the railways has been a rare success story. The project has succeeded beyond expectation. It has been widely approved and acclaimed by the passengers, in press and Parliament, and even by the Western media. It has helped in boosting the image of Indian Railways. It has increased confidence within the country to handle sensitive on-line real-time applications indigenously.

Some of the benefits derived from the system by the passengers, the railway reservation staff and the railway management are summed up below:

(a) *Benefits derived by Customers*

- The system provides universalised service, viz., reservations (as well as cancellations and modifications) by any train and any class are now available at any of the reservation counters anywhere including the satellite reservation offices;
- The system provides efficient service with shorter queues and substantial reduction in waiting time;

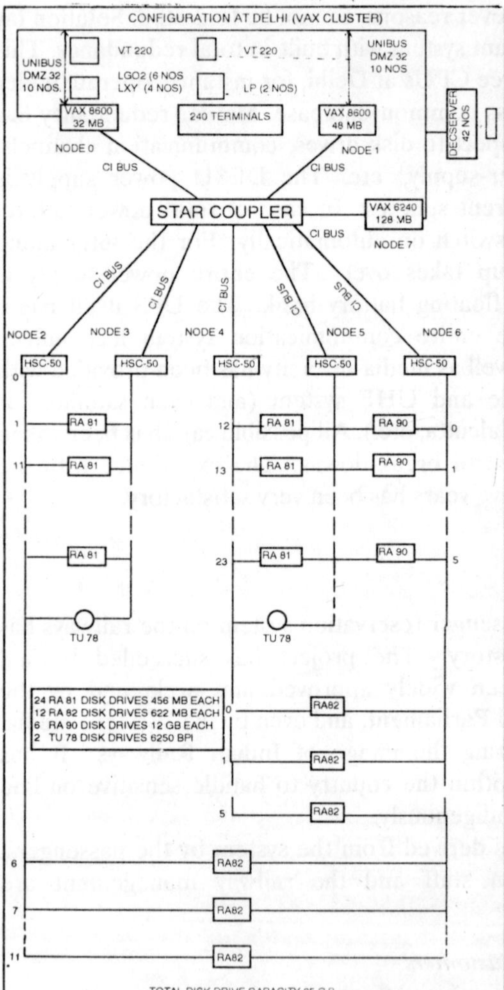


**FIG. 27.1: Passanger Reservations on Indian Railways: The Computer Solution**

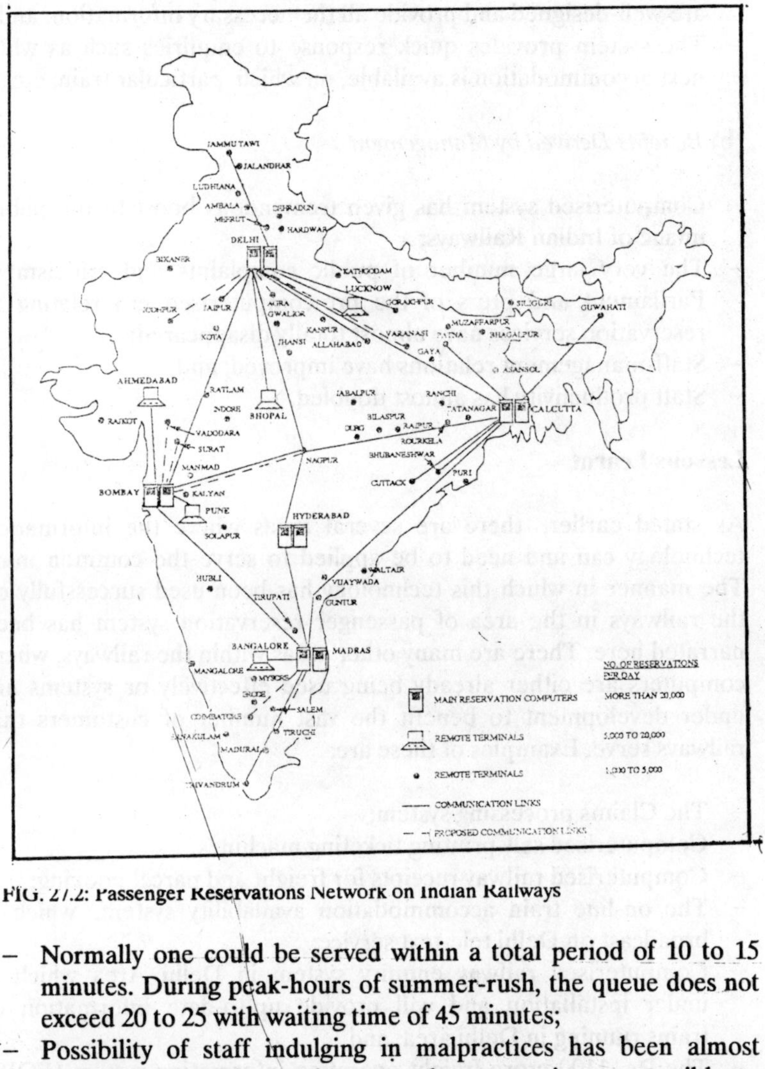


FIG. 27.2: Passenger Reservations Network on Indian Railways

- Normally one could be served within a total period of 10 to 15 minutes. During peak-hours of summer-rush, the queue does not exceed 20 to 25 with waiting time of 45 minutes;
- Possibility of staff indulging in malpractices has been almost totally eliminated. In the manual system, it was possible to manipulate records;
- With air-conditioning, improved layout and effectively designed direction-boards, the environment at reservation offices has improved substantially. Standing in a queue to get a train reservation is no longer an ordeal and often a pleasant experience;

- Tickets and passenger manifests are printed neatly and legibly, are well-designed and provide all the necessary information; and
- The system provides quick response to enquiries such as when next accommodation is available, on which particular train, etc.

(b) *Benefits Derived by Management*

- Computerised system has given tremendous boost to the public image of Indian Railways;
- The very large number of public complaints and criticism in Parliament and press of the pre-computerised era relating to reservation services have almost totally disappeared;
- Staff-management relations have improved; and
- Staff productivity has almost doubled.

**Lessons Learnt**

As stated earlier, there are several areas where the information technology can and need to be applied to serve the common man. The manner in which this technology has been used successfully on the railways in the area of passenger reservation system has been narrated here. There are many other areas within the railways, where computers are either already being used effectively or systems are under development to benefit the vast number of customers that railways serve. Examples of these are:

- The Claims processing system;
- Computerised self-printing ticketing machines;
- Computerised railway receipts for freight and parcel booking;
- The on-line train accommodation availability system, which is broadcast on Delhi tele-text service;
- Computerised railway enquiry system in Delhi Area which is under installation and will provide up-to-date information of trains running in Delhi area; and
- The Rs. 1100 crore freight operation information system (FOIS) which is under implementation.

However, whatever be the area of application, there is need to handle the projects with great care.

**Conclusion**

Implementing the project on computerisation of passenger reservation system (PRS) has been a unique and rich experience. It involved major technological change and more importantly acceptance of the change by the management and staff responsible for its operation. Some lessons learnt in the process are recorded below:

- Resistance to change is in-born in human nature. Change becomes much more difficult to implement in case it also simultaneously involves substantial technological changes. Skillful handling, with genuine concern for feelings and limitations of those involved in changes, is required. The system should be designed basically for those who will operate it, with their participation, catering for their needs;
- Major changes required a dedicated team to handle these. These cannot be handled effectively if entrusted as an addition to existing responsibilities. A dedicated team needs to be set up to perceive the project in its entirety and complexities — technical, financial, human, etc. — and plan careful implementation of change;
- Once appropriate personnel have been identified for a project, they should be involved from conception of the project to its implementation. The personnel in the team should not be changed in between. That the PRS project succeeded is due to the fact that personnel on the project were not changed in between. The success was theirs, not to be shared. If the project had failed, there were no scapegoats. Responsibilities, both for success and failure, were theirs. Their commitment to the project was total;
- Another important factor in the successful implementation of change is the quality of leadership. The choice of the team-leader is crucial. He should be dedicated to the project and possess capabilities of leadership to carry the team, management and staff with him. Flexibility to blend the technical and human needs to meet the organisation's objectives is an essential quality.
- Technological changes often demand fundamental changes in age-old rules and regulations. Management has to display courage and flexibiiity to accept and implement these changes. Financial powers should match the responsibilities entrusted at

each level. Conventional constraints need to be relaxed. New situations cannot be handled with old and rusted tools;

- Area chosen for change should be appropriate. There should be dissatisfaction with the existing system;
- Fears and apprehensions of staff and management should be identified and adequate care taken to remove these;
- The system should preferably be developed, designed, tested and proved in a limited area, as a pilot project, and perfected before extending it to the entire system;
- Management and staff should participate in development and implementation of the project. Rules and regulations framed for a different environment must be modified to meet new situations;
- New technology should be explained to the staff in a language they understand;
- Interaction between man and machine is crucial to success. The interface should be carefully designed keeping in mind interest of the men who will be required to operate it;
- Training staff to work with new technology and unfamiliar environment needs planning with great care. It helps to pick up trainers from amongst the staff and train them as trainers;
- Confidence must be built amongst the staff that their job, status and career-prospects are not threatened; and
- The system should be fault-tolerant with enough built-in redundancy against failures.

# 28

# AIRLINES

S.K. BOSE*

## Introduction

Indian Airlines started office-automation with the usage of unit record machine in the early 60's, with the objective to improve efficiency. A further step in automation began with the installation of a second generation machine in the late 60's, with the idea of developing conventional data processing applications. A centralised advance seat reservation system started functioning on IBM 1401 system in the year 1971.

Indian Airlines further strengthened the automation infrastructure with the installation of UNISYS 1100/80 (2*2) system (supporting batch, transaction and interactive-mode in both multiprogramming and multiprocessing environments with vast networking capabilities) at Delhi in the year 1983. The large-scale computerisation started in the year 1985 with the implementation of transaction-based on-line reservation system on the UNISYS 1100/80 (2*2) system. Since then, the UNISYS 1100/80 (2*2) system has been augmented to make it UNISYS 1100/80 (4*4) system, to keep pace with the fast-growing computing requirements of Software and data communication and in line with airlines' latest fly-by-wire fleet acquisition with an ultimate objective to achieve greater efficiency and better passenger services. The computerisation plans of Indian Airlines were carried out on linear approach keeping in view the available computing resources. The implementation of on-line transaction-based systems were carried out on the UNISYS 1100/80 system, whereas the batch applications were implemented on the super-mini HORIZON III. The computerised departure control sys-

---

* Indian Airlines.

tem was implemented on ORG-80/ORG-40 machine using the concept of decentralised distributed data processing.

### Current Hardware Configuration

Indian Airlines currently operates the following machines:

- Mainframe system;
  The UNISYS 1100/80 (4*4) configuration includes 4 CPUs with built-in back-up systems, a main storage capacity of 4 MB, mass-storage capacity of 24.8 GB on 40 disc drives, 7 tape drives, two 900 lpm printers and two general communication sub-systems;
- Super mini system;
  Two HORIZON III systems, with each having main storage capacity of 4MB, mass storage capacity of 1.5 GB. on 3 winchester drives, two streamer tape drives and one line printer;
- Check-in system;
  A pair of ORG-80 systems each at Delhi, Bombay, Calcutta and Madras and ORG-40 systems at Hyderabad and Bangalore for computerised check-in.

### Computerised Application Areas

These comprise the following:

- Passenger services system;
  (a) *Passenger reservations* : The system implemented in 1985 now handles about 30,000 reservations a day and works 24 hours a day with a success rate of 99 per cent. The system provides a wide range of functionality designed to meet domestic and international airlines reservation requirements. It supports a range of functions such as schedule and availability information, passenger name record creation, seat inventory control and modification with total security of the stored data;
  (b) *Message switching system* : The system provides a store-and-forward message-switching capability. The system is also used to process the reservation request via

IATA/AIRIMP message formats. This provides delivery of all type of administrative and reservation-messages from and to all stations on IA network and other airlines;

(c) *Automatic Ticketing* : The passenger name record details are used to print the tickets on the ticketing printer with automatic fare calculations;

(d) *Flight Information System* : The on-line system to provide latest information regarding flights arrival and departure status; and

(e) *Computerised Departure Control System* : The system works in a stand-alone mode with stand-by processor. Passenger name list is down-loaded automatically by centralised reservation system (UNISYS) to check-in system. The passenger record details are used in the processing of printing the Boarding cards;

- Online management information system :
  Data related to seat utilisation, load factor, estimated revenue/expenditure and flight-delays is extracted on-line from all the stations and a Mapper-based management information system is used to analyse the reports showing financial viability, capacity utilisation and delay statistics;
- On-line aircraft spares information system for A320 inventory;
- Indian Airlines employee's personnel information system;
- ULD system to control the movement of aircraft containers and pallets;
- Computerised flight plan processing.
  The system is used to generate navigational flight plans based on the latest meterological data and ATC parameters;

- Financial accounting applications:
  (i) Credit billing (passengers and cargo),
  (ii) Interline billing,
  (iii) Agent sale accounting,
  (iv) Passenger sales accounting,
  (v) Mail accounting,
  (vi) Sundry debtors,
  (vii) Payroll and P.F.,
  (viii) Fuel and oil accounting,
  (ix) Annual accounting,

(x) Monitoring of A/c components performance and life-span,
(xi) Aircraft component inventory control.

**Indian Airlines Data Communication Network**

Indian Airlines (IA) has one of the largest private communication network in the country. At present 72 stations (domestic, international and off-line) are connected on-line using high-speed dedicated Department of Telecommunication-leased circuits. The nodal centres at Delhi, Bombay, Madras and Calcutta are connected with three to four data circuits to computer centre forming a star network and outstations, in a region, are connected to nodal centre by means of a single data circuit. A total of 1056 CRTs, 458 dot matrix printers, 66 ticketing printers, 17 teleprinters, 6 ORG check-in systems and 12 telex machines are connected to the central computer at Delhi. The 8 foreign stations of Indian Airlines are connected to the computer at Delhi through the high speed SITA communication link (Type A). All international airlines are linked to IA computer system using low-speed communication link (Type B) of SITA.

The Air India computer system has a high speed link with the Indian Airlines computer system for online availability display of IAC flights on Air India communication network. A low speed TTY (Type B) link is also used for message interchange between the two airlines.

The different communication protocols used in the IA network are UNISCOPE 100 and P1024 (SITA standard).

**Derived Benefits from Computerisation**

These can be enumerated as follows.

- Efficient customer service,
- Instant display of flight schedule,
- Choice of alternate route or flights,
- Instant status of booking and automatic upgrading of waiting list,
- Display of fares,
- Display of passenger and meal lists,
- Elimination of duplicate bookings,
- Display of flight arrival and departure timings,
- Seat preference at check-in time,

- Electronic mail for information interchange,
- Better provisioning of aircraft-spares through inventory control,
- Accurate corporate financial accounting system,
- Effective performance monitoring of aircraft components,
- Processing of reservation requests from other airlines either on-line or through standard teletype messages without manual intervention, and
- Effective planning and control through on-line management information system.

**Conclusion**

The problems were encountered in the following areas :

- With the installation of UNISYS machine in 1983, one of the major problem was to move from the existing network of teleprinters to a CRT-based network for on-line reservations. This was achieved by installing indigenously developed multiplexers and concentrators (to handle both CRT and teleprinter traffic) at the nodal centres;
- The reservation network was quite unstable to start with, but over a period of time with better monitoring and coordination, the network stability has improved appreciably;
- The network still has the problems in the area of resiliency, limited protocol support, PDN connectivity, etc. These inadequacies will be removed with the installation of intelligent FEP and upgrading the nodal concentrators;
- Occasional database integrity problems due to software and hardware reasons have been overcome through the development of database recovery mechanisms; and
- The problem of meeting the peak-hour demand with the available computing resources has been tackled by the system-tuning and job-rescheduling.

# 29

# POLICE-I (General)

S.K. SHARMA*

## Introduction

In India, the major components of criminal-justice system are the police and certain other law-enforcement agencies, the law courts, government prosecution agencies and the defence lawyers, jails and other institutions for detention of offenders and various correctional and rehabilitation institutions. Policing and criminal law-enforcement is, by and large, a State subject under the Constitution of India, but the Central Government has been playing a major role in guiding and assisting the States in the modernisation and improved functioning of various components of the criminal-justice system in the States.

## History and Growth of Police Computerisation

As regards computerisation as a part of the modernisation of criminal-justice system, the Government of India has made a beginning with the crime, criminal and associated data with the police organisations initially. Other components of the criminal-justice administration have not gone in for computerisation in any planned manner as yet. The Indian Police, over the years, have sought to improve the efficacy of the existing information systems to fulfil their main role with greater efficiency and towards this end, various central police organisations have been set-up. The Central Finger Print Bureau (CFPB) in 1956, the inter-state crime records section of

---

* National Crime Records Bureau, Ministry of Home Affairs, Government of India.

the Central Bureau of Investigation (CBI) in 1964, the Directorate of Coordination Police Computers (DCPC) in 1976 and the National Crime Records Bureau (NCRB) in 1986 are some of the important milestones.

The year 1975-76 was a hallmark in the history of the Indian Police when the Ministry of Home Affairs (MHA) included the computerisation of crime-criminal information including finger-prints in its modernisation scheme for the State police forces which had been in operation since 1970-71. The main objective of DCPC was to promote and encourage computerisation in the States primarily for maintenance of crime records with financial assistance of MHA under the modernisation scheme having an outlay of Rs. 100 crores for 10 years. The labours of DCPC led to the development of computer-based crime-criminal information systems and installation of computers for this purpose in 12 States, besides the one at DCPC.

Modernisation of crime records entered a new phase in the year 1985 with the acceptance of the recommendations of the National Police Commission (NPC) by the Government of India. The NPC recommended that crime records bureaux be established at the Centre, State and District levels for more systematic and efficient collection and dissemination of crime-criminal information among various Central and State law enforcement agencies. The Commission envisaged that "an effective spread of the computer network" and formation of the crime record bureaux at various levels would form "the bed-rock of a new information system for the entire country". The perception of NPC was that when the crime record bureaux started functioning, they would be able to receive, store and furnish different types of data and information relevant to various requirements, such as, investigation and trial, study of the present scheme of court trials and procedures and sentencing policy, as also the conduct of the criminal, assessment of the effect of probation and correctional services, and to facilitate scrutiny of the various environmental factors promoting deviant behaviour and criminality in society, thus serving effectively the overall purposes of the crime-criminal justice system as a whole.

In pursuance of the recommendation of NPC, MHA constituted a task force in June 1985 to work out the modalities for the setting up of a National Crime Records Bureau. The task force submitted its report in September 1985 and upon its acceptance by MHA, NCRB was set up in January, 1986 as an attached office of MHA.

The following units which were already in existence as part of other central police organisations were merged with it:

(i) Directorate of Coordination Police Computers (MHA);
(ii) Inter-State data section of the coordination division of the CBI;
(iii) Statistical Section of Bureau of Police Research and Development; and
(iv) The Central Finger Print Bureau, Calcutta (CBI).

As per the resolution of the Government of India, NCRB is required to act as a central store-house of crime and criminal information, including those operating at national and international levels, for aiding the investigating agencies and the organisations concerned with criminal-justice system. It will receive from, and supply data to, penal and correctional agencies for their tasks of rehabilitation of criminals, remand, parole, premature release, etc. It is also required to coordinate, guide and assist the States in activising their crime records systems and advise MHA in regard to their performance and modernisation programmes. NCRB is also responsible to provide training facilities to the personnel of States and Central police organisations in respect of computerisation and crime records. It also collects and processes crime statistics at the national level.

**Impact of Computerisation on Crime Control**

The NCRB, from its very inception, has been well aware of the areas of weaknesses in the computerisation programme of the criminal-justice system in the country. In order to take stock of the situation, a study was undertaken by the Institute of Criminology and Forensic Science (ICFS) in the year 1986 on "Impact of Police Computerisation on Crime Control in India". The ICFS study has pointed out that while substantial data has been stored on computers, enquiries by the investigating officers have been few, and even in these cases, computer outputs did not really help investigators solve their cases. This study has, therefore, concluded that computerisation has had only a marginal impact on crime control.

Based on the findings and recommendations of the ICFS study, NCRB initiated discussions on the use of computer facilities in crime investigation with the functional-level police officers actually engaged in crime investigation and supervision with a view to assess their views and work out an Action Plan to rectify the shortcomings at the ground level so that police computerisation could proceed along meaningful lines. Accordingly, an Action Plan was prepared taking into consideration the views that emerged during discussions with a cross-section of investigators and supervisors across the country.

This Plan includes, the following:

(a) establishment of crime records bureaux at each district headquarter in States;
(b) evolution of a concept of integrated procedures and formats for use by the police, courts, prosecutors, jails and correctional/rehabilitation agencies, etc;
(c) introduction of new police forms integrating the police investigation and computerisation requirements;
(d) development of improved and more user-friendly crime-criminal information software packages;
(e) short and long-term telecommunication plans for data transmission;
(f) enhancing the training capabilities and capacity of NCRB to augment the number of trained technical staff manning police computer centres both at the State and district levels; and
(g) generating awareness among police ranks about the utility of computers in law-enforcement through appreciation training capsules as part of all police training programmes.

**Expansion of Computerisation Plans**

The computer systems now in use with the Indian Police were installed from 1976 onwards. Most of these systems have outlived their normal life and maintenance has become uneconomical and difficult due to non-availability of spares. The system software and software development tools available for the crime-criminal information system on these computers belong to 'second generation'. The application software is consequently quite rigid and not user-friendly and has, therefore, not proved popular with the police officers in the field.

There is a crying need for replacement of the old systems with a more user-friendly and need-based solution which provides improved data communication facilities in order to foster extensive use at the cutting edge levels of the police. Consequently, a detailed revised police computerisation plan based on maintaining threshold data at various levels on a need-to-know basis, was formulated by NCRB and approved in principle by MHA. Thereafter, an extensive feasibility study was carried out in collaboration with a professional software house to suggest computer configurations for the police all over India at district, State and national levels. The study also included concrete suggestions regarding data thresholds, volumes of data and broad types of enquiries for all the three levels. Based on the recommendations of the study, a comprehensive proposal for procurement of hardware and software of various categories was formulated involving financial implications of a non-recurring expenditure of Rs. 500 millions approximately.

It is felt that use of computers should be extended to all agencies of criminal justice system, over and above its use as an aid to the prevention and detection of crime. Far reaching possibilities will open up if other agencies of the Criminal-Justice System, viz., law enforcement agencies other than the police (including immigration organisations), courts, jails, probation officers, penal and correctional institutions also join in by contributing their related data towards building of a comprehensive computer-based integrated information system. Each of these agencies would then draw from the system, a far richer range of information than is available to them at present. It would help them to make a more effective contribution to the overall common objectives of a sound and effective criminal-justice administration.

The courts will be able to receive information from the computer system on their case pendency, data relevant to sentences in individual cases and case statistics, while the probation officers will be able to ascertain and determine social, economic and personal factors influencing criminal behaviour and use the same for effective supervision and rehabilitation in each case. Similarly, the system will enable the penal and correctional institutions to identify the factors which may help them in effecting classification and treatment of juvenile offenders. But, as earlier stated, most other constituents of the criminal justice system have not yet taken to automation in their day-to-day working. The police department has, however, given a lead in this area and made considerable advancement in the use of computers covering some of the aspects pertaining to other agencies involved in the administration of criminal justice system. Some of the important computer applications in the Indian Police are briefly described below:

(A) *Crime-Criminal Information System (CCIS)*

Data in respect of 19 offences which have inter-State ramifications are being collected from all the States and Union Territories (UTs). The computerised crime data-bank has about 75,000 records out of the estimated 150,000 convicted inter-State criminals. The State computer centres hold massive data on crime and criminals varying from 100,000 records in smaller States to about 1 million records in larger States in the present scheme of computerisation. Large volume of data in respect of stolen and recovered property (numbered or identifiable) is also stored on computers at a few States and at the national levels. Separate files are maintained for economic offenders and highly desperate criminals with about 6,000 records in each category. The information can be retrieved on various parameters of crime and criminals. These parameters include *modus operandi* (major, minor, method), place, property, day and time of the crime, special features of the crime and name, age, height, sex, physical features, identification marks and deformity of the criminals. The system has been recently modified to make it more user-friendly leading to nearly 150 per cent increase in its usage.

(B) *Fingerprints Analysis and Criminal Tracing System (FACTS)*

A semi-automated finger print system is already operational in some of the computer-using States. The finger prints are manually converted into a 40-digit specially designed code and stored on computers. In the retrieval process, an enquiry slip is similarly converted into a 40-digit code and matched on computers with the stored codes of finger prints. Since the semi-automated system suffers from certain disabilities, NCRB is engaged in promoting research and developmental activities in indigenous design of an automated finger-print identification system (AFIS). This system is being developed under the aegis of the Department of Electronics (DOE) with a R&D grant of Rs. 1.86 crores. The new system has been tested and the results have been found to be encouraging. The system is being installed at NCRB presently. MHA have been requested for inclusion of this machine in its modernisation scheme for the states. The total volume of records of fingerprints held at NCRB is around

1,500,000 and the record size in the States vary from 50,000 to 700,000 ten-digit slips. Besides, single-digit F.P. records and scene of crime finger-prints are also maintained at NCRB and in the States. However, due to the constraints of storage capacity of the system, it is proposed to initially computerise the records of the inter-State type of criminals at the national level and inter-district type of criminals at the State level. The remaining records will be computerised in the subsequent phases.

A close coordination between computerised finger-print records system and the reformative and correctional institutions can help in focusing the attention to the recidivists who can be identified most conclusively on the basis of finger-print records. Statistics of recidivism, socio-economic milieu and the age groups of the recidivist criminals and juveniles offenders are more easily available from this record and the outcome can enhance the capability of correctional institutions to assess the effectiveness of the reformation efforts and methodologies.

### (C) *Wanted Criminal Tracing System (AWPIS)*

The system has been developed to check the arrested persons against the wanted criminals data on computer to ascertain the complicity of the arrested persons in other crimes. This application has been implemented both at the State level for inter-district criminals and at NCRB for the inter-State criminals. Data collection is in progress in the States. So far, about 40,000 records of wanted persons have been collected at NCRB and the results achieved are highly encouraging.

### (D) *Property Co-ordination System (PCS)*

Property coordination system is operational at States and at NCRB for matching lost and recovered vehicles, fire-arms and cultural properties (idols, antiques). The data volume of the lost and recovered property at the NCRB are: vehicles (82,746), fire-arms (49,468), cultural properties (12,305) and counterfeit currency (32,814). On an average, 150 properties are being coordinated every month at NCRB alone at this stage when the data files are not complete and up-to-date. Useful application of this data is being made in a few States. A very innovative approach has been evolved to capture good quality data in respect of stolen motor vehicles from the

General Insurance Corporation(GIC) under an arrangement that will work to promote the effective performance of NCRB as well as GIC.

(E) *Crime Statistical System (CSS)*

The NCRB is responsible for compilation of the National crime statistics and brings out an annual publication titled "Crime in India" which gives a variety of statistics on crime and criminals of various categories, including juvenile and female offenders for police organisations, academic and research institutions and for researchers/ scholars of criminology. This publication was running 5 to 6 year behind schedule in 1988 when NCRB took over this responsibility. Due to system's approach and computerisation of statistics, this publication has now been brought up-to-date. Another publication brought out by NCRB annually is "Accidental Deaths and Suicides in India". This is presently in arrears and is on the threshold of computerisation in the near future.

(F) *Economic Offenders Information Bureau System (EOIS)*

Economic offenders' data has been computerised and computer master file has about 7,450 records of economic offences. The system is fully developed and tested and the Economic Intelligence Bureau of the Ministry of Finance has been making use of the system as per requirement. The information in respect of registered economic offenders can be retrieved on name, alias, sex, age, height, physical features, mark of identification, passport number, commodity involved, type of offences, area of operation, etc.

(G) *Terrorist-Information System (TIS)*

With a view to help the law enforcement agencies to fix the identity of criminals suspected to be terrorists, a computer-based data bank has been created at the NCRB. The volume of data is about 5,000 criminal records. Data received from various States/UTs was found to be deficient in several respects like physical features, finger-prints, photographs, etc. Necessary corrections and updation of data are underway in the States. The States/UTs have been advised to make use of the system. The information can be retrieved on various crime and criminal parameters.

(H) *National Information System for Drug and Narcotics (DNIS)*

There is need to establish a national information system to study the patterns of *modus operandi*, geographic dispersion and the commodities involved in the incidence of drug crime and trafficking, and for quick dissemination of information on criminals indulging in smuggling and trafficking of narcotic drugs and psychotropic substances. Since these offences have national and international ramifications, hence the need to modernise the information system to effectively help in combating this fast-spreading crime which is responsible, inter alia, for promoting many other forms of crime. Basic data collection formats have been finalised in consultation with the Narcotics Control Bureau (NCB) of the Ministry of Finance. Information requirements are being worked out and the system design is underway.

**Training in Computers**

Over the last decade and a half, extensive training programmes have been undertaken to generate computer awareness in general, as also to train policemen in various technical aspects of EDP. To date, over 7000 police officers of various ranks from the States and the central police organisations have been trained. Special courses to impart basic computer training have also been organised for personnel of the selected central and state police organisations as a campaign before introduction of computers in these organisations. It is one of the main objectives of NCRB to continue to generate more computer literacy and to remove 'key-board shyness' amongst the police officers.

The NCRB training wing is the only police agency imparting training to police officers on crime information management and computers. The training modules have been designed in such a manner so as to re-orient officers to modern methodologies and capabilities of computer-based information management in crime prevention and detection. The modules also include systems analysis and design, software development techniques, management aspects of databases and basic features of computerised systems manage-

To diversify the training activity of the NCRB on computers and management of crime information, regional training centres have been set-up in four locations in the country to penetrate deeper into the field organisations in the police and prepare the police personnel to the phase of computer usage at district, State and national levels.

The NCRB plans to involve the premier training and research institutions like National Police Academy, Institute of Criminology and Forensic Science, Indian Institute of Public Administration and others to undertake studies in the field of crime records system, crime records management, modernisation of crime records and organisational reforms which may be of help in crime control.

**Problems and Constraints**

(a) *Quality of Data*

A mention has been made above that the impact of computerisation on crime control has been only marginal and that the information furnished by the computer-based systems has not really helped in the investigation of cases. The reasons have been analysed and it has been found that the quality of information available in the basic records maintained at the police station level has not been satisfactory. This has happened because the crime investigation work has been increasingly losing priority in the face of ever-increasing demand on the police to attend to public order and the associated duties. It has also been experienced that the input fed into the computer has not always been accurate and complete. It has been recognised that good-quality data is the soul of any information system, more so of a computer-based information system. To overcome this problem and remove other inadequacies in the existing statutory forms and computer input forms, NCRB has evolved the idea of the integrated police forms which obviate the need to fill up separate forms for data entry. The MHA have recommended to all the States/UTs the adoption and implementation of these forms uniformly all over the country. Another approach adopted to improve the data quality is by providing data processing facilities at district headquarters so as to be close to the data generation sources, i.e., police station. The ideal would have been to provide data entry machines at the police station itself, but this stage has not yet come.

(b) *Data Collection Machinery*

Inadequate and defective data collection machinery in the States and shortage of qualified technical staff at the police computer centres are some other problems which have contributed substantially to the slow progress of the computerisation programme. In order to get on top of the problem and to bring about organisational changes to activise data collection and processing functions, it has been decided to create State and district crime records bureaux in line with the recommendations of the National Police Commission. Constant persuasion with the States has led to about 16 States having established such Bureaux at the State level in line with the model provided by NCRB. It is believed that the establishment of crime records bureaux will ensure closer interaction with the field staff on data collection matters. However, the experience so far has been that generally such bureaux are manned by personnel who lack the required motivation and ingenuity because of the unpopularity of such posts in the police. Thus these bureaux are still to become fully functional. Regarding shortage of qualified technical staff, efforts are afoot to evolve an effective personnel policy for manning the technical services in the police besides providing adequate financial incentives to the personnel working in these services.

(c) *Communication Facilities*

Another important reason for the sub-optimal utilisation of computers has been identified to be the lack of adequate communication facilities. The ICFS study has gone to the extent of pointing out that there should be Computer terminals even at the police station level. This is not feasible when efficient and reliable communication lines are not assured even at all the districts in some of the States. The efficacy of the existing computerised system has been considerably inhibited because of this factor. To provide good communication cover to the police forces in the country, a concrete plan for upgrading the existing telecommunication system has been proposed. The plan envisages linking of national capital to the State capitals, State capitals to the range HQs and range HQs to districts through dedicated voice-grade lines. The Police Stations are to be linked to the districts through MART system on VHF with connectivity to the public/police exchanges.

(d) *Attitudinal Problems*

One of the serious difficulties that have been faced in the police computerisation programme pertains to attitudinal problems. It has been found that most of the investigating officers do not show much faith or interest in collection of information through the use of computers for investigation of crime. There has been lack of communication between investigating officers and computer experts. Whatever may be the other shortcomings in the programme like lack of communication facilities, rigid formats of enquiry, ambiguous outputs, etc., it is felt that the system has not been exploited to the maximum by the users because of attitudinal problems. The systems and equipments can always be improved, but changing of attitude is a long-drawn process. The central agencies like NCRB have taken a number of steps directly or through State governments to overcome this problem.

**New Approaches Towards Solutions**

The NCRB has formulated broad outlines for a national plan for police computerisation under which computers will be installed at the district, State and national levels for information retrieval according to the requirements. This plan has already been approved by the Ministry of Home affairs and a monitoring committee for modernisation of crime records has been constituted. For effective implementation of this plan, necessary guidelines and operating procedures are under formulation. NCRB is also attempting to draft a model crime records manual for the States, incorporating therein the procedures for manual as well as computerised maintenance of records.

The problems and difficulties as depicted earlier notwithstanding, it is quite encouraging and gratifying that the police computerisation programme is making the desired headway. The ICFS study has brought out certain positive features of the computerisation effort put in during the last decade which are as under:

(i) The investigating officers (IOs) have acquired general awareness of computer's role in crime investigation;
(ii) 46 per cent of the IOs covered by the study are aware of the concept of computer processing;
(iii) 50 per cent of the IOs have actually taken help of computers in

crime investigation;

(iv) 33 per cent of the IOs "admitted" an increase in their output, i.e., disposal of cases because of help received from computerised information system;

(v) IOs expressed satisfaction to the effect that they could obtain, with the help of computers, list of criminals not only from their district but from other districts or from whole of the State within 24 hours;

(vi) 60 per cent of IOs showed awareness of computer-based property coordination and its utilisation in their work; and

(vii) Over the years, data has been added on to the computer files and inquiries made by IOs have also shown an increase progressively.

The observation of the ICFS study that the information given by computer-based system has not helped in solving criminal cases appears to be somewhat misplaced, because firstly, the information from the computer system may not necessarily solve a case directly and secondly, it is a human trait and a tendency on the part of the investigating officers to try and avoid giving credit for developing clues to any other agencies, including computers. The test of the efficacy of the computer system should be whether the investigating officers are supplying data to the computer regularly and whether they continue to make enquiries on the computer for seeking information. If these two factors show a progressive growth, as it does in the Indian context, it should be taken as a positive indicator that computerised system has not been rejected by the user. The graphs at Figures 29.1 and 29.2 would reveal that there has been an upward trend in data collection in the States as well as at NCRB. There has also been constant increase in the number of queries received at the computer centres and the responses sent to the investigating agencies.

**Computerisation of Interpol Data**

It would be relevant to make a mention of the efforts for computerising the INTERPOL data in criminal matters. The Central Bureau of Investigation of the Government of India has been functioning since 1967 as the National Central Bureau (NCB) for India for coordination with the ICPO — Interpol. This office is responsible for extending international cooperation in all criminal matters connected with foreigners who come to adverse notice of the law enforcement agencies of this country. The Central Fingerprint Bureau (CFPB), which functions as a part of NCRB, receives ICPO finger-print slips and look-out notices in respect of arrested, convicted, wanted, under surveillance and missing persons, etc., from all over the world sent by Interpol, Paris through the NCB-India. These notices, with or without finger-prints, are classified, tested and searched for duplicates before they are recorded. When an arrest or conviction of a foreign national takes place in India, the information is received through the concerned law-enforcement agency and the arrest/conviction details alongwith finger-prints of the subject is sent to the Interpol wing of the CBI for onward transmission to the ICPO-Interpol. Similarly, finger-print slips of persons arrested in foreign lands are also received in CFPB for search to establish the identity and antecedents of the concerned person and the result of search is conveyed back to the source. As on date, we have nearly 7,600 Interpol slips in our records.

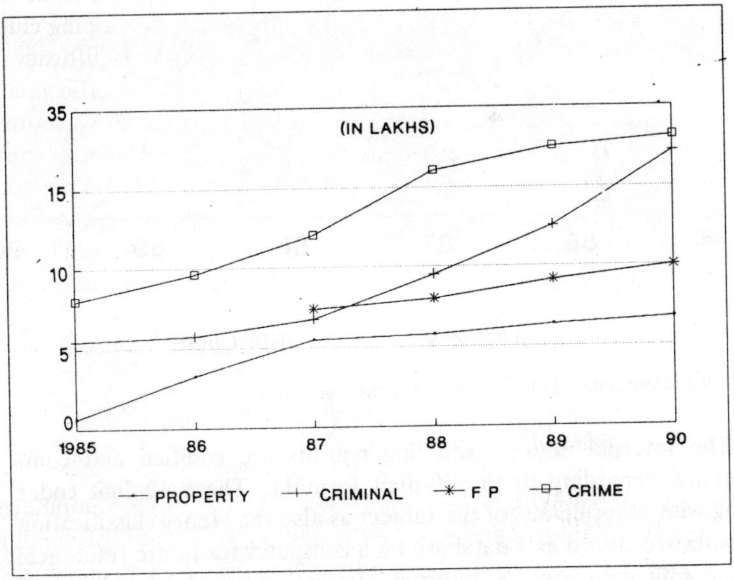


FIG. 29.1: Consolidated Data Growth in States (in Lakhs)

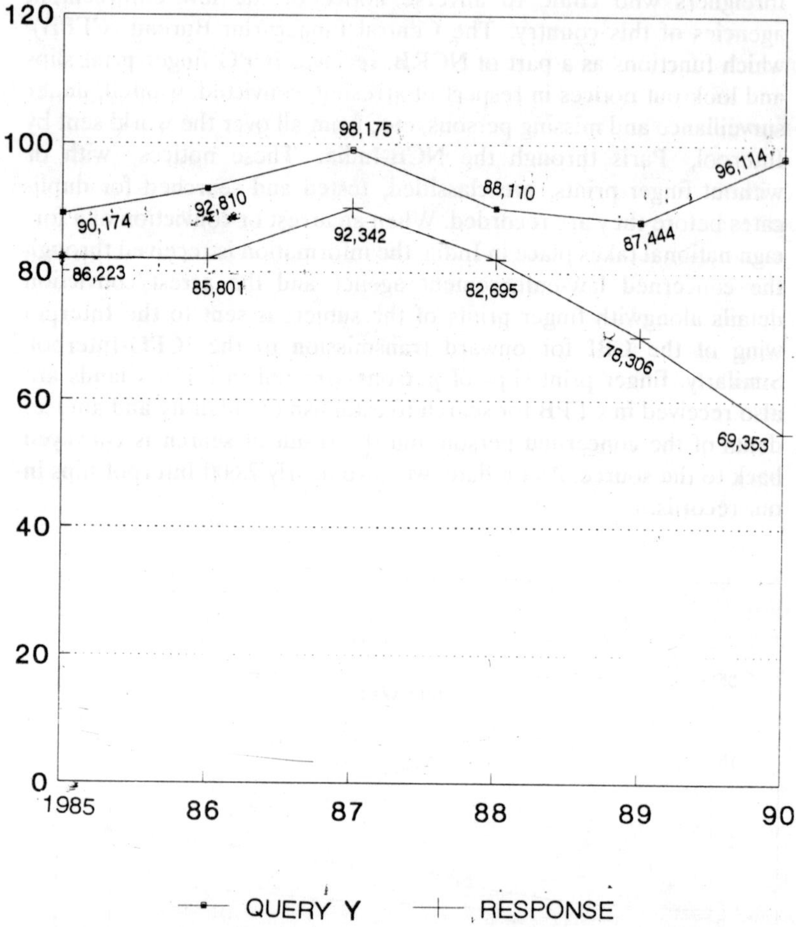


FIG. 29.2: Consolidated Queries and Responses at States

The Interpol notices with finger-prints are codified and computerised according to the 40-digit formula. These 40-digit codes along with other details of the subject as also the Henry classification formula are stored as a database on a computer for future reference. A separate data-base of Interpol criminals wanted by police and courts is also created by storing all available data other than the finger-prints. Finger-prints search references received through Interpol-India are similarly processed and the matching is done by the computer. The data is also used for generating variety of statistics on the international criminals nationality-wise, crime-wise, sex-wise, etc.

**Conclusion**

The use of modern IT tools, and more specifically computers, for rapid storage and retrieval of data required by various constituents of the criminal justice system cannot be over emphasised. Maintenance of proper, systematic and up-to-date records in respect of the persons who come in brush with the law is necessary so that all criminal justice agencies can be timely notified for appropriate action in a well co-ordinated and effective manner. We have only made a beginning with the police. For covering other components of the criminal justice system with an effective computer networking with proper linkages, massive funds for equipment and providing necessary infrastructural and communication facilities are required be required. There is no gainsaying that in a developing country like India, substantial part of the available resources will continue to be diverted towards the rural and other developmental activities and matters pertaining to crime and security will have comparatively lower priority in so far as resource allocation is concerned at the State and at the Centre. This poses a challenge to the IT industry and the professionals alike to evolve low-cost solutions for this high-profile application area. The high visibility enjoyed by the police among the people and the impact of its performance on the life of the common man should be used to prove the efficacy of the IT in everyday life.

# 30

# POLICE-II
# (Finger-Print Identification)

COLONEL P.P. VARMA*

## Introduction

Criminal justice is multi-faceted. Investigation and prevention of crime are among the important sub-sets of criminal justice. Identification of criminals through the well-established art of finger-print(FP) matching is a vital technique for both crime-investigation and prevention. Besides, the FP records help the reformative and the correctional agencies to identify the recidivists, who deserve the focus of our attention. In India, the first non-criminal application of identification through FPs is being considered for identification of people for payment of compensation to the victims of the worst-ever industrial tragedy of a world-wide notoriety involving leakage of poisonous gas at a Union Carbide chemical plant at Bhopal, India.

## History/Background

Historically, the art of finger-print identification was evolved originally by Sir Francis Galton in U.K. and later Sir E.R. Henry in India. The first finger-print bureau in the world was established in 1897 at Calcutta. The other countries adopted the system of identification through FP matching thereafter.

Identification through finger-print matching is based on the fact that for each human being, the finger-prints are Unique and Do Not change. A lot of other unique features like DNA signatures and

---

* National Crime Records Bureau, Ministry of Home Affairs, Government of India.

retinal eye-patterns have emerged recently as alternative individual identification parameters; but these are yet to get technology-proven over time and, more important, they have to first become economically viable for large-scale usage for adoption in a country of our size.

**Manual System**

The manual system, designed by Sir Henry and later modified by Chatterjee, has yielded the due dividends over almost a century now. Identification of individuals is required for two distinct types of cases, i.e., personal identification (PID) when the finger-prints are available for all the ten digits and chance-print identification (CPID) when single-digit prints are available — typically lifted from the scenes of crime. The 10-digit FP slips for PID are coded as per the Henry — Chatterjee classification system and the single-digit records for chance-print identification as per the Battley system of classification.

The manual system is simple, reliable, dependable and fool-proof but it is suitable only for small volumes of FP slips. With the massive growth of criminal records, the manual system has gradually become slow and in countries like India, where the records run into millions, the manual system has become too slow, tedious and difficult to manage the system effectively any more. Besides, the manual system suffers from a number of limitations like the following:

(a) Deterioration of prints over a span of time,
(b) Mis-filing due to ambiguous classification,
(c) Slow because of accumulation of records,
(d) Limited chance-print search capability,
(e) Limited chance-print database, and
(f) Difficult maintenance (deletion and updating).

Further, CPID, which is a very powerful tool for crime investigation and identification of a criminal, has several problems. These are characterised by the following:

(a) Availability of only partial and generally poor quality prints,
(b) Very few minutiae available for matching,
(c) Most of the time the class and the digit unknown,
(d) Reference points like core/delta not available, and
(e) Orientation not known.

The limitations of the manual system and the difficulties of manual record management were realised as early as 1970's and with the advent of computers, a computerised system of finger-print identification was the obvious solution.

**Evolution of Computerised FP Identification**

In India, the computerised method of identification has been evolved in two stages, i.e., the semi-automatic and the Automated FP identification systems. The semi-automatic era commenced in the early 70's while we are now on the threshold of being launched on to the automatic phase.

(A) *Semi-automatic Systems*

The semi-automatic systems aimed at quicker retrieval of the required finger-print slip from the manual records, which are binned according to the Henry classification system by taking the indirect advantage of the fast information-processing capability of computers, which became available in our country in the early 70's. The system consists of two distinct and complementary approaches which have been developed in different phases over a period of about two decades. One approach is of matching on a special 40-digit code and the other is on matching of names. The method of 40-digit coding is useful in cases where the information of the name is either not available or it is not reliable. Both these approaches are discussed briefly below.

(B) *40-Digit Code System*

In this, the 10-digit (10 fingers) finger-print record is coded additionally into a relatively more simple 40-digit code, with each finger being represented by a 4-digit code and stored in the data-base along with the corresponding Henry classification. The 4-digit code consists of the first two digits representing one out of the 22 specified and easily identifiable patterns and the next two digits giving information of the ridge-count between the core and the delta-positions. This 4-digit code is concatenated for the ten fingers in a definite specified sequence starting from the right-hand thumb to the little finger and continuing on to the left-hand thumb and the other fingers sequentially to form an ultimate string of 40-digits (Fig. 30.1). The search/query slip is similarly coded into 40-digits and matched on a computer with the stored data-base of the established and known criminals (Fig. 30.2). The computer usually produces a short list of possible matches, which can be manually examined and filtered on the basis of the other definite known information of the suspect and the suggested matches. The corresponding Henry classification reference obtained in the computer output enables quick access to the wanted record. The system also enables linking and updating of the criminal records in the crime-criminal information system. When conviction slips are received, on matching and linking up, the records with earlier Provisional Criminal Number (PCN) are updated with a Regular Criminal Number (RCN).

The system is, of course, useful for 10-digit searches for personnel identification (PID) only at present. It is functional at the national level at the National Crime Records Bureau and at 12 out of the 25 states in India, where third-generation computers have been installed in phases since 1976.

(C) *Name Indexing System*

This is a more recently developed system for cases where name information is reliably known. The system works on main-frame computers as well as on PC-ATs. In this, the data-bank is created by storing information of the criminal name, father/husband's name, primary classification, secondary classification of the right-hand index-finger and the Henry classification. Matching is done on all the parameters, i.e., the individual name, father's name, primary classification and the secondary classification of the right-hand index-finger. The computer output gives almost a unique match with the corresponding Henry classification in the output to enable quick access to the manual record. For name-matching, an algorithm based on SOUNDEX system, modified to suit Indian phonetic names of all the regions of the country, has been evolved. This algorithm has an accuracy of about 97 per cent. We are constantly endeavouring to identify and analyse the failure cases in order to improve the algorithm. The PC-version of the package is very useful for small-volume local data at smaller districts and at State level Finger Print Bureaux (FPBX).

| RT | RI | RM | RR | RL | LT | LI | LM | LR | LL |
|---|---|---|---|---|---|---|---|---|---|
| 08 03 | 05 04 | 13 06 | 14 04 | 15 05 | 01 00 | 06 04 | 04 00 | 13 05 | 14 05 |

Roman PATTERN CODE    Under line RIDGE COUNT

FIG. 30.1: 40 - Digit Coding Strategy (Semi - Automatic System)

SEARCH REFERENCE

04 08 09 10 01 13 14 15 21 **00 00 10 12 11 00 15 23 30 00**

——PATTERN CODES——→ ←——**RIDGE COUNTS**——→

↓

**MASTER RECORD**

04 08 09 10 01 13 14 15 21 **00 00 08 14 11 00 15 20 30 00**

——PATTERN CODES——→ ←——**RIDGE COUNTS**——

↓

TRACED

WHILE DECODING A MATCH, SYSTEM CATERS FOR LIMITED VARIETIES ON RIDGE-COUNTS WHICH MAY BE DUE TO HUMAN ERROR

FIG. 30.2: 40 - Digit Matching Strategy (Search Reference)

(D) *Future Perspective for Semi-Automatic Systems*

Although an automatic finger-print identification systems (AFIS) has been developed (as discussed below) and one such system is being installed at the national level for the inter-State type of criminals; but due to the exorbitant cost, it shall take quite some time before the fully computerised systems can percolate down to all the States and the district level FPBX. In the interim period, we envisage extended use of the semi-automatic systems. Even later, when the fully computerised systems are installed and several faster and accurate successful tracings are effected, we expect that the present dwindling confidence and faith in the finger-print matching technique will be restored among the various investigating agencies and the volume of queries will increase in a snow-balling manner. We are aware that very soon the volume of work-load would exceed the presently designed capacities of the computerised systems, despite the fact that we have catered for some expansion capability to a certain extent based on the existing average volume of search requests and the size of the data-base. It is during this period, before the capacities are upgraded, that the semi-automatic systems are envisaged to be used in conjunction with the fully automatic systems to share the load of work on a selective basis. It is with this perspective that we are still continuing our R&D efforts in improving the semi-automatic systems. One of the thrusts in our R&D endeavour is to develop an effective semi-automatic system for smaller volume chance-print identifications for use at districts and some of the smaller states. The other thrust is to improve on the matching algorithms for both 40-digit and name-indexing systems.

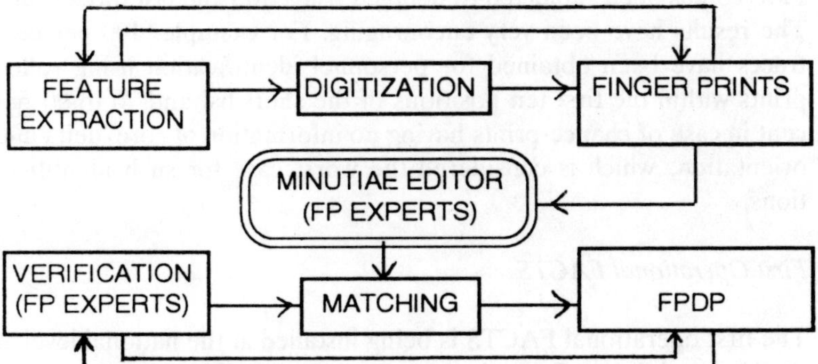


**FIG. 30.3: Finger-print Identification System**

**Automated Finger-print Identification Systems**

An Automated finger-print identification system with a commercial name of finger-print analysis and criminal-tracing system (FACTS), has been designed and developed indigenously within the country by own R&D effort which commenced in 1986. India happens to be the fifth country in the world to have acquired this expertise. The computerised system does not replace the FP expert but aids him in increasing the productivity and eliminates the drudgery of the manual system. It produces fast and accurate matching with a high rate of identification. It enables effective record management and provides connectivity to crime-criminal information system. It is modular in design and allows for upgradability.

The system caters for storage, retrieval and matching of 10-digit FP slips. The same system caters for single-digit records also. The search finger-prints are digitized, encoded for the various minutiae attributes and matched against the stored minutiae data base. Figure 30.3 gives the diagrammatic overview of the process. A short list of possible candidate slips is produced in the descending order of their probability and a FP expert physically verifies each one of them on the monitor by calling the corresponding stored images of the finger-print along with the image of the search-print. The system enables identification of personnel based on 10-digit rolled slips and also for the single-digit chance-prints lifted from the scenes of crime.

*Trials and Test Results*

FACTS has been subjected to detailed trials over the last three years. The results have been very encouraging. For example, 100 per cent traces have been obtained for personnel identification using rolled prints within the first ten positions of the short list and 70 to 90 per cent in case of chance-prints having no information of core/delta and orientation, which is considered the worst case for such identifications.

*First Operational FACTS*

The first operational FACTS is being installed at the national level at the National Crime Records Bureau at New Delhi. It is expected to be fully functional by mid-91. The initial database being created is of about 0.15 million records of inter-State type of criminals and will also include records of criminals of international notoriety as reported by the Interpol.

**Perspective Plan**

The futuristic plans aim for an ultimate nation-wide network of automated finger-print identification systems, improvements in the existing AFIS and the use of artificial intelligence technology to reduce dependence on the human finger-print experts. These thrusts are briefly described below:

A. *Networking of Automated Systems*

Research and development efforts are being made to develop lower capacity and low-cost automatic finger-print identification systems also. These will be commensurate with the requirements of the States and the districts of different sizes and would be compatible to the larger main system at the national level. A PC-AT 386-based prototype system is separately under development at present. Using the experience to be gained at the national-level system, smaller versions of the system are envisaged to be installed at the States and all the districts. These will be networked through a wide-area network (WAN) and would function on the principle of distributed data processing. The district systems would hold the total data of their jurisdiction, the State systems will hold data of inter-district type of criminals and the national level will store data of the inter-State type and the Interpol type of criminals. These systems will be co-located with the crime-criminal information system and the two systems will be closely integrated at each level for maximum exploitation by all the law enforcement, the criminal justice, the corrective and the reformative agencies. The communication network will be shared by both the crime-criminal information system as well as the automatic finger-print identification system. In the interim phase, as mentioned earlier, we plan to use the semi-automatic systems and may be later also, we may still have to use the semi-automatic systems as supplementary to the automatic systems on a selective basis.

(B) *Improvements in AFIS*

At the same time, our R&D effort is continuing to further improve the present AFIS. For instance, the present system requires the core/data positions to be identified on the monitor by a FP expert. This activity should be automatic in a computerised processing environment. Similarly, we want untraced search chance-prints to be checked against the library of the earlier untraced chance-print cases. The matching algorithms, based on the techniques of statistical cluster analysis of the minutiae attributes, also deserve attention for their continuous review and improvements based on critical examination of the results produced, particularly the failure cases.

(C) *Development of an Expert System*

The computerised systems developed so far are only an aid or a tool for the FP experts. Good finger-print experts themselves are a rare 'commodity' and require intensive training and extensive on-the-job experience before they can be deemed to be experts. Our thrust is, therefore, to exploit the artificial intelligence tools and develop a knowledge-based 'expert system'. Preliminary experimental work has been initiated in this field though it is in an embryonic stage as yet.

**Conclusion**

It is hoped that by the dawn of the 21st century, India would be fully geared up for effective computerised finger-print identification applications and would be able to actively and effectively contribute in this field towards the international co-operation for crime prevention and criminal justice.

# 31

# EMPLOYMENT

S.R. MAJUMDAR and Y.P. BHASKAR*

## Introduction

During the last half of the 20th century, the world has witnessed tremendous development in the field of science and technology so far as manufacturing process, factory management, product sophistication and equipment development are concerned. There has been a sea-change in the whole system of production and production plants in the modern world. The rate of technological advancement has been so rapid during this period that any process or processing systems introduced in our manufacturing plants lost its relevance almost instantaneously after its birth, increasing thereby the rate of obsolescence to an all-time high. In such a situation it was but natural that a world-wide rat-race started for continuous qualitative improvement of the means, methods and plants. History of last few decades, specially in the high-tech area, stands testimony to this. The advent of computer, in the meantime, has further radically changed the whole production scenario and practically revolutionised the industrial revolution itself.

Against the background of such a world-wide phenomenon, it is evident that the developing countries like India cannot sit tight with old-fashioned and out-dated technology. Due to sheer instinct to survive, the flood-gates of computers had to be opened in this country to usher in the magic-era of electronics in various walks of Indian economy. The need of the hour in this highly competitive world market is to endeavour for high production with constant improvement in the quality of products at reduced production cost. It is need-

---

* Directorate General of Employment and Training, Ministry of Labour, Government of India.

less to emphasise the importance of optimising the available resources at the command of a poor country like India and the introduction of computer in Indian trade, commerce and industry has to be seen from this angle.

**Present Need**

Rationalisation and optimisation of the work-place is probably the only answer to achieve the expected goal of technological excellence, thereby increasing the overall productivity which, inter alia, is directly proportional to the overall employment potentiality of our society as a whole. At the moment, to achieve this we have two main shortcomings: (i) smart method of working and (ii) smart workers.

In modern industrial situation the first lacuna is being overcome by the fascinating world of information technology. The introduction of computer in Indian industries and the ongoing advancement in computer and communications technology will certainly have profound effect on both the way people work and the management of work. It is interesting to note that both the technology itself and the expectations of the masses are moving up, forcing the modern management to provide smarter and smarter working methods.

In the world arena, information revolution has resulted in a quantum jump in information technology during the last couple of decades. This spectacular technological revolution has redefined the very nature of work. It calls for a new generation of skilled manpower capable to work with a combination of both cognitive and manipulative skills. The most important factor in modern manufacturing world today is the effectiveness of the work we do. To survive in the rat-race of competition, our work should be fast, highly responsive and absolutely result-oriented. Such a demand is aptly met by computerisation of production system. Computerisation which improves the functional efficiency is the most lucrative incentive towards industrial growth and ideal work culture that the science and technology has ever bestowed. Hence computers and information technology these days have a special place in almost all activities of our national economy such as:

(1) Business and administration
(2) Air and railway reservation
(3) Hospital records

(4) Banking and insurance
(5) Communication network and space science
(6) Land records maintenance
(7) DTP and documentation
(8) CNC technology and flexible manufacturing system
(9) Testing and inspection engineering
(10) Transport operation (as in flying by wire) and traffic signal regulation
(11) Data processing, MIS and CAD/CAM and system design
(12) Meteorology and weather forecasting
(13) Process simulation and process control engineering
(14) Entertainment electronics
(15) Diagnostic system
(16) Agriculture and mineral exploration, etc.

Even after hours of monotonous and repetitive human labour, the work efficiency in earlier era would not have been significant at all in comparison to the increased efficiency and the ease with which a modern operator works with his computerised production system. With computerisation of our work-place, not a single job has become redundant. On the other hand, newer job opportunities have been created which will certainly help us to ease the burden of unemployment in this country. One interesting aspect is that the computer and information technology enable us to visualise the various possibilities and manipulations of work parameters and their relative advantages and disadvantages to take a correct decision. Before going to the process of building the new product, we can simulate it well in advance, thereby, saving time and money, and avoiding mistakes, if any, and can modify it to our maximum satisfaction. The computerised communication network ensures better interaction between various nodal agencies in an organisation enhancing the productivity as a whole and reducing communication gap to the lowest. Hence, there is no doubt that this vital field of engineering marvel is on the increase in its application in factories, offices, hotels, libraries and everywhere.

**Newer Job Opportunities**

The tools and technology alone may not effect the improvement in employment generation. They must be synthesised with information on possible opportunities and be combined with skills and resources needed to capitalise on them. Together, these elements characterise the information revolution in which new ideas and new technology are critical factors of continued success in economy.

The information technology or computerisation has thrown to us a challenge to develop a new genre of skills capable to match its magical charm and efficiency. The latest needs of the employment market and information technology-related professions have given rise to a demand for manipulative and cognitive skills. A list of some of the newer professions in the world of computer and information technology business is given below:

(1) *System Analysts*

A typical analyst is a person armed with a diploma from a training institute with some programming background. Professionally qualified personnel such as engineers or MBAs, working in computer companies, would also have been through this route. Systems analysts work for the following organisations:

- Software companies, consultancies and data processing organisations;
- Private businesses, manufacturers, banks and insurance companies.

The Central Government too has a department for computerisation, called the National Informatics Centre (NIC).

(2) *Programming Personnel*

Wherever there is an analyst, a programmer cannot be far behind. They are also found in small companies that own a single PC where no analyst is employed. There the programmer's job involves analysis, programming and operations.

(3) *Personnel for systems software development (for operating system — OS)*

The systems software controls the way the computer works. It coordinates the hardware, whereas application software controls what the computer does. Work/vocation in systems software could mean the following:

- writing systems software during development of a new computer in association with hardware engineers and designers to decide the way the OS should work, develop (write out the "code") the OS and test it (make sure it works to specifications);
- writing system drivers (programmes that make the computer work with particular pieces of hardware, like printers, plotters etc.);
- testing of compilers/utilities;
- developing new utilities; and
- debugging OS problems.

A lot of the work in systems software is for the export market.

(4) *Data-base Administrators*

Companies are today consolidating the data in their computers. This means creating a data-base for information. The person responsible for this is called the data-base administrator. Only a few large companies have data-base administrators.

(5) *Computer Services Organisations*

The computer industry provides services to departments of the same company or external clients. Companies provide services ranging from renting PCs to publishing on a computer.

(6) *Consultants*

This growing species offers services ranging from helping customers select a computer to developing software. Consultants are such as, doctors providing feasibility studies, selection of hardware/software, software development, training and data processing.

(7) *Teaching and Training Personnel*

New-comers are not the only ones to be trained. The user-organisations (companies with in-house computers, also called the end-users) must have their personnel trained in computer usage. This requirement is met either through computer consultants or specialised training institutes.

(8) *Computer Maintenance Personnel*

With increasing dependence on computers comes a growing need for service technicians to maintain and repair them. In a computer manufacturing company, the maintenance people are field engineers. They work "in the field", on clients' premises. Actual repair of a computer that is "down" is a challenging and pains-taking work, requiring an analytical mind as well as technical knowledge. Computer technicians (or engineers) also install new equipment. They are mostly employed by equipment manufacturers. An emerging field is the third-party maintenance, in which companies other than the computer-manufacturers provide maintenance for a fee.

(9) *Computer Designers*

People in this field work on developing new designs and modifying earlier ones. Their work is in the fore-front of electronics technology and they are expected to be aware of the latest trends, products and developments in India and abroad. Their job is to ensure that their company builds the best possible machines at a reasonable cost. The computers must withstand the Indian environment – from 45 degrees to 0 degree C temperatures of offices without air-conditioning, with soft touch in the keys.

(10) *R and D Engineers*

Activity in hardware can also be in research and development. Here, one may work on chip and circuit design, computer architecture or the design of better peripherals (devices that are not part of the computer but work with it, such as a printer). R&D may also be in peripheral integration (say, making a printer work with one's company's computer).

(11) *Computer Manufacture Personnel*

A few companies have paid much attention to the specialised job of computer manufacture. Some of them with greater commitment to product quality than others have large, high-quality manufacturing outfits. Others use "screw-driver" technology (they get all the parts from outside and "screw together" the computer) and do not have any manufacturing capability worth speaking of.

Jobs in manufacturing range from component assembly to continuous testing and monitoring of the computer being manufactured.

**Effect on the Work and Work Culture**

Smart method of working and smart workers do not mean reduction in employment potential. It only asks us to sharpen our skill and organise our working environment. To explain it in simple terms, the person who recorded the data on a sheet of paper or perhaps in a ledger still does that job but may be on a computer terminal. During the process, he/she gets to know what is being done is right/wrong and its effects, e.g., a train seat-reservation operator knows whether the train is full or not and is able to satisfy the customer by going through all options of trains, classes of travel, dates of travel, etc.). Computerising the reservation procedure has reduced the time required to do a unit of a job and has satisfied the customer.

In the case of computerisation of the Railway reservations, a person can leave the counter within 15 minutes whereas, prior to computerisation, the same work needed 3 to 4 hours. In other words, in the same amount of time taken to do one reservation, more reservations can be done in addition to satisfying the customer and at reduced error-rate by shifting our method of working which is a necessity with our enormous growth in travelling population. It is important to note that the above change has not made the reservation clerk redundant. Hence it is clear that computerisation has not caused unemployment or snatched away employment opportunity. Instead, operators have less monotony and more satisfaction in the job thereby improving the overall productivity. The skullduggery of referring to many ledgers/cross references is avoided. But note the basic work is still done by the very same person, viz., entering/recording data.

From the above general example, it is fairly clear that the efficiency of the employee has been automatically improved, resulting in doubled or even tripled work output. In addition to the above, adopting the effective technology itself has given rise to employment in the form of people who are to involve in creating, producing, maintaining, managing and developing the technology. This indicates a double-folded improvement: one at the user's end of this effective and profitable technology and the other at the creator's and introducer's end of this technology.

With better information at the decision-makers hands, right decisions at the right time are possible leading to better products at reduced costs and greater business leading to higher employment in the production/service lines.

The chain-reaction of this brand of smart working creates newer job opportunities and employment in the following areas:

(i) creative and processing centre of the Information technology,
(ii) development of software,
(iii) maintenance of softwares,
(iv) maintenance of the hardware systems,
(v) research and development in the information technology itself,
(vi) marketing of information technology tools, and
(vii) training institutes in the use of information technology tools, etc.

In one of the reputed motor-tyre manufacturing companies, seven clerks looked after the incentive calculation for 1300 of its employees. A brilliant manager reformed the calculations that were being made and reduced the number of clerks to two only. Can it be said that this has caused unemployment or should this be called an improvement in management methods? This is an example of resource utilisation and efficient management without even introducing computers or any high technology machines. Information technology has given this intelligent management of resources and judicious utilisation of the same has paid tremendous benefits.

**Manpower Requirement and Training**

It is a fact that the computerisation in the country is plagued by shortage of trained manpower despite the fact that India is the home of the third largest pool of scientific and technical manpower. It is understood that during the period 90-94, almost 2000-2500 large branches of various banks in India with a daily work load of more than 750 vouchers will go computerised. The Rangarajan Committee of RBI in this context has emphasised that instead of reduction in the existing labour force in the banking industry, they may need the following:

(1) Data entry operators - 50,000
(2) Supervisory staff - 5,000
(3) EDP managers - 8,000
(4) Computer specialists - 2,000
(5) Trainers - 400

Moreover, about a lakh of officers have to undergo a computer appreciation course calling for a good number of computer trainers to be employed.

This single instance clearly shows the tremendous amount of future employment potential in this vital field of national economy. The demand-supply projections on employment by various committees set-up over the years, e.g., Rangarajan Committee for 1980-85, Sampath Committee for 1985-90, DOE, revised estimate for 1985-90 and demand projection in the Eighth Plan documents have all shown sizeable amount of gap between need and available manpower in this vital field. Accordingly, to tide over this problem, the role of non-government sector in training computer manpower slowly got acceptance by the trade and industry, and today the majority of computer personnel are being trained by these non-governmental computer training institutes.

Unfortunately, it is found that the unanticipated boom in demand for computer skills has spawned thousands of commercial ventures in computer education, a vast majority of which are unable to provide even the bare minimum quality for the exorbitant fees they charge. However, the present manpower requirement in this field are mostly met from the following sources:

| Sl. No. | Nature of job/category | Sources |
|---|---|---|
| 1. | Systems Analyst 'A' | IIM, Engg. Colleges with MBA, B.E./B.Tech., etc. |
| 2. | Systems Analyst 'B' | B.Sc. Computer Science |
| 3. | Programmer | Private Institutes, Societies, ITIs/ATIs |
| 4. | Computer Maintenance Engineers | Engineering Colleges, IITs |
| 5. | Software Engineers | IITs, Engineering Colleges |
| 6. | Data Entry Operators | ITIs, Private Institutes |

The Eighth Plan document projects the following gap between the supply-demand position in computer manpower during the Eighth Plan-period.

| Level | Requirement projected | Available Manpower | Gap |
|---|---|---|---|
| Ph.D | 255 | 240 | 15 |
| M.Tech. | 19,355 | 2,500 | 11,845 |
| B.Tech. | 23,945 | 7,000 | 16,945 |
| MCA | 40,040 | 18,000 | 22,000 |
| DCA | 98,880 | 80,000 | 18,880 |
| DCE | 18,340 | 7,000 | 11,000 |
| Total | 1,95,805 | 1,14,700 | 80,685 |

From the above, it is clear that this great employment avenue will wither away if our education and training programme does not handle the challenge with a war-footing agility. Hence to meet this gap a very good training network has to be established. Probably DGE&T, with active support from DOE, may revamp their available resources to tide over this gigantic task.

While many agencies under the State/Central government and private sector are organising variety of training programmes at various levels in the field of computers, the DGE&T in the Ministry of Labour, Government of India, is also conducting training programmes in the field of computers. Brief details of these training programmes are given below:

(a) The Advanced Training Institute for Electronics and Process Instrumentation at Hyderabad which was set-up with the assistance of SIDA and ILO offers short-term training programmes in the following areas in the field of computers: (a) Computer programming, (b) Basic language and computer control, (c) Microprocessor and their applications, (d) Problem-solving with Fortran, and (e) Computer applications for instructors;

(b) Some of these courses are also being offered at the Advanced Training Institute for Electronics and Process Instrumentation at Dehradun;

(c) A CNC training centre has been set-up at ATI, Madras, recently with the assistance of UNDP/ILO. This institute offers the following courses related to application of Computer in manufacturing:

(a) CNC turner operator and programming,
(b) CNC milling operator and programming,
(c) Computer-aided drafting/computer-aided manufacture (CAD/CAM), and
(d) Flexible manufacturing system (FMS). Similar courses will also be offered very shortly in ATIs at Bombay and Kanpur.

(d) To meet the requirement of data-entry operators and junior programmers, a scheme was implemented in the industrial training institutes located in different parts of the country in collaboration with the Department of Electronics. Originally two courses, viz., console operator-cum-programmer assistant and data preparation assistant were being offered. However, these two courses have now been amalgamated into one course, viz., data preparation and computer software which is of one-year duration.

**Conclusion**

The need of the day is improvement in economy and that is possible if we use our men most efficiently in an efficient environment. The needs of industry and business houses may change to keep pace with the state of art of technology and hence we should be ready to prepare those 'smart workers' to work in 'smart environment'. Then there arises no question of unemployment. On the other hand, the employment-avenue and the standard of living improves considerably.

To improve employability, there is no substitute for training. Probably DGET, DOE and Computer Society of India should take the lead to formulate and provide the state-of-the-art training in this unique field of technology so that the trained personnel can germinate the seed of development to lead the country to the 21st century.

# PART VI

## LEISURE SECTOR

(Focus on Individual)

# 32

# NEWSPAPERS AND MAGAZINES

PRADEEP GUPTA*

## Introduction

The publishing industry in India is highly competitive. A large number of newspapers and magazines are launched every year for the readers and advertisers. As a result of this, competition in the industry has not lagged behind in absorbing modern technology. In fact, some of the first application-specific computers, the photo-composing machines, were brought in by this industry and the industry has also been quick to automate the various functions. Significant level of computerisation has been achieved by the leading companies. As example, the top five publishing companies, viz., *Times of India, Hindustan Times, The Statesman, Indian Express and Living Media* have a total installed base of 1000 PCs and 17 medium range computers. At an average of 200 PCs per organisation, it is clear that the industry is serious about mechanising so as to be able to provide services to the readers and the advertisers.

## Application Areas

The application of information technology in newspapers and magazines can broadly be classified under two areas — production applications and commercial applications.

### (A) *Production Application*

Production applications are those which involve the editorial, design and production department of a newspaper or magazine. Compute-

---

* Cyber Media Limited.

rising the bread-and-butter function of a media company gives tremendous competitive advantage to the company. The applications are as follows:

*Text entry*

A large amount of text has to be processed periodically by any publication. A newspaper would be handling around 50,000 words daily. A magazine would have 100,000 words in each issue. This large amount of text handling makes this activity highly amendable to computerisation.

*Text editing*

Any story has to be edited for spelling mistakes, syntax, readability, correctness, consistency, house style, editorial policy, etc. It might even have to go through more than one editor. For example, one pass might look only at spelling mistakes, syntax and readability. In another pass, a copy-editor might look for technical correctness, etc. A computer facilitates the task considerably.

*Desk Top Publishing (DTP)*

The stories have got to be pieced together in a readable format. The design department, working on a set of rules, will lay the story out. This process was done earlier by literally 'cutting and pasting'. Today, computers help the design departments to work out attractive pages with much more flexibility than what was available in the earlier system. For example, in case a story is not filling up the complete page and is a few lines short, the designer can increase the point size of the headline or the size of an illustration/blurb and refit the balance text.

*News network*

Newspapers and magazines subscribe to a number of news agencies. Some have there own agencies which syndicate news to other smaller newspapers. The earlier systems of teletype were very slow. Today computers, communication links and store-and-forward technology (SFT) is used by most publications so that there is a quick access to events occurring around the world. Publications also have to have their own networks so that news from the bureaus is available immediately.

*Database*

Publications need access to past stories by multiple keywords so that the background information can be compiled fast, when required.

(B) *Commercial Applications*

The three major commercial applications relevant for a publication are circulation, advertising and accounts, described below:

*Circulation*

Publications have to keep track of their readers so as to be able to understand the profile of the readers, ensure maximum reach and retain its reader base. Most periodicals are habit-forming and, therefore, publishers have to ensure that competition should not find an entry into their reader base. So, it is necessary to monitor stand sales and subscribers so that there are minimum complaints from the readers.

Subscribers' records have to be maintained, receipts, renewals, etc., have to be generated, to ensure a lock-in with the subscriber. Organisations have to work out right address-slips so that the publication reaches the reader without any problem.

Publications usually have a very extensive retail network. There are a large number of vendors who might be picking from very few to very many copies. Complete vendor accounts have to be maintained.

Since a large part of the product is despatched through train, optimum-sized bundles have to be made. For example, if 54 copies of the newspaper and 5 copies of magazine A and 7 copies of magazine B are to be despatched, the circulation department has to work out the bundling procedure, since smaller bundles may get misplaced and larger bundles will create handling problems.

*Advertising*

The real revenue for a publication comes from the advertisers. A computer system keeps track of advertisement bookings, special requests, advertisement material, etc. After production and despatch, accurate records of each agency and client are to be kept to ensure best results for the company.

A publication may be a member of Indian Newspaper Society (INS). In this case, records have to be maintained for INS accredited advertisement agencies and certain specific reports are to be generated.

*Accounting*

Like all commercial organisations, a publisher has to keep a track of the accounts. Also, in case the publication wants newsprint quota, statements have to be generated to fulfil the requirements of the Registrar of Newspapers of India (RNI). Similarly, in case the organisation goes through Audit Bureau of Circulation (ABC), specific records have to be maintained.

**Organisational Objectives**

The basic objective of the publication in going in for computerisation can be described as follows:

(i) Reduction of lead-time between availability of news and printing. This gives a publication a competitive edge over rival publications. Incorporation of last minute changes and updates ensures enhanced sales;
(ii) Better readability by sticking to a house-style and ensuring that mistakes are kept to a minimum. Better readability is also ensured by having an attractive layout for each page;
(iii) Access to news agencies as well as to in-house information carried in past issues of magazine. Availability of news and inputs from other bureau offices;
(iv) Transmission of stories and pages in case of multiple editions;
(v) Lesser manual mistakes for subscription record, agents accounts, advertiser accounts, etc.;
(vi) Lean manpower; and
(vii) Timeliness of management information systems.

**Methodology**

(i) *Editorial*

The editorial matter is keyed in directly on the computer using standard word processing (WP) packages. Editorial matter may also come in through communication channels from news agencies, such as, UNI, PTI, Reuter, etc.; syndicate services such as Dev Features, Radiant Sport Management, etc.; and from bureaus located in different parts of the country.

After the information is available on the computer, it goes through multiple editing steps. Spellings may be checked using standard packages such as Spellchecker. It is desirable that the house style (whether to use the spelling 'program' or 'programme') is incorporated in the dictionary.

Various sub-editors, copy editors and technical editors might have to look at the matter to ensure high readability and correctness. This is achieved by using standard WP packages on which the text is edited. At this stage, the photographs are indicated which have to be incorporated in this story.

The editorial department also requires a lot of background information very quickly. Past issues are put on a data-base accessible through keywords. There are no good packages available for this, especially since the keywords may not be obvious at the time the data is put on the data-base.

(ii) *Production*

Once the matter is ready, the page lay-outs have to be prepared. This is done in a number of units by using special photo-composing and lay-out machines. Increasingly, general a purpose computers are being used for this purpose amongst whom the Macintosh has got a clear edge. A number of PC AT/386 type of machines are also being used. The packages preferred are Pagemaker and Ventura, depending upon the specific requirement of a publisher.

The pages are laid out using desk-top publishing (DTP) software. The designer gets a lot of flexibility and, in fact, can do things which were almost impossible manually. For example, there can be an odd-shaped illustration and the text can wrap itself around it. After the design is over, the output is taken out on a laser printer and is checked for correctness. Changes, if any, are incorporated and the final output is taken out on a high resolution laser printer or on a photo-composing machine compatible with the DTP system.

In case there are no photographs or illustrations (except line drawings), the output can be directly taken out on films, thus eliminating one step, i.e., processing of camera-ready artworks.

(iii) *Commercial*

There are no standard packages currently available in India for the various commercial activities performed by an organisation. Most organisations have gone in for customised packages for mechanising subscription records, agent accounts, advertising agency records and financial accounts.

(a) *Subscription system:* This system comprises four sub-systems, viz., receipt of subscriptions, maintenance of lists, renewal systems and management reports. Upon receipt of a subscription, a subscription code is allotted, the payment is accounted for, receipts are issued and the subscriber's record is created. Periodically, lists/stickers may be taken out for despatch of the magazine. Stickers may be taken out in a geographic sequence to facilitate posting. Lists may also have to be taken out for direct mailing to specific type of subscribers, etc. The renewal system ensures a 'lock-in' for a publication. A number of reminders may have to be sent. It is also necessary to analyse the reasons in case renewal is not made. Lastly, the software must give MIS reports so that the readership profile is available which is vital for soliciting advertisements. Special reports may have to be generated for RNI & ABC purposes.

(b) *Agents system:* This system comprises updation, despatch and accounting. Agents send their requisitions or changes on a daily basis in a highly unstructured format by way of postcards, telegrams, oral requests, etc. This has to be updated very fast. For instance, an agent may ask for higher despatch on the day following the budget. The system must generate a demand report so that the print run can be decided. Despatching includes bundling and label-printing so that the publication can reach the agent without errors and loss. The accounting sub-system monitors the billing and payment receipts. Again, special reports might be required in case the publication has to send statements to RNI & ABC.

(c) *Advertising:* The advertising system comprises advertisement booking, accounting and MIS. Advertisement bookings, special requests and material availability has to be monitored. This system also provides links to the production system so that the editorial and advertising mixture in each page can be planned. The system also does pagination. Subsequently, bills are raised, payments are accounted for and party accounts are prepared. In case of INS, special reports for INS accredited agencies are generated. Management reports help the publication to define its marketing strategies.

(d) *Financial accounts:* Standard packages have been used by various newspapers and magazines for computerising this activity. However, for ABC, RNI or INS requirements, special programmes are required.

**Benefits**

The benefits of computerisation clearly emanate from the objectives defined earlier, which can be summarised on follows:

(i) The ability to carry news fast and to make each individual item highly presentable and readable gives a newspaper/ magazine a competitive edge over rival publications;

(ii) Quick and extended accessibility of information from networks, bureaus, past stories, etc., helps a publication in better in-depth analysis of stories which again results in competitive advantage; and

(iii) Timeliness and accuracy of the commercial systems helps a publication to maximise reach and have satisfied readers, agents and advertisers;

**Problems**

The foremost issue is that the Indian computer industry has not responded to the needs of the publishing industry. In the process, they have lost a sizeable chunk of business which unfortunately has gone to imported systems. Looking at the size and maturity of the publishing industry, it is rather surprising that no computer manufacturer has looked at providing value added hardware which would have reaped rich dividends. This is not just a general sweeping statement but has a lot of merit as enumerated below:

(a) Presently, a publisher has to use a different system for text editing and production applications and a different one for commercial applications. There are excellent entry, editing and photo-composing systems but these cannot be used for general-purpose computing. Similarly, there are medium-range systems which would be able to handle the commercial applications but these can not be used for production applications because of lack of DTP software, language fonts-etc.

(b) As a result, a publisher has to go in for two different types of systems. A typical publication might go in for a number of steps: use PCs for text entry and editing, use Macs for DTP, take the photocomposed output on another machine and use a medium-range UNIX box for commercial work.

(c) The interesting thing is that the publishing industry is highly standardised and, therefore, it should be possible to offer a combined solution by doing a bit of system engineering. Unlike other industries, the method of operations for most publishers is identical. The degree of uniformity in the application areas is enormous. Yet the industry has to use multiple systems and has to keep on transferring data from one system to another. This is a waste of resources. The publisher would be very willing to pay for a CPU which could be useful as follows:

 (i) has entry/editing PCs, with WP software for required languages, hooked on to it,
 (ii) has communication abilities with other offices,
 (iii) possesses DTP software and full screen (19") monitors for layouts,
 (iv) hooks on to a Postscript-driven photo-composing unit with desired language fonts,
 (v) stores large amount of data for reference purposes,
 (vi) has terminals, disc space and software for commercial applications.

**Conclusion**

The publishing industry has had to pay precious foreign exchange for importing photocomposing equipment since their first priority was to automate the editorial applications. These machines have been of non-standard interfaces and, therefore, integration with other systems has not been possible. Only in recent times are standard Postscript-driven photo-composing engines available. The photo-composing industry has done this deliberately in the past so that high prices can be kept up, but no Indian manufacturer has ever attempted to take a lead in this area and come out with an integral solution.

The second major problem has been that of inadequate training. The publishing industry has tried to utilise existing manpower by training them in the use of computers. The people have basically learnt on the job. The knowledge-base, therefore, is inadequate. There are no specific programmes available where the users can learn how to utilise the technology available to them. The publishing industry has been a very rapidly growing industry and has the resources to pay, provided, proper training facilities are available.

It is not too late for the computer industry to tackle these problems. A solution will benefit the IT industry and the publishing industry both.

# 33

# TELEVISION

Y. VENKATESWARLU*

## Introduction

Doordarshan India is a vast organisation. It has programme-producing facility at almost all the State capitals, besides large set-ups at Delhi and other metropolitan centres. Presently, 528 transmitters have been installed across the length and breadth of the country for providing TV coverage to about 62 per cent of the population.

Television is just not a leisure-sector topic and it cannot be treated at par with other agencies like newspapers. We consider that Doordarshan is a catalyst to social reformation. In the past decade, Doordarshan has influenced the lives of millions of people across the country in their attitude, thinking and behaviour, etc.

Even before Doordarshan contemplated computerisation, computer-based technology had seeped into the organisation surreptitiously and this has proliferated into all key areas. Now, contrary to the popular belief, Doordarshan has state-of-the-art equipment for its programme production and transmission. Many of these equipments are micro processor-based or computer-controlled. In Central Production Centre at Delhi, a very advanced lighting control system, based on micro processors, has been installed and is in use.

## Application Areas

Computers can be gainfully utilised in almost all spheres of Doordarshan's activities. It can be introduced at headquarters at Delhi in a big way and followed with a need-based systems at zonal offices, different kendras and the other associated set-ups.

---

* Directorate General of Doordarshan, Government of India.

(A) *Project Monitoring*

At the headquarter, the work of the planning and development (P&D) unit involves planning the television service, preparing plan document, project notes for studio transmitter and satellite services, equipment configurations, equipment list, equipment specifications, preparation of drawings, designing the air-conditioning system and preparation of estimates followed by procurement action for the equipment to be procured from abroad as well as indigenous sources. In addition, the headquarter is also responsible for implementation of plans, execution of different projects monitoring their progress and eventually completing the projects. Thereafter, the maintenance wing of the headquarter takes over. For the several activities listed above, the correspondence and the follow-up action is presently being done manually with all its attendant disadvantages.

It is proposed to computerise some aspects of the above activities like preparation of equipment list, cable schedules, purchase follow-up, monitoring of equipment receipts and diversion of equipment from one project to another, preparation of budget estimates, etc. A software package is being developed for this purpose. This should enable maintenance of necessary databases and back-up information, avoiding duplication of effort, so that all concerned agencies can have ready access to the information.

Computerisation is bound to improve the efficiency and helps in better planning and monitoring of the projects. One of the biggest problems likely to be faced is pertaining to entering data of the on-going projects.

(B) *Central News Room Automation*

To just discuss another application area where computerisation is considered essential is the news room operation. Presently, the news room is connected to a number of wire agencies and the news fall is received through teleprinters. The clippings are circulated to all concerned, for preparation of news stories, deciding the visuals, deciding the run downs etc. Sometimes, it may so happen that the person concerned to take action regarding the particular news item is not readily available to take immediate action. Besides, access to archives is not readily available at present. The news production and presentation at present is almost manual. This not only puts severe limitations in preparation of news bulletins, but also effects the news presentation greatly. Many of the news organisations have computerised their operations and Doordarshan is also planning central news room automation.

All the news stories from wire agencies are entered directly into a central computer to which the news producers, editors will have ready access. This will help in systematic preparation of news bulletin, e.g, a sports producer will access his area in the computer to learn about the latest in the sports field. He will prepare these stories and contribute to the final bulletin. The News Editor may further work on these scripts if he so desires. He may also decide the visuals, the duration and the timing. The last-minute changes will be possible even while the news is on the air. Even the supporting equipment like teleprompter and videotape-recorders can be controlled by the central news room computer.

This will certainly make news production an enjoyable feat besides improving the presentation.

(C) *Teletext*

Teletext service was introduced by Doordarshan in Delhi in 1985. This service utilises the blank lines in the video signals for transmitting information in the form of magazines, each having a certain number of pages. With the help of a decoder, the viewer can view these pages.

The dedicated equipment in the teletext chain was based on computer technology. With the help of the National Informatics Centre (NIC), Doordarshan had introduced some utilities for editing the teletext pages. The software was configured around a MICRO-32 computer. The functions of the dedicated equipment have now been emulated on PCs. The entire set-up has been re-configured. The key equipment, the teletext broadcast controller (TBC), has also been emulated on PC. Dedicated PCs are now available for serving the different agencies utilising teletext service, like Indian Railways, Indian Airlines, etc.

(D) *Central Archives*:

Another important area where Doordarshan wants to computerise is in the area of central archives. A large number of programmes have archival value and these are to be preserved in proper conditions for future possible use. These tapes will be required for play-back by Doordarshan and also to be made available for other agencies for their use. Proper cataloguing of these tapes and a query system has to be developed so that in the shortest possible time, we can access the relevant tape.

A computer system is being planned for the above applications. The software services of outside agencies may also be used in the development of this system. This system will also eventually support the news section, helping the news room staff to select the required tape, visuals, etc., with the help of an elaborate query system. This will help in retrieving the tape in good time so that the material can be used in the same day's bulletins. It is assumed that around 50,000 tapes may have to be archived. This also includes tapes of archival value which are preserved at individual kendras.

In the recently concluded elections for the special telecast of election analysis and special election news bulletins, computers and NICNET were extensively used. These programmes were produced jointly by Doordarshan and NDTV. Computer hardware configurations and support software were developed by NDTV. A brief description of the system installed for the purpose is given below.

**Information System for Election Analysis**

The election information system was used for collecting, processing and presenting election results during the election analysis programmes of Doordarshan. It consisted of the following three components :

(a) *Data Collection*

The election results from various constituencies were received through NICNET, UNI and PTI and hotlines;

(b) *Studio Network*

A network of super-ATs was installed in the studio for compiling and processing information coming from the above sources;

(c) *Results Output*

The output consisted of graphics for broadcasting, reports on monitors and printers;

(i) NICNET

NICNET, as we know, is a satellite-based network installed by National Informatics Centre that links over 450 districts to a mainframe computer at New Delhi. These district centres were feeding election results to the central computer after every round of counting. This included both the fast-track information, i.e., which party has won or is leading in a given constituency and the detailed information containing votes polled by the major candidates and the total valid votes. The NICNET mainframe was connected to the studio network through a DoT line for automatic downloading of these election results.

(ii) UNI and PTI

UNI and PTI were sending election results through teleprinters installed at the studio;

(iii) HOTLINES

The studio was also connected to various State election commission offices through hotlines.

**Studio Network**

The studio-network consisted of four PC-ATs-(IBM-compatible 386 machines). There were two master computers, one of which was storing fast-track information and the other was storing detailed votes information. VT100 terminals were connected to these for entry of results coming through UNI, PTI and hotlines. One PC-AT was connected to NICNET central node at the C.G.O. complex. It was retrieving information packets sent by NICNET district centres and routing them to the two master computers. Another PC-AT was connected to the two masters which served as the back-up. Automatic periodic back-ups of the two databases were being taken so that operation could be shifted to the backup computer in case of a master crashing.

The election data on the two masters were being summarised continuously to generate various kinds of reports (latest party positions with gains and losses, vote shares, Swings for various parties, turnout percentage, etc.). These reports were being fed through RS-232 cables to the following :

(i) Graphics

The graphics subsystem consisted of two IBM PC-ATs having add-on video graphics cards to generate video signals. These were running software for displaying broadcast quality anti-aliased animated charts and text. Updates, showing latest position, were coming from the masters and within seconds they could be presented in the form of growing bars. This was used for showing the vote shares, vote changes, party positions and headlines during the programme.

(ii) Analysis

Printers and terminals were linked to the master computers which could be used for viewing the latest reports. These outputs were provided for special election bulletins.

**Conclusion**

In addition, a host of other uses to which Doordarshan can put the computer are: pay roll preparation, (already implemented), inventory management, personnel management, training, conference, etc.

In the years to come, Doordarshan should be one of the biggest computer-users in the country.

# 34

# BOOKS

SUGATA MITRA*

## Introduction

The application of computers to enrich the quality of life remains mostly a dream, here in India and elsewhere. At the same time, the fact that computers have changed the quality of our lives is undeniable. Computer applications have always suffered from a lack of definition of success. It is not very clear if a computer application can be called successful if it does any of the following:

(i) Earns a lot of money for its originator(s),
(ii) Increases human productivity,
(iii) Changes the way certain things are done,
(iv) Results in the sale and use of more computers or software,
(v) Alters human power structures or the society,
(vi) Alters human behaviour,
(vii) Some or all of the above.

Lack of a clear definition of success naturally also makes it difficult to decide when a computer application is unsuccessful.

The success or failure of computer applications is viewed very differently in different segments of society. One could thus devise these alternative definitions for a successful application.

## Successful Application

A successful computer application is defined as follows:

---

* NIIT Limited.

(A) One which is financially viable, that is, the cost of development and implementation is adequately less than the earnings from the application;
(B) One which is socially useful, that is, the application improves one or more of the important parameters of human society such as prosperity, power, happiness, productivity, and so on;
(C) One which actualises one or more capabilities of current science and technology, that is, it converts an idea into an event; and
(D) One which causes an irreversible change in the world, that is, a world with this application is substantially and irrevocably different from a world without it.

A computer application which satisfies all of the above definitions would, of course, be called a rip-roaring success. They are very few in number!

Definition (A) is usually adopted by traders and businessmen. Definition (B) is supported by governments. (A) and (B) together are acceptable to "good" industrialists and progressive bureaucrats. Definition (C) is a scientists definition while (C) and (D) together are what excites those inventors who do not mind a bit of fame and glory. It is very rarely that one comes across developers who can create applications where all four definitions apply. Edison, a rare example, was one such. In Table 34.1, we have tried to classify some important computer applications and also include some non-computer products to show how they compare.

For the purposes of this article, we propose the following definitions:

> "The success of a computer application is directly proportional to the number of human beings it affects."

This definition is restrictive and perhaps unkind. It merely measures change as a parameter of success. However, Nature too does the same. Evolution proceeds merely through change and benefits (or the lack of it) are not considered important. It is because of this unfortunate point of view that the above definition equates the success of communication technology with that of the hydrogen bomb.

It is with this restrictive definition in mind that the rest of this paper should be read.

TABLE 34.1: Important Computer Applications

| PRODUCT | DEF(A) | DEF(B) | DEF(C) | DEF(D) | AFFECTS... |
|---|---|---|---|---|---|
| Data-base management Systems | Yes | ? | Yes | ? | Many people |
| Computer-Assisted Communication | Yes | Yes | Yes | Yes | Almost everybody |
| The "Windows" environment | Yes | ? | Yes | ? | Few people |
| Computer-Assisted Medical imaging | Yes | Yes | Yes | Yes | Most people |
| The Electric lamp | Yes | Yes | Yes | Yes | Almost everybody |
| The Hydrogen Bomb | ? | ? | Yes | Yes | Almost everybody |

**New Applications Development**

Before undertaking to implement a new computer application, one would generally consider whether the new applications, (a) can be created, and (b) can be used. One could generally expand these considerations into a nine-element matrix, as shown in Table 34.2.

In India, most industries operate in the A1 area and hence most industrialists prefer to be middlemen selling someoneelse's technology. At best they may venture into B1 or C1 but seldom anywhere else.

The government, on the other hand, prefers to remain in the C3 area where accountability is low. At best, if they are adventurous, they enter B3, and usually fail. One may well recall the laudable, yet suicidal plunge of C-DOT into the A2 area.

It is interesting to note that most creative and ambitious students would like to work in areas A2, A3, B2, and C2, which are unattended in this country. Hence they leave. The ones who remain tend to vegetate in A1 or C3.

TABLE 34.2: Strategies for Development

| | A<br>Market Needs it Now | B<br>Market does not Know that there is Need for it | C<br>Market does not Need it Now, but will in Future |
|---|---|---|---|
| 1. Products Exist | - Become a distributor<br>- Make a better one<br>- Leave it alone | - Create awareness<br>- Create a need<br>- Become a distributor | - Hoard it<br>- Plan marketing<br>- Include in strategy |
| 2. Product does not exist but can be made | - Build it fast<br>- Don't try anything fancy<br>- Keep track of competition | - Get marketing advice<br>- Keep budgets low<br>- Watch competition<br>- Create a need | - Build a low-cost research team<br>- Keep track of university work<br>- Include in corporate planning |
| 3. Product does not exist and needs to be invented | - Invest in R and D<br>- Invest in media and PR<br>- Get funding | - Get government funding<br>- Start low cost R and D<br>- Invest in marketing | - Invest in research<br>- Start low-key need-building<br>- Participate in conferences and publish |

## Struggles with Indian Applications

Computers are now applied in many facets of Indian life. However, a list of these would neither be comprehensive nor throw much light on the application process. Instead, in what follows, we present three case-histories of applications where we were involved in the conception, development and implementation. We hope this limited experience will provide some insight into the general area of computer applications for common man.

(A) *The "Partners" Project*

In 1984, we developed a system which used about a hundred rules to attempt automatic matching of men and women in the indian "arranged" marriage format. The rules here are fuzzy and depend significantly on social parameters (e.g., caste, colour, etc.) not generally considered significant in other countries. The system seemed to produce good results and a businessmen attempted to set-up a service agency with it. This did not prove to be viable because the cost of educating the market and getting them to accept a non-human system proved to be too expensive. In the end, the product was sold to the *Times of India* and the *Hindustan Times* newspapers, both of which continue to use it as a value-addition to their matrimonial columns. In the last eight years or so, unofficial estimates from these organisations indicate that over 25,000 marriages have taken place using the output of this system. The Partners system has significantly affected the lives of 50,000 persons and, when it was developed, fell into the B2 category of Table 34.2. However, apart from meeting its development costs, it has not directly produced any money.

(B) *The "Jobads" Project*

In 1984, we were involved in purchasing and implementing one of the first LAN's in the country. This was a Convergent Technologies B-22 LAN driving a pair of Autologic APS-micro5 CRT typesetters. The user organisation was United India Periodicals, publishers of Patriot newspaper. After the system was implemented, we began development of software which would enable operator-independent typesetting and pagination of databases. This was a time when desk-top publishing was unknown and we published some of results. Subsequently, this work led to a concept where employment advertisements from various newspapers were abstracted, classified and paginated automatically into a tabloid magazine called JOBADS. The entire magazine was produced by a single operator and two terminals. It reached a circulation of 8000 in Delhi. However, the massive increases of newsprint prices and distribution costs (fuel) in 1987-88 made the publication unviable. Subsequently, the concept changed its form to where several existing publications used an abstracted jobs section as value-addition to their readers. During its publications, about a million copies of JOBADS were sold, and while it is only possible to guess from readers' letters, at least 5,000 persons obtained employment using the information from its columns. In the framework of this article, in 1985, JOBADS was a B3 type project and should perhaps have been taken up by the government.

## (C) *The "Yellow Pages" Project*

In 1985, the Department of Telecommunication (DoT) produced their "Blue Book" of officers using the database publishing technology developed for JOBADS. The data was ported from their PDP-11 to the B22 LAN and typeset automatically in just a few hours. This generated interest within the DoT in the area of telephone directory publishing. Telephone directories were published from DoT databases by entering the information all over again on typesetting systems. This caused great inaccuracies and delays. In 1986, TCS who were contractors to the government for telephone directory production used the Patriot LAN and we developed directory-typesetting software for them and paginated the Delhi telephone directory.

Subsequently, the government awarded a contract to Patriot for the production of the telephone directories of Delhi, Bombay and Calcutta for five years. This was followed by similar contracts for Hyderabad, Coimbatore, Madurai, Salem, Trichi, Orissa circle, etc., covering over 70 per cent of all telephone directories in India. These contracts were unique since the government would get all these directories free of cost from the contractor and would, in addition, receive a hefty commission (over Rs. 30 crores) from them during the contract period. In return, the contractor would be permitted to produce a classified business section in the directory — "Yellow Pages" as they are called all over the world. The contractor would retain all revenues from advertisements in these directories and use this to defray their costs and pay the royalties. United India Periodicals (UIP) set up a new company — United Database India (UDI) to handle this project.

Production of yellow page directories require three main kinds of software: direct marketing software to guide a large direct marketing and telemarketing team; data-base software to maintain data-bases of over two million subscribers; and typesetting software for both regular ("white") and yellow page directories. This software was available from the USA for around US $ 500,000 to run on the IBM or VAX mainframe platforms.

At UDI, the software was developed on PC-LANs communicating with Convergent B-25 LAN's for typesetting. The effort was about 20 Man-years completed in about 10 calendar months. LANs were set up at Calcutta, Delhi, Bombay and Hyderabad and first directories of Delhi, Bombay, Calcutta, Hyderabad, and the smaller cities produced in 1987-88. Over 10 million people consisting of telephone subscribers, business houses and other buyers and sellers used the output of these programmes, and their calling, buying and selling patterns altered accordingly.

The turnover of UDI and UIP rose from around Rs. 3 crores in 1987 to over Rs. 30 crores in 1990. The management and ownership, reeling under these unaccustomed figures, went through massive transformations. UDI continues to be one of the largest yellow page publishers in the world and one of very few to have its own LAN-based marketing and publishing systems. The yellow pages project represents a A1 type project, purely in the commercial domain.

**A Restrictive View of the Future**

Any predictions regarding future applications of computers is an exercise in fantasy. However, it is sometimes possible to indicate broad areas where computers will be used. Our work and experience are restricted to the small computer/PC, MS-DOS arena and it is in this domain that we would like to hazard some guesses.

We would expect PCs to move out of EDP on to the streets (so to speak !) in a short while. For this to happen, many tools will be required in the areas of graphics (particularly bitmaps), voice, music and sound, animation, Indian language processing, expert systems and neural networks. Table 34.3 shows some of the position these technologies occupy in the application-development matrix as of now (August, 1991). Tables 34.2 and 34.3, consulted together, can easily produce application projects and strategies.

**Conclusion**

In India, in our limited experience, a new application takes a long time to be acceptable. It is much more easily introduced with piggy-backing on some existing and accepted application. Funding for new applications development is almost impossible to obtain unless it is

TABLE 34.3: Positioning of Future Indian Applications (non-exhaustive)

| | A<br>Market Needs it Now | B<br>Market does not Know its Need | C<br>Market will Need it Later |
|---|---|---|---|
| 1. Products exist | - Bitmap editors<br>- Colour separators<br>- Voice cards<br>- Expert shells | - Video digitisers<br>- Music systems<br>- Transputers<br>- Voice mail | - Indian language interfaces<br>- Indian music<br>- CD ROMS<br>- Animation |
| 2. Product can be made | - Graphics data-bases<br>- Audio data-bases<br>- Canned Indian expert systems<br>- Technical training programs | - Indian language expert systems<br>- Speech recognition<br>- Process control for home use | - Neural net-work shells<br>- Voice/image based medical diagonstic systems<br>- Traffic and city planners<br>- Real-time newspapers |
| 3. Product has to be invented | - Ruggedised rural PCs<br>- Electronic telephone directories<br>- Indian games | - Energy management systems<br>- Tax monitoring<br>- Rural education<br>- Applicat-ions for the handi-capped techniques | - Integration of voices, image, expert systems, neural net-works and process control<br>- Image/data compression |

already ordered by an end-user. Consequently, new applications development is guided by the end-user's imagination which, in most cases, is dismal. There is not one Indian utility package in the world market (the last indian conceptual invention was the zero). There is not one Indian game in the market (the last invention was chess). If this situation is to be changed, Indian industry must learn to invest judiciously (but not cautiously) in the areas represented by the second and third rows of Tables 34.2 and 34.3. They must do so without any estimates of immediate profitability. They must do so without converting their R & D's into shops.

They must do so, knowing that it is the spearhead which is most likely to be bloodied and blunted.

35

# INDIAN LANGUAGES (GIST Application)

SUBASH PANI*

## Introduction

GIST (Graphics-based Information Systems) technology is the state-of-the-art and *de facto* standard for information technology applications in Indian languages. It is the result of sustained research started at the Indian Institute of Technology (IIT) Kanpur and now continued at the Centre for Development of Advanced Computing (C-DAC), Pune. The current implementation of GIST marks a major breakthrough for information technology applications in Indian languages providing a powerful yet flexible and simple solution being absolutely in tune with the current international industry standards and hardware/software.

The state-of-the-art GIST technology offers standard phonetic key board, use of Indian languages on the DOS, UNIX/XENIX platforms, use of all standard application development tools like dBASE, Lotus 123, Wordstar, etc., display of text entered in one language in another script through a few key strokes, concurrent use of multiple Indian languages along with English, standard print enhancement features, interfaces with standard DTP packages like Ventura and Pagemaker, printing in DMP and Laser printers, character generation for TV and a host of other facilities.

GIST itself has evolved over less than a decade as on today but in its innovative approach and technical quality it marks a quantum jump, an order-of-magnitude improvement over what was previously

---

* Orissa Computer Application Centre.

available and truly represents a giant leap forward. Although GIST has diverse applications within the broad spectrum of information technology-related activities, we will primarily concern ourselves with computer-based information system (CBIS), in view of its greater relevance and extensive use.

**Indian Languages — Special Feature and some Technology Issues**

Computers in their electric/electronic form are hardly half a century old. In India too, computers have been used for almost a similar period. However, serious efforts in developing computer applications using Indian languages has perhaps gone on for only about a decade. In order to appreciate the issues connected with computing in Indian languages, one has to understand the special features of Indian languages and the problems associated with their use for computing.

Firstly, India has not one language but a host of them. Of these more than a dozen can be categorised as major languages and even the Indian constitution has recognised them as such. While some of the languages share the scripts, most major languages have their own unique scripts. Secondly, while the Roman group of characters including English have a very small set of alphabets, albeit with capital and small letters, the Indian languages have the added complexity of a large number of conjuncts, besides a number of 'Matras'. Consequently, the complete character-set for each Indian language becomes very large, the number sometimes exceeding three hundred. Accommodating the complete character-set in any system to be used for computer representation, therefore, poses a fairly complex and difficult technology problem.

Each of these major languages, however, is not only spoken by a substantial number of people in terms of absolute numbers but, more importantly, a vast amount of work both in official matters and otherwise which is transacted in these languages is eminently suitable for computerisation. Non-availability of a cost-effective and technologically feasible solution for use of these languages in computers had been a major impediment in extending the benefits of information technology to a vast majority of Indian population, particularly in the areas of public administration and public services.

**Evolution of Technology in Indian Languages**

At this stage, it will be relevant to briefly outline the history of technology innovations in the use of Indian languages for different purposes. The mechanical typewriter was the first automated tool for representing text for different scripts. After independence, Hindi was declared as the national language, several attempts were made to develop Hindi typewriters. Since the English typewriter with the QWERTY key-board was the standard with which all typists in government organisations were familiar, the technology solution attempted was to fit in the Devnagari script within the existing English typewriter's key board layout.

As the complete character-set could not be accommodated within this QWERTY key-board layout, sacrifices had to be made by excluding several characters and virtually all conjuncts. Consequently, the solution was neither elegant nor functionally complete. Since the nature of Indian scripts is completely different from that of English, these attempts were somewhat like trying to fit a square peg in a round hole. The key-board had no relation to the frequency of use of different characters or with the natural classification of the Indian scripts which is based on phonetic grouping. No wonder, therefore, that in the initial stages these Devnagari typewriters were not popular and very few could develop the specialised skills to make use of these machines. Similar attempts were also made in the other Indian languages over a period of time with equally lack-lustre results. The need for developing an appropriate key-board for Indian languages in general as also for specific languages has, therefore, been the subject matter of research and study for linguists, printers, manufacturers of typewriters and related equipments as well as various government departments including the Department of Official Languages.

As for the printing industry, the first attempt to introduce the electronic technology was made in the photo-type setting machines in which the severe limitation of mechanical typewriter in terms of the character-set which could be represented was overcome. In the latter, each character was available in the shape of a metal font at the head of a lever connected to the individual keys of the typewriter. These were either a complete alphabet or a *Matra* or some other graphic form which was used for representing the script, either singly or in combination of some other letters or graphics. Since the concept of upper and lower case did not exist in Indian languages, each of the specific key could accommodate two such items for representation of the Indian scripts. In the photo-type setting machines, however, the characters were formed with combination of slices of characters, called 'char-slices', in a linear order.

To include the complete character-set, a large-key board was required which sometime had four overlays. Naturally the operation was quite clumsy and cumbersome and required long practice for specialised operators to make use of these machines and yet the productivity was not very high. Another problem related to the display of the characters in the screen on account of the formation of character through combination of parts of characters within the character-oriented display format originally designed for English. The results were far from satisfactory and, in fact, in some cases were quite unreadable. However, the key concept of forming the individual characters through a combination of char-slices contained in it a very fundamental concept about the representation of Indian characters which later evolved into the present system of GIST. Consequent on the availability of microprocessor-based systems, it was possible to avoid the multiple overlays of key-board and include the complete character-set through combination of different keys.

Along with this, the development of a common standard for the Indian languages key board was conceptualised by providing for the basic alphabets which are common to a larger number of Indian languages, particularly those derived from the Brahmi family of scripts. The latter include 12 of the 14 major languages in India. The basic phonetic units called *phonemes* in these languages are common to these languages and consequently they have fairly common set of alphabets though their script representations are different. This set consists of the vowels – Swarabarna, the consonants – Vyanjanabarna and various matras – basically in the nature of prefixes/suffixes as sound/phonetic modifiers. The set is also grouped into distinct logical units, sometimes called 'Vargas'. These common and basic alphabets could be accommodated within a set of 75 characters and all the conjuncts could be derived from a combination of these alphabets.

Following the above approach the Departments of Electronics (DOE), Government of India (GOI) standardised the key-board for Indian languages in 1986. This is known as INSCRIPT (Indian Script) key-board. As a result of the reduced number of basic units, this could use the standard QWERTY key-board layout. Based on the analysis of the frequency of use and for the convenience of typing, the layout has the vowels and consonant in separate pads in the left and the right part of the key-board. Since the basic alphabets are accommodated within the three touch-typable rows of the corresponding QWERTY layout, it provides considerable ease of use. The logical inter-relationship of the different parts of the layout makes it easy to learn and even non-typists and first-time users find it much simpler to learn when compared to learning the use of English typewriters. This has been more than amply demonstrated in the high-volume data entry work for the land records projects using Indian languages in various Indian languages.

**ISCII Code**

In a parallel development, DOE standardised a code for the representation of Indian languages in the shape of the Indian Standard Code for Information Interchange (ISCII) in the year 1986. This was subsequently revised in 1988. ISCII retains the standard ASCII-set in the lower half and the upper half contains characters required for all Indian scripts. All the composite characters in Indian languages are formed by a combination of the basic characters. The ISCII code is compatible with the ISO 8-bit recommendations. Later on, two variations of the ISCII code have been developed for handling the special problems associated with the IBM PC and compatibles (which do not follow the ISO 8-bit format) as well as some specialised software packages which use a 7-bit format. These are known as PC-ISCII and ISCII-7. The complete technical details of these standards are available with DoE.

**GIST Evolution**

GIST started as a research and development project in the IIT, Kanpur. Work on the GIST project, then called Graphics and Indian Script Terminal, started in 1983 as a sponsored project of DOE. Mohan Tambe, then a fresh alumni of the institute, was the project leader and continues to be the spirit behind the evolution of the GIST Technology.

In the words of the GIST Group, "Right from the beginning the goal was to provide a technologically perfect solution for the Indian scripts". Most of the earlier attempts had followed the character-generation approach and provided dedicated systems for specific applications like word processing. The GIST project, however, intended to provide a general-purpose computer for diverse applications. At this point, the specific goal of the project was to develop Indian language script processing facilities in the industry standard VT100/VT220 compatible multi-user terminal. Up front in the development efforts, the project adopted the graphics approach for representation of the Indian scripts in which display of the script is done dot-by-dot. A word on the display strategy would be relevant at this stage. The structure of the different Indian scripts vary widely but some of them are similar. Some are linear (Malayalam, Oriya, Tamil) and others are non-linear, etc) (Devnagari). In the latter, matras are sometimes positioned over preceding characters. Further, some have horizontal bars on top like Devnagari. The basic shapes also vary in as much as some have basically circles and half circles with a few vertical bars/horizontal bars, while others have more of square/triangular shapes.

Each script has, therefore, to be handled in somewhat unique fashion, though the underlying software strategy would be common. The latter consists of developing the appropriate graphic primitives which can be accommodated within the basic set and yet the combination, positioning and sizing of which would provide aesthetically pleasing and traditionally correct display of almost the complete alphabet set for the language. On account of the flexible size and the variable positioning of the matras, use of subscripts and conjuncts consisting of multiple characters, the problem becomes really complex.

A word on the display strategy would be relevant at this stage. To take care of all the complexities outlined above, an appropriate frame for the font is defined within which the various combinations are accommodated. For example, the following strategy is adopted for the Devnagari script. A few standard widths are defined to take care of the horizontal partition. In addition, different sizes of kerning spaces are defined to provide proportional spacing. Besides, there is an ascender space and descender space above and below the character space for vertical portions. The character space itself is further divided into appropriate zones. Due to this graphics orientation, the cursor occupies a flexible space on the video display. Due to the need for the high resolution display and other limitations, a standard video displays 14 lines of Indian characters. The exact number of characters which can be displayed horizontally would obviously vary.

The bit-mapped graphics technology requires high resolution

graphics display and substantial processing capacity. Fortunately, the availability of powerful Intel-8088 16-bit Micro-processor made this approach technologically feasible. Initially, the project took up implementation of the Devnagari script and used a custom key-board with alphabets laid out in a logical pattern. The initial system which was displayed in the International Hindi Sammelan was a resounding success and received enthusiastic support from all concerned. The initial model was in the shape of a terminal for a multi-user system. Then it was called Integrated Devnagari Computer (IDC). This was developed under the INTER-MDS development platform. The near-perfect solution not only provided the necessary confidence to the development team but also whetted the appetite of the user-groups for additional features and functions.

The systems were also displayed in the CSI exhibitions and exposed the possibilities in the area of information technology applications in Indian languages to a larger audience. Simultaneously, a dialogue was started with the industry for commercial production of GIST systems. Initially, the cost appeared to be quite high. However, the availability of the 32-bit Motorola 68000 micro-processor made it possible to provide the complete solution in a single compact-board with less than 50 chips, while making available far greater power than the earlier version. In July 1986, GIST technology was transferred to six manufacturers for commercial production of GIST systems.

Since then, GIST has evolved on many fronts. In due course, GIST adopted the ISCII standard and the INSCRIPT key board. The availability of IBM PCs in the 80's and their enormous popularity as well as the availability of a large number of high-quality packaged software also brought up new challenges for further development of GIST. It was quite natural, therefore, to expect that GIST be made available on the PC and compatible platforms. In 1987, the first IBM PC plug-in card incorporating GIST was introduced.

Simultaneously, work on the development of appropriate font-sets for GIST machines was also taken up. Today, clear-print quality-fonts with a 24-dot height and proportional spacing for most major Indian languages is available as part of the GIST firmware. These can be used with standard 24-pin dot-matrix printers or even with 9-pin printers, though, in the latter case, the printing has to be done in more than one pass. Drivers are provided for several standard printers like EPSON, Godrej, L&T, and for line printer of Mannesman Tally/LIPI.

From October 1988, the GIST project has been adopted by the Centre for Development of Advanced Computing (C-DAC) at Pune as one of its sub-missions. The scope of the project has also been expanded substantially from the original objective of providing a script terminal. In fact "the orientation is now towards delivering an international standard solution in a much broader domain of information technology". While on the script front the boundaries of the Brahmi group has been crossed and GIST solutions for the Perso-Arabic group of languages like Urdu, Arabic, Persian, Sindhi and Kashmiri are already available, work on the more complex Asian scripts like Sinhalese, Tibetan, Burmese and Thai is also on hand. It is relevant to mention that GIST solution is also available for the Russian language. On the application domain, several new solutions have been provided which include desk-top publishing, interface for photo-type setting machines in shape of remote data-entry terminals, character generation for television, etc.

A related development is in the area of fonts. An Indian standard font code (ISFOC) has been defined which is useful in providing the detailed specifications for font development. On account of the use of a variety of *Matras* and a large number of conjuncts including some superscripts and sub-scripts, a whole lot of technical issues are involved in the preparation of fonts for Indian languages. Again, these vary from language to language. While it would not be possible to give a comprehensive or detailed account of these technical issues within our ambit, suffice here to say that GIST provides the necessary technology solution for developing a large variety of fonts for specific applications like printing, video display and computer screen display and interfaces for standard desk-top publishing (DTP) softwares like Ventura and Pagemaker, etc.

Currently, GIST also includes a built-in script processor which has most of the standard print-enhancement facilities like bold-facing, underlining, italics, shadowing, etc. Post-script language interface has also been provided for full functionality in terms of use of the DTP packages.

In this context, a mention has to be made regarding rapid and sudden expansion the DTP applications in the country in the last five years. In the mid-eighties, particularly after the liberalised computer policy of 1986, a large number of Apple Macintosh systems were imported to the country. The availability of easy-to-use font-designing software saw a sudden rise of interest in Indian language computer applications, particularly word processing, DTP and computer linked photo-type setting. Though the character-oriented approach was followed and had its own limitation and a large number amateurs got into the act, yet a variety of fonts was available. Some pioneering work in this regard has been done by the Indian Typographical Research Institute of Pune which already had long experience in font design — both metal cast and films for photo-type setting machines. Since the DTP provided an affordable alternative to the more expensive photo-type setting machines, the use of computers for Indian language applications proliferated in a big way. Today, a good number of regional newspaper and publishing houses use these dedicated DTP systems with Indian language fonts, specialised or general purpose word processors and standard DTP softwares like Ventura and Pagemaker. Although a sub-optimal, somewhat inelegant and technologically imperfect solution, these have nevertheless played a very vital role in bringing Indian language computing to a large body of users and the market place.

**Milestones of GIST**

GIST provides a very neat solution for Indian language computing. At the core of the technology is the concept of a phonetic key-board which can be used for most major Indian languages like Hindi, Marathi, Gujarati, Gurmukhi, Tamil, Telugu, Bengali and Oriya, etc. The generation of characters in the screen and printer is graphics-oriented with each character, combined characters (juktaksharas) and matras being formed as per the unique features of the specific language, through combination, positioning and manipulation of the sizes of some graphic primitives. While the earlier photo-type setting machines had unique and large multi-level key-boards to accommodate the complete character-set of an Indian language, the initial PC-implementations, mostly on the Apple Macintosh platform, offered purely word processing facilities with substantial limitation on the character-set. Besides, each vendor offered his own non-standard solution. GIST implements the Indian Standard Code for Information Interchange (ISCII) along with fonts developed as per the Indian Standard Font Code (ISFOC) guidelines.

Another major breakthrough was achieved in the year 1988 by providing facilities for concurrent use of English and any one or more of Indian scripts. This highly ingenuous solution made use of the least commonly used character "x" to mark the starting point for an Indian script. By embedding appropriate control character for denoting the specific Indian language selected, it was possible to provide for use of multiple-language scripts within the same text. The character 'x' is otherwise used to represent the *Nukta* character which is also less frequently used within the total character set of Indian languages. By repeating this character twice, the actual representation of *Nukta* character is achieved. Those familiar with the use of C language will find a parallel in the use of escape, "\" character used as a delimiter. Similar delimiter is also used by most word processing packages for embedding control characters for appropriate print enhancements. This strategy provides full functionality for mixing of different Indian scripts which co-exist with the English script, while providing an absolutely simple method for user interface. Once the user gets into the Indian script mode through the appropriate key combinations, he can select the script of his choice from a menu. It is relevant to mention that at this stage the development platform for GIST was UNIX/XENIX.

The next important milestone in the evolution of GIST was the development of an application-specific integrated circuit (ASIC) chip, GIST-9000. Completely designed by the GIST Team at C-DAC, this ASIC chip has been fabricated at VLSI Technology Incorporated (VTI), USA. This ASIC chip works in tandem with the Motorola MC-68008 Processor. Although the latter uses 8-bit data-bus, through appropriate technology innovations full functional compatibility and performance quality has been achieved at par with the earlier 68000 based cards. The use of the ASIC chip has reduced the card-size dramatically and also brought down the total number of chips to about 9, compared to the standard full-length IBM PC GIST card containing some 49 ICs. Currently, GIST is also being tried on the LAN environment. The development platform is the SUN work stations and several special-purpose hardware and software.

A second-round technology transfer has been made in the year 1990 and currently another round is in progress. For the script-font, C-DAC has now a full-fledged team exclusively looking after font design. In this, C-DAC has also been working in close collaboration with some other development organisations, notably Orissa Computer Application Centre (OCAC) for some specific languages. The font-development platform has been standardised with the FONTOGRAPHER software on the Apple Macintosh platform, used concurrently with the Publisher's Type Foundry (PTF) software on the IBM PC platform. For technical reasons, separate fonts have to be developed for the Post Script and non-Post Script printers, dot-matrix printers, computer screens and video terminals. For the non-Post Script printers, the fonts have to be developed for each of the font size proposed to be used. Therefore, it would be more appropriate to say that a font-family has to be designed to meet the complete requirement of languages for different applications. While work on Devnagari script has made substantial progress, similar work has also been taken up for other languages also. On the *Ratha Yatra* day at Puri in 1991, the first set of non-Post Script ORIYA fonts for laser printers titled 'SARALA' jointly developed by C-DAC and OCAC team was dedicated, as shown in Figure 35.1. Devanagari and Bengali scripts were also successfully used with the caption editors to provide the required graphic support in the national television network by Doordarshan to display election information.

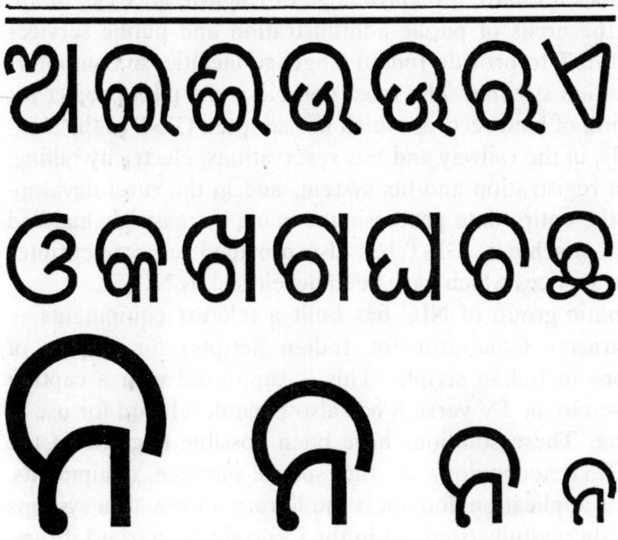

FIG. 35.1: Some sample Oriya Fonts

**Application Domains**

With the current level of technology, the application domains for GIST has truly no frontiers. Anything and everything, where information technology can be used and data and text needs to be stored and displayed in Indian languages, is a potential domain for GIST application. The arrival of GIST has truly heralded the liberation of computer applications in Indian languages from the narrow world of text processing. While even in the area of text processing, an easy-to-use solution is available for use of multiple languages, additional facilities like simultaneous transliteration into different Indian languages as well as representation in the Roman (English) script with the standard diacritic marks, interface for desk-top publishing software and facilities for Type Setting Terminals have considerably expanded the use of computers for the entire printing and publishing industry. However, the most important benefit of GIST has been in the area of data processing. Since a vast majority of the population in this country does not have the knowledge of English, a variety of applications in the areas of public administration and public services have utilised GIST to provide Indian language facilities in computer-based information systems. The most notable is the pilot project for computerisation of land records which has adopted GIST as the standard. Similarly, in the railway and bus reservations, electricity billing, motor vehicle registration and tax system, and in the rural development sector, the entire data processing is being increasingly handled with the GIST machines. GIST has also provided telex, teleprinter and video-text services which have been developed by NITEL.

The telematic group of NIC has built a teletext equipments — CGIST (Character Generator for Indian Scripts) for display of colour captions in Indian scripts. This is supported with a caption editor. A close-circuit TV version has also been developed for use in the Lok Sabha. These solutions have been possible because of the underlying GIST technology in the special-purpose equipments. Another major application domain is the library information systems and has been successfully tried out in the Central Secretariat Library. GIST facilitates display of information about Indian books in Indian scripts. Additionally, there is facility for automatic transliteration between different Indian scripts and also Roman scripts with diacritic marks. On the last-mentioned item, a standard has been evolved jointly by the National Library, Central Secretariat Library and the

Library of Congress (USA).

**Future Trends: Problems and Prospects**

In the short period of less than a decade, GIST has matured like a precocious child. It is still growing ever more rapidly and is bound to pervade many new application areas. Of these, one major thrust-area is speech-recognition and speech-synthesis for which serious research is currently being undertaken in the Tata Institutes of Fundamental Research. A natural extension of this would be knowledge-based computer systems (KBCS) incorporating the Indian languages, and natural language processing in Indian languages and optical character reading (OCR) systems for recognising Indian script characters. Another interesting possibility is the use of multiple Indian languages for simultaneous subtitling. This can be achieved through multiplexing and appropriate coding and decoding mechanism in the main transmitters and relay transmitters of Doordarshan. In such a system when a regional language film is being transmitted, it will be possible for viewers of different regions of the country to see the subtitles in their local languages.

Another exciting possibility is in the area of computer-aided education (CAE). An elaborate network of video-based distance education system is available in the country under the auspices of UGC, IGNOU and the different State-level institutions including the educational television units (ETV). High-quality video-visuals can be produced in one location and can be combined with audio/graphic inputs in multiple languages. In this last area, the latest technological innovation in the information technology field in the shape of multimedia systems can be utilised. In other words, GIST can work in tandem wilt multi-media systems to combine graphics, data, text, sound and animation to provide complete and near-natural representation of information.

A few problems, however, exist and need to be taken care of if we want GIST to become ubiquitous and useful. While the technology innovations have been far reaching, dramatic and in many ways almost epoch-making, in terms of intensive use and technology absorption by computer vendors, service organisations and end-users, the progress has not kept pace. Even though the first GIST terminal was available in 1986, very few major computer manufacturers took interest in the developments and absorption of technology in the initial stage. In fact, when this author conducted a thorough and comprehensive bench-marking and evaluation of computer hardwares for the pilot project for land records in Orissa towards the middle of 1989, the major manufacturers including the top ones had practically no knowledge of GIST. At the insistence of OCAC, vendors like WIPRO, SIVA, HCL and PCL hurriedly procured GIST cards and terminals, and were able to demonstrate GIST solutions. Although a few of the manufacturers have obtained technology transfer from C-DAC, one cannot say that they have internalised the GIST technology in their organisations. They have not invested enough in terms of technology absorption and there is inadequate expertise with the major computer manufacturers. Some expertise is, however, available with the few dedicated card and terminal manufacturers like QUARK and AEM. However, even with the latter, adequate expertise in the areas of operating systems and application development tools, application software development and high-volume data processing is almost totally absent. C-DAC, by its nature and mandate, is not in a position to take up activities in the last group. GIST is a technology and GIST-based equipments are tools for solving real-life problems.

There are, however, organisations like Orissa Computer Application Centre (OCAC) which have more expertise in the last-mentioned area and are also intensive users of the GIST technology, particularly in the areas of computer-based information systems and high volume data processing. They also have a group of technical personnel well-versed with the application softwares, application development tools and operating systems. A time has come when a proper synergy and symbiosis has to be achieved between the C-DAC the primary technology innovators, the dedicated card and terminal manufacturers, the computer systems manufacturers, dealers, suppliers and system integrators-cum-consultancy organisation like OCAC and the major end-users. GIST is a technology and GIST-based equipments are tools for solving real-life problems. To use the cliche, the taste of the pudding is in the eating. By adopting the above-mentioned strategy, the real benefit of GIST can permeate the everyday life of the common man of India.

## Conclusion

GIST which originally started with the limited objective of providing an Indian script (initially only Devnagari) terminal has come a long way towards being a general-purpose IT solution for diverse applications. Nothing brings this more dramatically into focus than the metamerphosis of the name itself. Originally, it was Graphics and Indian Script Terminal. At one point, it was called Graphics and International Script Technology and, later, it was Graphics-based Information System Technology. In the latest literature of C-DAC (September 1991), it is described as Graphics and Intelligence based Script Technology. GIST as a product has undergone major upgrades and is more mature today than its 1986 version but, more importantly, in the extension of application domain, its metamorphosis has been most significant and spectacular. The growth and success of GIST has been possible not only because of internally sound technology, but to a large extent due to concurrent development of important standards like ISCII and ISFOC.

GIST, an innovative product of Information Technology, is a technological marvel. Few would have realised its true significance for the Indian nation. Information technology is bound to be the driving force of the economic activities, not merely for the developed countries but also for the newly industrialised countries (NICS). As IT permeates the fabric of national life, the availability IT solution in diverse fields in Indian languages could not have been more timely. The Indian nation is well-known for its great intellectual contribution to the human civilisation. When mankind is moving towards the information age, the vast majority of the people of this great nation would have been denied access to the latest tools and technology on account of lack of knowledge of English. By providing a high-guality product of this technology, using the Indian language, GIST has provided this great nation a legitimate place in the international arena. The product is sound, robust, of excellent technical quality and, most important, also absolutely easy to use. It has opened the gates of the wonderful world of information technology applications to every Indian. In fact, it has gone one step ahead and has established a standard which can be conveniently adopted by the international community, as has already been amply proved by use of Russian with GIST. In this sense, GIST is truly India's gift to the world.

# 36

# ART AND CULTURE

DR. B.C. KAILAY*

## Introduction

Information technology which has converged computers and communication, has revolutionised the working environment. Today, the computers are being used as a tool as well as meta-tool (which creates tools) and a medium as well as meta-medium (a medium which creates media).Capabilities for sharing information, knowledge and experience without physical proximity through computer networks have enhanced the perceptual, conceptual and physical understanding of the whole world.

Latest technical developments have helped to provide an integrated environment as a tool for conceiving, representing, realising, processing, ordering, experimenting, investigating, producing and disseminating information (textual, visual and sound) available in different media like prints, photographs, video, audio, etc. It provides multi-dimensional medium to express concepts and ideas in various dimensions of human experience and stimulate participation and creativity.

## Art and Culture

The term culture has been generally used to refer to the finer aspects of life such as artistic and creative achievements and their dissemination especially with reference to the aesthetic dimensions of man. Broadly, culture stands for the beliefs, ideas, customs, laws, morals, arts and other capabilities and skills acquired by man as a member of

---

* National Informatics Centre, Planning Commission and Indira Gandhi National Centre for the Arts.

society. Culture determines everything in this sense and even society itself is a product of culture.

There is now a growing recognition that culture, like our environment, is at the core of all development activities. Culture is what gives a society its sense of direction and togetherness, as also a perception of values and excellence. Programmes and projects conforming to improving the standards of living by economic growth alone lose their meaning and relevance if society ceases to care or does not care adequately for its heritage and life style, both of which are the essential determinants of culture.

The world decade (1988-98) for cultural development was proclaimed by the General Assembly of the UNESCO. Two of the objectives approved for the decade were "formulating international cultural identities" and "promoting international cultural cooperation". In pursuit of these objectives, UNESCO resolved in its Resolution DR 228 in October 1987 to promote scientific studies of lifestyle, using sophisticated modern information technology for the multimedia computerisable documentation and to facilitate the cross-cultural understanding, perception and knowledge of lifestyles of different communities.

In a further Resolution DR 249 in October 1987, UNESCO stressed the need and urgency for developing integrated original data-bases and information systems for the storage, retrieval and dissemination of data on art and cultural heritage. Yet in another Resolution DR 32 in August 1989, UNESCO reaffirmed the objectives to promote the development of specialised regional information network for South and South-East Asian countries on cultural heritage.

The preservation, promotion and enrichment of the cultural traditions of the country have continued to be the vital concern of the Department of Culture (DoC) in Ministry of Human Resource Development. The Department has sought to maintain the vibrancy of these traditions through a network of institutions and supportive schemes.

DoC administers a series of innovative and supportive schemes which have a vital role in the dissemination of culture. Some of the important functions of the Department are to protect and preserve monuments and antiquities; to administer libraries and museums of national importance; promote performing, plastic and literary arts, and to administer scholarships in the field of art and culture. The

Department coordinates matters relating to incoming and outgoing exhibitions, such as, Festivals of India. It is also the agency for National Council of Arts. DoC has 10 subordinate offices and 23 autonomous institutions. These include Archaeological Survey of India, Anthropological Survey of India, National Archives of India, National Museum and Central Secretariat Library.

In 1985, Government of India (GOI) set-up the Department of Arts, for the sole purpose of establishing the Indira Gandhi National Centre for the Arts (IGNCA). Actions were initiated by the Department for nucleating the programmes of IGNCA as per the conceptual plan of the Centre. IGNCA has been conceived to serve as a major resource centre for the arts and an important ingredient in the activities of the Ministry of Human Resource Development. Through its multi-disciplinary programmes, it will : catalyze an integrated perception of the Indian tradition in art and culture; stimulate awareness of and sensitivity to the precious heritage; refine perception and understanding of the heritage. It thus aims at regenerating wide-spread appreciation of the depth and range of Indian tradition. The main focus of IGNCA is to comprehend the outonomy of arts and creativity within the context of Indian world-view. It has addressed itself to identify inter-related concepts, theories of aesthetics, structure (at the level of text, context and form) and artistic process with the experience of art manifestations. In other words, the Centre aims to underline the thread of unity among ideation, life-style and the plurality of artistic manifestation in different forms. To achieve the objectives, diverse inter-disciplinary and multi-disciplinary research programmes at the level of publication, training, creative activities and presentations are being undertaken.

Art and culture includes material/information on written (published/unpublished), static visuals (paintings, sculptures, architecture/monuments, crafts/artifacts, etc.), kinetic visuals (dance, drama, fairs/festivals, rituals, life-style, etc.) and oral (musical performances, recitation, speeches, interviews, etc.). This large volume of widely diversified material/information in multilingual forms is available in original and in various media such as microfilm/microfische, photographs, negatives, slides, films, audio/video cassettes, etc., wide-spread in different places in the world.

## Use of Technology in Art and Culture

Art and culture has always relied on technology of the times and, conversely, art and artist affect technology as the needs of artist to convey a particular vision lead to enquiries and innovation. It is essential to select, adopt and experience emerging technologies and make them available to large community of artist and scholars.

To enhance research capacity of the scholars/institutions as well as wide dissemination of comprehensive and integrated cultural information, multi-media technology has the potential to be used as a tool for: capturing, structuring/processing, presentation/visualisation, study/research/investigation/analysis, learning/teaching, archiving/ preservation, production, medium and dissemination. Brief description about the use of technology in these areas is given below :

### (A) *Capturing*

Flat-bed scanners and optical-character recognition systems are used for capturing the textual and visual information in computational form. Scan-digitising facilities are available for the audio-visual (static and kinetic).

### (B) *Structuring/Processing*

Image and sound processing tools are useful as an integral part of data-base management of textual, images and sound information. The ability to display more than one image simultaneously on the screen is essential for comparative purposes. This combined with a zoom feature allows the researcher to view details alongside a perspective, or to compare details. Adjustments in brightness and contrast allow the researcher to locate and examine obscure details in the background (not visible to the naked eye) in a photograph, print or painting. These tools are being extensively used in a number of on-going multi-media projects at the University of California, Berkeley.

### (C) *Presentation/Visualisation*

Historically, the artists have been interested in utilising computers to investigate imaginary and concrete worlds through visualisation. The pre-visualisation and visualisation of artworks has been affected by the development of new tools. Computers provide immediate feed-back and can be used in a spontaneous fluid manner for exploring the visual dynamics of a composition.

There was an interesting demonstration at the Annual 'SIGGRAPH 90' Conference on 3-dimension computer-controlled kinetic sculptures with the flexibility in their motions and physical appearance. These sculptures were composed of iron powder in a computer-controlled magnetic field. They are sometimes referred to as "living landscape" or "dancing trees". The designer and producer of this was of the view that one could think of them as visual analogues for musical instruments. Alternatively, one could think of them as non-human dance group that can be choreographed. Thus one can have a visual symphony perhaps performed by the deaf.

He further stated that technology can be a medium for emotional expression just like painting, dance, theatre or writing. It need not be used only for making tools for extending our intellectual capabilities but can equally be used for extending our empathy and compassion, increasing the emotional understanding of ourselves. He also ex-pressed that the extent to which our current technology is cold and emotionally sterile, is attributed more to our cultural biases than to anything intrinsic to the technology itself.

### (D) *Study/Research/Investigation/Analysis*

Computers are being used effectively as an analytical tool for the art/historical analysis. In AT&T Bell Laboratory a computer-aided study has been made by Prof. Lillian F. Feldmann Schwartz, on Leonardo Da Vinci's famous painting of Mona Lisa. She has also studied the works of Picasso, Matisse and Van Gogh, among others.

A collaborative project of the Vatican Library, the University of Pittsburgh and OCLC, has taken the earliest printed books (including colour illuminations) housed in the Vatican Library for multi-media presentation.

"Perseus", a multi-media data-base project has been undertaken at the Harvard University, to study ancient Greek literature, history and archaeology. All information is linked so that the paths can be used as a note-taking device for individual research and as an ex-pository tool for other readers. Although the source material within the database may not be changed, it will be possible to create new links and paths for navigation as well as to add supplementary information.

In his study, Prof. Kirti Trivedi of IIT, Bombay, has mentioned that the procedure and methods used in the design and construction of Hindu temples bear a striking resemblance to many of the procedures in computer graphics, including discretisation, fractalisation, extensive use of recursion and procedures involving self-similar iteration. The instructions for these operations are given in the procedures described in ancient texts on architectural practice (called Vastu-Shastras); and many of these instructions are in the nature of general programmes from which different temple forms may be generated. He has further proposed that these temples may be viewed as 3-dimensional fractal models and that the use of fractal geometry procedures has a special symbolic meaning in the generation of the forms of Hindu temples.

### (E) *Learning/Teaching*

Computer-Assisted Instruction (CAI) and intelligent tutoring system (ITS) are available for teaching different artistic activities. A computer-based multi-media tutor for beginning piano students, developed at Carnegie Mellon University is available.

"Thangka Painting" project developed at Xerox Palo Alto Research Centre, USA, by using interactive video and touch-screen technology aims to preserve the 2000 years old art of Tibetan Thangka painting and disseminate the craft.

### (F) *Archieving/Preserving*

All over the world, there is a trend to use optical/laser technology for archiving the static (not likely to change) information. Most of the multi-media projects have been developed with an aim to preserve the valuable cultural heritage.

### (G) *Production*

Multi-lingual desk-top publishing systems are used for text processing, formating, page layout and quality printouts. It is possible to get computer outputs on paper, slides, microfische, etc. Animation and graphic packages allow for creating animated sequences and high quality 2D/3D-graphics.

Recently, desk-top systems are made available for in-house production of interactive compact disc (CD)-ROM and video/laser disc.

(H) *Medium*

More important, however, is the significant potential of the computer in the evolution and development of new modes of artistic expression. The computer is a multi-dimensional medium that provides the artists with different modes of communication or expression of concepts or ideas. These modes include visual imagery, text, sound, music, movement or animation.

The computer is becoming increasingly important in the fine arts. Sculptors use the same kind of 3D-modelling software finally available to industrial designers for exploring forms and ideas beforehand instead of building maquettes. Painters, print-makers and photographers can move images back and forth between physical media and the computer to discover and refine visual imagery difficult or impossible to realise in other ways.

The computer enables the artist to simulate real objects and environment as well as represent them which are not intended to exist in the world where constraints such gravity, scale and engineering criteria do not apply. It allows to visualise and conceptualise in 2D/3D-environments including the use of motion or stereoscopy to enhance the impression of space. No other tool or medium provides this diversity of expression in one device.

(I) *Dissemination*

The multi-media technology has been extensively used for the dissemination of centuries-old pieces of art-works preserved in many museums in the world. Such interactive presentations are accessible for active viewer participation. Instead of passively reading exhibit labels or attending lectures or films or videodisc, now the user can pick and choose what they want to learn.

There is an automatic audio-visual system operational at National Museum of Ethnology, Osaka in Japan which facilitates the user to access information on any exhibit or video programmes available on the optical discs by their identity no., geographic area selection, by any topic/theme, etc.

In Emperor-I project, developed at Boston, USA, they used Digital Equipment Corporation's interactive video information system (IVIS) and prepared two double-sided video discs. These two double-sided 12" video discs, consist of 216,000 frames of visual images and a two-hour narration/music on double sound-tracks in English and Chinese regarding the site artifacts belonging to the period of the First Emperor of China. Video disc production was tcompleted at the Athena Labs at MIT, USA.

An interactive video disc programme on Greek vases which has been in operation since 1986 and other interactive video disc programme on the subject of illuminated manuscripts was put into the public use in 1989 at the J. Paul Getty Museum in USA.

An interactive video disc on the master pieces of Louvre Museum in Paris, is available for viewing on the stand-alone optical disc drive.

To develop intuitive user-interface for the naive users, Prof. Howard Besser from University of Pittsburgh is working with Prof. Todd Cavalier of Carneigh University, responsible for the Great American History Machine project.

**National Efforts in Using Technology in Art and Culture**

National Informatics Centre (NIC) has been providing information technology support to all government departments in the country for almost last two decades. In 1986, NIC established its cultural informatics unit (CIU) for the computerisation work of Department of Arts and Department of Culture. In both these Central government departments, the computerisation work was started ab initio. HP 3000/42, NEC-S 1000/20D system terminals, 386-based computers and a number of PCs were operationalised for the development of information systems.

In the last four years, the computerisation requirements were analysed; hardware and software were selected, acquired, operationalised, maintained and personnel for technology support were trained; entire software support as per the scholars/users need was provided and the scholars/users were trained for effective technology utilisation; R&D projects have been initiated taking into consideration the long-term objectives as well as trends in information technology.

The status of computerisation is given below under two broad headings : Department of Culture and Department of Arts/IGNCA.

(A) *Department of Culture*

DoC has organised cultural statistical unit to formulate cultural policies, execution and management of cultural projects and programmes, to meet the statistical requirements of UNESCO and other national bodies. To build up a comprehensive and scientific data collection system, an Expert Advisory Committee on Cultural Statistics and five sub-groups in different functional areas, such as, archaeology, archives, museum and art galleries, creative arts, libraries and art education were formed for collecting data from all the cultural organisations in India. Input formats were designed and standardised. Data is being compiled from all sources throughout India.

Information systems have been developed to monitor : The status of cultural exchange programmes (CEPs) running between India and other countries; the cultural activities of zonal cultural centres (ZCCs); the action plan of the department for the current year and the annual expenditure.

Feasibility reports for the computerisation work were prepared for Archaeological Survey of India, Anthropological Survey of India, National Archives of India, Sangeet Natak Akademi and Central Secretariat Library.

The following information systems have been developed for other associated organisations of DoC:

(i) *Monuments Information System*: There are about 4000 monuments under the care of Archaeological Survey of India (ASI). The conservation and preservation programme for these monuments include structural repairs as well as chemical preservation. A large amount of data for each monument such as, location of the monument, ownership status, demarcation details, tourist facilities, loose sculptures, etc., is required to be maintained for monitoring and planning as well as actual execution of structural repairs/conservation from time to time. The input format for capturing the relevant information was designed and circulated to all circles for data collection.

(ii) *Antiquities Information System*: A data-base has been developed to maintain information of all antiquities spread all over India which are registered under AAT Act, 1972 in India.

This data-base includes information on: Registration No., location in data bank, category of antiquity material, description, status of preservation, approximate date/period, owner's name and address, mode of acquisition, location of antiquity/security, name and address of registration officer, transfer of ownership, if any, with name and address of new owner, name and address of new RO of the jurisdiction etc. The data entry/validation/updation work is in progress at the head office of ASI on Janpath, New Delhi.

(iii) *National Archives Reference Information System*: National Archives of India (NAI) is a huge repository of documents related to Government of India, their predecessors, eminent persons of the world, etc. It is estimated that there are six hundred million records in multi-media form. One of the main activities of the National Archives is to make available this valuable information to the public, scholars and government officials. Year-wise index registers sorted on the subjects are available for manual reference. An information system for the reference of scholars to locate the desired information has been developed. Arrangements are being made by NAI for data entry.

(iv) *"People of India" Information System*: A data-base was developed including information about 780 ethnographic traits about more than 4000 communities under 'People of India' project undertaken by Anthropological Survey of India, Delhi. Comprehensive details for each community are in the categories : general information, history, present day distribution, natural environment and population. Community identification markers, constitutional status, food habits, staple food, drinks, fruits, changes in food habits, social divisions, functions, changes in surname, marriage, rules regarding remarriage, family, rituals, religion, occupation, socio-religious movement, employment, etc.

Implementation handbook along with complete data on floppies in dBASE format with menu-based user-interface for accessing information, was formally released to public on Ist October 1990.

(v) *Sangeet Natak Information System*: In the first phase, it has been planned to develop data-bases in Sangeet Natak Akademi regarding : The artists including their background, address, their standing in the field, proposed/considered year of award/fellowship/sponsorship, etc.; financial assistance directly to institutions and through State governments including year, amount, group/institution, field of performing arts, etc.; different functions/festivals/programmes including theme/occasion, time/duration, place, who presided, etc. and different multi-media (books, periodicals, photographs, tapes/cassettes/discs, films, art objects, etc.), their contents and exchange status.

(B) *Department of Arts/IGNCA*

GOI has designated IGNCA as the nodal agency for all matters relating to the setting up of a national information system and data bank (NISDB) on art, humanities and cultural heritage. Technical standards including hardware and software requirements will be prescribed by National Informatics Centre (NIC) for all agencies under the Central and State governments for purposes of storage, retrieval and dissemination of data on arts, humanities and cultural heritage for the development of a national network in this area. Further, IGNCA has been authorised to issue suitable instructions to all departments of the Central government for obligatory filling of data and information on standard formats with IGNCA, in the area of arts, humanities and cultural heritage and also advise the State governments for cooperation of their agencies in this respect. IGNCA has taken various steps for the implementation of the above government decision, as it involves inter-departmental and inter-agency planning, coordination and integration in respect of the technical and administrative aspects of the work for organising the national data bank.

The Government of India has also set-up a Standing Technical Group (STG) under the chairmanship of Additional Secretary and Director-General of National Informatics Centre (NIC) to advise IGNCA on the hardware and software requirements for setting up NISDB. This multi-disciplinary STG includes experts from various Government departments/organisations, namely Department of Space, Ahmedabad; Department of Atomic Energy, Bombay; Department of Electronics, New Delhi; Department of Science and Technology, New Delhi; National Remote Sensing Agency (NRSA), Hyderabad; National Centre for Software Technology (NCST),

Bombay and Central Scientific Instrumentation Organisation (CSIO), Chandigarh.

The Centre has been further identified by UNESCO as a nodal agency for developing regional databases for South and South-East Asian countries on art, cultural heritage and lifestyle through the applications of modern information technologies for standardisation, exchange and dissemination of data. It has been planned to hold consultation meeting of experts of member-countries of South and South-East Asian region for networking specialised information systems and cultural heritage.

In order to create a strong foundation for all research work in IGNCA, massive programmes of collecting source material has been launched. The source material includes : printed material (multilingual), microfilms/microfische, audio-visual, graphic material, photographs, slides, audio/video tapes, etc. Personal collections will include both 2D and 3D art objects. An enormous amount of source material have already been gathered from many parts of the world. Three multi-disciplinary programmes on unified themes have been held : Kham (space), Akara (calligraphy) and Kala (time). Each one of these programmes brought to IGNCA, scholars of various disciplines from all over the world to discuss perennial themes which cut across civilisations, cultures and disciplines. Side by side with the seminars, exhibitions on these themes, in audio-visual form, were also held. The series will continue.

**National Information System and Data Bank (NISDB) on Art, Humanities and Cultural Heritage**

It is desirable for any systematic study or research on any aspect/theme/area in any field, to first scan the references available from the secondary/primary sources. The scholars/users further narrow down the focus on the specific references for detailed study of relevant information available in multi-media forms.

To facilitate the study/research in the field of art and culture, the Centre has envisioned to develop a unique reference and research base of cultural source material in multi-media forms under one roof. To provide easy, integrated and interactive access, the creation and maintenance of this comprehensive multi-media base in digital or digitally accessible format is planned.

A realistic and practical phased approach for setting up the

NISDB has been envisaged. In the first phase, after analysis, detailed profiles including the needs for computerisation and user requirements/expectations alongwith work plan were prepared. In the second phase, nucleus hardware and software was acquired, operationalised, personnel for technology support were trained and prototype descriptive data-bases were developed including information on : catalogues of manuscripts; manuscripts; sound recordings; art objects; audio/visual material; Library information; multi-lingual thesaurus; multi-lingual glossary on basic terms; financial accounting; resource persons/general addresses, etc. Over the period, these data-bases were evolved based on the users/scholars feedback and input formats for all theses categories of information were standardised. Data entry/validation work is in progress. In the third phase, the development of multi-media presentations and networking is envisaged.

A uniform coding scheme has been evolved and used in all the data-bases to minimise storage requirements and inconsistency in data for the following categories of information:

- Places, states, countries, regions (based on geographical/ political/economical factors) of the world;
- Names of persons and their variants;
- Types of material and modes of acquisition;
- Subjects/disciplines/terminologies used in the field of art and culture;
- Scripts/languages of the world; and
- Names of institutions in the world, etc.

Thesaurus structure is being developed for subjects/disciplines/ terminologies used in the field of art and culture.

All data-bases have been designed to achieve integration of them in the long run.

Brief description about the above-mentioned databases is given below :

(i) *Union Catalogue of Catalogues (CATCAT)*

A large number of printed catalogues of Indic manuscripts are available in different institutions, universities, archives, libraries and private agencies in India and other countries. There are more than

3000 libraries, museums and other private/public repositories in the world who have Indian manuscripts. So far approximately 2000 catalogues of Indian manuscripts have been published. Such catalogues are classified under different categories, i.e., descriptive, alphabetic, report or handlist type. Descriptive catalogues are generally classified as language-wise or subject-wise. Thus to locate any relevant manuscript (published/unpublished), exhaustive information about the available catalogues of manuscripts is essential.

Information from more than 1000 catalogues has been computerized and can be retrieved by title, catalogue, repository, subject/theme, language, etc.

(ii) *Manuscripts (MANUS)*

The manuscripts of Indian origin are available all over the world in different repositories. They are in various scripts, covering a large number of subjects. Some of them include illumination and illustrations which provide solid foundation for the critical analysis of history and art. Over a period of time, different scholars have made valuable comments including interpretations on the contents of different manuscripts in the form of commentaries. The total collection would be roughly of the order of 2 to 3 crores. The descriptive reference information about the contents of these manuscripts is being included in the data-base.

Information about all the manuscripts available on the 84 identified fundamental Sanskrit texts, under the KALA KOSHA fundamental text-series programme, is being computerised. This will provide the base for the variant readings of manuscripts for critical editions.

(iii) *Sound Recordings (SOUND)*

This includes information on Shri S. Natarajan's recordings and some vedic chantings of Ranayaniya and Jaiminiya Sakha of Samveda, Paippalada of Atharva Veda-etc. Further information of various audio-visual recordings available with various agencies in India and abroad will be included.

(iv) *Art Object (PICTO)*

This data-base will include information on 2D and 3D art objects. At present information on Elizabeth Brunner's paintings, Dr. Mathpal's rock cave paintings and musical instruments of Shri S. Krishnaswami's collection available with IGNCA have been computerised.

(v) *Kala Kosha Terms (KKTERM)*

KKTERM data-base for Kalatattvakosha has been developed. Under this project, 250 terms have been identified for the glossary (Kalatattvakosha). In the initial phase, data relating to these terms which is in Roman as well as Devnagari script is being computerised. This will help the scholars in the preparation of comprehensive text-reference for each term, verification of bibliographic references and cross-references of quotations and terms in different texts. For example, final printouts of indexed terms with their occurrences in the given slokas related to Dattilam text were prepared.

(vi) *Library Information Management System (LIMS)*

An integrated library information management system (LIMS) is under development. This includes cataloguing information about all the books and periodicals available in IGNCA library. A user-friendly query-interface with screen-based menus/options for locating library books is operational.

(vii) *Audio-Visual Information Management System (AVIMS)*

This includes cataloguing information about audio-visual material available in IGNCA.

Millions of Indic manuscripts are no longer accessible to research scholars in the original. It is proposed to develop a microfilm/microfische library of unpublished manuscripts in India and foreign collection. This is a long range programme, which will cover private and public libraries in India and abroad. Steps have been initiated to acquire on a selected basis microfilm/microfische, from the collection of Durbar Library, Nepal; Staas Bibliothique, Berlin; Bibliothic Nationale, France and British Library, UK.

It is possible to store and retrieve indexing information on microfilm/microfische by using desk-top PC alongwith microimage terminal with the ability to receive commands from the computer to search the film, display and to make prints.

(viii) *Preparation of Multilingual Thesaurus*

This project is undertaken in the Loka Parampara Section of Janapada Sampada Division. Initially each project will be subdivided into modules like multilingual bibliography, physical environment, cartography, etc. Besides these modules, the other modules will be based on the preparation of a thesaurus — compilation of vocabulary with reference to water, fire, ether, air and earth, body, environment, flora, fauna, soil, food, agriculture, etc. and the rituals related to each of the above.

User-friendly software with screen-based menus has been developed with the facility to enter multi-lingual data on different terms with their corresponding meanings under different levels of categories as envisaged in the chart developed for the project. One can list out all the related terms and their meanings on terminal as well as take printouts by specifying either the terms (in full or partial), keywords, category description or category code.

All these data-bases are being extensively used by the research scholars/users from IGNCA as well as from outside. One such use is described below by taking an illustrative example of manuscripts :

To start with, the reference information about Union Catalogue of Catalogues of manuscripts (CATCAT), described earlier, is being used as the *First Level*.

Further, these manuscripts are in various scripts, covering a large number of subjects. Some of them include illuminations and illustrations which provide solid foundation for the critical analysis of history and art, over a period of time, different scholars have made valuable comments including interpretations on the contents of different manuscripts in the form of commentaries. The total collection would be roughly of the order of 20 to 30 million. The descriptive reference information about the contents of these manuscripts will form the *Second Level*.

Even a rough estimate is difficult to make regarding the total number of folios of manuscripts because of the fact that the range varies from 10 pages to 1,000 pages for many manuscripts. As envisaged, selected manuscripts will be maintained in digitised form based on the needs of different research programmes and users.

This maintenance of cultural material in digital or digitally accessible form are being used as the *Third Level* by the scholars interested in studying the original text in these manuscripts.

The *Fourth Level* will include cross-references on artist, subject, place, availability in other media, etc. For example, on *Gitagovinda* theme, there are thousands of manuscripts, paintings and songs. Therefore, for integration, the documentation of cross-references is essential.

Similarly, four levels of computerisation has been envisaged for other categories (textual, visual, sound) of cultural heritage material/information.

A few R&D projects, initiated taking into consideration the long-term objectives as well as trends in IT, are described below.

## Research and Development Projects Undertaken

### (A) *Integrated User-friendly Query Interface*

It has been considered that graphical user-interface with pull-down menus and windows is more intuitive than line-oriented interfaces. Pull-down menus provide users with many options to choose from without cluttering up the screen. Windows allow the users to perform more than one task simultaneously with each task taking place in a separate window on the screen. Thus for effective user-interface, three levels to access comprehensive information in an integrated way have been envisaged.

At the *first* level, graphical icons using query by forms, set-up on screen, are used for query formulation. These query-formulations are being further converted into standard query language (SQL) for actual retrieval of information from the data-base. These two steps have been maintained to allow interchangeability between back-end DBMS packages. The user can select any field and can form query by logical (=,>,<) and/or boolean (and, or, not) operators to retrieve records of interest. The selected records alongwith other multi-media information about visual or audio information will be presented on the screen for further processing. Prior knowledge or definite perspective for retrieving the information is pre-requisite but at the same time, it is experienced that art scholars are motivated to further explore the retrieved information by intuition or association. Thus use of expert system with comprehensive dictionary/thesaurus has been considered as an essential tool for the art scholars.

In developing user-interface to access information from MINISIS data-bases, it was found that MINISIS DBMS package does not allow for interactive selection of the display format which was a basic limitation experienced by the users. Therefore additional facility to MINISIS DBMS package of defining interactive display formats during the query session was developed. This major achievement was demonstrated at the Ninth MINISIS Users Group (MUG) conference held at Ottawa in Canada, organised by the International Development Research Centre (IDRC) in 1988, the developer of MINISIS package.

At the *second* level, once the textual, visual and audio information are located, the users are provided with text (Indian languages) processing, image processing and audio processing tools for further processing or display. Also, facility for storage and retrieval of Roman characters with diacritical marks and Devnagari script data has been developed, which will be further extended to other Indian scripts.

At the *third* level, users are provided with visual sorting and hyper-media tools to organise retrieved information as per their needs and save them as subset to be studied in more detail at a later time. The ultimate aim is to use information processing technology as an effective communications and thinking tool.

(B) *Indian Languages Processing Tools*

In India, there are 14 distinct scripts with 1652 languages/dialects, thus making it a unique country with a society and culture based on many languages and literature. The multi-lingual society and its synchronisation depends upon the dissemination of information concerning languages and culture. The capabilities of digital computers, to act as large intelligent information banks and as powerful information processing agents, open up a large potential area for processing of Indian languages and scripts. So far in all computers, facilities provided for desk-top publishing system or multilingual processing have been developed with the Roman script as logical base and using the principles of linear composition and matrix-bound letters, based on the nature of Indian languages. They can never be adopted to handle the total requirements of Indian language text processing.

Font lay-out styles typically present in our ancient manuscripts cannot easily be created in these systems which are necessarily print-oriented.

In Roman script, in general, the composition of text is linear and characters are placed one after the other in linear succession without overlapping. On the other hand, text-composition in Indian scripts includes fusion of two or more characters to render a single character and overlapping of neighbouring characters horizontally as well as vertically.

A committee of distinguished linguists and computer specialists worked to study various script patterns, their inter-relationship and the variations in forms and phonetic levels to finalise transliteration system among Indian scripts. Similar systems under development at different places like CMC, Hyderabad; Tamil University at Tanjore; French Institute of Indology, Pondicherry; Stanford University at Stanford, USA, etc. were surveyed. Based on the pure consonant approach, working table of phonetic equivalences with a meta-script has been considered for the development of transliteration system among Indian languages.

It is interesting to note that the phonetic division of Indian alphabets into vowels and consonants serves as a common base for all Indic scripts. The consonants are further grouped as guttural (throat), palatal (palate), dental (teeth), labial (lips), etc. according to their source centres in the human body which help produce these sounds. Thus Panini's phonetic classification has served as a base for such groups in all Indian scripts.

In view of the ultimate aim to develop natural language interface as the primary mode for computer communication, a phase-wise plan to develop following tools for Indian language processing is under implementation :

*Phase I*

(a) Uniform coding scheme specific for Indian language processing;
(b) Desk-top publishing and electronic typesetting in Indian language;
(c) Multilingual data-bases, authority files and thesaurus; and
(d) Machine transliteration between Indian scripts and Roman script.

*Phase II*

(e) Indian script pattern recognition;
(f) Domain specific machine translation among Indian languages; and
(g) Natural language user-interface.

*Phase III*

(h) Speech synthesis in Indian languages;
(i) Automatic conversion to text from verbal descriptions; and
(j) Human-computer conversation in natural languages.

(C) *Desk-top Publishing System*

'Vidura' multilingual electronic publishing system was indigenously designed and is under development, specifically to cater to the requirements of Indian languages. The design of Vidura is based on the ancient but precise principles laid by the ancient Sanskrit Grammarian *Panini*. Further generic fonts lay-out styles created, can be used to compose text in different styles. The system including Devnagari and Roman script has been developed on PC which will be further extended to other Indian scripts. This has also facility to mix graphics with textual data.

Also a computer-aided tool has been developed which can be used by the font designer/calligraphist to design interactively different fonts for a given script. Further facility has been developed to use these fonts in the 'Vidura' system. This project is assigned for development to the National Centre for Software Technology (NCST), Bombay.

The first phase of development of 'Vidura' DTP system including Devnagari and Roman script was completed. A demonstration of this was held for Member-Secretary and all other heads of division of IGNCA. Further development of this package to include diacritical marks with Roman script and additional Bengali, Tamil and Oriya scripts are in progress.

(D) *Interactive Multi-media Presentation*

During the last five years, IGNCA has been exploring ways and means to acquire knowledge and expertise from different institutions in the world involved in the documentation of cultural heritage. Experts from National Museum of Ethnology, Japan; Palo Alto Centre, Xerox Park USA; Pittsburgh University, USA, etc. involved in the multi-media documentation were invited to imbibe experience and expertise. As a first step to undertake the development work, conceptual design needs to be drawn. To assist in drawing the conceptual design, an expert from Palo Alto Centre, Xerox Park, San Francisco who was involved in the development of multi-media project on "Thangka Painting", was invited to IGNCA. After four weeks of intensive discussions with subject experts and computer experts, a conceptual design for the project on *Gita Govinda* was drawn. A report on this has been prepared. For this development work, configuration of hardware and software has been finalised. The development work is in progress.

In the available expert systems, descriptive models are being used to represent knowledge and to draw inferences from the knowledge-base. Efforts are being made to link interpreted textual outputs with the visual and oral information for multi-media presentations.

(E) *Holography Display System*

To provide a forum for creative and critical interaction between and among the diverse arts through multi-media projections, holograms of different art objects/art traditions were considered as an alternative media.

Recent developments in display holography have made it possible to depict and preserve precious and ancient art objects in their true 3D perspective size, textures and shades of an object which are very crucial for art analysis. They further provide advantages such as portability, durability for archieving and ease of display. Since masterpieces cannot be shifted from remote and poorly preserved corners, it is through the intermediary holography that these valued treasures can be satisfactory preserved elsewhere for close and intimate human perception.

Another important aspect of these precious and ancient art objects is their restoration. Due to the passage of time and environmental effects, these art objects (sculptures and paintings) have been, by and large, unable to retain their original colour, shine, texture and form. There have been a gradual erosion of this artistic and cultural wealth which in the recent past became a cause of great concern all over the world. Holography offers a unique solution for their restoration by employing highly sensitive holographic interferometry for non-destructive diagnosis of incipient faults or critical damages, such as, detachment between the primary layers and the underlying support in precious ancient paintings and timely detection of micro-cracks and cleavanges in ancient sculptures and monuments caused due to aging. This will enable the caretakers to initiate action for their timely restoration without in any way injuring the art objects.

Two holograms of an art object were prepared by Central Scientific Instruments Organisation (CSIO). They were shown in 1989 and appreciated by Member-Secretary of IGNCA. Further plan for making holograms is being drawn.

Standing Technical Group recommended that R&D work for "holography display system" may be initiated for preservation and display of historical and cultural treasures. The following phases of development have been considered :

*Phase I*:

Transmission holograms of single colour of still objects can be taken up in the laboratory itself. Techniques for colour holographs should be developed;

*Phase II*:

Spatial dedicated equipment which can be transported for in situ recording of the holograms of historical and cultural objects may be developed;

*Phase III:*

A system for holographic images with manipulative stereo capabilities and 3D-animation with digital manipulation of environment may be developed.

(F) *Portable Manuscript Acquisition System*

Manuscripts of Indian origin are available on palm-leaf/barched leaf/bhoj-patras/papers/metal/stone, all over the world in different repositories. They are in various scripts, covering a large number of subjects. Some of them include illumination and illustrations which provide solid foundation for the critical analysis of history and art. Over a period of time different scholars have made valuable comments including interpretations on the contents of different manuscripts in the form of commentaries. The total collection would be roughly of the order of 20 to 30 millions. A large number of these manuscripts are of peculiar size of 5" X 25" or 30".

Standing Technical Group recommended the development of this system and suggested that CCD camera with suitable resolution may be considered for grabbing quality images from old manuscripts. Various R&D organisations were consulted to take up this time-bound development work. As an immediate feasible solution, NIC has initiated this development work at its Hyderabad regional office.

In addition to the above described databases and R & D activities undertaken, the following software has been developed :

(a) To include Devnagari script for storage and retrieval of data from the databases using MINISIS database package;
(b) To transfer the hit file from different queries on MINISIS databases to PC terminal and locally printing the file on dot matrix printer;
(c) Interactive user-defined display formats for the contents of inverted file used by MINISIS;
(d) Data export of dBase-III files to MINISIS structure and vice-versa;
(e) MINISIS interface with IMAGE data-base system;
(f) Data export of MINISIS database file on HP 3000 system to INQ data-base structure on NEC S-1000 computer system;
(g) To include diacritical marks along with Roman characters for retrieval and storage of data in the MINISIS databases;
(h) User-friendly query-interface with screen-based menus/-options for retrieving information about resource personnel as well as general addresses for correspondence;
(i) User-friendly query-interface as well as report-generation software for bibliographic information.

Multilingual thesaurus, controlled vocabulary and uniform coding schemes have been evolved to facilitate integration and inter-linking relevant information.

## Networking

IGNCA has planned to develop networks of communication with other national and international centres of arts and culture and to affiliate with universities and other institutions of higher learning within India and abroad, toward the conduct and recognition of related research in the arts, humanities and cultural heritage. A global computer network of all cultural institutions with IGNCA as nodal agency is envisaged through National Informatics Centre Network (NICNET). The idea has been further developed in a recent meeting of some of the Asian experts under the sponsorship of UNESCO and the idea of a cultural heritage information network (CHIN) has been evolved.

**Conclusion**

As the new computer applications in this field are emerging continuously, the adoption of emerging technologies have to be an evolutionary process and investments need to be continuous. Systematic and regular evolution of information system and induction of technology need to be balanced with the most effective methods of adopting and using it. The use of computer must selectively grow out of the principles of inquiry and expression of the user's as well as developers. It is also equally important to study carefully the effects of these emerging technologies on our cultural expectations.

37

# GAMES AND SPORTS

V.V.S. MURTHY*

## Introduction

Sports are playing a vital role in everyday life by inspiring people to participate in the games by either playing or seeing. Sports cover a whole gamut of events ranging from musical chairs, tug-of-war, street circus feats to competitive sports such as archery, gymnastics, athletics, tennis, golf, cricket, etc., where skill, physical fitness, technique, accuracy and competitiveness play a crucial role. Sports also provide enjoyment to viewers and listeners through suspense and thrills accompanying it, making it a patronisable event through which money and sponsorship flow in. It is also prone to gambling in some countries where bookings and stakes are a common practice on the outcome or the result of the competition. The information technology is rapidly revolutionalising the sports arena, which is making greater impact on the development of sports in its various facets.

In the paper, it is proposed to cover the details on the development of management information systems for providing decision support to the Department of Youth Affairs and Sports and to Sports Authority of India by National Informations Centre (NIC), for helping in the administration and development of sports in the country. The priority areas have been chosen on the basis of wide range of discussions held with sports administrators and policy-makers. It has been planned to develop appropriate expert systems in areas where the decision support could be sought from these systems.

---

* National Informatics Centre, Planning Commission and Sports Authority of India.

**Computer-based Methodology**

National Informatics Centre has installed a local area network of super-PC/AT computer with terminals to cater to the data compilation and information retrieval needs of the schemes of the Department of Youth Affairs and Sports at Shastri Bhavan, New Delhi. NIC has also installed a dedicated telephone data circuit for connecting the Department to the NICNET making it capable of accessing the data-base systems and general packages like GIST, census and electronic mail on NEC S1000 super computer installed at NIC headquarters. As NIC has established State and district computer centres and linked them through the satellite network communication system, it should be possible for the department for establishing a quick communication with any part of the country for its information processing needs. It has deputed software professionals on a full time basis to the department and Sports Authority of India for the development of MIS on priority areas and providing analytical tools through consultations with the administrations of sports policies in the country.

National Informatics Centre, which is providing information technology support to all government departments in the country for almost past two decades, has provided computer hotline support with Cyber-170/730 system for the successful conduct of IX-Asian Games in 1982 at Delhi and developed softwares in a record time for supporting all the important activities of the organisation of the competitions. This covered personal information of participants and officials, accreditation, sports performances in all the major international tournaments with world records, generation of score sheets and result sheets for all the competitions and quick information dissemination to TV, Radio and press personnel. It has also computerised the world events which took place subsequently at Delhi, namely, for the World Table Tennis Championships and the World Railway Games by providing computer hardware at the locations of the events, and developing and installing the software for supporting various activities for the efficient conduct of games.

*NIC-Ministry Coordination Committee*

NIC-Ministry Coordination Committee has been formed under the chairmanship of Secretary, department of Youth Affairs and Sports, having officials from the Youth aand Sports Wings and NIC as members, with the objective of ensuring effective utilisation of NICNET facilities by creation of data-bases for monitoring departmental schemes, having inputs from feeder data-bases to be created at state and district level, data-bases on the information criteria for effective organisation and implementation of various departmental schemes.

*Development of Management Information Systems*

The following outline some of the areas where the automation has been attempted leading to the decision support for administration and policy-making for the Department of Youth Affairs and Sports and Sports Authority of India. The sports persons are playing important role in effective development of sports in the country. They are a vital component of the development of sports, the progress of which very much depends on the achievements of the sports persons. Various schemes are formulated by Government of India, such as, sports infrastructure development in NSTC Schools, assistance through State sports councils for the creation of sports facilities, adoption of children through national sports talent contest, adoption of sports persons through special area games, sports hostels and SPDA centres, encouraging sports talent through sports scholarships and by providing coaches for giving expert coaching in all the major sports schemes of Central and State government administrations.

The proformae have been designed and are being implemented covering the over-all progress and achievement of sports persons. The development of the proformae is very essential as it envisages uniformity and accuracy of the data, if compilation has to be attempted from different locations and to avoid communications gaps. The proformae designed includes the results, techniques used, measurement of physical fitness, physiological and nutritional inputs, design of training schedules, etc. The preparation of an athlete for a competition of any level requires the knowledge of targets set for achievement in a designated competition, optimised nutritional inputs, physical fitness norms for the specific sports discipline, etc., depending on age group and sex. The norms for the physical fitness and genetic parameters designed for Indians will help in knowing the gaps existing in comparison with similar norms of the other sports forward countries.

Apart from these, it is also vital to know the styles and techniques adopted by the opponent in contact games like wrestling, judo, boxing, etc., or games like tennis, table tennis, football, basket-ball, volley-ball, etc., for adopting, getting trained and in acquiring the appropriate styles and techniques. The proformae, which have been developed in consultation with various subject-experts of the country belonging to various fields of sports sciences, reflect the current trends of information technology adopted throughout the world covering most of the sports disciplines, like the usage of sports teachers and latest techniques used for anaerobic threshold measurement. The basic ingredients of the proforma are given below:

(a) *Personal Information Criteria*

These are for sports persons like sports person identification number, name, address, knowledge of languages, details of sponsorship, etc.

(b) *Socio-Economic Information*

This includes details like the family background, income of the family, number of brothers and sisters and their genetic norms.

(c) *Physical Fitness Information*

It includes anthropometric parameters like height, weight, other body measurements like skin-fold thickness for measuring body-fat percentage, posture-profile evaluation, flexibility-profile evaluation and muscular profile, etc. This will help in evaluating the uniform muscular growth and posture profile.

(d) *Aerobic fitness Profile*

This includes aerobic capacity, ventilatory threshold, respiratory functions, bio-chemical parameters and other tests useful for measuring the endurance. It leads to the evaluation of the oxygen in-take and anaerobic threshold which are very vital in determining the training received by the sports persons and also helps in the design of individual training schedules.

(e) *Training Schedules*

These are required to be designed by a coach for a sports person in consultation with physical fitness and physiological experts requires inputs of the sports person regarding the past performance in competitions, physical fitness tests' results and physiological parametres, especially the anaerobic threshold value which forms the basis for the design of training schedules for arriving at targeted performance in a phased manner. These have to be designed for a specific discipline for an individual, depending on the age-group and sex. In case of team events, it is also required to design training schedules group-wise and on individual basis. The techniques used in the training for various disciplines require to be standardised as far as possible to make them uniform and timely feedback on the attainment of performance levels to enable corrective measures to be taken by national coaches.

(f) *Psychological Profile*

It includes the parameters comprising the psychological preparedness of the sports persons, evaluated by measuring the reaction time, anxiety level, etc., of the sports persons.

(g) *Medical and Clinical Data*

It includes the parameters of sports injuries, general medical back ground, clinical parameters, etc. The data are being collected and compiled on a regular basis, helpful in knowing at any point of time the status of health, injuries and recovery phase of a sports person, which are very useful components in selection process.

(h) *Nutrition Data*

It includes the parameters of sports persons about regular diet-sequence while in session or during break. Approximate quantity of food-items with name of the items are required to be specified to calculate the calorific input and to relate it with the actual work-load in calories spent while in training or in competitions in assessing the actual requirements and expected intake for the sports persons. The analytic group of NIC is planning to design an economic menu programme incorporating optimum nutritional inputs catering to the needs and tastes of sports persons of various age groups representing different sports disciplines.

(i) *Facilities*

This proforma enquires about the facilities made available to sports persons for practising during training period and coaching camps. It also projects the requirement of equipment and consumables for practice and competitions. The central technical stores, which caters to the equipment needs of various state sports councils and sports federations in the conduct of competitions and coaching camps, is being automated, helping in its smooth operation through projection of re-ordering levels, planning the procurement of equipment from within the country and abroad.

(j) *Competitions/Coaching Camps Directory*

The national and international competitions taking place across the world at different locations are being compiled using this directory. It also gives the disciplines in which the competitions are held, duration, the number of officials, sports persons and countries participated. It also serves as a calendar of the competitions and coaching camps for the events likely to be held in the next one or two years.

(k) *Performance of Sports Persons*

These are the crucial proformae which determine the progress achieved in the country in a particular discipline by the performances and achievements of sports persons. The performae have been designed and being implemented for all the Olympic sports disciplines covering different are groups with appropriate world, Asian, National, State competitions' records for sub-junior, junior and senior sports persons. This will be very handy for selection purposes, the design of individual and group-training schedules and in knowing the best performances of an individual in measurable events like athletics, gymnastics-etc. In team and contact sports events, the proformae have been designed keeping in view the team and individual contributions in relation to opponent teams or individuals. The statistics on the sports persons' performances both individual and teamwise in games like cricket, tennis, table tennis, football, etc., are very handy in giving running commentaries and in publishing statistical records books.

**Specific Applications**

The proformae indicated above are implemented, in phases, for schemes like national sports talent contest, special area games, sports hostels, talents' progress and achievements monitoring.

(a) *National Sports Talent Contest*

National sports talent contest conducted at national level has been computerised covering the participants' personal details, their performance in the competitions and motor-quality tests for generating the merit-list very quickly after the end of competitions, which is very handy for the selection committee for screening the performances.

The status of selected children joining the NSTC adopted schools is being monitored. The allotment of schools depending on the region, medium of instruction, availability of hostel, discipline, type of school, etc., is being made giving options of the schools available for admitting the children. The infrastructural information available and details of grants given to each school have been computerised. The details of coaches posted in adopted schools with reference to their postings and leave information is being monitored. It is required to monitor the progress of children in terms of their sports and academic performance. Also, the achievements and performance of coaches is required to be formatted and monitored.

(b) *Special Area Games*

The natural talent, selected by Sports Authority of Indian under special area games from remote and tribal areas in sports disciplines like archery, gymnastics, athletics, football is being monitored in terms of personal, socio-economic, psychological, yoga, physiological and performance formats periodically to enable the review team for examining the progress made by each athlete from a starting level to a stage where they could be able to participate in national and international competitions, to suggest corrective steps required to be taken in the training schedules so as to attain the targeted performances. The Canadian norms have been adopted to Indian environment for interpolating the Indian sports persons performance. This software helped in making the selection of talents on the spot.

*Sports Hostels*

A feasibility study has been conducted for the information requirements of sports hostel in terms of the above criteria for monitoring the progress of sports persons and other managements information. A prototype software is being attempted for efficient organisation of sports hostel activities.

(c) *National Elite Sports Talent*

The front-line sports persons who are likely to participate or are participating in major national and international competitions are being given special attention in terms of arranging national coaching camps and special competitions for having exposure before actually participating in the targeted events. Attempts are being made to have their performance records and other performance-dependable parameters to have a very good insight into their past performance and in assessing their potential of winning a medal in a targeted competition. As a by-product of the software being developed, the details of sports persons receiving awards and scholarships are also being compiled.

(d) *Development of Expert Systems Concerning Sports Persons*

There is a lot of scope and necessity for the development of expert systems in the sports administration and policy planning especially in the selection or sports persons and in the design of training schedules in the specific sports disciplines and for different age-groups.

(e) *Sports Infrastructure Information System*

The department is releasing the grants for the construction of sports structures in various States/UTs by processing the applications of voluntary organisations and other government organisations, forwarded by State administrations. Currently, an information system has been designed and implemented for monitoring the release of grants to various agencies, the grant released for a particular sports structure, the receipt of utilisation certificates, status of construction and the commitment of funds by State government. The system is being used for generating letters through data-bases for the head of various State sports organisations giving the status of pending structures and release of grants by Central government and balance of commitments from State government.

It is also required to devise a system incorporating sports census, as a feedback for considering of a sports structure in a particular location. Apart from this, the applications received from various organisations are required to be processed, based on the specified criteria for helping in the selection of the sports structures to be recommended for the release of grant.

(f) *Sports Protocols*

The sports protocols executed by the Government of India with other countries are required to be monitored in terms of their implementation, action plan, agencies involved, etc. for efficiently organising the implementation of protocols. A software has been developed for covering the monitoring of implementation, visiting of teams abroad and receiving of teams, dates of protocols' implementation. The protocols covering 9 countries, numbering about 310 which are exhaustive and up-to-date, are compiled and are being monitored.

During the second phase of protocols' computerisation, it is proposed to analyse the impact of protocols in terms of development and progress of sports in the country. Another aspect to be considered for the successful implementation of the protocols, is to develop the data-base of countries with their achievements in sports for helping in decision-making in signing protocols for matching sports disciplines.

### (g) *Sports Federations*

The sports organisation and development agencies in the country, namely, sports federations, have a vital role to play in the proper planned development of sports in the country. The action plan for the conduct of competitions and coaching camps in various sports disciplines for senior, junior and sub-junior levels on a continuous basis forms its major activity. The organisation and constitution of a sports federation, are also required to be considered.

Currently, a sports federations' data-base has been developed concerning a profile of officials of various federations; the clearances being issued by the department at cost or no cost for participation in international competitions; and the reports are being generated indicating the clearances issued during a particular period. For an effective planning of sports in the country, an advance planning for at least next two or three years is essential and required to be monitored. It is also required to complete the results of the competitions, participated by Indian players in the country and outside on a continuous basis for helping in the evaluation of progress made and achievements in specific sports disciplines.

### (h) *Prize Winning Schools*

The schools, winning the competitions at block-level, are being awarded a prize-money for showing excellence in each discipline. The award-money, being presented to the winning school, is required to be used for the development of sports infrastructure of the school.

An information system has been developed covering the schools winning the award at the block level. Letters have been written by the Secretary (YA&S) to various principals of the award-winning schools regarding the status of receipt of the prize winning money, the mode in which prize money is being utilised by the school and sending of the utilisation certificates. The receipt of acknowledgement of the letter and status of receipt of utilisation certificate from each of the schools have been monitored.

### (i) *National Coaching Scheme*

SAI coaches are posted in agencies like NSTC Schools, SAG centres, sports hostels, university field stations, regional coaching centres.

etc., for providing expertise and guidance to players at different locations. An information system has been developed for supporting the details like personal, experience, leave postings, etc., to enable the administration to readily get integrated information on the coaches, who are remotely located. Various reports like coaches posted outside their native zone, coaches currently posted in a particular place exceeding certain number of years, coaches having experience of specified years, etc., can also be generated.

The demand of coaches from various zones has been compiled in relation to the existing number of coaches to evaluate the number of vacancies in a particular agency/zone/discipline to help the administration to plan for future recruitment/transfers.

(j) *Bharatiyam*

SAI has constituted the Bharatiyam directorate to generate awareness and develop physical fitness culture. It is providing training facilities in Bharatiyam elements to students of various schools in the country through the State administrations. The teachers from various schools are being provided training in Bharatiyam elements who in turn train the students of the respective schools. During Bharatiyam '89, a programme was organised by SAI for the Nehru Centenary Celebrations. The details of teachers, students trained from various states have been compiled by the directorate.

NIC is assisting in the creation of data-bases concerning statewise students/teachers trained from time to time, action plan of Bharatiyam in the conduct of training and display programmes, the budget available for training and allied activities and release of grants to various states and UTs.

(k) *SPDA Centres*

The proformae have been designed to monitor the construction and operation of SPDA centres proposed to be constructed in various parts of the country. The proformae designed cover the following areas:

(a) Monitoring the status of construction of SPDA Centres,
(b) Status of release of grants to a centre,

(c) Directory of schools falling in the range of a SPDA Centre,
(d) Advisory committee,
(e) Performance of SPDA trainees,
(f) Action plan of an SPDA centre,
(g) Progress of achievements in sports and academic fields for the inmates.

(l) *Processing for the Award of Sports Scholarships*

SAI is the nodal agency for the award of sports scholarships to sports persons showing excellence in senior, junior and sub-junior states at international, national, State and university levels. It invites applications from players sponsored by federations for consideration for the award of scholarships. The forms are received for fresh and renewal cases separately. An information system has been designed and developed for the preparation of merit list in various categories like national, State level and senior, junior, sub-junior stages, etc., based on the performance in competitions. These merit-lists are very handy for the experts in their decision-making for the award of scholarships.

**Conclusion**

In conclusion, co-ordination of the government and voluntary organisations working for the development of sport and games are enumerated below:

(a) *Nehru Yuva Kendras*

Nehru Yuva Kendras which have centres established in all the districts of the country have the coaching and training facilities for sports persons in the region. NYKs' contribution in broadbasing of sports in the country could also be useful in the generation of sports talent.

(b) *University Grants Commission*

UGC is also receiving the grants for providing sports facilities at universities and colleges under national sports organisation scheme for promoting sports and games. The talents available at university level could be compiled and made available for selecting talent at inter-university, inter-State and world-university competitions by creation of an information-base covering the talent from these institutions.

(c) *Sponsors of Sports Persons*

The public-sector organisations like Railways, Indian Telephone Industries and private organisations like Mahendra and Mahendra, Tata-Steel, etc., are providing sports facilities and offer jobs for encouraging talent through their sports-quota reservations. By compilation of the facilities offered by various organisations which are working for the development of sports, it could be possible to coordinate the efforts of these organisations in an effective and efficient manner.

(d) *Employment Exchange and Compilation Employment Avenues for Sports Persons*

Many public sector and private organisations reserve certain category of posts for sports persons. A compilation of the vacancies of sports persons is helpful in publishing these vacancies. Similarly, the eligible sports persons' bio-data with the necessary parameters could be compiled for matching against the compiled vacancies.

# PART VII

# CONCLUSION

# 38

# USER REVIEW

DR. VINAY DHARMADHIKARY* and B.C. KAILAY**

The Working Conference was organised by Computer Society of India (CSI) under the convenorship of Dr. Utpal K. Banerjee to lead to an in-depth discussion on the various aspects. On 11 September 1991, the following sectors had come for discussion: crops and seeds, road, railways, airlines, drinking water, weather, CRISP, rural development agriculture, geo-mapping, district planning, environment and power. Senior professionals presented their papers, followed by an intensive discussion. In continuation of the discussion, there was a User Review Session at the end of the day which was chaired by Dr. J.G. Krishnayya, with rapporteurs Dr. Vinay Dharmadhikary and Dr. B.C. Kailay. The following points came up for general consideration:

1. Since the conference was on "IT for Everyday Life" and in India, 85 per cent of life is in rural area, it was decided to focus on IT for rural sectors and we should see how the conference could make effort in strengthening the national policy-making and how this could be implemented in all sectors;
2. In the past, slogans were used by CSI, e.g., IT was more important than *Roti-Kapada-Makan*, as raised by President of CSI (Dr. R.K. Datta). It was a Midas touch, as stated by the Electronics Secretary (Mr. N. Vittal) and we should focus on what, achievements in key economic sectors can IT claim to support such slogans in day-to-day life;
3. DG-NIC (Dr. N. Seshagiri) said he expected 75 per cent

---

* Department of Electronics, Government of India.

** National Informatics Centre Planning Commission, Government of India.

utilisation of NICNET and other NIC investments and that NICNET could act as a launching pad for private sector data-base industry also. How the tangible benefits from such utilisation could be documented and publicised by professional body life CSI should be examined;

4. Food Corporation of India, moving Rs. 12,000 crores worth of grains per year, has been using NIC services. How much loss was saved and services improved by FCI attributable to NIC services?
5. In banking sector, who was responsible for spearheading massive re-training of bank employees and the unions to remove their resistance?
6. NIC is creating 4 computer-aided instruction centres using multi-media technology capable of 32,000 trainees per year. Who is prioritising trainee segments to have the maximum visible and perceptible impact in everyday life?
7. The police network across the states was a must and NIC has the capability and has proved successful in 1991 elections. But when and how can a national time-table be made for POLICENET?
8. A time-bound action-plan, naming individuals, needed to be developed to facilitate full utilisation of all "Public Domain" Software developed using central and State government grants and any departments/agencies. This should be made available to users at cost, and CSI or DOE should take up this task;
9. Single clearing, houses or data-bases were needed to be developed, to avoid unconscious duplication and overlap of software development projects;
10. NIC resources were not being made easily available to non-profit organisations, NGO sector as well as eminent researchers and organisations like CSI should take up this and evolve a concrete mechanism;
11. Major software projects (e.g. CAM by IIM's or CAD by ITT's) were being funded by the Government of India, but researchers often refused to give software documentation to enable others to use, as it was not in our culture. Institutions and individuals needed to be publicly held accountable to cause better utilisation of all R&D projects. What can organisations like CSI or NASSCOM do about documentation?

12. Can NIC be helped to create a comprehensive village-level data-base for all users instead of each department/ government agency doing surveys separately?
13. Almost all sectoral secretaries of Government of India were asked to send senior decision-making representatives to the conference to evolve a IT use plan. Instead, many ministeries were either absent or gave publicity information normally available in annual reports and other public documents with hardly a commitment to develop a national-level action plan;
14. Each ministry could be asked to provide to CSI and action plan of using IT for wealth generation and improving everyday life;
15. All NRDMS centres under DST need to be locked together with NICNET centres and NNRMS;
16. Twenty-nine State-level departments collected information at village and district level which needed to be integrated into NIC's DISNIC;
17. How could CSI present material to the Raja Chelliaya Committee on Tariff for reducing IT cost, such as, VCR at Rs. 5,000 and PC at Rs. 10,000, etc.?
18. An action plan for IT use in water sector has been developed by CWC, but there was no process (or time-table) to get a national-level action plan discussed and adopted by Ministry of Water Resources and the concerned State Departments;
19. Information collected/repositing with government but not utilised/disseminated to actual users meant a tremendous opportunity loss. Could CSI take up this potential gold-mine with government especially with the Department of Electronics of Planning Commission?
20. Successful and intensive pre-planning and employee-orientation, achieved in the railway computerisation, could be adopted in the banking sector and other transaction-intensive sectors to get out of present bottlenecks mentioned by the Prime Minister to Shri N. Vittal. For example, only one branch per year was allowed to be computerised. Thus, another 25 years would be needed for IT to be used in the banking sector. Could CSI take this up?
21. The Ministry of Surface Transport could be asked to develop a IT plan in their sector, after examining BEST, APSRTC and other city transport corporation successes and failures;

22. The major scheme of Dr. Seshagiri on electricity construction project computerisation was not making much substantial difference in CEA operation;
23. Power generation plants were operating at 20 per cent to 40 per cent capacity utilisation despite CEA's efforts. What and how much could IT do to solve this?
24. SAIL experience with IT showed that with a little investment in making information available, control and efficient resource utilisation, productivity improvement, etc., cannot but follow. Perhaps CEA and Ministry of Power could also attempt this?
25. An organised forum for IT users was needed cutting across all sectors, so that problems with IT vendors, maintenance problems, software documentation, etc., could be aired and actioned in time-bound way;
26. A code-of-ethics should be determined for IT vendors to be eligible for membership of CSI;
27. CSI could make a check-list of all preparations for the intending purchasers before a computer was purchased, so that idling of IT equipment due to lack of preparations could be avoided;

The following recommendation were made by Mr. B.M. Khanna, CGM now chairman and Managing Director of MTNL:

28. Absence of good documentation lead to enormous wastage. DOE should be induced to intervene in this problem;
29. Hardware maintenance was very poor. We need a programme to develop a testing and certifying process for "Certified Hardware Maintenance Organisations", whose bills for maintenance work would be acceptable without question. CSI should investigate into this;
30. Special pay should be paid to computer workers. They should get certificates after training. After working on computer for some time, they should get Rs. 100 or so as special pay;
31. (Recommendation made by Dr. A.K. Jain of SAIL)
    Larger users need a User Forum for all manners of technical, managerial and vendor-related matters. The issue should be discussed in detail;
32. (Recommendation made by Dr. Subramanim of NIC)
    A Training Institute for the banking informatics was overdue.

This should be looked into carefully;

33. Successful introduction of IT in large organisations required a team of carefully selected individuals (users *plus* IT professionals) whose 100 per cent Job was to achieve IT success, and who would be assured to be not transferred till completion, (as seemed to have happened in the Indian Railways in the passenger reservation systems (PRS);
34. Financial powers should match the responsibilities entrusted at each level, relaxing or breaking age-old rules and regulation;

The Working Conference, in continuation, had an in-depth discussion in the following sectors on the 12 September 1991: health, education, art and culture, police, finger-printing, entertainment, etc. A User Review Session was organised, following the proceedings and the presentations of paper by senior professionals which was chaired by Mr. Subas Pani, with the help of rapporteurs Dr. Vinay Dharmadhikary and Dr. B.C. Kailay. Good and interesting ideas meant for CSI and similar organisations came up in these discussions as follows:

1. In most of the key economic and social sectors (with the exception of Indian railways, SAIL and a few handful of others), there did not seem to exist any comprehensive vision and strategy for IT use to improve tangible benefits to common man. CSI and DOE should contribute towards it;
2. (a) Many large PSUs (Coal India, MTNL, ONGC, etc.) had bitter experiences of being cheated or disappointed by a large number of IT vendors with millions' worth of IT equipment lying idle or unutilised. CSI or DOE should develop an implementable action plan instead of accepting this as fact of life in Indian Culture;

   (b) Exemplary successes had been achieved in SAIL in making the same IT vendor equipment work, through standardisation, vendor qualification and rate contracts. CSI and MAIT members should be approached by BIS for developing code-of-ethics;
3. CSI as the only non-vested-interest IT users' lobby was ideally suited to undertake the mission for dividing IT use-strategies within such vital sectors at health,

education, social welfare, women and child development, etc., where the government ministries were conspicuous by their non-participation and inability to do so;

4. SAIL reported that a Rs. 4,000 crore grandiose IT plan developed by a PSU in IT field, failed to take off, whereas a trojan-horse approach of a young electronics professional coming on deputation to SAIL has yielded excellent results;
5. It was often observed that more often than not, general-purpose PCs get used for extremely limited functions like word-processing, data-entry, etc. Examples of SBI, etc., showed that for properly planned requirements, customised special-purpose machines for data-entry only, word-processing only, etc., may be more cost-effective nationally, if CSI and DOE could take a leadership and bring some fruitful results;
6. CLASS programme of DOE and NCERT was an example of virtually running aground without anybody being held accountable to the speeches and promises in Parliament, IT conventions, etc.;
7. IT has enabled such quality improvement in newspaper and magazine industry in the USA that small ones are as good and effective as large ones, but in India this has not happened due to certain impediments. CSI/DOE should work for plans for the removal of such impediments;
8. Several import-bans and duty anomalies were reported by a media-use expert, which were disputed by Dr. B.C. Kailay of NIC. If these hurdles were indeed verified, then CSI & DOE should take up these issues to revolutionise, cost-effectively, the media content and quality where IT can be the key-catalyst;
9. Doordarshan did not seem to have a well though-out, IT-use strategy to improve their core-functions and their efficiency;
10. Full capabilities of GIST and TDIL did not seem to be well-understood nor used by either computer professionals nor general potential users. If this was India's gift to the world, could CSI champion this cause?
11. A vision could be evolved for CSI with an accountability. A secretariat with enough competence and strength

might be needed which would help in the smooth functioning of this professional body;

12. CSI should prepare convincing documents with success stories such as Indian railways, SAIL, etc, who had tremendous usage of IT in their fields and send it to the top-level officers in various sectors where IT-use strategy did not exist so far;
13. In many organisations, institutions and companies, PCs were installed as show-pieces like getting offices air-conditioned, etc.;
14. Government/PSU purchase procedures allowed hardware to be purchased much more easily than software, because specific applications for software purchase were often thwarted since three quotations could not be obtained, etc. CSI/DOE should make this easy for the user like purchase of books.

In a nutshell, we should see how IT can be used extensively in public domain and bring it to the common masses through different media.

**Lessons Learnt by the Railways**

1. Resistance to change is in-born in human nature. Change becomes much more difficult to implement in case it also simultaneously involves substantial technological changes. Skilful handling, with genuine concern for feeling and limitations of those involved in changes, is required. The system should be designed basically for those who will operate it, with their participation, catering for their needs;
2. Major changes require a dedicated team to handle these. These cannot be handled effectively if entrusted as an addition to the existing responsibilities. A dedicated team needs to be set-up to conceive the project in its entirety and complexities (technical, financial, human, etc.) and plan careful implementation of change;
3. Once appropriate personnel have been identified for a project, they should be involved from conception of the project to its implementation. The personnel in the team should not be changed in between. That the PRS project succeeded is due to the fact that personnel on the project were not changed in

between. The success was theirs, not to be shared. If the project had failed, there were no scapegoats. Responsibilities, both for success and failure, were theirs. Their commitment to the project was total;

4. Another important factor in the successful implementation of change is the quality of leadership. The choice of the team leader is crucial. He should be dedicated to the project and possess capabilities of leadership to carry the team, management and staff with him. Flexibility to blend the technical and human needs to meet organisation's objectives is an essential quality;
5. Technological changes often demand fundamental changes in age-old rules and regulations. Management has to display courage and flexibility to accept and implement these changes. Financial powers should match the responsibilities entrusted at each level. Conventional constraints need to be relaxed. New situations cannot be handled with old and rusted tools;
6. Area chosen for change should be appropriate. There should be dissatisfaction with the existing system;
7. Fears and apprehensions of staff and management should be identified and adequate care taken to remove these;
8. The system should preferably be developed, designed, tested and proved in a limited area as a pilot project and perfected before extending it to the entire system;
9. Management and staff should participate in development and implementation of the project. Rules and regulations framed for a different environment must be modified to meet new situations;
10. New technology should be explained to the staff in a language they understand;
11. Interaction between man and machine is crucial to success. The interface should be carefully designed keeping in mind interest of the men who will be required to operate it;
12. Training staff to work with new technology and unfamiliar environment needs planning with great care. It helps to pick up trainers from amongst the staff and train them as trainers;
13. Confidence should be built amongst the staff that their job, status and career prospectus are not threatened; and
14. The system should be fault-tolerant with enough built-in redundancy against failures.

# INDEX